Pure and Simple Politics

THE AMERICAN FEDERATION OF L
POLITICAL ACTIVISION, 1881–1917

Scholarship on American labor politics has l
view that the American Federation of Labor, the
zation in the early twentieth century, rejected po
of economic strategies. Based on extensive rese
political party records, this study demonstrates tha
devoted great attention to political activity. The or
strategy, however, which Julie Greene calls "pure
itics," dictated that trade unionists alone should shape
politics. Exploring the period from 1881 to 1917, *Pu
Politics* focuses on the quandaries this approach genera
ican trade unionists. Politics for AFL members became
tested terrain, as leaders attempted to implement a strateg
rank-and-file workers rejected. Furthermore, its drive to ac
ical efficacy increasingly exposed the AFL to forces beyond
as party politicians and other individuals began seeking to
labor's political strategy and tactics.

The recipient of fellowships from the American Historical As
ation, the Josephine de Karman Foundation, and the National Endowm
for the Humanities, Julie Greene is Assistant Professor of History
the University of Colorado at Boulder. She has also taught at the Un
versity of North Carolina at Chapel Hill and the University of Missour
at Kansas City. Julie Greene's writings have appeared in *Labor History*,
Radical History Review, *Nebraska History*, and *Frontiers: A Journal
of Women Studies*.

Pure and Simple Politics

THE AMERICAN FEDERATION
OF LABOR AND POLITICAL
ACTIVISM, 1881–1917

Julie Greene

CAMBRIDGE
UNIVERSITY PRESS

PUBLISHED BY THE PRESS SYNDICATE OF THE UNIVERSITY OF CAMBRIDGE
The Pitt Building, Trumpington Street, Cambridge CB2 1RP, United Kingdom

CAMBRIDGE UNIVERSITY PRESS
The Edinburgh Building, Cambridge CB2 2RU, UK/http://www.cup.cam.ac.uk
40 West 20th Street, New York, NY 10011–4211, USA/http://www.cup.org
10 Stamford Road, Oakleigh, Melbourne 3166, Australia

© Cambridge University Press 1998

First published 1998

Printed in the United States of America

Typeset in Times Roman

Library of Congress Cataloging-in-Publication Data
Greene, Julie, 1956–
    Pure and simple politics : the American Federation of Labor and political
activism, 1881–1917 / Julie Greene.
        p.   cm.
    ISBN 0–521–43398–3
    1. American Federation of Labor – History.   2. Trade unions – United
States – Political activity – History.   3. Labor movement – United
States – History.   4. United States – Politics and government.
I. Title.
HD8055.A5G784   1998
331.88′32′0973 – dc21   97–25547
                                                                          CIP

*A catalog record for this book is available from
the British Library*

ISBN 0 521 43398 3 hardback

For my parents
William H. and Helen Greene

Contents

Acknowledgments

This book has been made possible by a large community of friends, colleagues, and institutions who provided generous and stimulating support. Together they made my work a delight, and it is a great privilege now to express my thanks.

A number of organizations provided essential financial support for this project, and I am very grateful to all of them: the Josephine De Karman Foundation, the American Historical Association Albert Beveridge Fellowship, the National Endowment for the Humanities, Yale University, the University of Missouri at Kansas City, and the University of Colorado at Boulder.

Archivists and staff members at many institutions worked hard to answer my questions and locate materials for me, and I thank each of them: Library of Congress, National Archives, New York Public Library, Chicago Historical Society, University of Chicago, Yale University Library, Duke University, University of Michigan, University of North Carolina at Chapel Hill, University of Illinois, Illinois State Historical Society, Indiana State Library, the George Meany Archives (AFL-CIO), University of Wisconsin at Madison, California State University at Northridge, University of Missouri at Kansas City, and University of Colorado at Boulder. I am especially grateful to Joe Sullivan at the Library of Congress and to Peter Albert and the late Stuart Kaufman at the Samuel Gompers Papers, University of Maryland.

As a graduate student, I enjoyed working with an inspiring and supportive group of scholars. I learned the craft under the guiding hand of David Montgomery, who brilliantly and compassionately pushed me to refine my analysis. His written comments on dissertation chapters continue to shape my thinking even now. David Brion Davis provided a model of intellectual scholarship, kindly took an interest in a subject far from his own specialty, and helped strengthen both my argument and my writing. David Plotke shared with me his expertise in political science, helping to discipline and focus my ideas. Several other scholars generously shared their ideas and approaches with me: My thanks to John Agnew, Nancy Cott, and especially to Terrence McDonald. In my earliest days as a student of history, I learned to appreciate the discipline from three historians who do not specialize on the United States, and to each of them I remain fondly indebted: William Hunt, John Broomfield, and Zara Steiner.

Graduate students also teach each other, and I luckily moved among people doing fascinating work both in New Haven and in Ann Arbor, the latter my home while I completed the dissertation. For sharing their ideas with me, I am indebted to Cecelia Bucki, Toni Gilpin, Joanne Goodwin, Ileen DeVault, Peter Hinks, Robert Hinton, Tera Hunter, Brian Lloyd, Daniel Letwin, Priscilla Murolo, Rebecca Reed, Karin Shapiro, and Whitney Walton. In its later stages, this book found a challenging audience among graduate students in my courses at the University of Colorado: I am grateful to all of them and particularly to Carol Byerly, John Enyeart, Thomas Krainz, Todd Laugen, and Gerald Ronning. For able assistance with research, my appreciation goes to Erika Fedge, Nicki Gonzales, and Christopher Riggs.

As this book developed, it benefited tremendously from close readings by, and conversations with, an exceptional group of scholars. Because each of them has published work that influenced my own, their comments and suggestions proved a wonderful inspiration. For their assistance with sections of this manuscript, I am deeply grateful to James Barrett, David Brody, John Buenker, Robert Cherny, Alan Dawley, Melvyn Dubofsky, Leon Fink, William Forbath, Nelson Lichtenstein, Gwendolyn Mink, Bruce Nelson, Grace Palladino, Elisabeth Perry, David Roediger, Steven Sapolsky, and Richard Schneirov. Serveral brave souls read the entire dissertation and helped me shape it into a book: With pleasure, I thank Eric Arnesen, Gary Fink, Steve Fraser, Michael Kazin, Joseph McCartin, and especially Bruce Laurie.

Some friends and family provided a different sort of sustenance by opening their homes to me. From them I learned that a friendly hearth can transform a grueling research trip into a wonderful adventure. Thus, my great thanks go to Eileen Boris, Nelson Lichtenstein, Ileen Devault, David Fasenfest, Toni Gilpin, Robert Hinton, Annie Sailer, Mervat Hatem, Gary Issac, Sarah Greene, William Tucker, Diane Meisenhelter, Amy Stanley, and Craig Becker. Long discussions with some friends whose work diverges quite sharply from my own also proved remarkably helpful. For their friendship, I am grateful to John Stack, Jeffrey Longhofer, Judy Ancel, Heidi Gottfried, Rickie Solinger, Jennifer Patchen, and the late Richard McKinzie.

Since moving to Boulder two years ago, I have happily found myself surrounded by a distinguished and stimulating community of historians. In different ways, they have shared this project with me, providing comments, reactions, and ideas. I am grateful to every member of the University of Colorado's History Department for their support and encouragement, and especially to Lee Chambers-Schiller, Philip DeLoria, Barbara Engel, Susan Kent, Patti Limerick, Gloria Main, Ralph Mann, Mark Pittenger, and Thomas Zeiler. My heartfelt thanks also to Walter Stone and Susan Brumbaugh for their assistance with data from the Inter-University Consortium for Political and Social Research.

Two friends must be singled out for the remarkable role they played in this project. Dana Frank not only shared with me her love of labor history, she also read more drafts of this project and listened to more tales of Samuel Gompers than anyone had a right to expect. Along the way, she taught me a great deal and worked relentlessly to help me refine my ideas. Shelton Stromquist, whose own work on labor and politics provided such a splendid example, has served this project as a voice of influence and inspiration for several years. As the project's official reader at Cambridge University Press, Shel understood the book I wanted to write and helped me achieve it.

At Cambridge University Press, Frank Smith has proved himself a remarkable editor, providing careful and stimulating reactions to the project at every stage. I am grateful also to Ernest Haim and Peter J. Zurita for their skilled work on the manuscript. My enthusiastic family has tolerated and supported this project for many years. I celebrate all of them: Donna and Kenneth Stevens, Molly and William Lairamore, Susan and Robert Dale, Sarah Greene and William Tucker, Chris and Christy Greene, and Alex Greene. And my affectionate thanks to Elaine Maffie for her friendship and love.

I owe a special debt to my parents, William H. and Helen Greene. My first and best teachers, they introduced me to ideas and passions that have become central to my life and to this book. From them emerged my fascination with politics, with history, and with the world of industrial labor. If my life combines these things in a way quite different from their own, they nonetheless have supported me with humor and wisdom. I admire both my parents tremendously, and this book is dedicated to them.

Finally, James Maffie has lived this project too, sharing with me his incomparable talents and ideas. Critiquing my writing with clarity and precision, Jim made this a much better book. Meanwhile he continues to make my life, daily, more joyful. For all this and more, I am deeply grateful.

Introduction

During the late nineteenth and early twentieth centuries, the American Federation of Labor (AFL) developed a distinctive and influential approach to political action. Rather than creating an independent party of American workers, akin to the British Labour Party or the German Social Democratic Party, AFL members and leaders struggled to find another route to political effectiveness. Along the way, they experimented with diverse political strategies, committing vast resources and generating passionate debates.

AFL President Samuel Gompers first articulated the political approach that would come to dominate the American labor movement. In the 1890s he argued forcefully, and ultimately successfully, that "party slavery" constituted a major source of tyranny in American life. Seeking to reject partisan commitments, the AFL turned to lobbying. In the early twentieth century, when an expanding federal bureaucracy and a growing anti-union movement among American employers together defeated AFL lobbying efforts, Gompers and other leaders reluctantly embarked on a more strenuous strategy. They ambitiously entered electoral politics, urging some two million AFL members across the nation to support pro-union candidates. Ultimately, they hoped to encourage class consciousness through a "strike at the ballot box." The AFL leaders would soon learn, however, that achieving their political goals remained elusive.

At the heart of labor's political effort stood several conundrums. In a political system dominated by the two major parties, should the Federation remain independent and eschew partisan alliances? Or should it ally with one of the major parties or even with an alternative like the Socialists? Could AFL leaders possibly engage in electoral politics without dividing their ranks or, equally fearsome, facing embarrassment if trade unionists refused to join the effort? And could AFL leaders encourage limited engagement in electoral politics without losing control over the political future of the labor movement? Rank-and-file trade unionists had their own ideas about the shape American labor politics should take. Many of them favored Socialist or Labor Party activities, whereas others simply wanted their local labor councils and state federations of labor, rather than the national leadership, to stand at the heart of any political movement.

But how could rank-and-file unionists shape the political direction of their movement, lacking as they did the resources and influence possessed by national leaders? Such questions weighed heavily on the minds of trade unionists during the early twentieth century; answers would not come easily.

These political quandaries belie some of our common assumptions about the character and activities of the American Federation of Labor in its early decades. Since the early twentieth century, when John Commons and his colleagues wrote their classic studies, scholarship on American labor politics has been dominated by the view that the AFL rejected political action and pursued instead economic- and union-centered strategies. The AFL may have occasionally lobbied the government but beyond that, it is said, the Federation stayed out of politics.[1]

But did it? With this question, I began researching the American Federation of Labor's activities during its early decades, from the origins of its predecessor, the Federation of Trades and Labor Unions, through the election of 1916. Much to my surprise, I found that the American Federation of Labor devoted a great deal of attention to political activity during its early decades, and this activity helped shape both American politics as well as the character of the AFL itself. Accordingly, this book explores the AFL's evolution during its early decades as a way to understand the origins, character, and significance of trade union–centered political action that so dramatically distinguishes the case of the United States from labor movements in other countries. It will trace the AFL's approach to electoral politics, its relationship to the party system, and its strategies of mobilization. Two key arenas will require a close focus: the relationships within the AFL, in which members and leaders debated political strategies and exposed their own differences along the way; and the relationship between the AFL and other groups, such as Democratic Party politicians, state bureaucrats, open-shop employers, and workers not invited to join what was, after all, a highly exclusivist trade union federation. I call the strategy developed by the AFL "pure and simple politics," and with this phrase I hope to suggest a number of things.

Samuel Gompers coined the phrase "pure and simple" in 1893, at a time when, as president of the young AFL, he was already battling against Socialists for control over the institution. During this fight, he portrayed Socialists as "outsiders," regardless of their trade unionist credentials. "I cannot and will not prove false to my convictions," he proclaimed on one occasion, "that the trade unions pure and simple are the natural organizations of the wage workers to secure their present and practical improvement and to achieve their final

[1] Michael Rogin, "Voluntarism: The Political Functions of an Antipolitical Doctrine," *Industrial and Labor Relations Review*, 15 (4), July 1962, 521–35; David J. Saposs, "Voluntarism in the American Labor Movement," *Monthly Labor Review*, 77 (9), September 1954, 967–71; Ruth L. Horowitz, *Political Ideologies of Organized Labor* (New Brunswick, NJ: Transaction Books, 1978); Marc Karson, *American Labor Unions and Politics, 1900–1918* (Carbondale: Southern Illinois University Press, 1958); Philip Taft, *Labor Politics American Style: The California State Federation of Labor* (Cambridge: Harvard University Press, 1968).

emancipation."[2] In the years since Gompers made this statement, "pure and simple" has become a common phrase for his brand of conservative unionism. For decades, the phrase was used mainly by radical critics of the AFL, who disdained what they perceived as the narrow and conservative outlook of Gompers and his allies. Today, the term remains pervasive in histories of the AFL, though ironically its meaning has grown less clear over time. It can refer generally to conservatism within the trade union movement, or to anti statism,[3] or perhaps most commonly to a wholesale rejection of politics. Bruce Laurie writes in his insightful book on nineteenth-century labor, for example, that "Pure and simple unionism scorned social reform for the here and now, and sought to better conditions in the workplace within the framework of the existing order." Norman Ware, on the other hand, an early historian of the AFL, equated pure and simple unionism with a complete rejection of politics and political ambitions.[4]

With the phrase "pure and simple politics," I hope to suggest that any assumption like Ware's is inaccurate. "Pure and simple" unionism should not be equated with nonpolitical unionism, nor should we perceive the AFL as the archetypal nonpolitical or antipolitical labor institution. In linking this study of a politically active organization with the concept of pure and simple, I hope to return us closer to Samuel Gompers's original intention. The early AFL *was* a political organization, but quite distinctly in its own way. Pure and simple politics meant, first of all, that only trade union members and leaders should determine the shape of American labor politics. It entailed, secondly, a highly independent approach to political activity. Formally, AFL policy was strictly nonpartisan; in practice, it involved a close but contingent partnership with the Democratic Party that hinged on the party's responsiveness. Thirdly, as scholars before me have demonstrated, AFL political policy remained resolutely antistatist during this period. Rather than seeking ambitious social reforms, AFL leaders sought to achieve their very modest goals within the existing political system.[5]

Exploring the evolution of American labor politics with a spotlight on the AFL requires that we situate ourselves in a particular context of working-class history. This project will examine the national level of American politics, for during this period, power moved upward from local and state levels and many working-class institutions began trying to influence national policymaking and

---

[2] Samuel Gompers, *Seventy Years of Life and Labor* (New York: E. P. Dutton, 1925), 1:385.

[3] By using the term antistatism, I mean an approach to politics that opposes most forms of state intervention and perceives government as a negative influence that should remain as limited as possible. Antipolitics, on the other hand, refers to trade unionist strategies that reject activities in the political sphere as a means to achieve labor's goals, preferring instead strictly economic action.

[4] Bruce Laurie, *Artisans into Workers: Labor in 19th Century America* (Toronto: Hill and Wang, 1989), 177; Norman Ware, *The Labor Movement in the U.S., 1860–1890* (New York: Appleton, 1929), 42, 350.

[5] See, for example, Louis Reed, *The Labor Philosophy of Samuel Gompers* (Port Washington, NY: Kennikat Press, 1966); and Fred Greenbaum, "The Social Ideas of Samuel Gompers," *Labor History*, 7 (1), Winter 1966, 35–61.

politics. It will concentrate not on radical parties, but on America's trade union movement and particularly the AFL, for the latter dominated the labor movement by 1900 both politically and economically. Likewise, this project will highlight not the legislative arena, but rather the relationships between organized labor and the mainstream political parties. Workers achieved relatively little in shaping national legislation during this period, primarily because the antistatism of major leaders such as Samuel Gompers precluded a powerful role in that sphere. Instead, organized labor made its power felt more through its energetic political mobilization and nervous negotiations with the major parties. The American Federation of Labor trailblazed in these areas during the Progressive era, articulating organized labor's voice on political questions at the national level, forming an alliance with the Democratic Party, and attempting to offer political guidance to the mass of American workers.

The Historians and American Labor Politics

Scholars have long been interested in the political potential of American workers. In 1906, Werner Sombart cast a long shadow over our understanding of U.S. labor politics by framing the issue negatively in his essay titled "Why Is There No Socialism in America?" He answered his question by arguing that in the United States, class consciousness was wrecked on the shoals of material prosperity.[6] Since that time, historians have directed their attention more to explaining the political incapacity of the working class and their unions than to exploring their actual political practices. Particularly in recent decades, diverse arguments have been offered to explain why class has played so small a role in American politics, why workers eschewed socialism, and why labor failed to exercise significant influence. In the 1960s and 1970s, for example, the dominant school of political historiography argued that ethnic, cultural, and religious factors determined citizens' voting behavior in the years between 1870 and 1910, and thus that class was not a significant factor.[7] More recently, legal historians have

---

[6] Werner Sombart, *Why Is There No Socialism in America?*, trans Patricia M. Hocking and C. T. Husbands (White Plains, NY: International Arts and Sciences Press, 1976; originally 1906).

[7] See, for example, Richard Jensen, *The Winning of the Midwest: Social and Political Conflict, 1888–1896* (Chicago: University of Chicago Press, 1971); Paul Kleppner, *The Cross of Culture: A Social Analysis of Midwestern Politics* (New York: The Free Press, 1970); idem, *Continuity and Change in Electoral Politics, 1893–1928* (New York: Greenwood Press, 1987); Robert Cherny, *Populism, Progressivism, and the Transformation of Nebraska Politics, 1885–1915* (Lincoln: University of Nebraska Press, 1981). For criticisms that this school neglected class as an influence on political behavior, see Allan Lichtman, "Critical Election Theory and the Reality of American Presidential Politics, 1916–1940," *American Historical Review*, 81 (1976), 317–51; idem, "Political Realignment and 'Ethnocultural' Voting in Late Nineteenth Century America," *Journal of Social History*, 16 (3), Spring 1983, 55–82. Richard L. McCormick, "Ethnocultural Interpretations of Nineteenth Century American Voting Behavior," *Political Science Quarterly*, 89 (2), June 1974, 351–77.

argued that judicial hostility turned workers away from the political sphere: Because hard-won labor reforms could always be ruled unconstitutional by a judge, workers decided not to waste time on political mobilization.[8] Now within women's history, an important new school is looking at white middle- and upper-class women's contributions to early twentieth-century state formation and particularly the origins of social welfare policies. As Kathryn Kish Sklar has written in a widely read article, between 1880 and 1915, "prodigious political mobilization by middle-class women formed the largest coalitions that broke through the malaise and restructured American social and political priorities at the municipal, state, and federal levels." Sklar builds her argument on a premise of working-class political failure. Seeking to highlight the remarkable role played by American women, she argues that gender acted as a "surrogate" for class in American politics.[9]

In each of the previous arguments, a presumed absence looms far larger than any working-class political presence. These and other studies have indeed helped us understand why workers failed to accomplish more politically in the decades from 1880 to 1930. Workers were divided by craft, skill, region, gender, ethnicity, and race. Working people also divided along political grounds. Disfranchisement excluded female, African-American, and recent immigrant workers from electoral politics. White male workers themselves divided their loyalties among the Democratic, Republican, or Socialist parties, or rejected politics altogether. Until the 1930s, this prevented them from uniting in sufficiently large numbers to exert a major influence on the course of American politics. Yet even if working people did not unite at the ballot box in the decades before the Great Depression, and even if they failed to build a Socialist or Labor Party capable of dominating working-class political culture, it does not follow that they engaged in no political activity or that their efforts had no impact at all.

During an earlier period in American labor historiography, scholars lavished more attention on the political activity of working-class institutions like the AFL. John R. Commons, Philip Taft, Selig Perlman, and other scholars linked to the Wisconsin school of labor scholarship documented the significant political presence maintained by AFL leaders. Yet they celebrated the AFL's emphasis on economic action and stressed the limits on its political action. This assessment shaped future decades of labor historiography. As Selig Perlman described the evolution of the AFL, its leaders rejected the political panaceas pursued by the

---

[8] William Forbath, *Law and the Shaping of the American Labor Movement* (Cambridge: Harvard University Press, 1991); Victoria Hattam, *Labor Visions and State Power* (Princeton: Princeton University Press, 1991).

[9] Kathryn Kish Sklar, "The Historical Foundations of Women's Power in the Creation of the American Welfare State, 1830–1930," in Seth Koven and Sonya Michel, eds., *Mothers of a New World: Maternalist Politics and the Origins of Welfare States* (New York: Routledge, 1993), 45; Theda Skocpol, *Protecting Soldiers and Mothers: The Political Origins of Social Policy in the United States* (Cambridge: Harvard University Press, 1992), rejects Sklar's surrogate argument, yet she agrees with Sklar in seeing working-class politics as an arena of failure and missed opportunity.

Knights of Labor for a path to economic success paved by conservative business unionism.[10] Although early trades unionists such as Gompers and Adolph Strasser began as Marxists, they soon discovered that class consciousness in America was and could only be limited. This new species of labor organization "grasped the idea, supremely correct for American conditions, that the economic front was the only front on which the labor army could stay united," in the words of Selig Perlman, and this appraisal underpinned their successful, economistic, trade unionism.[11]

Historians influenced by the Wisconsin school elaborated these ideas into a larger claim that the AFL's character derived from a consensus among its members and leaders that an antipolitical and especially antisocialist approach would best serve their interests. That consensus in turn derived primarily from the middle-class psychology of American workers. According to Marc Karson, "The American worker feels middle-class and behaves middle-class. To understand his politics, one must recognize his psychology, a large part of which is middle-class derived." Their middle-class psychology led workers to support both American capitalism and individualism. "When Socialists criticize the self-interest and acquisitive spirit of capitalism, the worker feels under attack for within himself, he knows, burns the capitalistic spirit."[12]

With the emergence of the "new labor history" in the 1960s, historians shifted their attention away from institutions, politics, and the state. Labor historians began examining community and workplace relationships at the expense of institutions. The impressive work published on politics by scholars such as Melvyn Dubofsky, John Laslett, Leon Fink, Mari Jo Buhle, and Nick Salvatore tended to explore moments of militancy and radicalism. As a result, the political activities of the Knights of Labor, the Socialist Party, or the Industrial Workers of the World have many students, whereas the politics of conservative or moderate workers for many years awaited their historians.[13]

---

[10] Selig Perlman, *A Theory of the Labor Movement* (Philadelphia: Porcupine Press, 1928), 198–9. See also John Commons et al., *History of Labour in the United States* (New York: Macmillan, 1918, 2 vols.). For other discussions of the AFL that indicate the influence of the Wisconsin school, see Gerald Grob, *Workers and Utopia: A Study of Ideological Conflict in the American Labor Movement, 1865–1890* (Chicago: Quadrangle Books, 1961); Marc Karson, *American Labor Unions and Politics, 1900–1918* (Carbondale: Southern Illinois University Press, 1958); and Selig Perlman, *History of Trade Unionism in the United States* (New York: Macmillan, 1922).

[11] Perlman, *A Theory of the Labor Movement*, 197–8.

[12] Karson, *American Labor Unions and Politics*, 290–6. For other "psychological" arguments about American workers, see Perlman, *A Theory of the Labor Movement*; and Marc Karson, "The Psychology of Trade Union Membership," *Mental Hygiene*, 41, January 1957, 87–93.

[13] Examples of works in labor history focusing on politics include Nick Salvatore, *Eugene V. Debs: Citizen and Socialist* (Urbana: University of Illinois Press, 1982); David Montgomery, *Beyond Equality: Labor and the Radical Republicans, 1862–1872* (New York: Alfred Knopf, 1967); Leon Fink, *Workingmen's Democracy: The Knights of Labor and American Politics* (Urbana: University of Illinois Press, 1983); Alan Dawley, *Class and Community: The Industrial Revolution in Lynn* (Cambridge: Harvard University Press, 1976); Melvyn Dubofsky,

Several studies provide important exceptions to these trends in labor historiography by shifting our focus from the national to the state level of labor politics. In 1962, Michael Rogin employed the term "voluntarism" to describe an AFL "pragmatic philosophy" that urged workers to rely on "their own voluntary associations" and opposed alliances with a political party or state intervention. Rogin stressed the political consequences of voluntarism: It was an "antipolitical doctrine" that denied unions "the right to act politically." According to Rogin, local and state labor movements broke with the antipolitical orientation of the national AFL leadership. They lobbied actively and pursued a broader spectrum of social legislation.[14] Gary Fink's excellent study of the Missouri State Federation of Labor, published in 1973, expanded on Rogin's ideas. Like Rogin, Fink found that local labor leaders "placed a much greater emphasis upon the exercise of [their] potential political power and influence than did the national leadership." He also argued that critical differences existed between the national and local levels of organized labor. Local workers rejected the antistatism of the national AFL, and they moved close to rejecting its emphasis on nonpartisan campaign strategies.[15]

In 1968, Philip Taft's study of the California State Federation of Labor, which looked at the period after World War I, presented a very different interpretation. He argued that the California federation pursued a pragmatic and moderate political vision, one closer to the political vision of the AFL national leaders. Presenting labor politics as a sphere remarkably free from internal conflict, Taft proposed that national AFL leaders allowed local and state leaders to make their

We Shall Be All: A History of the Industrial Workers of the World (New York: Quadrangle Books, 1969); Mari Jo Buhle, Women and American Socialism, 1870–1920 (Urbana: University of Illinois Press, 1981); Richard Oestreicher, Solidarity and Fragmentation: Working People and Class Consciousness in Detroit, 1875–1900 (Urbana: University of Illinois Press, 1986); Henry F. Bedford, Socialism and the Workers in Massachusetts, 1886–1912 (Amherst: University of Massachusetts Press, 1966); William Dick, Labor and Socialism in America: The Gompers Era (Port Washington, NY: Kennikat Press, 1972); Chester McArthur Destler, American Radicalism: 1865–1901 (Chicago: Quadrangle Books, 1966); James R. Green, Grassroots Socialism: Radical Movements in the Southwest, 1895–1943 (Baton Rouge: Louisiana State University Press, 1978); John H. M. Laslett, Labor and the Left: A Study of Socialist and Radical Influences in the American Labor Movement, 1881–1924 (New York: Basic Books, 1970); Richard Schneirov, "The Knights of Labor in the Chicago Labor Movement and in Municipal Politics, 1877–1887," Ph.D. diss., Northern Illinois University, 1984.

[14] Michael Rogin, "Voluntarism: The Political Functions of an Antipolitical Doctrine," Industrial and Labor Relations Review, 15 (4), July 1962, 523, 531. Voluntarism is a profoundly slippery term, meaning different things to different people. It seems derived from the language and concepts of AFL leaders like Samuel Gompers, but in fact he discussed voluntary relationships only in the last months of his life. Because of such problems, this study will not rely on the term or the concept of voluntarism. For more on the concept's history, see Julia Greene, "The Strike at the Ballot Box: Politics and Partisanship in the American Federation of Labor, 1881 to 1917," Ph.D. diss., Yale University, 1990.

[15] Gary Fink, Labor's Search for Political Order: The Political Behavior of the Missouri Labor Movement, 1890–1940 (Columbia: University of Missouri Press, 1973).

own political decisions and the latter in turn sought simply to carry out the wishes of their rank-and-file members. The absence of a labor party in the United States, he concluded, derived from the lack of interest in such an effort exhibited by ordinary American workers.[16]

By the 1980s, labor historians had begun to rediscover politics and the state as an important sphere of working-class experience, so much so that the work carried out by Rogin, Taft, and Fink no longer seemed unusual. The movement began among political scientists as a small group of "new institutionalists" responded to the influence achieved by social historians.[17] Soon the movement took shape in the rallying cry first articulated by Theda Skocpol in her essay "Bringing the State Back In." Challenging social historians' "society-centered" analysis of historical change, and their emphasis on social forces and phenomena, Skocpol proposed instead a "state-centered" methodology that envisions the state as autonomous and hence as a central causal agent in American society, economics, and politics.[18]

Skocpol's influential work has encouraged labor historians to explore new aspects of workers' relationship with politics and the state. David Montgomery's 1987 synthesis of labor history, *The Fall of the House of Labor*, signaled this growing interest. Historians with diverse approaches, from Melvyn Dubofsky to Shelton Stromquist and Cecelia Bucki, as well as political scientists such as Amy Bridges, Karen Orren, and Martin Shefter, have all shed new light on working people's politics. Unlike many earlier studies, these have not focused on radicalism, but on more moderate and widespread political approaches.[19] Such work

---

[16] Philip Taft, *Labor Politics American Style: The California State Federation of Labor* (Cambridge: Harvard University Press, 1968), 4–7.

[17] James G. March and Johan P. Olsen, "The New Institutionalism: Organizational Factors in Political Life," *American Political Science Review*, 78 (3), September 1984, 734–49; Rogers M. Smith, "Political Jurisprudence, the 'New Institutionalism,' and the Future of Public Law," *American Political Science Review*, 82 (1), March 1988, 89–108.

[18] Theda Skocpol, "Bringing the State Back In: Strategies of Analysis in Current Research," in Peter B. Evans, Dietrich Rueschmeyer, and Theda Skocpol, eds., *Bringing the State Back In* (New York: Cambridge University Press, 1985), 3–37; Skocpol, *Protecting Soldiers and Mothers*; Stephen Skowronek, *Building a New American State: The Expansion of National Administrative Capacities, 1877–1920* (New York: Cambridge University Press, 1982).

[19] David Montgomery, *The Fall of the House of Labor: Workplace, the State, and American Labor Activism, 1865–1925* (New York: Cambridge University Press, 1987); Melvyn Dubofsky, *The State and Labor in Modern America* (Chapel Hill: University of North Carolina Press, 1994); Shelton H. Stromquist, "The Crucible of Class: Cleveland Politics and the Origins of Municipal Reform in the Progressive Era," *Journal of Urban History*, 23 (2), January 1997, 192–220; Cecelia F. Bucki, "The Pursuit of Political Power: Class, Ethnicity, and Municipal Politics in Interwar Bridgeport, 1915–1936," Ph.D. diss., University of Pittsburgh, 1991; Joseph McCartin, "Labor's Great War: American Workers, Unions, and the State, 1916–1920," Ph.D. diss., State University of New York at Binghamton, 1990; Alan Dawley, "Workers, Capital, and the State in the Twentieth Century," in J. Carroll Moody and Alice Kessler-Harris, eds., *Perspectives on American Labor History: The Problem of Synthesis* (De Kalb: Northern Illinois University Press, 1989), 152–200; Colin Davis, "Bitter Storm: The 1922 National Railroad Shopmen's Strike," Ph.D. diss., State

as Michael Kazin's fine *Barons of Labor* have rekindled interest not only in politics, but also in the AFL. Exploring labor politics in San Francisco during the Progressive era, and following a line of argument pursued decades earlier by Gary Fink and Michael Rogin, Kazin demonstrated that workers there were politically and socially active and engaged.[20]

Two recent studies, each coincidentally stressing a single factor of causation, bear with special relevance on the political history of the AFL. William Forbath, in *Law and the Shaping of the American Labor Movement*, and Gwendolyn Mink, in *Old Labor and New Immigrants*, both argued that historians need a new explanation for the exceptionalism of the American working class. How should we explain the triumph of conservative craft unionism that rejected broad visions of social and political change? Forbath and Mink found their explanations, respectively, in the courts and in immigration. According to Forbath, "judge-made law and legal violence limited, demeaned, and demoralized workers' capacities for class-based social and political action." Judicial hostility and repression made inclusive unionism and broad reform efforts seem costly, encouraging Samuel Gompers and his allies to stress economic action and only very narrow and limited political concerns.[21]

Pure and Simple Politics will complement Forbath's study by focusing on the major parties and the ways that turn-of-the-century partisan culture shaped the political environment in which the AFL operated. It differs in seeing the evolution of American labor politics as caused by many factors rather than simply the judiciary. Furthermore, I will argue, Forbath's approach does not help us explain the trade unionists' aggressive political activism around the injunction and other issues. Judicial hostility helped push trade unionists into more, rather than less, political engagement.

For her part, Gwendolyn Mink holds that immigration "played the decisive role in formulating an American version of labor politics." Exploring immigration's influence with an emphasis on demographic change, the split labor market, segmentation of the American working class, and nativism among white native-born workers, Mink demonstrates how waves of immigration from Europe

University of New York at Binghamton, 1989; Amy Bridges, *A City in the Republic: Antebellum New York and the Origins of Machine Politics* (Ithaca, NY: Cornell University Press, 1987); Martin Shefter, "Trade Unions and Political Machines," in Ira Katznelson and Aristide Zolberg, eds., *Working-Class Formation: Nineteenth Century Patterns in Western Europe and the United States* (Princeton: Princeton University Press, 1986), 197–278. A fine example and summary of the growing literature on labor politics is David Brody's essay "The Course of American Labor Politics," in idem, *In Labor's Cause: Main Themes on the History of the American Worker* (New York: Oxford University Press, 1993), 43–80. See also David Brody, "The American Worker in the Progressive Era," in his *Workers in Industrial America: Essays on the 20th Century Struggle*, 2nd ed. (New York: Oxford University Press, 1993), 3–47.

[20] Michael Kazin, *Barons of Labor: The San Francisco Building Trades and Union Power in the Progressive Era* (Urbana: University of Illinois Press, 1987), 3–7, 277–90.

[21] Forbath, *Law and the Shaping of the American Labor Movement*, 3, 25, 168.

and Asia reinforced occupational and ethnic divisions within the working class. Ultimately, in Mink's view, these forces gave rise both to the craft exclusionism of the AFL and its conservative political orientation: "racial nativism became a driving force behind union politics" and AFL voluntarism became its ideological formulation. Mink's argument on the demographic and segmenting impact of immigration is useful, but the interpretation of the relationship between immigration and AFL politics in *Pure and Simple Politics* will diverge significantly from hers. Although the AFL leaders clustered around Samuel Gompers certainly cared deeply about immigration restriction, it never became a central force or a litmus test for determining their political alliances, nor can it explain why the Federation entered politics so energetically after 1903. Other issues like judicial hostility and even the eight-hour day for government workers ranked much higher in the hierarchy of political issues on which AFL leaders concentrated.[22]

Unlike studies proposing a single-factor explanation, this project interprets the political evolution of organized labor in the United States as deriving from a variety of factors, influences, and contingencies. The unusual nature and character of the American state, with the courts and political parties exercising such a powerful role, greatly shaped the labor movement. Far from a static force during these years, the federal government underwent a transformation as the executive branch expanded its powers and intervened more directly both in domestic and international affairs. In addition, anti-union employers' organizations aggressively mobilized in the years after 1900, contesting labor's power on shop floors across the country and, increasingly, through skilled use of the courts, the parties, and the U.S. Congress. These forces not only helped push politics to the center of labor's agenda, they also shaped the specific political strategies labor activists developed for combatting their enemies and achieving their visions.

Yet the working class and its institutions stand at the heart of this story. Working people in the United States by the turn of the twentieth century were profoundly divided amongst and against themselves. Immigration and the gradual entrance of women, children, and African Americans into the work force reshaped the gender and racial characteristics of the class. By 1900, one could

---

[22] For an example of immigration's subordinate position in the AFL's political universe, one might consult "Labor's Protest to Congress," *American Federationist* (hereafter cited as *AF*), 15 (4), April 1908, 261–6, the document generated by the AFL to list its main demands during the critical campaign year of 1908. Immigration is not mentioned in the document. Similarly, after the 1912 election, Gompers visited President-elect Woodrow Wilson to discuss labor's political goals, and again immigration was not on the list (see Chapter Eight). I am not arguing that immigration never mattered to AFL members and leaders, but rather that it played a less central role than various other issues. Gwendolyn Mink, *Old Labor and New Immigrants in American Political Development: Union, Party, and State, 1875–1920* (Ithaca, NY: Cornell University Press, 1986), 67 and 53. See also Julia Greene's review of *Old Labor and New Immigrants* by Gwendolyn Mink, *International Labor and Working-Class History*, 34, Fall 1988, 122–6.

see in the United States a bifurcated working class, dominated by a minority of skilled workers, predominantly white native-born men, who made higher wages and exercised more power on the shop floor than did other workers. These skilled craftsmen were also far more likely to enjoy full political rights, exercising the franchise and participating enthusiastically in the era's partisan political culture. The labor organization they created, the AFL, not only stood at the center of the labor movement by the end of the nineteenth century, it also excluded the vast majority of workers. Semiskilled and unskilled workers, those most likely to be female, new immigrants, or workers of color, seldom found the AFL a welcoming place. Yet they continued to exert a tremendous influence on labor's strategies. Their labor militancy, especially in the years after 1909, and their involvement in more radical political and economic organizations, issued a constant warning to AFL leaders and members – one that did not always go unheard – of the dangers and risks of conservative craft unionism.

Although the AFL represented only a privileged segment of the working class, it nonetheless emerges as central to understanding the evolution of American labor politics. As the most powerful institution representing any part of the working class, the AFL's project to develop a national political policy was a formidable one. Furthermore, this effort held significance for every working person in America, including those whom the AFL excluded. Understanding the AFL's political evolution thus requires an exploration of the different and rivaling voices within the Federation. Power relations within the AFL were complex and political decisions highly contested. Scholars long ago demonstrated the AFL's vulnerability and its dependence on powerful affiliated unions such as the carpenters and the miners. Federation leaders like Samuel Gompers always had to be sure their policies enjoyed support among a critical mass of affiliated international unions, which thus exerted a significant influence. Yet for all the careful attention national leaders gave to the wishes of international affiliates, when it came to their relations with more politically oriented affiliates, the central labor unions and the state federations of labor, a different approach dominated. The national leaders of the AFL possessed a great deal of power and they frequently employed it aggressively in an attempt to keep local affiliates under control.

Yet the trade unionists who belonged to the AFL defied many efforts to control their activities. Geography, ethnicity, religion, and partisan loyalties all served to give AFL members strikingly different approaches to politics. At no time during the period explored by this book did AFL members easily unite behind a single approach to politics. It was partly this diversity and division along political lines that made the AFL's nonpartisan politics so appropriate. But other divisions also separated AFL members and leaders besides the question of which political party to support. Local- and state-level unionists wished to choose their own political strategies and alliances, and they disapproved of national leaders' efforts to steer them in one direction or another. Thus, the AFL's effort to mobilize trade unionists behind a political program in 1906 and

1908 would generate powerful tensions within the Federation. Furthermore, when it came to the tactics of mobilization, as we will see, local-level trade unionists made very different choices than their counterparts at the national level.

This study is therefore most interested in the relationship between AFL workers and the larger political culture in America at the turn of the century. As such, voting behavior itself will not be central to the story. A meticulous calculation of voting statistics at the ward and precinct levels would enhance our understanding of workers' voting behavior. My main concerns, however, lie instead in the complex processes through which the AFL decided its political strategies and experimented with mobilization tactics and political alliances. Thus, I focus on the activities and beliefs that created labor's political culture in the weeks and months before election day. I seek to examine who controls the political decisions made by organized labor, how demands and pressures from below influence their formulation, and the consequences of political strategies as diverse as mass mobilization and elite lobbying tactics.

This, then, is a book about the political possibilities faced by different groups within the American Federation of Labor, and the political choices they made. It will explore diverse political strategies and styles, and the debates those political decisions generated. It will weigh the AFL's decision to embark on a campaign of mass mobilization, as well as its retreat into a more narrow and less popular version of labor politics in the years after 1909. All these factors came together to create one very important part of labor's political culture in the decades before World War I. They shaped both the way the "labor question" would be treated in the public and political spheres, and relations within the AFL itself.

State and Society in Progressive America

The larger environment in which trade unionists experienced and acted on politics changed rapidly at the turn of the century. Because this transformation so profoundly shaped the context in which AFL members and leaders made their political decisions, it requires a brief exploration. What relationship existed between state and society during these years, and how does an organization like the AFL fit into the equation?

Before the Progressive era, the federal government possessed only limited powers relative to individual states. Amidst such a radical decentralization of power, two key players provided a source of unity: the major parties and the judiciary. In the phrase coined by Stephen Skowronek, this was "a state of courts and parties." As early as the 1830s, party organizations developed extensive mechanisms for establishing discipline, and thus became the most effective public instruments for wielding power in nineteenth-century America. Amidst a fervid partisan culture based on rock-solid loyalties, the two parties competed fiercely against one another. The courts, as Forbath has explored, played a central role by defining the relationships between federal and state governments and the proper functions of each.[23]

After 1896, the hegemony of the major parties grew fragile as they faced challenges from many quarters. Meanwhile, state bureaucracies expanded and grew more interventionist, as described most eloquently in Stephen Skowronek's *Building a New American State*. Skowronek presents a "state-centered" analysis of turn-of-the-century American politics, one that emphasizes the activities of state managers and the influence exerted by preexisting state institutions. Along with scholars such as Theda Skocpol, Skowronek recommends that we reject "society-centered" approaches that would reduce complex political transformations to the effects of broader socioeconomic changes.[24] Although this project has been profoundly influenced by the work of Skowronek, it takes a different approach. The work and conceptualizations of social historians who see ordinary people exercising agency in American history remains extremely useful. Following their lead but interested in the political sphere, my work focuses on the relationships between state and society. How and when do society and state interpenetrate each other? How does their relationship change over time? How do social groups articulate demands and pressure the state to respond? How do they create institutions that, in ways not always pleasing to the social groups from which they sprang, negotiate with the state? Although seeing both state and society as influential players in their own right, this project is most interested in the interactions between the two.[25]

A careful examination of the relationship between state and society is especially important in the case of the United States, with its tradition of weak government. Arguments for "state autonomy" seem least useful conceptually in the case of the United States, where even Skowronek claims that the parties, instruments of mass democracy, possessed far more power than did the state bureaucracy. The parties' central role suggests a need to look closely at organizations that exercise power, as well as the relationship between them and those they seek to represent. Even during the Progressive era, when state managers began to emerge as independent and powerful players, the structure and culture of the party system remained strong and enduring. Even the most powerful federal bureaucracies were embryonic at this stage. As a result, whichever party won the presidency continued to exert a major influence on the government's character.

---

[23] The term "party state" comes from Stephen Skowronek, *Building a New American State: The Expansion of National Administrative Capacities, 1877–1920* (Cambridge: Cambridge University Press, 1982), 24–35.

[24] On the decline of the parties, see Walter Dean Burnham, "The System of 1896: An Analysis." in Paul Kleppner et al., *The Evolution of American Electoral Systems* (Westport, CT: Greenwood Press, 1981), 147–202. On the state's expansion, consult Skowronek, *Building a New American State*; Skocpol, *Protecting Soldiers and Mothers*; and Evans, Rueschemeyer, and Skocpol, *Bringing the State Back In*.

[25] For a view close to my own, see Charles Bright and Susan Harding, "Processes of State-making and Popular Protest: An Introduction," in their edited collection *Statemaking and Social Movements: Essays in History and Theory* (Ann Arbor: University of Michigan Press, 1984).

Thus, in the Progressive era, one sees an expanding but still weak state bureaucracy, deteriorating discipline among the parties' rank and file, and widespread attacks on the power of the judiciary. Amidst this reformulation and recreation of the state, new organizations sprang up across the nation to offer citizens innovative ways of influencing the state and participating in political decision making. Potentially, they represented a further flowering of American democracy: Although the structure of American politics made it exceptionally difficult for independent or radical party politics to succeed, the organizations that represented employers, doctors, farmers, and workers, along with many other groups, provided a new if imperfect way for specific social groups to shape their government. Their potential was especially important given the remarkable "substanceless" character of American parties: As broad coalitions, the parties were often found wanting by any specific social group.

Yet even at their best, the new organizations and institutions represented a double-edged sword. Although they gave a distinct voice to farmers, employers, workers, and other social groups, they were themselves part of a larger concentration of power occurring within the state bureaucracies, in the parties, and across American society. The "organizational revolution" was one key part of a shifting of power from the local communities, to the state, and upward to the national level. As Samuel Hays described many years ago, there emerged an upward shifting of power both in public and private affairs during this period.[26] For example, the economy was transformed at the turn of the century as consolidation – commonly referred to as the great merger movement – restructured corporate America. The expansion of state bureaucracies so ably described by Skowronek forms one part of this centralization of power. Another part involved a shifting of responsibilities from municipal governments upward to the state level, and from state legislatures upward to the federal level. But it also emerged throughout American society, as groups struggled to develop their voices at the national level. As the boundaries between different levels of government shifted and the federal government assumed an expanded range of powers and responsibilities, social groups scrambled to exert influence at the national level of American politics. Thus, the small and rapidly growing organizations that represented different constituencies themselves underwent a dramatic transformation during these watershed years. Headquarters were established in Washington, D.C.; lobbying activities took up a greater part of their time. In the process, many of these organizations grew less democratic and less representative of the social group from which they had sprung.

In sum, understanding the relation between state and society at the turn of the century requires that we focus on two overlapping but contradictory processes. On the one hand, the ability of social groups to influence their government in

---

[26] Hays, "Political Parties and the Community-Society Continuum." See also idem, *The Response to Industrialism* (Chicago: University of Chicago Press, 1957); and Robert Wiebe, *The Search for Order, 1877–1920* (New York: Hill and Wang, 1967).

some ways increased during this period, as the state underwent a thorough reconstruction and its main pillar, the political parties, began to deteriorate while the new state bureaucracies had not yet consolidated their power. Within this vacuum of power, new organizations pressed the demands of various social groups, and a diverse range of activities – strikes, protests, riots – less directly placed pressure on the state. While these developments pointed to a more porous interaction between state and society, a second process simultaneously began to insulate the state from societal pressures: a broad concentration of power that took place within and outside of the state in the economic, political, and social realms. Both these processes can be seen at work in the players that dominate this study: the political parties and the union movement. As the parties declined they struggled, often successfully, to hold onto their powers and protect themselves from other pressures. Meanwhile as the AFL developed a national voice, it simultaneously grew less democratic and more exclusivist as the conservative leaders allied around Samuel Gompers consolidated their control over the entire labor movement. The tensions and debates generated as trade unionists shaped and reacted to all these changes will be a central concern of this book.

The chapters that follow are organized in a rough chronological order, and they fall into three major parts. Part One explores the rise of the AFL. Chapter One traces the social and economic roots of the AFL and its evolution into a conservative and exclusivist organization representing the interests and outlook of skilled workers, most of them white, native-born, and male, by the end of the 1890s. Chapter Two looks at the AFL's political evolution during the Gilded Age, tracing the triumph of a political strategy favored by Samuel Gompers, one that rejected "party tyranny" and relied instead on nonpartisan tactics like lobbying to win specific labor demands. Chapter Three analyzes the forces that encouraged Federation leaders, by 1904, to reach beyond their limited lobbying tactics and experiment with electoral politics. In particular, the chapter explores the impact of a more interventionist state and an increasingly aggressive anti-union movement led by the National Association of Manufacturers.

Part Two examines the AFL's "strike at the ballot box," that is, its aggressive move into electoral politics in 1906 and 1908, in which leaders exhorted trade unionists to support and mobilize behind prolabor candidates. Chapter Four focuses on the AFL's campaign strategy in 1906, which stressed congressional campaigns, looking in particular at the different decisions made by national- and local-level trade unionists. The next two chapters analyze the AFL's mobilization campaign during 1908, when a presidential election significantly altered the terrain of American labor politics. Chapter Five depicts the Federation's support for Democratic Party candidate William Jennings Bryan and the origins and nature of its unprecedented alliance with the Democratic Party. Chapter Six assesses the impact this alliance exercised on the AFL. The Democratic-AFL partnership that year put the labor movement at the heart of American politics, yet the consequences proved surprising. To the chagrin of AFL leaders, they became an object of criticism and their institution, a center of disaffection.

Defeated in most of their goals in 1908, Federation leaders retreated from their dramatic mobilization campaigns in the years that followed, but refused to disengage from politics altogether. Meanwhile, trade unionists at the local level intensified their participation in Socialist and Labor Party activities. These activities formed one part of a larger shift in American political culture, as progressive reform activities reached their height and the role of the state became a dominant issue. Part Three examines the AFL's political goals and strategies amidst these changing circumstances. Chapter Seven explores the AFL's reevaluation of political strategy that followed on its 1908 defeat, as well as the new emphasis on lobbying and discrete alliances with Democrats that resulted. Finally, Chapter Eight focuses on AFL politics after the election of Democrat Woodrow Wilson to the presidency in 1912. A Democratic presidency seemed to bring the AFL closer to the pinnacles of political power, yet the politics of reform in these years marginalized Federation leaders even as new actors proved increasingly influential.

PART ONE

The Rise of Pure and Simple Politics

I am willing to subordinate my opinions to the well being, harmony, and success of the labor movement; I am willing to sacrifice myself upon the altar of any phase or action it may take for its advancement; I am willing to step aside if that will promote our cause; but I cannot and will not prove false to my convictions that the trade unions pure and simple are the natural organizations of the wage workers to secure their present and practical improvement and to achieve their final emancipation.

Samuel Gompers, *Seventy Years of Life and Labor*,
vol. I, p. 385

CHAPTER ONE

Building the Federation

In early December of 1886, thirty-eight trade unionists converged on Druids' Hall in Columbus, Ohio, hoping to create a new nationwide labor federation. They represented young unions like the Tailors, Bakers, Iron Molders, Bricklayers, and Printers. At the movement's head stood three unions: the Cigar Makers, famed for their effective institution-building tactics and represented by Adolph Strasser and Samuel Gompers; the Federation of Miners and Mine Laborers, led by John McBride and Christopher Evans; and the Carpenters and Joiners, headed by Peter McGuire, "one of the coolest and shrewdest men in the labor movement." Most delegates had roots both in socialist organizations and in the Knights of Labor. Now, however, they wanted an organization that would place national trade unions at the movement's center, displacing politics and social reform and guaranteeing autonomy to the various trades.[1]

The organization these men created, the American Federation of Labor, soon eclipsed the dying Knights of Labor. Although the AFL represented a diverse group of unions, by 1900 it would be dominated by the business unionism of conservative affiliates like the cigarmakers and the carpenters. Although industrial unions like the miners played an important role in the AFL, craft unionism would triumph over broader strategies for reaching out to the American working class. And even though the AFL was born amidst a complex mixture of radical and independent politics, it achieved fame for eschewing these in favor of a limited and nonpartisan lobbying program. During its early decades, then, the AFL underwent a complex transformation, one which can be understood only by investigating who it represented, what relationship its leaders and members possessed to the larger working class, and how internal power struggles influenced its evolution during the critical early decades.

---

[1] "Federation of Trades," *New York Tribune*, Dec. 9, 1886, in Stuart Kaufman, et al., eds., *The Samuel Gompers Papers*, Vol. 1, *The Making of a Union Leader, 1850–1886* (Urbana: University of Illinois Press, 1986).

The Social Roots of the AFL

The trade unionists who united in the American Federation of Labor formed a select group: They were predominantly skilled workers and typically male; ethnically, their roots most often lay in England, Ireland, Germany, or Scandinavia. Possessing significant power on the shop floor and earning relatively high wages, America's own "labor aristocracy" grew more distant from other workers during the late nineteenth century as its members struggled to maintain their enviable position amidst complex challenges.

The hothouse conditions characterizing Gilded Age industrialization brought rich rewards to some Americans, but penalties awaited others. Employers, for example, felt squeezed by a tumultuous economy. Intense competition among manufacturers, the long deflationary crisis of 1873 to 1897, declining profit margins, and record bankruptcy rates together made for an explosive business climate. A period bracketed by major depressions (1873–8 and 1893–7), the Gilded Age experienced industrial growth overall but of an increasingly unstable nature. After the 1870s, the periods of expansion grew shorter and the rate of growth in the Gross National Product dropped by nearly half.[2]

Businesspeople explored two main avenues to overcome such economic miseries. They joined together in alliances to prevent the cutthroat competition that led prices to spiral downward. With time, this approach would grow more complex and give birth to the merger movement of 1895 to 1904, in which some 1800 firms disappeared to reemerge as combinations like American Tobacco and Standard Oil.[3] Until then, however, employers stuck to less formal but typically unsuccessful attempts to restrict output.

Employers also responded to declining profit margins by cutting production costs, thereby generating the ceaseless industrial conflict that marked the Gilded Age. Both skilled workers' power in the workplace and their relatively high wages hampered efforts to reduce costs. Thus, employers sought not only to cut wages – undoubtedly the most common strategy – they also struggled to diminish unions' strength and where possible to eliminate skilled workers through mechanization or division of labor. In the long run, such tactics diluted skill and exercised a homogenizing effect on American workers, but during the Gilded Age, the effects varied significantly from one industry to the next.

The iron and steel industry, for example, suggested how mechanization and employer intransigence could devastate a work force. Beginning in the 1870s, new technology gradually made skilled puddlers and rollers less essential to production. In the Homestead strike of 1892, Carnegie and Frick exploited the new circumstances to break the Amalgamated Association of Iron, Steel, and Tin

---

[2] In the 1870s, the rate of growth in the GNP, in constant prices, was an annual average of 6.5 percent; it dropped to 3.6 percent by the mid-1890s. See David M. Gordon, Richard Edwards, and Michael Reich, *Segmented Work, Divided Workers: The Historical Transformation of Labor in the United States* (New York: Cambridge University Press, 1982), 100–2.

[3] Naomi R. Lamoreaux, *The Great Merger Movement in American Business, 1895–1904* (New York: Cambridge University Press, 1985), 2.

Workers, one of the most powerful unions in the country at that time. Following this defeat, wages fell while the union's work rules disappeared. As David Montgomery argues, skilled workers continued to play a central role in the mills, but one that intensified their isolation from other workers. After the strike, Frick reorganized the job structure to make skilled blowers, melters, and rollers into supervisors of other men. Although the number of skilled steelworkers decreased during this period, their distance from those they supervised increased dramatically after 1892 as the steel industry expanded.[4]

Workers in many other industries, notably cigarmaking, tailoring, and furniture making, similarly confronted skill dilution and new machinery during the nineteenth century. Printers, however, differed: Although employers introduced linotype, workers successfully controlled access to the machine-tending positions this created. Carpenters and metalworkers provided yet another response to industrialization. Although carpenters faced a range of woodworking inventions after 1871, their skills remained essential to the trade throughout the twentieth century. Meanwhile, industrialization created a range of new construction skills, as electricians and structural ironworkers joined the carpenters' ranks. In metalworking, too, industrialization created new skills, especially the tending of sophisticated machines, keeping the machinists' trade a skilled craft beyond the nineteenth century.[5]

In short, although the threat of skill dilution loomed over Gilded Age craftspeople and occasionally became a reality, industrialization had a more complex and less even impact than one might assume.[6] In fact, skilled workers' numbers overall did not significantly decline. Assessing their numerical strength between 1870 and 1910, Andrew Dawson found little change: In 1870, skilled workers constituted 20.5 percent of the nonagricultural working class; in 1880, 17.6 percent; in 1890, 19 percent; in 1900, 17 percent; and in 1910, 18.5 percent.[7] Rather

---

[4] David Montgomery, *The Fall of the House of Labor: The Workplace, the State, and American Labor Activism, 1865–1925* (New York: Cambridge University Press, 1987), 41–2; David Brody, *Steelworkers in America: The Nonunion Era* (New York: Harper & Row, 1960).

[5] Andrew Dawson, "The Paradox of Dynamic Technological Change and the Labor Aristocracy in the U.S., 1880–1914," *Labor History*, 20 (3), Summer 1979, 325–51; Robert Christie, *Empire in Wood: A History of the Carpenters' Union* (Ithaca, NY: Cornell University Press, 1956), 26, 108; and John Jentz, "Skilled Workers and Industrialization: Chicago's German Cabinetmakers and Machinists, 1880–1900," in Hartmut Keil and John Jentz, eds., *German Workers in Industrial Chicago, 1850–1910: A Comparative Perspective* (DeKalb: Northern Illinois University Press, 1983), 73–85.

[6] For this point made from the perspective of English history, see Raphael Samuel, "Workshop of the World: Steam Power and Hand Technology in Mid-Victorian Britain," *History Workshop Journal*, 2 (3), Spring 1977, 6–72.

[7] I have rounded off Dawson's figures, which are based on the following trades: enginemen, firemen, and conductors; carpenters and joiners; masons (brick and stone); painters, glaziers, and varnishers; paper hangers; plasterers; plumbers and gas and steam fitters; mechanics; glassworkers; blacksmiths; machinists; steamboiler makers; wheelwrights; cabinetmakers; coopers; gold- and silverworkers; bookbinders; engravers; printers; lithographers and pressmen; and model makers and patternmakers. See Dawson, "The Paradox of Dynamic Technological Change," 330–1.

than facing elimination, America's labor aristocracy enjoyed greater prestige and better economic rewards than most workers during this period. Skilled workers saw their wages increase much more dramatically than those of other workers during the late nineteenth and early twentieth centuries. Peter Shergold argues that the gap between skilled and unskilled workers' earnings was much greater in the United States than in Great Britain, particularly after the 1890s' depression ended. Similarly, Andrew Dawson has demonstrated that between 1890 and 1914, a period when all manufacturing workers saw their wages rise on average by 54 percent, skilled workers' wages rose by 74 percent and unskilled workers' wages increased by only 31 percent.[8]

Broader changes during these decades heightened skilled workers' isolation. Most dramatic, perhaps, was the social re-creation of the American working class. Between the 1870s and 1890s, the working class was ethnically rather homogeneous. Most workers came from northern and western Europe and ethnicity did not separate skilled and unskilled workers: Though Germans dominated skilled occupations to the disadvantage of Irish workers, both ethnic groups were well represented across skill levels. According to JoEllen Vinyard's study of Detroit, for example, 39 percent of German men in 1880 held skilled jobs and 36 percent worked at unskilled labor; by contrast, 28 percent of Irish men possessed skilled occupations and 42 percent were unskilled laborers.[9]

During the 1890s, and especially when recovery from the depression set in, these older immigration patterns gave way as large numbers of immigrants entered the United States from central, southern, and eastern Europe. In 1896, for the first time "new" immigrants outnumbered the "old" (191,545 new vs. 137,552 old immigrants entered the country), and in the following years, until 1915, their numbers rose dramatically (320,981 new immigrants entered the United States in 1900; 610,818 in 1903; 971,715 in 1907; and 894,258 in 1914).[10] Usually lacking in industrial skills, these Italian and Slavic immigrants formed a new unskilled working class. Working as laborers on railroads and in mines, as operatives in textile mills, or as homeworkers in the clothing industry, they typically performed the heaviest, most tedious, and worst paid work in America after the 1890s. The "new" immigrants' seemingly exotic customs and dress, their Catholic or Jewish religion, and their lower standard of living separated them from more privileged workers. But the fundamental difference between old

---

[8] Peter R. Shergold, *Working-Class Life: The "American Standard" in Comparative Perspective, 1899–1913* (Pittsburgh: University of Pittsburgh Press, 1982), 45–57; Dawson, "Paradox of Dynamic Technological Change," 332–4.

[9] JoEllen Vinyard, *The Irish on the Urban Frontier: Nineteenth Century Detroit, 1850–1880* (New York: Arno Press, 1976), 144, cited in Nora Faires, "Occupational Patterns of German-Americans in Nineteenth-Century Cities," in Hartmut Keil and John B. Jentz, eds., *German Workers in Industrial Chicago, 1850–1910: A Comparative Perspective* (DeKalb: Northern Illinois Press, 1983), 37–51.

[10] Bureau of the Census, Department of Commerce, *Historical Statistics of the United States, Colonial Times to 1970* (Washington, DC, 1975), 1:105–6.

and new immigrants remained skill: As immigration from northwestern Europe dried up, as their children and grandchildren became craftspeople, and as new immigrants flooded into unskilled and semiskilled positions, the skilled trades included fewer and fewer foreign-born workers.[11]

Not all of the new immigration came from Europe. Mexican and Asian immigrants also entered the United States in greater numbers by the late nineteenth and early twentieth centuries. Though their numbers were small compared to the influx of southern and eastern Europeans, they reconstructed the work force of certain industries in the western states by the early twentieth century. Like European immigrants, Asian and Mexican workers both found their wage-earning opportunities limited almost exclusively to unskilled tasks. Both groups could be found working predominantly in agriculture. Mexicans, for example, constituted 40 percent of the beet farming work force in Colorado's South Platte Valley and 100 percent of the same industry in California's Imperial Valley. Mexicans also found jobs throughout the West in construction, mining, and railroad maintenance labor. Chinese, Japanese, and Filipinos centered their work in California agriculture, but gradually employment became more possible in laundries, cigar-making, menial restaurant work, and lumber and railroad industries.[12]

More gradual changes also transformed the working class's social character during this period. Women, children, and African-Americans all increased their labor force participation, and in each case, they worked primarily in low-paid, unskilled jobs. The number of working women rose significantly between 1890 and 1910, from 3.7 million women workers in 1890 (18.2 percent of the working class) to nearly 5 million in 1900 (20 percent of all workers).[13] The most common job held by women remained domestic service well into the twentieth century: In 1900, approximately one-third of all women wage earners worked as household servants. African-American women chose domestic service or laundry work when they could, preferring it to agricultural labor. For native-born white women, vocations like teaching and nursing grew increasingly important at the turn of the twentieth century, as did clerical, sales, and other service jobs. Almost 40 percent of women worked at manual jobs, but nearly always in unskilled or semiskilled positions that proved difficult to organize. The classic female industrial job involved tending a machine in a New England textile factory. Meanwhile, by 1900, more than 250,000 children under the age of fifteen

---

[11] Shelton Stromquist, "Looking Both Ways: Ideological Crisis and Working-Class Recomposition in the 1890s," unpublished manuscript, 1984, 58.

[12] See Lawrence A. Cardoso, *Mexican Emigration to the US, 1897–1931* (Tucson: University of Arizona Press, 1980), 24–7; Albert Camarillo, *Chicanos in a Changing Society: From Mexican Pueblos to American Barrios in Santa Barbara and Southern California, 1848–1930* (Cambridge: Harvard University Press, 1979), 165–9; Yasuo Wakatsuki, "Japanese Emigration to the US," *Perspectives in American History*, 12, 1979, 409; and Ronald Takaki, *Strangers from a Different Shore: A History of Asian Americans* (New York: Penguin Books, 1989), 87–92, 182, 319.

[13] *Historical Statistics of the United States: Colonial Times to 1957* (Washington, DC: U.S. Government Printing Office, 1960), 131–2.

worked for a wage in American mines and factories, typically in highly tedious and unskilled jobs.[14]

The vast majority of African-Americans lived and worked in the rural South until well into the twentieth century. As late as 1910, 80 percent of blacks worked either in southern agriculture or as household servants. When the Civil War ended, the number of African-Americans holding skilled industrial jobs actually decreased as whites determined to control well-paying positions. Over the next two decades across the South, the rise of craft unionism and the apprentice system aided white workers' efforts to win control over jobs, especially in the building trades and on the railroads. Yet significant numbers of African-American men continued to work at industrial jobs in the South, retaining some jobs in the building trades and increasing their numbers in extractive industries like lumber and mining. They also worked occasionally in northern industries like mining. Beginning around 1900, the number of African-American men in industrial jobs began steadily to increase. In an era of increasing Jim Crow segregation, this created great animosity among white workers toward their black counterparts, and the number of strikes by white workers protesting the employment of black workers more than doubled during the decade from 1890 to 1900. In addition, blacks seeking industrial employment often faced violence and death threats from white workers. African-American women also worked in large numbers: In 1870, 49.5 percent of them were in the labor force, and that figure remained relatively constant throughout the late nineteenth century. Like white wage-earning women, African-American women typically worked as domestic servants or at related tasks like laundering or cooking.[15]

By the late nineteenth century, then, skilled workers emerged as a distinct social group, isolated and different from other workers, due to a dramatic social and economic remaking of the working class. On a daily basis, their wage labor differentiated them from other workers because they possessed a skill that brought both higher wages and power to affect their immediate environment. After 1890, this fundamental difference became overlaid with ethnic, gender, and racial distinctions. Increasingly, most unskilled workers were female, southern or eastern European, and/or African-American, and most skilled workers were native-born or northwestern European whites as well as being almost

---

[14] Alice Kessler Harris, *Out to Work: A History of Wage-Earning Women in the United States* (New York: Oxford University Press, 1982), esp. 108–41; Tera Hunter, *To 'Joy My Freedom: Southern Black Women's Lives and Labors after the Civil War* (Cambridge: Harvard University Press, 1997); Alice Kessler-Harris, "Where Are the Organized Women Workers," *Feminist Studies*, 3 (1/2), Fall 1975, 92–105; and *Historical Statistics*, 139–40. For a comparison of men's and women's job choices, see Ileen A. Devault, "'Give the Boys a Trade': Gender and Job Choice in the 1890s," in Ava Baron, ed., *Work Engendered: Toward A New History of American Labor* (Ithaca, NY: Cornell University Press, 1991). American Social History Project, *Who Built America?* (New York: Pantheon Books, 1992), 2:175.

[15] Arthur Ross, "The Negro in the American Economy," in Arthur Ross and Herbert Hill, eds., *Employment, Race, and Poverty* (New York: Harcourt, Brace, and World, 1967), 3–48; William H. Harris, *The Harder We Run: Black Workers since the Civil War* (New York: Oxford University Press, 1982), 10–28, 37–41.

exclusively male. As historian Shelton Stromquist notes, these differences became reinforced by changes in urban structure: The rise of streetcar suburbs
removed craftspeople and their families from older working-class neighborhoods
and added a spatial component to the growing social gulf separating skilled and
unskilled workers.[16]

Skilled workers inhabited a culture that reflected and reinforced their increasing separation from other workers. As David Montgomery has noted, a mutualism rooted in working-class solidarities formed the dominant element in their
culture. Thus, George E. McNeill would write in 1899, "The Organization of
laborers in Trades Unions recognizes the fact that mutualism is preferable to
individualism." On the shop floor, this translated into the "stint," or output quota,
because workers saw unlimited production as leading to lower piece rates and
unemployment. Closely joined to the mutualism, in the craftsmen's world view,
stood the principle of "manliness." According to David Montgomery, who first
described manliness as an important aspect of skilled workers' culture, possessing a "manly bearing" provided shorthand slang for the dignified posture workers
should hold both toward the boss and toward one another. The concept suggested
a proud worker unwilling to placate or beg his employer. More recent work on
working-class manliness has expanded on its nature and functions: It connoted
competency, physical prowess, assertiveness, and independence. Furthermore,
the culture of manliness not only united workingmen against their employers,
as Montgomery described it, but also united them against those perceived as
outsiders: women, girls, and boys. Ava Baron, for example, has shown how workingmen intertwined notions of manliness with efforts to control apprenticeship
procedures. Mary Blewett has described a craft workers' version of manliness in
Fall River, one closely tied to the family wage (a wage that allowed the hus-
band to be the only support of his family) and male control over the union.[17]

---

[16] My argument in these pages has been greatly influenced by Shelton H. Stromquist, "Looking
Both Ways: Ideological Crisis and Working-Class Recomposition in the 1890s." Also very
useful on these questions is Andrew Dawson, "The Parameters of Craft Consciousness; The
Social Outlook of the Skilled Worker, 1890–1920," in Dirk Hoerder, ed., *American Labor and
Immigration History, 1877–1920s: Recent European Research* (Champaign: University of Illinois
Press, 1983), 135–55; Sam Bass Warner, *Streetcar Suburbs: The Process of Growth in Boston,
1870–1900* (Cambridge: Harvard University Press, 1962); and Theodore Hershberg, ed.,
*Philadelphia: Work, Space, Family, and Group Experience in the Nineteenth Century: Essays
Toward An Interdisciplinary History of the City* (New York: Oxford University Press, 1981).

[17] Montgomery, *The Fall of the House of Labor*, 4, 17–20, 171, 204–6; Ava Baron, "An
'Other' Side of Gender Antagonism at Work: Men, Boys, and the Remasculinization of
Printers' Work, 1830–1920," in idem, ed., *Work Engendered: Toward a New History of
American Labor* (Ithaca, NY: Cornell University Press, 1991), 47–69; Mary Blewett, "Man-
hood and the Market: The Politics of Gender and Class among the Textile Workers of Fall
River, Massachusetts, 1870–1880," in Baron, *Work Engendered*, 92–114; Gail Bederman,
*Manliness and Civilization: A Cultural History of Gender and Race in the United States,
1880–1917* (Chicago: University of Chicago Press, 1995); Elliott J. Gorn, *The Manly Art:
Bare-Knuckle Prizefighting in America* (Ithaca, NY: Cornell University Press, 1986); Anthony
E. Rotundo, *American Manhood: Transformations in Masculinity from the Revolution to
the Modern Era* (New York: Basic Books, 1993).

Often, too, manliness became closely intertwined with a racial consciousness. In a remarkable reformulation of American labor history, David Roediger has suggested that a racial consciousness of their own whiteness helped unite white workingmen during the nineteenth century. Roediger's work has focused thus far on the antebellum period, and more work is needed to comprehend the subtle dynamics of whiteness and its transformation during the post–Civil War period. Yet it seems clear that as the "age of emancipation" gave way to the triumph of Jim Crow segregation, white working-class culture, too, became pervaded by notions of racial supremacy. In the labor journals and periodicals of the late nineteenth century, one regularly sees craftsmen proclaiming their identity as not mere men, but *free, white* men. Even in moments of celebration, skilled white workers often demonstrated that their identification as "union men" meshed closely with a white racial consciousness. A poem written by Michael McGovern during this period described iron puddlers' festivities after the signing of a new scale:

> There were no men invited such as Slavs and "Tally Annes,"
> Hungarians and Chinamen with pigtail cues and fans.
> No, every man who got the "pass" a union man should be;
> No blacksheep were admitted to the Puddlers' Jubilee.

By the late nineteenth century, as social dynamics such as mass immigration and the entry of more women and children into wage work transformed the working class, such racial and gender identifications as these began to play a different function, reinforcing the sealed character of a distinct social group constituted by skilled workers.[18]

Craftsmen's recreation also reflected the male world in which they worked. No institution occupied a more central position in working-class leisure than the saloon, which served as a place to talk with friends or workmates, to gossip or learn about job possibilities, to celebrate a wedding or to pick up mail. In saloon culture, the common ritual of "treating" one's friends provided a way, as Roy Rosenzweig has suggested, for workers to reinforce through non-economic means the mutuality pervading their lives. Jack London described the custom in his novel *John Barleycorn*, for example, commenting that "I had achieved a concept. Money no longer counted. It was comradeship that counted." Yet saloons also reflected the gender segregation that prevailed in working-class America. Although women and men both enjoyed alcohol in the nineteenth century, the former almost always drank at home. When women did appear in the local saloon, they apparently were exempt from "treating" rituals: In this case,

---

[18] Montgomery, *Fall of the House of Labor*, 25; David Roediger, *The Wages of Whiteness: Race and the Making of the American Working Class* (London: Verso Books, 1991); Bederman, *Manliness and Civilization*; Eric Arnesen, *Waterfront Workers of New Orleans: Race, Class, and Politics, 1863–1923* (New York: Oxford University Press, 1991); Peter Rachleff, *Black Labor in the South: Richmond, Virginia, 1865–1890* (1984; rpt. Urbana: University of Illinois Press, 1989); Alexander Saxton, *The Indispensable Enemy: Labor and the Anti-Chinese Movement in California* (Berkeley: University of California Press, 1971).

as in others, male workers' mutualism had become an exclusive preserve. Other activities popular with working-class audiences, such as theater and sporting events, likewise catered primarily to white male audiences.[19]

In the late nineteenth century, in short, skilled workers' relationship to other workingpeople grew more complex and troubled. Although in many cases their skills remained viable, they faced innumerable threats to their privileged position and could look around to see less fortunate craftsmen who had lost their autonomy, their monopoly over craft knowledge, their high wages, and much of their prestige. At the same time, skilled workers evolved into a separate social grouping because the unskilled and semiskilled working class became composed of immigrants, women, African-Americans, and children. As the chasm widened, unskilled and semiskilled workers seemed, to craftsmen, poised to exploit any opening for new jobs at the expense of those with skills. This social distancing of the skilled workers, combined with the threats they faced as a result of industrialization, would play an important role in the labor movement's evolution at the turn of the twentieth century.

Preserving the Trade Unions

Beginning in 1852, workers in diverse trades began creating national unions to represent their interests. As industrialization created a new national market, standardized products, and stronger businesses in closer touch with one another, more workers found they needed institutions capable of reaching beyond the local or state level.

In seeking to create national unions, workers confronted formidable obstacles in the form of uncompromising employers, an unstable economy, and harassment from the judiciary and the police. These pressures and workers' responses to them influenced the shape of the young labor movement and encouraged a dramatic change of direction during the Gilded Age. In the 1860s, the organized

---

[19] Typically, saloons and theaters were segregated on the basis not only of gender but also ethnicity and race, because they appealed to specific ethnic groups. See Roy Rosenzweig, *Eight Hours for What We Will: Workers and Leisure in an Industrial City, 1870–1920* (New York: Cambridge University Press, 1983), 59–64 (the Jack London quote is on p. 60); Francis Couvares, *The Remaking of Pittsburgh: Class and Culture in an Industrializing City, 1877–1919* (Albany: SUNY Press, 1984), 31–50; David Brundage, *The Making of Western Labor Radicalism: Denver's Organized Workers, 1878–1905* (Urbana: University of Illinois Press, 1994), 66–8; and Jon M. Kingsdale, "The 'Poor Man's Club': Social Functions of the Urban Working-class Saloon," *American Quarterly*, 25, October 1973, 472–89. After 1900, new leisure opportunities would emerge, such as amusement parks and nickelodeons, where women were more welcome. With time, movie houses replaced saloons as centers of sociability, and women played an integral role in this new environment. The limited research so far conducted, however, suggests that African-Americans continued to feel exempted from the movies and amusement parks. See, in addition to Rosenzweig, John F. Kasson, *Amusing the Millions: Coney Island at the Turn of the Century* (New York: Hill and Wang, 1978); Kathy Peiss, *Cheap Amusements: Working Women and Leisure in Turn-of-the-Century New York* (Philadelphia: Temple University Press, 1986).

labor movement rested largely on local unions, felt profoundly the influence of socialism, and devoted itself to political agitation. By 1900, the labor movement had become nationwide, its leaders had centralized their power and reinforced it with business unionist strategies, and although socialism remained important, it had been pushed to the margins of the movement and no longer served as a central inspiration. Furthermore, as efforts to unionize unskilled workers faded, craft consciousness increasingly dominated the movement.

The young cigarmaker named Samuel Gompers typified many of these trends. Born in England in 1850, Gompers emigrated to the United States with his Dutch Jewish parents in 1863. Living in New York, Gompers joined his cigar-making father at the trade, and both joined the Cigar Makers' National Union in 1864. The boy's interests remained distant from the labor movement, however, until 1873 when a new job introduced him to socialism and trade union-ism in one fell swoop. Working in a shop owned by the German socialist David Hirsch, Gompers entered a fascinating milieu of politically active cigarmakers. Among others, he met Ferdinand Laurrell, a Swedish socialist and a leader in the International Workingmen's Association. Introduced by Laurrell to socialist philosophy, Gompers set about learning German so he could read works by Marx, Engels, and Lassalle in the original.[20]

Laurrell also stressed to Gompers the importance of economic organization and the benefits of trade unionism. Radicals like Adolph Strasser, Peter McGuire, and John Swinton, on the other hand, favored the Lassallean approach based on political agitation. As Stuart Kaufman has shown, political versus economic activity emerged as a central division in the International during the depression of the 1870s. Seeing economic organization as the key to working-class eman-cipation, Gompers and Laurrell joined forces with activists like J. P. McDonnell, David Kronburg, and Friedrich Bolte.[21] Within this environment, Sam Gompers first articulated the principles that would motivate his life.

An influential pamphlet by German socialist Carl Hillman, written in 1873 and entitled "Practical Suggestions for Emancipation," provides insight into the trade union–centered approach Gompers was then discovering. According to Hillman, trade unions provided workers with the tool needed to end class rule. Because workers naturally distrusted political parties and showed more interest in immediate concerns like wages and hours, Hillman argued, "it is a fatal error to subordinate the trade union movement directly to the purely political party movement." Workers should focus instead on building strong union organizations, with health and death benefits, and thereby maintain their members' loyalty.

---

[20] Samuel Gompers, *Seventy Years of Life and Labor: An Autobiography* (New York: E. P. Dutton, 1925); Stuart Kaufman, *Samuel Gompers and the Origins of the AFL* (Westport, CT: Greenwood Press, 1973).

[21] Kaufman, *Samuel Gompers*, 34–55; Mark Erlich, "Peter J. McGuire's Trade Unionism: Socialism of a Trades Union Kind?", *Labor History* 24 (2), Spring 1983, 165–97; H. M. Gitelman, "Adolph Strasser and the Origins of Pure and Simple Unionism," *Labor History*, 6 (1), Winter 1965, 71–83.

And at the heart of such unions must be democratic organization. Rather than giving senior craftsmen dictatorial control, unions must follow the principle of equal rights and equal duties: "Even the chairman must not have any privileges. He must be considered an executive only and not a policymaker." Hillman's pamphlet did not exclude politics from labor's future. Once the movement matured sufficiently to create a national federation of unions, he stressed, politics would become more important as workers recognized that they and the Social Democrats shared common interests.[22]

Gompers and his comrade Adolph Strasser would become well known to American labor activists for initiating strategies of business unionism in the Cigar Makers' International Union (CMIU). Ironically, before that, the two men achieved a name by fighting exclusivist union practices. In 1872, Strasser organized a new union for New York City cigarmakers, one open to anyone in the trade, regardless of method or place of work, sex, or nationality. This union, the United Cigarmakers, constituted Strasser's response to CMIU regulations that prohibited "bunchmakers" (workers who used a mechanical mold to press tobacco into shape) from membership; most Bohemian cigarmakers were bunchmakers, so they could not join the union. The United Cigarmakers also initiated key changes in union organization, including collection of regular dues by shop stewards, creation of a central board of administration with delegates representing the various shops, and a system of unemployment and strike benefits. In 1875, the CMIU changed its regulations to admit new members without regard to sex or method of work, and chartered Strasser's union as local 144.[23]

Members of the new local elected Gompers as their first president and Strasser as financial secretary. The two began working to extend their policies of inclusive membership, high dues, centralized administration, and benefits throughout the CMIU. In 1877, the CMIU convention elected Strasser president, and in the following years, with assistance from Gompers, Laurrell, and others, he reorganized the union. As Strasser explained to union members in the pages of the new CMIU journal, both American and English experiences proved the need for a more efficient and more protective structure. Thus, he acted to make the CMIU more centralized (e.g., giving the executive board control over a strike fund and the power to shift funds from richer to poorer locals), more benevolent (adding sick and death benefits), and more wealthy (establishing uniform dues and an initiation fee). By the early 1880s, Strasser and his allies had transformed the CMIU into a model of business unionism based on centralized control, membership

---

[22] Carl Hillman, "Practical Suggestions for Emancipation," Leipzig, 1873, in Kaufman, Gompers Papers, 1:23–44. Kaufman points out that Gompers acknowledged his intellectual indebtedness to Hillman's pamphlet in his autobiography (21–2).

[23] For the United Cigarmakers' Constitution, see "Concerning the Cigarmakers," Social-Demokrat, October 24, 1875, in Kaufman, Gompers Papers, 1:60–6. See also Kaufman's comments, "Samuel Gompers and Early Cigarmakers' Unions in New York City," 45–7; and Thomas Capek, The Czechs (Bohemians) in America: A Study of Their National, Cultural, Political, Social, Economic, and Religious Life (Boston: Houghton Mifflin, 1920), 71–3.

benefits, and financial efficiency. In following years, the new approach proved advantageous: Through the 1880s, Strasser happily reported on the union's growing number of locals and its greatly improved strike record.[24]

Amidst this reconstruction of the CMIU, Strasser had somehow lost his original instinct for broad solidarities. He had apparently learned one key lesson from the 1877 cigarmakers' strike and the depression of the same decade: The union should focus on protecting its core of skilled, white, and male workers. After 1877, Gompers and Strasser attempted to outlaw tenement cigar production rather than organize its mainly female and immigrant work force. This decision, along with the centralized structure they imposed and their mainstream political tactics, gave rise to pervasive criticism from union members. In 1882, a nationwide secessionist movement developed after Strasser voided the results of an election won by Socialists in New York City. The group of Germans and Bohemians, many of them Socialists, pulled out of the CMIU and formed the Cigar Makers' Progressive Union. As Patricia Cooper noted in her study of the cigarmaking trade, this was not simply an ideological battle between socialists and conservative unionists. The cigarmakers' Progressive movement seems instead to have been motivated by a wide range of criticism: Some workers, usually Socialists, criticized the "bourgeois" political tactics or the business-like strategies of the CMIU; immigrants complained about English-speaking workers' domination over union affairs; yet other workers attacked the CMIU as undemocratic, and demanded more local autonomy and better organizing efforts among tenement house and team workers. All these criticisms reflected internal tensions the CMIU, like other trade unions, would contend with well into the twentieth century.[25]

Amidst these complex alliances, the CMIU leadership began simultaneously to define itself in opposition to socialism. As early as 1883, Adolph Strasser testified to the U.S. Senate on relations between labor and capital and observed that "socialistic feeling" did not belong in the CMIU: "We have no ultimate ends. We are going on from day to day. We are fighting only for immediate objects – objects that can be realized in a few years."[26]

The business unionism pioneered by Strasser and Gompers competed with other trends in the American labor movement during the late nineteenth century. Only slowly did their tactics of centralization, protection, and financial efficiency

[24] "Constitution Proposed by the 12th Convention of the CMIU," September 15, 1879, and Stuart Kaufman, "Samuel Gompers, Adolph Strasser, and the Reform of the CMIU," both in Kaufman, *Gompers Papers*, 1:141–51 and 1:71–72; Patricia Cooper, *Once a Cigar Maker: Men, Women, and Work Culture in American Cigar Factories, 1900–1919* (Urbana: University of Illinois Press, 1987), 19–22.

[25] Cooper, *Once a Cigar Maker*, 23–5; see also Eileen Boris, "'A Man's Dwelling House Is His Castle': Tenement House Cigarmaking and the Judicial Imperative," in Baron, *Work Engendered*, 114–41.

[26] United States Congress, Senate Committee on Education and Labor, *Report of the Committee of the Senate upon the Relations between Labor and Capital . . .* , 48th Congress, 4 vols. (Washington, DC, 1885), 1:460.

emerge as the dominant model for union organization. During the 1880s and 1890s, many unions, like the United Mine Workers, the Brewery Workers, the Bakery Workers, the Boot and Shoe Workers, the International Association of Machinists, and the Furniture Workers, to list only the most important cases, experimented in varying degrees with socialism and populism and with the inclusive structure of industrial unionism (i.e., unions structured to organize all workers in a trade). The Cigarmakers' approach did quickly influence unions like the Typographers, Iron Molders, and the Carpenters. During the 1890s, many other unions would embrace business unionism as the economic depression and defeats confronted by socialism persuaded many activists of the advantages of more pragmatic strategies. But in the short run, Strasser's and Gompers's innovations in the CMIU remained largely limited to that organization – until, that is, they ascended to prominent positions in the movement to create a nationwide federation of trade unions.[27]

To comprehend the origins of that national federation, the role played by the Noble and Holy Order of the Knights of Labor (KOL) requires attention. Formed in 1869 by Philadelphia garment cutters, the Knights functioned as a secret but otherwise fairly typical craft union for several years. Its founder, Uriah Stephens, modeled the Order on fraternal organizations like the Masons and the Knights of Pythias. The Knights remained a loose gathering of local assemblies until 1878 when it first elected national officers. Only in 1882 did the Knights completely relinquish their code of secrecy, allowing their name to be spoken in public. By this time, the Knights had acquired characteristics quite different from the craft unions. The Order aspired to lofty ideals: Its principles stressed that people, like nations, should be measured by their moral worth rather than by their material wealth. The movement's leaders emphasized social reform as much as traditional unionism, eschewed strikes, and rejected political action as a way to achieve change. Despite this, rank-and-file Knights embraced both strikes and politics, with some success, as means to realizing their goals.[28]

---

[27] John H. M. Laslett, *Labor and the Left: A Study of Socialist and Radical Influences in the American Labor Movement, 1881–1924* (New York: Basic Books, 1970); Stuart Kaufman, *A Vision of Unity: The History of the Bakery and Confectionery Workers' International Union* (Urbana: University of Illinois Press, 1987); Melvyn Dubofsky, *Industrialism and the American Worker, 1865–1920* (Arlington Heights, IL: Harlan Davidson, 1985), 64–7; Andrew Roy, *A History of the Coal Miners of the U.S.: From the Development of the Mines to the Close of the Anthracite Strike of 1902* (Columbus, OH: J. L. Trauger Printing Co., 1907); Robert Christie, *Empire in Wood: A History of the Carpenters' Union* (Ithaca, NY: Cornell University Press, 1956).

[28] Richard Oestreicher, "Terence Powderly, the Knights of Labor, and Artisanal Republicanism," in Melvyn Dubofsky and Warren Van Tine, eds., *Labor Leaders in America* (Urbana: University of Illinois Press, 1987), 30–61; Bruce Laurie, *Artisans into Workers: Labor in Nineteenth Century America* (New York: Noonday Press, 1989), 141–75. For a contemporary view of the Knights, see also Roy, *History of Coal Miners of the U.S.*, 262–72; on the political activity of the Order, see Leon Fink, *Workingmen's Democracy: The Knights of Labor and American Politics* (Urbana: University of Illinois Press, 1983).

The Order's divergence from craft unionism could be seen in its structure. Knights encouraged mixed assemblies of workers from different trades as a way to overcome craft divisions. They also admitted any producers who accepted the Order's principles, as long as they were not parasites on the body politic: Landlords, lawyers, and liquor dealers could not join, but honorable manufacturers and employers were welcomed. The Knights' inclusiveness also made membership possible for women (their numbers, which included housewives as well as wage-earning women, reached 10 percent of the total Knights' membership at their height), for African-Americans (though typically in segregated assemblies, their numbers, too, reached an estimated 10 percent, or approximately 60,000), for immigrants, and more generally for unskilled workers. Yet the racism of some Knights became apparent in their response to Chinese workers: By the mid-1880s, anti-Chinese sentiment in California led to a boycott of Chinese-made cigars. As one speaker summarized the conflict at a Knights rally, "This is the old irrepressible conflict between slave and white labor. God grant there may be survival of the fittest." Determined to assist God's plans, the Knights promoted a "white" union label to help employers and consumers discriminate against Chinese workers.[29]

The Knights proved the most influential labor organization of the late nineteenth century, and long after it had faded, the labor movement would be led by people who received schooling under its umbrella. As union pioneer Andrew Roy wrote in 1907, many United Mine Workers' leaders "took their first lessons in public speaking in the local assembly room of the Knights of Labor." Shelton Stromquist has demonstrated how many Gilded Age unionists shared a commitment both to craft unions and to the Knights.[30] Yet, gradually, a tension emerged between the Order and the trade unions. The trade unionists' disagreement with the Knights centered on three problems, which in turn would influence the nature of the young AFL. Trade unionists criticized the Knights of Labor because of its preoccupation with social reform (it supported cooperatives more generously than strikes, for example) and willingness to include nonworkers; its centralized structure and the dominant role played by Terence Powderly; and its jurisdictional encroachments on territory trade unionists believed belonged to them.[31]

The carpenter Peter McGuire perhaps best represented the many Knights whose loyalties shifted away to the craft union movement. Born in 1852, McGuire grew up in New York City and became active in various radical causes from his teens

---

[29] Or as a writer in the San Francisco *Truth* complained, "The Chinese restriction bill is a weak and sickly invention designed to lull us into security while this silent invasion proceeds. Let us all, men and women, unite for the common purpose of race and national preservation." Saxton, *The Indispensable Enemy*, 180, 218. See also Susan Levine, *Labor's True Women: Carpet Weavers, Industrialization, and Labor Reform in the Gilded Age* (Philadelphia: Temple University Press, 1984); and Rachleff, *Black Labor in the South.*

[30] Stromquist, "Looking Both Ways."

[31] The best source on the relationship between the trade unions and the Knights is Norman Ware, *The Labor Movement in the United States, 1860–1890* (New York: Vintage Press, 1964; originally 1929). See also Stuart Kaufman, "The KOL, the Trade Unions, and the Founding of the FOTLU," in Kaufman, *Gompers Papers*, 1:159–61.

onwards. By the mid-1870s, McGuire was deeply influenced by Ferdinand Lassalle, who stressed that workers should employ political rather than economic tactics in order to capture the capitalist system. McGuire agitated on behalf of both the Knights of Labor and the Socialist Labor Party. Between 1876 and 1881, McGuire's views shifted dramatically and he began to see trade unionism as central to the workers' struggle. It could discipline and educate workers, and by introducing them to practical reforms, trade unionism would ultimately bring workers to socialism. Hoping to promote trade unionism, McGuire returned to his trade in 1880. In 1881, he created the Brotherhood of Carpenters and Joiners, soon to become one of the most successful American unions. Still a committed Socialist, McGuire advocated an activist-centered trade unionism, one based on his admonition to "organize, agitate, and educate."[32]

McGuire belonged to a growing group of Knights members who opposed their organization's leadership and saw it as unsupportive of trade unionism. In 1879, the KOL General Assembly passed a resolution declaring that "locals formed . . . exclusively in the interest of any one trade are contrary to the spirit and genius of the Order as founded. . . ." It required that any such locals must be subordinated to the District Assembly and must admit workmen of all trades.[33] As a result of these disagreements, several unhappy Knights convened in August 1881, in hopes of creating a rival organization of trade unionists. Their meeting led to the creation, in November 1881, of the Federation of Trades and Labor Unions (FOTLU, the immediate predecessor to the AFL). A KOL Executive Board member described this gathering to Powderly and noted the role played by dissident Knights: "I tell you these men dreaded the K. of L. and nearly in every instance these men were K. of Labor."[34]

Despite the presence of KOL members at the founding meeting of the FOTLU, delegates chose a plan of representation that privileged national and international unions. The latter would be represented by a graduated number of delegates depending on their size, but local assemblies or councils were granted only one delegate each, regardless of their size. The 1882 FOTLU convention changed this plan to allow more equal representation for KOL district assemblies and local labor bodies, but by then the Knights had decided the FOTLU did not warmly embrace them. Knights of Labor members gradually ceased participating in the new federation.[35]

The Federation of Trades and Labor Unions modeled itself explicitly on the British Trades Union Congress. It was intended as an annual congress of unions

---

[32] Christie, *Empire in Wood*, 29–45; Mark Erlich, "Peter J. McGuire: Socialism of a Trades Union Kind?" *Labor History*, 24 (2), Spring 1983, 165–97.

[33] Ware, *The Labor Movement*, 172–3.

[34] Myles McPadden to Powderly, November 23, 1881, in Kaufman, *Gompers Papers*, 1:162; Ware, *The Labor Movement*, 168–75.

[35] "Adjourned Sine Die," news account of 1881 FOTLU Convention in the *Pittsburgh Commercial Gazette*, November 19, 1881, in Kaufman, *Gompers Papers*, vol. 1; idem, "The KOL, the Trade Unions, and the Founding of the FOTLU," *Gompers Papers*, 1:159–63.

that would exist both to encourage the formation of labor organizations and to represent labor's legislative and political interests.[36] In fact, the FOTLU faced a critical shortage of funds and quickly became a moribund organization. Yet its emergence quickly intensified competition between the trade unions and the Knights of Labor. As early as 1882, this competition prompted P. J. McGuire to assess the role the FOTLU should play for American workers. He stressed that organization by trades would be necessary and beneficial as long as industry prevailed. Likewise, a federation of trade unions organized along industrial rather than political lines would serve as the "most natural and assimilative" way to bring workers in different trades together while maintaining the autonomy of each. According to McGuire, the labor movement needed both a public and a secret side: FOTLU would dominate the former, while the KOL could rule in labor's secret world. The two sides could work together harmoniously if not for "overzealous" men in the Order "who busy themselves in attempting the destruction of existing unions to serve their own whims and mad iconoclasm." In denouncing both the KOL and politically based labor movements, McGuire sharpened the conflict between the rival organizations and set new priorities for the FOTLU.[37]

In the next years, jurisdictional conflicts reinforced these programmatic ones, as the KOL fought trade unions for control in the building and printing trades, iron molding, granite cutting, and other industries. Squabbling broke out over issues such as KOL failure to honor trade union strikes or boycotts.[38] In 1882, the Knights' General Assembly reversed its position on organization by trades and voted to encourage the formation of trades assemblies. This decision led the Order to compete more aggressively with trade unions for workers' loyalties. In 1885, for example, the General Assembly decided to create a national assembly of miners, which then began competing directly with the recently founded National Federation of Miners.[39] Meanwhile, bitter conflict broke out between the two institutions in the cigarmaking industry as the Knights began aggressively to organize workers believed by the CMIU to be within its province. In 1886, KOL leaders ordered cigarmakers to choose between membership in the Order or in the CMIU, an action that shocked trade unionists and stoked higher the fires of anti-KOL militancy.[40]

---

[36] "The Labor Congress," news account in the *Pittsburgh Commercial Gazette*, November 18, 1881, Kaufman, *Gompers Papers*, 1:221–9.

[37] P. J. McGuire to the officers and delegates of the 1882 FOTLU Convention, November 20, 1882, in Kaufman, *Gompers Papers*, 1:279–81; for the significance of this, see Gompers, *Seventy Years*, 1:233.

[38] Laurie, *Artisans into Workers*, 172.

[39] Ware, *The Labor Movement in the U.S.*, 174–90; Roy, *A History of the Coal Miners*, 262–73.

[40] Strasser to Powderly, March 6, 1886, in Kaufman, *Gompers Papers*, 1:382; "Document 160" from the KOL, *Record of Proceedings of the General Assembly of the Knights of Labor of America, . . . Richmond, Virginia, October 4 to 20, 1886*, in Kaufman, *Gompers Papers*, 1:435; idem, "The Culmination of the Rivalry between the CMIU and the Cigarmakers' Progressive Union of America," in Kaufman, *Gompers Papers*, 1:365–7.

By this time, the FOTLU had become virtually useless as an organization and could provide little assistance to trade union leaders in their battle with the KOL. In this context, trade union activists needed either to reach an agreement with the KOL or create an alternative federation capable of protecting their interests. They first tried the former solution, meeting in May 1886 with KOL leaders in hopes of a reconciliation. This effort failed, and the KOL's demand in October that cigarmakers choose between it and the CMIU extinguished hopes of a peace agreement.[41] In November 1886, the presidents of the Steelworkers, Iron Molders, Cigarmakers, Miners, and Carpenters called for creation of a nationwide trade union federation.[42]

This led thirty-eight trade unionists to convene at Druids' Hall in Columbus, Ohio, in December and create the new American Federation of Labor. In the deliberations that founded the AFL, one could see the impact of the war between the KOL and the unions. In the eyes of trade unionists, their conflict with the Knights had centered on the latter's determination to suppress trade unions in preference for broader social reform priorities. Hence the new federation centered around trade unions and sought to unite the various trades in a beneficial alliance while giving to each one complete independence and autonomy. Similarly, the delegates wanted their new federation to be pragmatic and to focus on economic action. As president, unionists chose thirty-six-year-old Sam Gompers, the street-smart vice-president of the CMIU known for his antagonism toward the KOL. The AFL's constitution provided for federal trade unions that could recognize workers of diverse trades when no single trade dominated. This decision undercut the need for flexible KOL structures like the mixed assembly. By providing for unified action on strikes and boycotts, the delegates sought to give each union the resources of a national organization, providing another way to obviate the need for the KOL.[43]

Although the founding of the AFL helped push the U.S. labor movement into a new era, many years had yet to pass before the AFL would be synonymous with antisocialism, centralized union bureaucracy, craft consciousness, and the tactics of business unionism. The early AFL included many unions that organized on industrial rather than craft lines, that eschewed the centralized structure and high dues advocated by the CMIU, and that followed socialist or populist philosophies: unions like the miners, bakers, and furniture workers. The lines were drawn differently in 1886. Gompersism did not yet dominate the Federation, and officials like miner John McBride, who disagreed with Gompers on so much, noticed instead the key area of agreement. Rejoicing at the accomplishments of the AFL's founding convention, McBride proclaimed: "we have preserved the

---

[41] Kaufman, "The KOL," *Gompers Papers*, 1:385–7.

[42] P. J. McGuire et al. to the Officers and Members of All Trade Unions, November 10, 1886, in Kaufman, *Gompers Papers*, 1:450–1.

[43] *New York Tribune*, "The American Federation," December 12, 1886, in Kaufman, *Gompers Papers*, 1:467–70.

trades unions."[44] To understand the triumph of Gompersism that would shortly come, we shift our attention to the 1890s and the transformation of America's labor movement.

Gompers and the Triumph of Conservative Unionism

During the next decades, the American Federation of Labor emerged as the dominant labor federation in the United States. As economic depression, mass immigration, internal migration, and a new white racial consciousness in the dawning era of Jim Crow together transformed the working class, so also did they influence the labor movement's direction. Through the AFL, skilled workers' increasing isolation from other workers became institutionalized. By 1900, despite important exceptions, the AFL stood for craft consciousness, conservative business unionism, national trade unions' dominance over local labor, nonpartisan political strategies, and membership practices that excluded most women, nonwhites, and unskilled workers from the organization.

When he began leading the AFL, Samuel Gompers was already known as a militant defender of trade unionism. A brilliant strategist and an energetic organizer, Gompers seemed highly promising as the new federation's first chief. He was also known as a carousing man, one who appreciated good fun, decent cigars, and plenty of barroom drinking. Gompers's rotund physique – he stood five feet four inches tall with nearly two hundred pounds of bulk – was made more imposing by his "coal black hair worn almost long enough to sweep his coat collar," "his fierce black mustache and goatee, and something of a bull dog look of determination about his jaws and mouth. . . ."[45]

During the AFL's first decade, Gompers focused on building the institution. He quit the cigarmaking trade for a full-time salary of $1,000 per year. Four years later, his salary had been raised only to $1,500, still less than he could earn at cigarmaking. In these early years, Gompers ran the AFL from a series of small rooms – a tenement donated by the CMIU initially, then a front room of his own apartment. Normally an errand boy assisted him, and sometimes a clerk. By 1896, the AFL began to acquire the trappings of a viable institution: Frank Morrison of the Typographers worked alongside Gompers as full-time secretary, aided by two stenographers and an office boy. They now worked in a permanent three-room office in Washington, D.C.[46]

---

[44] *New York Tribune*, "Trades Union Leaders Contented," December 13, 1886, in Kaufman, *Gompers Papers*, 1:470–1.

[45] Bernard Mandel, *Samuel Gompers: A Biography* (Yellow Springs, OH: Antioch Press, 1963), 88; "Organized Labor," Mobile *Daily Register*, May 18, 1895, in Kaufman, *Gompers Papers*, 4:25; "Gompers in Town," *Indianapolis News*, April 19, 1890, in Kaufman, *Gompers Papers*, 2:297.

[46] Frank Morrison to Isaac Mitchell, August 29, 1902, *American Federation of Labor Records: The Samuel Gompers Era*, microfilm edition (Microfilming Corporation of America, 1979), (hereafter referred to as *AFL Records*), reel 59; Mandel, *Samuel Gompers*, 90–3, 171–3.

Gompers worked relentlessly at his new endeavor, singlehandedly building the Federation into an influential unifying force for the labor movement. He edited the AFL journal, first called the *Union Advocate* and, after 1894, the *American Federationist*. He carried on a voluminous correspondence with labor activists across the United States and abroad. In 1889, he undertook his first speaking tour throughout the United States, visiting fifty cities in three months to expound on the merits of trade unionism. Beginning in 1887, Gompers also worked to build a corps of volunteer organizers. These activists received no pay from the AFL, although often local unions found a way to reimburse them for their costs. Volunteer organizers established local unions in varying trades and emerged as important factors in the union movement's expansion.

The AFL confronted three great challenges during its first decades. Competition from the Knights of Labor posed the first challenge, and although that continued to be a problem after the AFL's founding in 1886, the Order rapidly disintegrated under the pressures of internal rivalries, employers' aggressive opposition, and the backlash against radicals and labor after the Haymarket incident of 1886. The second great challenge emerged in the AFL's ideological split, as Socialists grew better organized and conservatives like Gompers and Strasser grew more vocal in their antisocialism (we will explore this in Chapter Two). The third challenge, the most threatening of all, was the great economic depression of 1893 to 1897.

The depression began with a financial panic in the spring of 1893. By the end of the year, approximately 15,000 businesses and 400 banks had declared bankruptcy. Five years later, when the depression ended, thousands of others had joined them. Businesses lucky enough to survive tolerated low profit margins, and sought to recover lost ground by cutting wages or laying off workers. For workers, this meant widespread unemployment, part-time work, and reduced wages. The AFL estimated in 1893 that more than three million workers were unemployed. Most unions watched as their numbers – and their revenues – declined dramatically. Economic recession during the mid-1880s had hurt the young union movement, whereas the 1870s depression had virtually eliminated it. Surviving the 1890s depression became the AFL's first major achievement.[47]

Yet the labor movement did not emerge unscathed from the crisis. The depression made broad solidarities among workers more difficult to achieve, while it bolstered business unionists. Industrial unionism formed an important part of the labor movement – both inside and outside of the AFL – at the beginning of the 1890s. The American Railway Union, formed in 1893 and led by Eugene Debs, provided the most dramatic example of industrial unionism. Government intervention into the fateful Pullman Boycott shattered the union, threw many of its members permanently out of their jobs, and imprisoned its famous leader. Within

---

[47] Philip Taft, *The A.F. of L. in the Time of Gompers* (New York: Harper, 1957), 123–4; Gilbert C. Fite and Jim E. Reese, *An Economic History of the United States* (Boston: Houghton Mifflin, 1973), 272.

the AFL, a number of industrial unions, most of which had resisted the businesslike tactics pioneered by the CMIU, found the depression difficult to weather. Examining the fate of industrial unions during the depression, Shelton Stromquist has demonstrated that by 1900, they had retreated from or abandoned many of their principles of broad solidarity. Although the United Mine Workers (UMW) remained progressive and organized along industrial lines, for example, socialists grew less powerful and leaders like Michael Ratchford and John Mitchell moved the UMW closer to Gompers's vision of business unionism. The Boot and Shoe Workers' union, another influential industrial union, shifted policy in 1898 and established higher dues and benefit features after years of opposing such tactics.[48]

As industrial unionism retreated, the policies of conservative craft unionism grew more pervasive. The United Brotherhood of Carpenters and Joiners (UBCJA) typified this transformation. As Robert Christie documented in *Empire of Wood*, during the 1890s the Brotherhood split between two groups. One group, headed by founder P. C. McGuire, emphasized unionism as activism and as agitation. McGuire himself established high dues and benefits in the union and had long praised their advantages in creating a stable and wealthy union. But the other group, headed by "professional organizers" (as Christie called them), often business agents, fought to wrest control away from McGuire and intensify the union's reliance on practical businesslike tactics. This meant, for them, a centralization of the union bureaucracy, provisions for full-time organizers, a conciliatory approach toward relations with employers, and an aggressive position in jurisdictional conflicts. It took a decade, but by 1902, the professional organizers had defeated McGuire and the UBCJA was rapidly emerging as a model of business unionism.[49]

Other unions, like the Bakers, joined the UBCJA's march toward craft consciousness and business unionism during this same period.[50] Some advocates of industrial unionism remained in the AFL, but now they seemed besieged. At a time when skilled workers felt threatened by immigrants, African-Americans, and women entering the work force in large numbers, one consequence of business unionism and craft consciousness became more apparent: a strong trend toward exclusivist membership policies among the national unions belonging to the AFL.

Like other indicators of conservative craft consciousness, the exclusivism of AFL unions grew more pronounced as the nineteenth century drew to a close.

---

[48] Another indication of the fortunes of broad solidarities: For years, many members of industrial unions maintained membership in both their union and in the Knights of Labor. After 1895, Gompers found himself and his Federation sufficiently strong to halt dual memberships. Stromquist, "Looking Both Ways," 22–4, 51–4.

[49] Christie, *Empire in Wood*; Mark Erlich, "Peter J. McGuire's Trade Unionism: Socialism of a Trades Union Kind?" in *Labor History*, 24 (2), Spring 1983, 165–97.

[50] Stuart Kaufman, *A Vision of Unity: The History of the Bakery and Confectionery Workers International Union* (distributed by the University of Illinois Press by arrangement with the Bakery, Confectionery, and Tobacco Workers International Union, 1986).

A relative openness toward women and African-American workers in the 1880s had virtually disappeared by 1900, as skilled craftsmen's social relationship to other workers grew more contentious and more distant. Several reasons exist for this. The craft structure of AFL unions marginalized semiskilled or unskilled workers, which included most female, African-American, and immigrant workers.[51] The tactics of business unionism further discriminated against unskilled workers, because high dues and initiation fees could not be afforded by any but relatively prosperous craftspeople.

The AFL never came close to matching the commitment of the Knights of Labor to recruiting women and blacks. Yet during the 1880s, both groups could be found on union rosters. Gompers was alert to the need to organize both female and African-American workers, if only to protect his white male members. Speaking in Mobile, Alabama, in 1895, for example, he stressed that improving (white) workers' conditions required organizing African-Americans. "If the negro laborers are allowed to continue to receive these low wages they will inevitably drag you down to their level. . . . Help him to organize. I do not want you to dance with him, or sleep with him, or kiss him, but I do want you to organize with him."[52]

Yet Gompers's commitment to organizing other than white male workers remained limited. Unions with exclusionary "whites only" clauses in their constitutions posed a problem for AFL leaders, who disliked the clauses but hesitated to confront powerful affiliates over the issue. In 1890, the AFL convention refused to issue a charter to the National Association of Machinists because of such a clause. But by 1895, Gompers had found a solution. The machinists struck the clause from their constitution but continued to restrict membership to whites through their initiation rituals. Gompers urged the Locomotive Firemen to join the AFL two years later, by following the same route. Gompers denied that the AFL compelled its affiliated union to admit African-Americans, arguing only that an organization should not "declare against accepting the colored man *because he is colored.*" On the other hand, it would be appropriate to exclude individuals from membership, whatever their race or nationality, if they allied themselves with the employer against the union members. Therefore, according to Gompers, the Firemen's union should eliminate the whites-only clause in its constitution and then refuse admission to African-Americans because they assist employers during strikes, not because of the color of their skins. The Firemen

---

[51] It is important to note that although many "craft" unions did not limit their membership to the most highly skilled craftspeople, they not only preferred skilled workers as members, they also privileged skill in a number of ways. See Christie's *Empire of Wood* on the UBCJA for an example of how one influential union attempted to distinguish between the most highly skilled and the less skilled workers, showing little interest in organizing the latter.

[52] Mobile *Daily Register*, May 18, 1895, "Organized Labor," *Gompers Papers*, 4:26. Similarly, Gompers emphasized the importance of organization for women. See New Orleans *Times Democrat*, May 23, 1895, "Women Wage Earners," in Kaufman, *Gompers Papers*, 4:30–3.

refused to affiliate with the AFL, declaring that its members "do not care to belong to an organization that is not honest enough to make public its qualification of membership."[53]

By the early twentieth century, as Jim Crow segregation swept the South, AFL leaders grew more indifferent to racism within the institution. The AFL began allowing unions to affiliate even if they had whites-only clauses in their constitution, and when the Federation agreed to organize black workers, it placed them in segregated locals. In 1902, W. E. B. Du Bois released a study of union racial practices that found that forty-seven unions had not a single black members, and another twenty-seven included only a handful of African-Americans. Only one union, the United Mine Workers, followed nondiscriminatory policies in regard to African-American workers. Twenty thousand black workers belonged to the UMW, more than half the total black membership of the entire AFL in 1902. When Du Bois communicated his findings to Gompers, the latter denied their accuracy and then refused any further discussions.[54]

The AFL leaders' attitude toward eastern and southern European immigrants followed a similar, though less extreme, pattern. In the 1880s, official AFL pronouncements regularly declared a willingness to unite old and new immigrants regardless of ethnicity. Through the mid-1890s, AFL leaders typically granted requests for organizers fluent in Bohemian or Italian. But even as prejudice toward African-Americans grew more pronounced within the AFL, and as the flow of immigrants from eastern and southern Europe intensified, the latter began to be seen as a similar threat to the (white) American way of life. By the first years of the twentieth century, AFL leaders had begun fighting aggressively for literacy tests and other means of restricting immigration.[55]

Workers of Asian descent failed to receive even the gestures toward inclusion that Gompers granted to African-Americans in his early years. Like many white workers, Gompers articulated a racist rage toward Chinese, Japanese, Korean, and Filipino workers. When discussing Asian workers, Gompers made clear his belief in the superiority of whites. His clearest statement in this regard came in the infamous pamphlet he co-wrote, titled *Some Reasons for Chinese Exclusion: Meat Vs. Rice, American Manhood Against Coolieism – Which Shall Survive?* in which Gompers argued that the Chinese were by nature immoral:

[53] Samuel Gompers, "Why Affiliate with the Federation," *Locomotive Firemen's Magazine*, 20, July 1896, 64–7, in Kaufman, *Gompers Papers*, 4:213; Philip Foner, *History of the Labor Movement in the United States*, Vol. 2, *From the Founding of the AFL to the Emergence of American Imperialism* (New York: International Publishers, 1955), 349.

[54] Herbert Hill, "The Racial Practices of Organized Labor: The Age of Gompers and After," in Herbert Hill and Arthur M. Ross, eds., *Employment, Race, and Poverty* (New York: Harcourt, Brace & World, 1967), 365–402. On the main characteristics of black unionism, see Eric Arnesen, "'What's on the Black Worker's Mind?' African-American Workers and the Union Tradition," *Gulf Coast Historical Review*, 10 (1), Fall 1994, 5–18.

[55] Foner, *History of the Labor Movement*, 2:204–5; Saxton, *The Indispensable Enemy*; and Gwendolyn Mink, *Old Labor and New Immigrants in American Political Development: Union, Party, and State, 1875–1920* (Ithaca, NY: Cornell University Press, 1986).

"The Yellow Man found it natural to lie, cheat and murder and ninety-nine out of every one hundered Chinese are gamblers."[56] Regularly, Gompers argued that Asian workers as a group could not be assimilated into American society because they were "semicivilized," that is, "docile and menial, their wants most primitive." Though Gompers saved his most virulent racism for Asians, in his eyes they shared important characteristics with other immigrants and with African-Americans: White skilled workers feared the low wages, the poor living conditions, and the limited diet with which these groups contended. In an age of tumultuous change, skilled workers of the AFL feared they might end up living the same way. As Gompers put it, "the caucasians are not going to let their standard of living be destroyed by negroes, Chinamen, Japs, or any others."[57]

The AFL similarly grew less interested in organizing women of any race between 1890 and the early 1900s. In 1892, Gompers convinced the AFL Executive Council to appoint a National Organizer for Women, but by 1895, the federation included no female organizers on its roster. Although the nature of women's job participation helps explain the AFL's reluctance to organize them (their often short-term employment, their concentration in sectors difficult to organize along the lines developed by craft unions, such as domestic service, and the young age of most women workers), other factors also played a critical role. As Alice Kessler-Harris has documented, AFL unionists commonly believed that women belonged in the home and this influenced their leaders' decision to attempt eliminating women from the work force rather than encouraging them to organize. As a trade unionist wrote in 1897, "The demand for female labor ... is an insidious assault upon the home ... it is the knife of the assassin, aimed at the family circle." Even when a union admitted women, it discouraged their full participation by holding meetings in saloons or scheduling them at late hours.[58]

Broad solidarities, then, met with a miserable fate in the labor movement between 1886 and 1900. The Knights of Labor disintegrated, industrial unionism declined, and the AFL grew less open to women and African-Americans. One last source of inclusiveness in the American labor movement during this period could be found in the central labor unions and trade assemblies that dominated working-class institutions at the local level. Local federations organized on a geographic basis, embracing workers within a given region regardless of craft divisions. Hence, they provided a forum for more inclusive solidarities.

[56] Saxton, *The Indispensable Enemy*; Hill, "The Racial Practices of Organized Labor," 388–91.

[57] R. Todd Laugen, "Racial Americanisms: Labor Anti-Imperialism, 1897–1902," unpublished seminar paper; Saxton, *The Indispensable Enemy*, 273.

[58] Kessler-Harris, "Where are the Organized Women Workers," *Feminist Studies*, 3 (1/2), Fall 1975, 92–105; for a subtle interpretation of gender and the definition of craft membership, see Ava Baron, "An 'Other' Side of Gender Antagonism at Work: Men, Boys, and the Remasculinization of Printers' Work, 1830–1920," in Baron, ed., *Work Engendered*. On male workers' beliefs about women and work, see also Martha May, "Bread before Roses: American Workingmen, Labor Unions and the Family Wage," in Ruth Milkman, ed., *Women, Work and Protest: A Century of U.S. Women's Labor History* (Boston: Routledge and Kegan Paul, 1985), 1–21.

During the late nineteenth century, the AFL worked to suppress the central labor unions, seeking to bring local workers under the control of the national trade unions.

The founding of the AFL elevated the national trade unions to a dominant position in the labor movement. Reacting against the Knights, the trade unionists who created the AFL sought to base it on the singular principle of trade autonomy. They intended their Federation to be weak and subordinate to the trade unions, so the latter's autonomy would never be in question. This principle defined the options available to Gompers and other AFL leaders. The AFL could not specify unions' disciplinary activities, audit their membership or finance records, establish economic standards for collective bargaining, or assess and distribute a strike fund. What limited powers the AFL possessed Samuel Gompers and the Executive Council were often reluctant to use. In 1899, for example, the AFL acquired the power to assess a limited "defense fund," a per capita tax of one cent per week, which was limited to ten weeks of any year. The AFL rarely made use of this power. It more often raised money by appealing to the generosity of its affiliates than by mandatory assessment.[59]

Yet however weak the AFL might be, its presiding officer was an unusually strong leader. President of the AFL for all but one of its first thirty-eight years, Gompers developed a comprehensive and effective power base within the AFL. Extremely sensitive to the needs and interests of AFL affiliates (particularly powerful ones like the Carpenters and the Miners), Gompers effectively wielded his own power, in alliance with like-minded leaders, to steer the AFL in a conservative direction.

[59] Lloyd Ulman, *The Rise of the National Trade Union: The Development and Significance of its Structure, Governing Institutions, and Economic Policies* (Cambridge: Harvard University Press, 1966). Other useful sources on this point include Lewis Lorwin, *The American Federation of Labor: History, Policies, and Prospects* (Washington, DC: The Brookings Institution, 1933); Theodore Glocker, *The Government of American Trade Unions* (Baltimore: Johns Hopkins University Press, 1913); William Kirk, *National Labor Federations in the United States* (Baltimore: Johns Hopkins University Press, 1906); George Barnett, "The Dominance of the National Union in American Labor Organization," *Quarterly Journal of Economics*, 27 (May 1913), 455–81.

The AFL's relationship with its affiliates raises questions that go beyond the scope of this book. The UBCJA provides a classic example of a powerful union able to wield great influence with the AFL's leadership: See Robert Christie, *Empire in Wood*. Conversely, to explore Gompers's interventionist side, consider the United Metal Workers, discussed in Bruno Ramirez, *When Workers Fight: The Politics of Industrial Relations in the Progressive Era, 1898–1915* (Westport, CT: Greenwood Press, 1978), 104–14; and in Montgomery, *Fall of the House of Labor*, 311–12. The AFL awarded almost all workers in the Metal Workers' jurisdiction to other unions and, as Montgomery writes, "consigned the United Metal Workers Union to extinction." Last, Elizabeth and Kenneth Fones-Wolf argue that Gompers and the AFL intervened more frequently and effectively in the affairs of the affiliates than scholars have realized. Examples include Gompers's actions to assist dissident rank-and-file movements protesting corrupt but powerful union leaders. See their "Rank-and-File Rebellions and AFL Interference in the Affairs of National Unions: The Gompers Era," *Labor History*, 35 (2), Spring 1994, 237–59.

Gompers's extensive travels allowed him to create a wide network of allies, based in large part on the chain of volunteer organizers across the country. In the public mind, the AFL was largely synonymous with the person of Gompers. By the mid-1890s his role as editor of the *American Federationist* gave Gompers another way to shape opinion. Because of all this, it could be very advantageous to know Gompers and to be well-liked by him. He could help a union by supporting its boycott or label drive, by deciding a jurisdictional dispute in its favor, or by assessing a tax for strike support. Gompers could also assist individuals by giving them a prestigious job with an affiliated trade union, a labor newspaper, or a local or state federation.[60]

The volunteer and salaried organizers played an important role in Gompers's power base. They provided the AFL president with a network of loyal lieutenants who could supply information and help implement the national leader's decisions at the local level. By 1900, nearly 700 trade unionists held commissions as volunteer organizers for the AFL, and this number would reach 1,300 by 1908. The AFL also began to hire permanent paid organizers in 1899. Within a decade, the Federation was spending more than $59,000 to hire fifty organizers, and at least one leader, AFL Secretary Frank Morrison, saw salaried organizers as the key to organized labor's future expansion.[61] Delegates to the annual AFL convention did not elect the paid organizers as they did other AFL officials; instead, Gompers handpicked them. The organizers answered only to Gompers or to close allies such as Frank Morrison.[62]

Gompers's power within the labor movement became most visible at the annual AFL conventions. As president, Gompers could manipulate the proceedings of the convention to assist himself and his allies, but much more importantly, he appointed the members of all committees. These committees were the first to consider all delegates' proposals. If the committee did not support the proposal, delegates would have a difficult time passing it. Occasionally, when his allies could not afford the cost of their AFL dues, Gompers arranged to pay for them

---

[60] C. Wright Mills described Samuel Gompers as the first labor leader to join the "national power elite." Though this would happen only later in Gompers's life, even during the 1890s, he had risen to an unusual level of national prominence. See C. Wright Mills, "The Labor Leaders and the Power Elite," in Irving Horowitz, ed., *Power, Politics, and People: The Collected Essays of C. Wright Mills* (1939; rpt. Oxford: Oxford University Press, 1967), 97–109.

[61] On the number of organizers in 1908, see "Secretary Morrison's Report," *Report of the Proceedings of the Twenty-Eighth Annual Convention of the American Federation of Labor* (Washington, DC: National Tribune Co., 1908), 42; Frank Morrison to W. C. Hahn, September 16, 1908, Frank Morrison Letterbooks, Perkins Library, Duke University (hereafter cited as Morrison Letterbooks). For historians' discussions of AFL organizers, see Warren Van Tine, *The Making of the Labor Bureaucrat: Union Leadership in the United States, 1870–1920* (Amherst: University of Massachusetts Press, 1973), 154–5; Mandel, *Samuel Gompers,* 100–1; and Ulman, *Rise of the National Trade Union,* 420–2.

[62] At the 1897 convention, full power over the organizers was given to the Executive Council. See the American Federation of Labor, *History, Encyclopedia, Reference Book* (Washington, DC: AFL, 1919), 306–9.

so they would be allowed to attend the annual convention. In addition to this, many of Gompers's top organizers attended the conventions and mobilized energetically to build support among delegates for the issues favored by the AFL.[63]

Gompers and his allies at the helm of the country's unions agreed on one essential principle: The national and international trade unions should dominate the labor movement. Indeed, one of the AFL's most important services to the trade unions lay in stripping the central labor unions of their most essential powers. This transformed the labor movement's structure and influenced both its political and economic future.

The central labor unions were structurally and functionally analogous to the AFL itself. They carried out many of the duties on a local level that the AFL shouldered nationwide: They looked after legislation, coordinated organizing efforts, and reconciled divisions within the labor movement.[64] At the same time, they functioned very differently from the national trade unions. A national union covered an expansive region but included among its affiliates locals for only one trade. City federations covered only a limited geographic area, but locals of many different trades affiliated with them. This gave local federations the same potential for uniting workers across different crafts, and thus for encouraging broader solidarities, that industrial unions possessed. Last, although local federations carried out important economic tasks, they also engaged more often in political activity than did the national unions.

The reasons for the local federations' political orientation are varied. By their nature, local federations represented workers' class (rather than trade or craft) interests, because they consisted of locals from many different trades. In addition, local federations' work was largely carried out by volunteers – and thus by the most committed, and often most class conscious, of the local activists. Gary Fink notes in his study of Missouri labor politics that local unions and federations were closer to the political and economic problems of working-class people, and therefore they developed a more pragmatic and practical approach. Furthermore, local bodies were not only more responsive to their constituencies, but also potentially more democratic. If an issue appealed to local workers, the central labor union could quickly act on it; within a national union, on the other hand, by the time an issue had traveled up to the highest levels of the union bureaucracy, it could easily be squashed. Of course, a local federation could be

---

[63] Mandel, *Samuel Gompers*, 101–2.

[64] William Maxwell Burke, *History and Functions of Central Labor Unions*, in *Studies in History, Economics and Public Law*, 12 (1), edited by the faculty of political science at Columbia University (New York: Macmillan, 1899); Frank Morrison to the Secretary, Jackson (Tennessee) Trades Council, August 22, 1906, Morrison Letterbooks; *Report of the Proceedings*, 1908, 265; Gary M. Fink, *Labor's Search for Political Order: The Political Behavior of the Missouri Labor Movement, 1890–1940* (Columbia: University of Missouri Press, 1973); Irwin Yellowitz, *Labor and the Progressive Movement in New York State, 1897–1916* (Ithaca, NY: Cornell University Press, 1965).

no more democratic than its constituent local unions. In practice, the character of local federations varied considerably.[65]

During the late nineteenth century, central labor unions often led battles for shorter work days or founded political parties. In 1886, for example, a movement for political reform spread quickly across the country, and in many cities it was led by central labor unions. New York's Central Labor Union provided the most famous case of this when it nominated, and almost elected, the single-tax agitator Henry George for mayor. This focus on politics continued well into the twentieth century, even as local federations lost most of their powers, and provided a source of tension throughout the Progressive era.[66]

The labor movement, of course, had originated at the local level. Local unions came first, but by 1827, the first citywide federation emerged in Philadelphia. Such local federations continued to dominate the labor movement at least through the Civil War. Even after the 1860s, local federations became influential at times of crisis. During the depression of the 1870s, many of the national unions disappeared and local federations took over, providing the labor movement with direction and stability.[67]

By the 1880s, central labor unions and local unions across the country waned in influence as national unions rose to power. As a national union established control over beneficiary features, strike funding, and negotiations with employers, it undercut the economic power of local unions.[68] Dominance over local federations emerged more gradually, but at each stage, the AFL served the national unions as an invaluable ally. AFL leaders helped limit the power of local federations at AFL conventions, and worked to eliminate many of the local federations' economic powers.

The first constitution of the Federation of Organized Trades and Labor Unions gave most voting power to the national unions. Voting was on a proportional basis, allowing unions with fewer than 400 members to have 1 delegate; fewer than 4,000 members, 2 delegates; 8,000 members, 3 delegates; 16,000 members, 4 delegates; and so on. Local federations received only one delegate, regardless of their size.[69] The AFL maintained this structure and convention delegates

---

[65] David Montgomery provided me with important insights into the political orientation of local federations. See also Fink, *Labor's Search for Order*, 180–2; and for a similar argument, see Ulman, *Rise of the National Trade Union*, 342.

[66] Ulman, *Rise of the National Trade Union*, 342; David Scobey, "Boycotting the Politics Factory: Labor Radicalism and the New York City Mayoral Election of 1884," *Radical History Review*, 28–30, 1984, 280–326.

[67] Ulman, *Rise of the National Trade Union*, 341–3; John Commons et al., *History of Labour in the United States* (New York: Macmillan, 1918); and George Barnett, "The Dominance of the National Union," 457.

[68] Barnett, "Dominance of the National Union," 460; see also Ulman, *Rise of the National Trade Union*, and Van Tine, *Making of the Labor Bureaucrat*.

[69] Barnett, "Dominance of the National Union," 462; Ulman, *Rise of the National Trade Union*, 379–80. An 1882 addition limited local assemblies of the Knights of Labor and local unions to one delegate regardless of their size, whereas state federations received two delegates.

passed more sweeping changes in 1887. A notable resolution provided that if a roll-call vote was requested, each delegate, *except* those representing local or state federations, would cast one vote for every hundred members represented. Thus on any critical question, the local and state federations could be rendered insignificant. Delegates even discussed one proposal to exclude local federations from the AFL altogether. But this was unnecessary, because the new voting structure solidified the national unions' control over AFL conventions. In 1900, local federations attempted unsuccessfully to overturn these changes.[70]

Meanwhile, between 1886 and 1902, the AFL eliminated local federations' major economic powers. In successive years, central labor unions lost the right to call strikes, to begin boycotts, to intervene in collective bargaining, or to negotiate jurisdictional disputes between unions. Central labor unions' powers regarding strikes and boycotts particularly threatened the national unions, in part because sympathetic strikes often could be run most effectively by a local federation. Central labor unions also lost the right to determine who could or could not affiliate with them. By the early twentieth century, they could not exclude any local union that wanted to affiliate, except for those hostile to the AFL – which they were required to exclude.[71]

A local federation that refused to obey these regulations could lose its charter. Local unions typically withdrew from any local federation lacking a charter, either on their own initiative or at the urging of their national unions. The AFL then normally sent organizers out to build a new local federation. Thus, by 1912, only two independent central labor unions still existed in sizeable cities, in contrast to more than 630 local organizations affiliated with the AFL.[72]

In practice, the AFL limited but did not destroy the power base of local labor movements. Particularly between 1910 and 1922, more militant central labor unions would reemerge. As David Montgomery has documented, citywide strikes during and after World War I in Seattle, Kansas City, and other cities resulted in tense negotiations between the national AFL and local bodies across the country. But even here, the exceptions suggest the significance of the rule. Seattle, for example, became atypical because the local federation had almost unlimited support from the region's trade unionists (and the latter included approximately 50 percent of the city's wage earners). Only strong local backing made it possible for central labor unions to exercise an independent will, because Gompers and the AFL would likely oppose such actions from the start.[73]

---

[70] Barnett, "Dominance of the National Union," 461–2; Ulman, *Rise of the National Trade Union*, 381.

[71] Ulman, *Rise of the National Trade Union*, 382–6.

[72] Barnett, "Dominance of the National Union," 466–8. On the AFL's handling of the independence of central labor unions, see also Jacques Rouillard, "Le Québec et Le congrès de Berlin, 1902," *Labour/Le Travailleur*, I, 1976, 69–91.

[73] David Montgomery, "New Tendencies in Union Struggles and Strategies in Europe and the United States, 1916–1922," in James Cronin and Carmen Sirianni, eds., *Work, Community, and Power: The Experience of Labor in Europe and America, 1900–1925* (Philadelphia: Temple University Press, 1983), 88–116; and Montgomery, *Fall of the House of Labor,*

By reining in the local labor movements, the AFL exercised new control over bodies that constituted the political heart of the AFL bureaucracy.[74] Simultaneously, AFL leaders had reduced the paths available for building an inclusive and progressive labor movement. Its founders created the AFL to be a weak federation, one that upheld the principle of autonomy for its affiliates. Yet the AFL did not extend that principle to local federations. Although they retained some ability to act on their own, particularly on political matters, by the beginning of the twentieth century, local federations had lost most of their economic functions. Thus, the United States, unlike many European countries, possessed no institutional basis after 1900 for a labor movement independent of the national unions.[75]

Skilled craftsmen created the American Federation of Labor at a time when they were fast becoming isolated from other workers, jealous of those workers' efforts to win craftsmen's jobs, angry at their willingness to work for low wages or to live in conditions of squalor, and scared that they themselves might descend to a life of meanness. Those poor wages and miserable tenement homes gave unskilled workers a great need for protection and assistance from a nationwide movement of unions. But increasingly, America's leading labor organization excluded most workers through a variety of prohibitions, from the indirect effects of high dues and initiation fees, to the more explicit rituals that admitted only workers of a certain race.

Conservative craft unionism was not born but built, step by step, as potential paths to inclusive strategies gradually disappeared over the course of the late nineteenth century. The decline of industrial unionism, the waning of the Knights of Labor, the dominance over local labor organizations exercised by the AFL – together these events narrowed the outlook of skilled workers already facing great pressures from mass immigration, economic upheaval, and employer assertiveness. With skilled craftsmen facing options and conditions so different from other workers, only an inclusive labor movement could unite the working class. Instead, labor's dominant institutions reinforced and heightened the divisions within the working class, representing one privileged segment to the disadvantage of other workers.

411–64. On Seattle, see also Dana Frank, *Purchasing Power: Consumer Organizing, Gender, and the Seattle Labor Movement, 1919–1929* (New York: Cambridge University Press, 1994), 15–39.

[74] In general, the same restrictions described here applied also to the state federations of labor. This did not have quite the same significance, however, because the state federations had never been important in the same way as the central labor unions, and never possessed much economic power to begin with. For more information on their role, see Kirk, *National Labor Federations*, 36.

[75] Contrast these circumstances to those prevailing in France (with the existence of the *bourse du travail*) and in Italy (the *camera del lavoro*). For more information, see Peter Schottler, *Naissance des bourses du travail: un appareil idéologique d'état à la fin du XIXe siècle* (Paris: Presses Universitaires de France, 1985); and David Montgomery, "New Tendencies in Union Struggles," in Cronin and Sirianni, eds., *Work, Community and Power*, 100–1.

The Revolt Against
Party Slavery

Some Gilded Age workers lived amidst a heady swirl of political opportunities. Whether they chose soldierlike loyalty in the ranks of the major parties or alternatives like socialism, greenbackism, populism, or anarchism, workingmen regularly asserted their wish to influence the future of American society and government. Yet as a group, workers also faced severe limitations on their political influence. The conservative nature of the major parties, institutional discrimination against third parties, and ethnic divisions that made some workingmen Democrats and others Republicans, all placed obstacles in front of even those most empowered workers, the white men possessing citizenship. Far more striking was the way America's political system victimized female, Asian, and (in most cases) Native American and African-American workers through disfranchisement. European immigrants lacked the franchise until they became citizens, and for many of them, voting continued to seem unattractive even after that. These barriers extinguished any possibility that American workers could become a united political force during the Gilded Age.

Like the working class from which it sprang, the American Federation of Labor was pervaded by political debate during its early decades. Many among the AFL's skilled craftsmen agitated as part of the single-tax, socialist, or populist movements. Others supported the Democratic or Republican parties. By the 1890s, though, a bitter fight had erupted among AFL members over which political strategy the labor movement should pursue. Should trade unionists emphasize economic or political activity? And if the latter, should they ally with a political party or remain independent? Socialists pushed the AFL to adopt a political program that reflected their goals, populists advocated an alliance with the People's Party, whereas those unionists known as "philosophical Anarchists" rejected political tactics and championed economic struggle instead. Amidst the maelstrom of these political divisions, Samuel Gompers and other trade unionists began articulating a distinctive political vision, one that would ultimately attract a large and diverse group of AFL members to its support. This political vision emphasized that the trade unions stood at the heart of the labor movement, and it allowed no interference by either mainstream or radical political parties. Indeed, union leaders like Gompers skillfully employed antiparty rhetoric to win unionists over to his position, charging that political parties enslaved workers and stole their freedom. Instead of party politics, Gompers relied on limited and nonpartisan political tactics to further the interests of the trade union movement. By the end of the nineteenth century, Gompers's political vision had won a narrow triumph and rose to dominance in the AFL. Along the way, this "pure and simple" approach channeled workers' tumultuous political passions into the service of conservative trade unionism.

The Problem of Working-Class Politics

Scholars commonly stress the American political system's openness to working-class participation. In fact, a close look at suffrage requirements suggests dramatically diverse conditions depending on one's gender, race, and citizenship status. By 1900 the political system was closed to the working class as a whole, although a minority segment of that class – native-born white men – enjoyed a remarkable degree of political equality. Thus the American working class increasingly experienced a political as well as an economic and occupational bifurcation: Native-born white men not only commanded the better-paying skilled jobs available to workers, but they also were most likely to enjoy full suffrage rights.[1]

White women watched their franchise gradually expand between 1880 and 1920, as states or cities granted them suffrage rights. Yet they did not achieve political equality nationwide until passage of the nineteenth amendment in 1920. Historians such as Paula Baker and Estelle Freedman have described how middle-class white women inhabited a distinct political culture during the Gilded Age, one founded on voluntary social reform activities and interest group tactics.[2] African-Americans experienced very different conditions. After emancipation, black men enjoyed relatively unrestricted political freedom for several

---

[1] For an argument regarding the openness of the American political system, see Martin Shefter, "Trade Unions and Political Machines: The Organization and Disorganization of the American Working Class in the Late Nineteenth Century," in Ira Katznelson and Aristide R. Zolberg, eds., *Working-Class Formation: Nineteenth-Century Patterns in Western Europe and the United States* (Princeton: Princeton University Press, 1986), 197–278, esp. 243.

[2] See, for example, Paula Baker, "The Domestication of Politics: Women and American Political Society, 1780–1920," *American Historical Review*, 89, June 1984, 620–47; Ruth Bordin, *Woman and Temperance: The Quest for Power and Liberty, 1873–1900* (Philadelphia: Temple University Press, 1981); Estelle B. Freedman, "Separatism as Strategy: Female Institution-Building and American Feminism, 1870–1930," *Feminist Studies* 5, 1979, 512–29; and Kathryn Kish Sklar, "Hull House in the 1890s: A Community of Women Reformers," *Signs*, 10 (4), Summer 1985, 658–77. On the history of women's suffrage, see Ellen Carol DuBois, *Feminism and Suffrage: The Emergence of an Independent Women's Movement in America, 1848–1869* (Ithaca, NY: Cornell University Press, 1978); and Eleanor Flexner, *Century of Struggle: The Woman's Rights Movement in the United States* (Cambridge, MA: Belknap Press, 1959).

years. During the 1870s and 1880s, as Neil McMillen has shown in Mississippi, campaigns of organized violence intimidated black men into relinquishing their political rights before legal disfranchisement occurred. Then, between 1889 and 1903, measures such as poll taxes and literacy tests swept through the South and severely limited African-American men's ability to vote. J. Morgan Kousser has demonstrated that such restrictions produced a dramatic decline in political participation: Throughout the South, voting among African-American men decreased between 1888 and 1904 by an average of 62 percent.[3]

Similarly, as immigrant workers flooded into the country during the nineteenth century, helping to make and remake the American working class, their alien status damaged workers' political capacity. Until they lived in the United States for seven years and achieved citizenship, European immigrants did not enjoy full political rights. Many immigrants returned home after a brief stay in the United States. Others became globetrotters, entering the United States and returning to their home on a seasonal basis, and hence delaying or rejecting U. S. citizenship. Because the dream of returning home remained with some immigrants long after they had established roots in the United States, citizenship was not always a part of their plans.

These factors limited full political rights to a minority of American workers. In America's industrial cities, where 30 to 50 percent of workers might be foreign-born, the added impact of female and black disfranchisement could exclude as many as two-thirds of the working class from electoral politics. Women, blacks, and immigrants often participated in oppositional or mainstream politics, but rarely could they cast a ballot. This helped create a working-class political culture in which antistatism, syndicalism, and a distrust of the political system all flourished. With many workers disfranchised and thus limited in their ability to influence the government's character, their political abilities focused defensively on preventing the state from invading their homes, communities, and private lives. These same factors similarly shaped the culture of electoral politics. Because elections involved only white and native-born men as either candidates or voters, party rhetoric and tactics focused on appealing to them and ignored other social groups. Partisan culture united enfranchised workers with men of other classes in a masculine culture during political campaigns. Though more research is needed on the ways and degree to which women played a role in party politics before winning the vote, it seems clear that a celebration of "manliness," and closely linked qualities such as pride, independence, and equality were central to the sphere of electoral politics. Not coincidentally, these latter values also formed part of the legacy of republicanism, which continued to exert

---

[3] Neil R. McMillen, *Dark Journey: Black Mississippians in the Age of Jim Crow* (Urbana: University of Illinois Press, 1990), 35–71; and J. Morgan Kousser, *The Shaping of Southern Politics: Suffrage Restriction and the Establishment of the One-Party South, 1880–1910* (New Haven: Yale University Press, 1974), 11–44, 239–42.

a profound influence on American political culture at the turn of the twentieth century.[4]

Even enfranchised workers, meanwhile, found their political influence splintered by ethnocultural ties to different parties, local-level alliances with urban machines, and regional divisions (the urban industrial Northeast versus the less developed, more rural South and West). American politics, as numerous scholars have documented, simply did not rotate on the axis of class during the late nineteenth century. Ethnicity, religion, and geography predicted an individual's political affiliation and voting preference more reliably than did class. These dynamics gave the Democratic Party a slight edge among workers (its emphasis on personal liberty attracted Irish- and German-American workingmen), but other workers, including German Protestants, Scandinavians, and many Britons (especially, in each case, if they resided in northeastern cities), leaned toward the Republican Party with its focus on the tariff as the key to prosperity and its record in the Civil War.[5] Equally important, many workingmen found themselves touched most directly not by national parties at all, but by local machines. Whether Republican or Democratic, political machines could provide minimal welfare protection and politicians more responsive to labor's demands than those at the state or federal level.[6]

Yet urban machines did not seek out workers as potential partners. Their leaders intended instead a paternalistic relationship, with workers serving as grateful recipients of gifts from a generous protector. When workingmen returned

---

[4] John Bukowczyk, "The Transformation of Working-Class Ethnicity: Corporate Control, Americanization, and the Polish Immigrant Middle Class in Bayonne, N.J., 1915–1925," *Labor History*, 25, Winter 1984, 53–82; David Scobey, "Boycotting the Politics Factory: Labor Radicalism and the New York City Mayoral Election of 1886," *Radical History Review*, 28–30, September 1984, 280–326; on the masculine character of electoral politics, see Paula Baker, "The Domestication of Politics"; Bruce Laurie, *Artisans into Workers: Labor in Nineteenth-Century America* (New York: Hill and Wang, 1989).

[5] Richard Jensen, *The Winning of the Midwest: Social and Political Conflict, 1888–1896* (Chicago: University of Chicago Press, 1971); Paul Kleppner, *The Cross of Culture: A Social Analysis of Midwestern Politics* (New York: The Free Press, 1970); Robert Cherny, *Populism, Progressivism, and the Transformation of Nebraska Politics, 1885–1915* (Lincoln: University of Nebraska Press, 1981); Walter Dean Burnham, *Critical Elections and the Mainsprings of American Politics* (New York: W. W. Norton, 1970). Although most scholars agree that ethnocultural ties provide important predictors of political affiliation, many have also noted the limitations of these studies. Because class is rarely examined as an influence in determining political behavior, and because it overlaps with ethnicity and religion in complex ways, the ethnocultural school's findings on class and politics are not wholly reliable. See, for example, Allan J. Lichtman, "Political Realignment and 'Ethnocultural' Voting in Late Nineteenth Century America," *Journal of Social History*, 16 (3), Spring 1983, 55–82; idem, "Critical Election Theory and the Reality of American Presidential Politics, 1916–1940," *American Historical Review*, 81 (2), April 1976, 317–51; Richard L. McCormick, "Ethnocultural Interpretations of Nineteenth Century American Voting Behavior," *Political Science Quarterly*, 89 (2), June 1974, 351–77.

[6] Shefter, "Trade Unions and Political Machines," 197–278.

their gaze to the national level, the parties offered little more. Having exercised full suffrage rights since Andrew Jackson's reforms, many white workingmen felt deeply loyal to one or the other political party. The mass campaigns and torchlight parades so characteristic of Gilded Age partisan culture engaged working-class as well as middle-class Americans. Issues the parties stressed, like the tariff, prohibition, or states' rights, could appeal mightily to workingmen. But in fact, with issues like these, the parties could not become vehicles for significant social transformation in workers' interests. Both the Republicans and Democrats were fundamentally probusiness parties and they shared the anti-labor bias of American employers. The candidates each party put forward, their platforms, and the legislation they sponsored all demonstrated an unwillingness to appeal to workers *as workers*.

These barriers to mainstream political power encouraged workers' participation in oppositional politics. At the local, state, and national levels, workers experimented with a wide variety of alternative political movements. Especially at times when labor conflict erupted, workers pressed their demands through political activity. During the depression of the 1870s, especially after the great railroad strike of 1877, the cause of greenbacks, inflated currency, and (especially in California) opposition to Chinese immigration fueled workers' political activity. Amidst the Great Upheaval of the mid-1880s, another period of economic recession, workers employed the Knights of Labor and Henry George's single-tax theories to fight for reform. Then, as the nation fell again into economic depression between 1893 and 1897, political solutions suggested by socialists and populists grew popular among workingpeople.[7]

The most dramatic period of working-class political mobilization undoubtedly came between 1885 and 1888, when KOL local and district assemblies made their bids for power. Leon Fink has analyzed the political movements that sprang up in 189 towns and in all but four of the thirty-eight states and territories. Scores of workingmen achieved electoral victories: The winners included sheriffs, mayors, and reportedly one dozen congressmen (most of them on fusion tickets). These movements pursued a broad spectrum of goals, according to Fink, from increased control over local police, to minimum wage and maximum hours laws, more money for amenities like street lights and children's education, and punitive taxation of unoccupied land. Meanwhile, outside the sphere of electoral politics, female Knights members articulated a gendered vision of social reform,

---

[7] Selig Perlman, "Upheaval and Reorganisation," in John Commons et al., eds., *History of Labour in the United States* (New York: Macmillan, 1918), 2:240–68; Paul Kleppner, "The Greenback and Prohibition Parties," in Arthur M. Schlesinger, Jr., ed., *History of U.S. Political Parties* (New York: Chelsea House, 1973), 2:1549–81; Irwin Unger, *The Greenback Era: A Social and Political History of American Finance, 1865–1879* (Princeton: Princeton University Press, 1964), 348–95; Scobey, "Boycotting the Politics Factory"; Chester McArthur Destler, *American Radicalism, 1865–1901* (Chicago: Quadrangle, 1966; orig. 1946); Peter Alexander Speek, *The Single Tax and the Labor Movement*, Bulletin No. 878, Economics and Political Science Series, 8 (3) (Madison: University of Wisconsin, 1917).

one that focused on supporting suffrage and equal pay for women while fighting against liquor and the saloon.[8]

The Gilded Age also saw ambitious efforts to unite workers and farmers and thereby achieve a progressive program of social and political reform. In the 1870s, the Greenback movement remained limited and marginal until workers, incensed by events during the labor conflict of 1877, joined its ranks. Never completely agreeing with the stress placed on currency inflation, labor activists won the addition of several labor-related planks to the Greenback platform in 1878. These included standard labor demands such as legal reductions in the hours of work, creation of a Bureau of Labor Statistics, and an end to both prison labor and Chinese immigration. This new unity between workers and farmers produced the party's most successful year, as it polled more than one million votes in 1878 and elected fifteen congressmen (though most were elected on fusion tickets). Weakest in the South, the party grew stronger in the central and western United States and made its biggest gains, thanks to working-class supporters, in the East. But after the 1878 elections, the party's internal divisions, especially between western agrarians and eastern labor activists, pulled it apart. As Paul Kleppner has argued, once the depression ended, the potential for common ground between workers and farmers diminished. Workers grew less tolerant of a political movement built on currency reform or demands for lower railroad rates, and rapidly disappeared from the party.[9]

Almost twenty years later, the next battle to unite farmers and workers emerged. This time the Populists, again stressing the evils of a corrupt financial system, turned to workers for support. In much of the South and West and in mining areas in Illinois and Ohio, workingpeople joined the Populist crusade. Wage earners actually dominated the movement in states like Montana and Colorado and wooed farmers to join them. The leaders of the Knights of Labor, a wilting organization by the early 1890s, threw their fortunes together with the People's Party, founded in 1892. But in the East, the Populist Party had little influence and industrial workers there remained unmoved by the farmers' crusade. As in the 1870s, workingpeople found that the silver issue (and generally the Populists' focus on financial and distributive mechanisms) did not sufficiently address their problems and needs.

Workers' suspicions became even more evident in the 1896 election, when William Jennings Bryan attempted unsuccessfully to ride farmer-worker unity to the White House. Workingmen divided between the two parties, motivated

---

[8] Leon Fink, *Workingmen's Democracy: The Knights of Labor and American Politics* (Urbana: University of Illinois Press, 1983), 25–32; and Susan Levine, *Labor's True Woman: Carpet Weavers, Industrialization, and Labor Reform in the Gilded Age* (Philadelphia: Temple University Press, 1984), 118–27.

[9] Kleppner, "The Greenback and Prohibition Parties," 2:1559–63. For the labor planks added to the platform of the National (Greenback) Party, see the "Toledo Platform of the National Party, 1878," in Arthur M. Schlesinger, ed., *History of U.S. Political Parties*, 2:1599–1601.

more by traditional loyalties for either party and by the Republican promise of economic prosperity, than by Bryan's silver rhetoric. Nonetheless, the dream of uniting progressive farmers and workers would continue to inspire political activity for the next two decades. Bryan emerged from the 1896 campaign convinced that farmer-worker unity held the key to Democratic electoral victory. This made labor central to his and the Democracy's calculations until at least World War I.[10]

Socialist organizations competed with the major parties for workers' loyalties during the Gilded Age. Its major institutional representative during the late nineteenth century was the Socialist Labor party (SLP), but the ideological appeal of socialism reached far beyond that organization. The SLP's leaders and members were largely Germans (only 10 percent of its members were native-born), and its meetings were conducted in German. A rather sectarian approach accompanied the SLP's narrow ethnic base. Thus, as Morris Hillquit noted in his history of socialism, throughout the SLP's career its leaders' main goal consisted of "Americanizing" their organization.[11]

"Americanization" seemed closer to the SLP's grasp when an imposing intellectual, Daniel DeLeon, became active in the party's affairs in 1890. A year later, he rose to the editorship of the SLP newspaper, the *People*, a post he would hold until his death in 1914. Quickly DeLeon assumed control over the SLP – he offered the party not only a leader with command over the English language (born in Venezuela, DeLeon had been in the United States since 1872), but a brilliant speaker, writer, and polemicist.[12] DeLeon entered a party very much in the doldrums: Its influence had declined over the 1880s, first because of competition from the anarchists' International Working People's Association, and second due to the same post-Haymarket repression that helped kill the anarchists' movement in the United States. Yet DeLeon's rise did not solve the SLP's problems, and in the following years, its membership never rose above 5,000. Although he provided the party with an articulate leader, DeLeon also intensified its doctrinaire rigidity, allowing no questioning of his authority and expelling from the SLP anyone who disagreed with his pronouncements. According to Mari Jo Buhle, by the mid-1890s, most prominent women had left the party in response to DeLeon's attacks. The character of DeLeon's

---

[10] Destler, *American Radicalism*; Melvyn Dubofsky, *Industrialism and the American Worker, 1865–1920*, 2nd ed. (Arlington Heights, IL: Harlan Davidson, 1985), 72–5; Jensen, *Winning of the Midwest*.

[11] Morris Hillquit, *History of Socialism in the United States* (New York: Dover, 1971; originally published in 1910), 193–4. See also Henry Bedford, *Socialism and the Workers in Massachusetts, 1886–1912* (Amherst: University of Massachusetts, 1966); Howard H. Quint, *The Forging of American Socialism* (New York: Bobbs-Merrill, 1953).

[12] Glen L. Seretan, *Daniel DeLeon: The Odyssey of an American Marxist* (Cambridge: Harvard University Press, 1979). Samuel Gompers, who came to despise DeLeon, remarked of his heritage: "DeLeon came of a Venezuelan family of Spanish and Dutch Jewish descent with a strain of colored blood. That makes him a first-class son of a bitch." Ironically, Gompers himself descended from Dutch Jews. Quoted in Seretan, *Daniel DeLeon*, 102.

leadership particularly damaged SLP efforts to work harmoniously with groups like the AFL.[13]

Socialism during the Gilded Age transcended the SLP's boundaries and pervaded the labor movement in a subtle and immeasurable way. We saw in the last chapter that many labor leaders, like Gompers, McGuire, and Strasser, received their introduction to socialism and labor activism at the same time. It was the idea and the culture of socialism, not its institutional expression, that persuaded so many.[14] The Knights of Labor, the Greenback movement, and Populism all attracted socialists; some of them affiliated with the SLP but many did not. In the AFL during the 1890s, an important role would be played by activists like P. J. McGuire or William Mahon of Detroit, men who identified themselves as socialists but who disliked the SLP and opposed it on important questions.

Even this brief overview of workers' political activity during the Gilded Age suggests two clear themes. First, workingpeople energetically explored a wide range of political solutions and panaceas in response to the pressures of industrialization. Political activism and a sense of political urgency infused the labor movement from the first days of its postbellum rebirth in the 1870s. But secondly, the plethora of activities workers engaged in suggested also the limitations of labor politics. No single political solution to industrialization suggested itself to workers, who divided their energies among an increasingly splintered group of options. The fragmented oppositional culture confronted a political system that discriminated against third parties, and a working class that possessed strong ties already to the two major parties. Thus, although Gilded Age conditions encouraged radical labor politics, they also made success extremely difficult to achieve. In the late nineteenth century these two sides of American labor politics deeply influenced trade unionists struggling to determine the AFL's political direction.

The Birth of "Pure and Simple" Politics

Although the early AFL emerged out of a politically charged labor movement and its members engaged energetically in the populist and socialist movements, ironically the AFL's founding represented the advance of economic over political action. The conservative trade unionists clustered around Samuel Gompers

---

[13] On DeLeon's style, see Bedford, *Socialism and the Workers in Massachusetts*; Seretan, *Daniel DeLeon*; Mari Jo Buhle, *Women and American Socialism, 1870–1920* (Urbana: University of Illinois Press, 1981), 92. For membership figures, see Paul Buhle, "Socialist Labor Party," in Mari Jo Buhle, Paul Buhle, and Dan Georgakas, eds., *Encyclopedia of the American Left* (New York: Garland, 1990), 713–14. Consult also Bruce C. Nelson, *Beyond the Martyrs: A Social History of Chicago's Anarchists, 1870–1900* (New Brunswick, NJ: Rutgers University Press, 1988).

[14] For a useful exploration of socialism in one city, see Richard Schneirov, "The Knights of Labor in the Chicago Labor Movement and in Municipal Politics, 1877–1887," Ph.D. diss., Northern Illinois University, 1984.

gradually developed a distinctive approach that, without rejecting politics altogether, nonetheless emphasized the trade union as the central institution in working-class life and opposed interference from political parties. By the 1890s these divergent tendencies, combined with pressures generated by economic depression, gave rise to a tense and highly significant battle within the Federation over labor's political future.

More than anyone else, Samuel Gompers served as the architect of AFL political strategy during its early decades. We saw in Chapter One that Gompers received his initiation to trade unionism by socialists like David Hirsch and Ferdinand Laurrell. However, the socialism that engaged Gompers stressed the trade union and its economic activity as the key to a maturing labor movement. He adhered to the "Marxist," rather than the Lassallean, socialist tradition.

Gompers also inhabited a larger world, the urban environment of New York City, during nearly thirty formative years of his life. He arrived in New York from Britain during the Civil War, shortly after the 1863 race riots against the draft had been suppressed by regiments ordered away from Gettysburg. Standing with his relatives, young Sam watched as his father shook hands with an African-American man who had aided him during the journey. Noticing their encounter, "A crowd gathered round and threatened to hang both father and the Negro to the lamp-post."[15]

New York City, Iver Bernstein has shown, pulsed with working-class political experimentation during the mid-nineteenth century. As early as the Industrial Congress of the 1850s, workers struggled over the nature of their relationship with Tammany Hall. After the Civil War ended, William M. Tweed rose to lead Tammany with a machine that reconciled the demands of wage earners and elites. As Bernstein demonstrates, the white working class helped Tweed Democracy gain power and later contributed to its demise. Beginning in 1869, working-class resentment of Tammany intensified. Labor's reform movement that year united members of the German Arbeiter Union with the English-speaking Workingmen's Union. Together they vowed to sever ties with the major parties, declaring that "both of the existing parties are corrupt, serving capital instead of labor." Within this milieu of antipartyism, Sam Gompers received an early education in political strategy.[16]

Working in the CMIU a decade later, Gompers first deveolped his own double-fisted political style. First, use lobbying tactics to win legislation. Second, prohibit direct ties between the union and political parties. Gompers and Strasser won approval for exactly these two propositions at the CMIU's 1879 convention. Then they employed the approach in an ambitious campaign against tenement house production of cigars. Focusing on the New York state legislature,

---

[15] Samuel Gompers, *Seventy Years of Life and Labor: An Autobiography* (New York: E. P. Dutton, 1925), 1:23–4.

[16] Iver Bernstein, *The New York City Draft Riots: Their Significance for American Society and Politics in the Age of the Civil War* (New York: Oxford University Press, 1990), 75–124, 195–236, and esp. 224.

in 1881, the CMIU leaders attempted to elect senators and assemblymen who would help them pass their legislation. This was an early effort to "elect friends and punish enemies," the approach that would become so familiar in the early twentieth-century AFL. The project taught Gompers to exploit limited nonpartisan tactics like petitions, appearances before legislative committees, and letters to political representatives. Both in 1883 and 1884, the legislature passed a bill prohibiting tenement house production, but each time employers successfully challenged the bill in court.[17]

This political project became a source of criticism in CMIU Local 144 as trade unionists, often socialist German immigrants, challenged the union's leadership. While fighting for his bill in the New York legislature, Gompers furiously responded to the argument that political work should wait until labor could elect its own men to Congress. Even then, he countered, there would still be a president with veto power and a Supreme Court with ability to rule a bill unconstitutional. Hence it would be criminal to wait before seeking to win labor's demands through political activity. Some labor men, he said, wish to defeat labor's bill so they can prove trade union politics a failure. To the contrary, Gompers concluded, "any politics that is inconsistent with the politics of Trades Unions, is capitalistic."[18]

A few years later, amidst the political upheaval of 1886, Gompers supported Henry George's bid for the mayoralty of New York City. Although Gompers seemed ambivalent about participating (he editorialized in a New York newspaper that workers should hesitate before engaging in political activity), he served as secretary of the committee running George's campaign and headed its Speakers' Bureau. He spoke regularly on behalf of George's candidacy, sometimes as often as three or four times daily. At one meeting Gompers proclaimed, "I have been working for organized labor for twenty-five years and have never declared myself a politician. Now I come out for George as a trade unionist and intend to support him with all my might." After George's defeat, the movement supporting him split in two, with SLP activists opposing the United Labor Party. Such factionalism reminded Gompers of the virtues of nonpartisan politics.[19]

---

[17] Gompers, *Seventy Years*, 1:183–98; and editors' comments, Stuart Kaufman et al, *The Samuel Gompers Papers: The Making of a Union Leader, 1850–1886* (Urbana: University of Illinois Press, 1986), 1:72 and 1:170.

[18] Samuel Gompers to the Editor of the *Cigar Makers' Official Journal*, January 1882, in Kaufman, *Gompers Papers*, 1:252–4. Reflecting on this statement days later, Gompers noted that such politics were not only capitalistic but also middle-class.

[19] Gompers served in 1886 on a special committee of the State Workingmen's Assembly designed to elect friendly representatives to the state legislature. For Gompers's account of his role in the George campaign, see *Seventy Years*, 1:311–24. For more accounts of Gompers's speeches on behalf of George, see the excerpts in Kaufman, *Gompers Papers*, 1:431–2. Useful sources on the campaign include Speek, *The Single Tax and the Labor Movement*, 247–426; Scobey, "Boycotting the Politics Factory"; and Philip Foner, *History of the Labor Movement in the U.S.*, Vol. 2, *From the Founding of the A.F. of L. to the Emergence of American Imperialism* (New York: International, 1955), 115–24.

During the same period, he served as president of the New York State Working-men's Assembly and directed its efforts to win state legislation, thereby gaining more experience with lobbying techniques.[20]

The American labor movement had relied on nonpartisan tactics for decades before Samuel Gompers rose to prominence. George Henry Evans's land reform movement in the 1840s and early 1850s sought federal legislation to make pub-lic lands available to all citizens. Toward this end, Evans formed the National Reform Association. Its members pledged not to support any political candidate who disagreed with the association's goals.[21] Similarly, Ira Steward's movement to win a shorter workday prompted the creation of approximately eighty Grand Eight-Hour Leagues between 1864 and 1873. Steward devised a nonpartisan strategy for winning his desired legislation. Eight-hour activists submitted their program to every candidate, from governor down to the humblest city officials, and asked them one question: "Will you, if elected, vote for this bill?"[22]

The Knights of Labor also pioneered in the use of nonpartisan tactics. In 1879, the KOL leadership attempted to limit members' political work, prohibiting the discussion of politics during meetings and confining political action to endorse-ments of that party most willing to support labor's demands. These efforts to prevent KOL members from political engagement, as Leon Fink documented, failed. Yet in many ways, the KOL nonpartisan focus foreshadowed the AFL's twentieth-century efforts. In 1886, for example, KOL members sought to elect friendly candidates to Congress. Terence Powderly claimed the Knights that year had elected one dozen congressmen.[23]

The creation of the Federation of Trades and Labor Unions in 1881 and its supersession in 1886 by the AFL did not represent the triumph of economic action

---

[20] Samuel Gompers, "An Address before the New York State Workingmen's Assembly," January 18, 1887, in Kaufman, *Gompers Papers*, 2:4–9.

[21] Philip Foner, *History of the Labor Movement in the United States*, Vol. 1, *From Colonial Times to the Founding of the American Federation of Labor* (New York: International, 1947), 183–8.

[22] Steward and Gompers were close associates and co-members of the Economic and Soci-ological Club during the 1870s. John B. Andrews, "Nationalisation," in John Commons et al., eds., *History of Labour in the United States*, 87–93; Selig Perlman, "Upheaval and Reorganisation," in ibid., 302–3, 531; Perlman, *A History of Trade Unionism in the United States* (New York: Macmillan, 1922), 46–50; David Montgomery, *Beyond Equality: Labor and the Radical Republicans, 1862–1872* (Urbana: University of Illinois Press, 1981), 249–60.

[23] Gerald Grob, *Workers and Utopia: A Study of Ideological Conflict in the American Labor Movement 1865–1900* (Evanston, IL: Northwestern University Press, 1961), 79–98. Powderly consistently worked to prevent the KOL from forming partisan attachments until members voted him out of office in 1893. When the KOL formed a National Union Labor Party and then sought to influence the presidential campaign of 1888, Powderly insisted on main-taining the Order's nonpartisan strategy. Powderly also opposed working with the People's Party, and only in 1893, under new leadership, did the KOL break firmly with its non-partisan legacy and begin working with the Populist movement. Besides Grob, see Norman Ware, *The Labor Movement in the United States, 1860–1895: A Study in Democracy* (New York: Vintage Books, 1964), 350–70; Perlman, "Upheaval and Reorganisation," 439–70.

and the abolition of politics from trade unions. The question of trade unions' relationship to political action would not be decided until the 1890s. The founding of FOTLU, for example, actually suggested a new emphasis on political action. Modeled on the British Trades Union Congress, FOTLU's leaders focused somewhat more on political than on economic action. A legislative committee functioned as FOTLU's executive board, and the committee's secretary served as chief executive for the entire federation. Yet FOTLU soon began deteriorating as an organization, and its leaders achieved little economically or politically.[24]

The founding of the AFL subtly shifted the balance between political and economic struggle toward the latter. The secretary of the legislative committee no longer served as chief executive of the organization; instead, delegates created the offices of president, two vice-presidents, a treasurer, and a secretary. A core of conservative unionists, notably Gompers, Strasser, and McGuire, exercised significant control over the young AFL from its first days. The election of Gompers to the presidency, well known for his opposition to the KOL, his reliance on limited political tactics, and his commitment to craft unionism, suggested the desires of delegates. Their war with the Knights intensified trade unionists' frustration with social reform while it strengthened the hand of those favoring economic strategies, and this showed up in the AFL's early priorities. Although the AFL constitution included federal labor legislation as a major goal, in practice, Gompers and other leaders focused almost entirely on institution building during the early years. If called on to discuss political questions, Gompers stressed that building unions was a more important arena than politics. When labor did tackle politics, he argued in 1887, it should work toward "present and tangible results."[25]

Yet there was more to the AFL than Gompers and his allies, and many AFL members envisioned a different approach to politics. We saw in Chapter One that several AFL affiliates, for example the Boot and Shoe Workers and the Bakers, embraced socialism during the early history of the AFL. Other unions, notably the Miners, pursued a broad range of political options from mainstream party politics to socialism and populism. The AFL welcomed socialists and they returned the affection, especially after KOL chief Powderly enraged many

---

[24] Mark W. Moore to All Trades and Labor Unions of the U.S. and Canada, September 15, 1881, Kaufman, *Gompers Papers*, 1:164–5; "Champions of Labor," *Pittsburgh Commercial Gazette*, November 15, 1881, in Kaufman, *Gompers Papers*, 1:211–12; "The Labor Congress," *Pittsburgh Commercial Gazette*, November 18, 1881, in Kaufman, *Gompers Papers*, 1:224–6; Perlman, "Upheaval and Reorganisation," 318–24; Bernard Mandel, *Samuel Gompers: A Biography* (Yellow Springs, OH: Antioch Press, 1963), 48. On the early Trades Union Congress, see Ross M. Martin, *TUC: The Growth of a Pressure Group, 1868–1976* (Oxford: Oxford University Press, 1980).

[25] "The American Federation," *New-York Tribune*, December 12, 1886, in Kaufman, *Gompers Papers*, 1:469–70; Perlman, "Upheaval and Reorganisation," 410–11 and 495; on Gompers's political views, see the interview with him in the *Leader*, July 25, 1887, in Kaufman, *Gompers Papers*, 2:46–8; and "Four Questions," *New Yorker Volkszeitung*, December 3, 1888, in Kaufman, *Gompers Papers*, 2:162.

socialists by refusing to support clemency for the Haymarket martyrs.[26] Thus, in the 1880s, while Gompers and his allies sought to steer the Federation toward nonpartisan and nonradical political action, many other voices spoke persuasively for a different approach. Turbulent politics surrounded the AFL, as workers formed labor parties or worked through the socialist or anarchist movements, but within the Federation the 1880s proved to be the calm before a very big storm.

That storm hit between 1890 and 1896, as political turmoil tore the AFL apart. It began in 1890 when President Gompers determined to take a stand against party politics in the trade unions. The New York Central Labor Federation (CLF) had voted to admit a section of the Socialist Labor Party as an affiliate. Gompers declared that a political party should not be allowed representation in a trade union organization. Hence, he refused to issue a charter to the Central Labor Federation and referred the matter to the 1890 AFL convention. The CLF chose one of its SLP members, Lucien Sanial, to attend the convention and make its case.

In the convention debate over the matter, Gompers defended himself against the charge that he had become an antisocialist: "there is not a noble hope that a Socialist may have that I do not hold as my ideal." Nonetheless, he argued, "The Socialist Party and the Trade Unions . . . differ [inherently] in their methods." Indeed, Gompers framed the issue as a choice between the trade unions and political parties like the SLP. In his vision, only one could stand at the heart of the labor movement, and he sided firmly with the unions:

I am willing to subordinate my opinions to the well being, harmony, and success of the labor movement; . . . I am willing to step aside if that will promote our cause; but I cannot and will not prove false to my convictions that the trade unions pure and simple are the natural organizations of the wage workers to secure their present and practical improvement and to achieve their final emancipation.

In the heat of political battle, Gompers had created the concept of pure and simple unionism, one with which he would always be identified. The convention rewarded Gompers by agreeing strongly with his position, 75 percent voting against admitting Sanial and against chartering the CLF.[27]

Somewhere, Gompers had learned to choose his battles wisely. This incident placed him in a strong position, because it was hardly a radical notion that a party ought not to be a trade union affiliate. After all, even Frederick Engels agreed! Gompers wrote to ask Engels for his opinion, and the socialist pioneer wrote a friend about the matter soon afterwards. As a federation of unions, Engels said, the AFL has the right to reject any organization that is not a trade

[26] Laurie, *Artisans into Workers.*

[27] Gompers to Ernest Bohm, November 7, 1890, in Kaufman, *Gompers Papers,* 2:377–8; "Plotting Against Gompers," *New York Daily News,* December 4, 1890, in Kaufman, *Gompers Papers,* 2:383–5; "President Gompers Speech" at the annual convention of the AFL, 1890, in Kaufman, *Gompers Papers,* 2:400–1. For the coining of "pure and simple," see Gompers, *Seventy Years,* 1:385.

union. Rejection had to come, Engels concluded, "and I, for one, cannot blame Gompers for it."[28] In winning this battle, Gompers struck a blow for one of his key beliefs: Party politics must be kept out of the trade unions. Moreover, this battle enlisted antipartyism in an innovative way, using it not for opposition to the *major* parties, but as a basis for attacking a *socialist* organization.

In the next years, American workers confronted new problems that intensified the political clamor within the AFL. In 1892, major defeats in strikes among iron and steel workers in Homestead, switchmen in Buffalo, and miners in Tennessee and Coeur d'Alene heightened class tensions and made trade unionists wary of a purely economic struggle. Judicial hostility, which by 1906 would provoke a political crisis in the AFL, first emerged in these years as a block to trade union success. A labor injunction, for example, helped break the American Railway Union's boycott against the Pullman Company in 1894. Yet this famous case simply climaxed a number of judicial precedents established in the preceding year. Meanwhile, the economic crisis that began in 1893, the worst depression to that time, hit workers with high unemployment rates, slashed wages, and short time. The depression radicalized some workingpeople and encouraged many others at least to seek political solutions.[29]

As a consequence, labor-populist coalitions grew more popular, particularly in Ohio, Wisconsin, and Illinois, where miners, railroad workers, and machinists, among others, mobilized to assist the new People's Party. In July 1892, the People's Party convened at Omaha and nominated General James Weaver for president; later that year, Weaver received more than one million popular votes. Beyond the enthusiasm for Populism, urban workers in cities throughout the United States joined forces with local-level movements pushing for political reform. Meanwhile, delegates at the 1892 AFL convention endorsed government ownership of the telegraph and telephone systems and instructed the AFL Executive Council to begin working to increase union political activity.[30] As labor's interest in populism grew, a prominent socialist from Chicago, Thomas J. Morgan, prepared an eleven-point program and introduced it to the AFL's

---

[28] Engels to Hermann Schlüter, January 29, 1891, reprinted in Karl Marx and Frederick Engels, *Letters to Americans, 1848–1895: A Selection*, ed. Alexander Trachtenberg (New York: International, 1953), 233.

[29] Perlman, "Upheaval and Reorganisation," 495; Felix Frankfurter and Nathan Greene, *The Labor Injunction* (New York: Macmillan, 1930); Christopher Tomlins, *The State and the Unions: Labor Relations, Law, and the Organized Labor Movement in America, 1880–1960* (New York: Cambridge University Press, 1985).

[30] Foner, *History of the Labor Movement*, Vol. 2; Chester McArthur Destler, *American Radicalism*, 162–211; Stromquist, "Looking Both Ways: Ideological Crisis and Working-Class Recomposition in the 1890s," unpublished manuscript. Mandel, *Samuel Gompers*, 151; Lewis Lorwin, *The American Federation of Labor: History, Policies, and Prospects* (Washington, DC: The Brookings Institution, 1933), 35; "List of Resolutions of a Political Nature," *American Federationist* (hereafter cited as *AF*), 3 (8), October 1896, 174–5. Convention delegates also passed a resolution in 1892 declaring that partisan politics did not belong in the trade unions.

1893 convention. Morgan's program generated tremendous political debate for the next two years and provided the centerpiece for one of the most significant political battles in AFL history.

"Tommy" Morgan was an Englishman, founder of the Chicago Trades and Labor Assembly, and that city's most prominent socialist. He worked in the early 1890s to build an alliance in Illinois between urban radicals and rural populists, and led Chicago's delegation to the 1893 populist convention. Inspired by the British labor movement's effort in independent labor politics, Morgan hoped to commit the populists and the AFL to a list of demands closely modeled on British workers' activity. His political program catalogued eleven progressive demands. The most controversial plank, the tenth, was avowedly socialistic, demanding "the collective ownership by the people of all the means of production and distribution." Other planks called for the eight-hour workday, sanitary inspection of workshop, mine, and home, municipal ownership of street cars and gas and electric plants, and nationalization of telegraphs, telephones, railroads and mines.[31]

At the 1893 AFL convention, delegates voted to send Morgan's program out to be voted on by the affiliated unions. Over the next twelve months the labor movement debated its political future. The AFL journal, the *American Federationist*, ran regular articles arguing over the program's merits. Compared to socialists like Morgan or J. Mahlon Barnes, who wrote in defense of the program, or critics like John O'Brien, who rejected any political activity as useless, Gompers seemed to be staking out a centrist position. In his first essay in the new AFL journal, Gompers wrote: "In politics we shall be as we always have been, *independent*. Independent of all parties regardless under which name they may be known." Gompers argued that trade unions needed political action, but he rejected any reliance on a political party. A new and radical organization like the People's Party, in this formulation, was no better than the major parties.[32]

Thus, when AFL convention delegates voted, also in 1893, to form an alliance with the farmers' organizations, Gompers dug in his heels and stalled. Though AFL leaders obediently sent a delegation (Gompers, Frank Foster, and P. J. McGuire) to confer in June 1894 with representatives from the KOL, the railroad brotherhoods, and the National Farmers' Alliance, during the meeting Gompers rejected a KOL proposal to support People's Party candidates. He declared that "the Federation cannot with judiciousness imperil the economic integrity of its affiliated bodies by espousing partisanship, even in a third party form." Furthermore, Gompers retorted, because the unions were simultaneously debating the Morgan program, the AFL committee could not "assume to speak for the vast body of our membership, or pledge them to the support of any particular platform of principles."[33]

[31] Thomas J. Morgan, "The Programme," *AF*, 1 (1), March 1894, 7; Destler, *American Radicalism*, 167–71.

[32] Captain John O'Brien, "The Aspirations of the Trade Union Movement," *AF*, 1 (9), November 1894, 190; Samuel Gompers, "Salutary," *AF*, 1 (1), March 1894, 10–11.

[33] "Convention Notes," *AF*, 1 (11), January 1895, 266–7.

Even as Gompers spoke, the AFL's affiliated unions were overwhelmingly approving Morgan's platform. Only one union, the Bakers, entirely rejected the eleven planks. A few unions struck out or modified plank 10. But the vast majority of unions approved the program without changes: This included the UMW, ironworkers and steelworkers, tailors, painters, brewery workers, street-railway employees, shoe workers, textile workers, machinists, and mule spinners. A new commitment to political action seemed certain for America's labor movement. Also in 1894, more than 300 trade union members ran for office, most of them on the People's Party ticket, though only half a dozen celebrated a victory.[34]

But Gompers and his allies were determined to keep labor free from partisan allegiances. As delegates gathered in Denver for the AFL's 1894 convention, most planned to vote for the program. Gompers, however, kicked off the convention with an address stressing the many political defeats suffered recently by trade unionists. Disruptive as those local-level defeats had been, he argued, the disaster would have been greatly compounded if they occurred under the auspices of the AFL.[35] Then followed a two-day debate over the merits of Morgan's political program. Although initially it seemed the program would pass easily, opposition to it had grown. At one level, the battle centered on parliamentary procedure. Opponents to the program proposed that the preamble, which praised British labor for adopting an independent political movement, be voted on separately. Delegates thereupon voted it down. Next, a motion that delegates vote separately on each plank won approval. Despite this maneuver, delegates approved each plank except the tenth. In place of collective ownership of the means of production, delegates passed a new plank demanding abolition of "the monopoly system of land holding." Yet when delegates took a final vote on the entire program, they rejected it by a vote of 1,173 to 735.[36]

This was an odd turn of events to be sure. The affiliated unions had almost unanimously instructed their delegates to support the program. Nonetheless, those delegates voted to ignore their instructions and defeated the program by nearly 62 percent. What happened? It took more than parliamentary tactics to defeat the program. The most important key to defeating Morgan's plan was Gompers's carefully defined approach to politics. Rather than opposing political activity altogether, he stressed the evils of party politics, particularly for the immediate future. This allowed him to build a broad coalition that united, first, trade unionists like John Lennon (of the Tailors) or P. J. McGuire who favored political activity but feared committing to partisanship; and, second,

---

[34] Perlman, "Upheaval and Reorganisation," 511–14.

[35] Ibid., 512.

[36] J. F. Finn, "A.F. of L. Leaders and the Question of Politics in the Early 1890s," *Journal of American Studies*, 7 (3), December 1973, 243–65; American Federation of Labor, *A Verbatum Report of the Discussion on the Political Programme, at the Denver Convention of the American Federation of Labor, December 14, 15, 1894 [sic]* (New York: The Freytag Press, 1895); "Convention Notes," *AF*, 1 (11), January 1895, 266. For the vote, see William Dick, *Labor and Socialism in America: The Gompers Era* (Port Washington, NY: Kennikat Press, 1972), 42.

trade unionists who opposed any political activity and favored instead a complete reliance on economic action. This latter group included both the philosophical anarchists – for example, the printer August McCraith and the baker Henry Weismann – and conservative unionists like printer John O'Brien. With these diverse groups united behind him, Gompers succeeded in isolating those Socialists and Populists desiring an immediate partisan affiliation.

It is important to note that many within Gompers's coalition explicitly supported political action. A number of these men, for example John Lennon and William Pomeroy, supported the populist movement. Many, like William Mahon, identified with the socialist movement, but refused to support a program that threatened to disrupt the AFL. Others such as Walter Macarthur and P. J. McGuire clearly supported political action but opposed *party* politics within the AFL. Macarthur was determined, as he put it, "to conserve the [AFL] . . . and to keep the virus of politics out of it. I am in favor of political action. What bothers me is how to do it. I am satisfied that we cannot do it as trade unionists and preserve the efficiency of the trades unions. . . ." Once we have "preserved the unions," Macarthur concluded, we can launch a political movement.[37]

Though they failed to pass the program, those who supported it did defeat Samuel Gompers's bid for reelection to the AFL presidency. They united with the miners to elect UMW leader John McBride, a victory that suggested not only a great desire among AFL delegates for more politics (McBride appeared more supportive of independent labor politics than did Gompers), but also for a shift away from East Coast leadership (that the convention was held in Denver clearly contributed to Gompers's defeat). Unfortunately, McBride's tenure as chief of the Federation was greatly damaged by illness and charges of corruption. The next year the convention returned to the East coast and Gompers defeated McBride for the presidency by a narrow vote of 1041 to 1023. That same year, delegates attempted to reintroduce Thomas Morgan's program, but the measure lost. Instead, delegates adopted and inserted into the AFL constitution a declaration that "party politics shall have no place in the conventions of the AFL." Reflecting later on his successful reelection to the presidency, Gompers attributed it to this triumph within the AFL of nonpartisan politics.[38]

Gompers's Political Vision

Returning to head the AFL in 1895, Gompers and his allies moved quickly to consolidate their control over the organization. AFL leaders recalled all organizers' commissions, inspected each one, then reappointed those whose support they

---

[37] Finn, "A.F. of L. Leaders," 243–65; for the Macarthur quote, see American Federation of Labor, *A Verbatum Report [sic]*, 6.

[38] Lorwin, *American Federation of Labor*, 40; Marc Karson, *American Labor Unions and Politics: 1900–1918* (Carbondale: Southern Illinois University Press, 1958), 21; Gompers to W. H. Milburn, Denver *Evening Press*, September 23, 1896, *The American Federation of Labor Records: The Samuel Gompers Era* (microfilm edition, 1979), Microfilming Corporation of America (hereafter cited as *AFL Records*), reel 59.

could count on.[39] In addition, Gompers now knew that whoever sought to lead the Federation must assert a political as well as an economic vision. In a calculated response to the upheaval of 1893 and 1894, he and other leaders began firmly to articulate and implement a more detailed political program based on their vision of trade union–centered and nonpartisan political action. AFL headquarters shifted from Indianapolis to Washington, D.C., so its leaders and lobbyists could pursue a legislative program. And the AFL leaders began a careful effort to win their members' support for that program through regular articles in the *American Federationist*. At the same time, Gompers and his allies launched more aggressive attacks on socialism, targeting especially the leaders of the Socialist Labor Party, mainly through the pages of the *American Federationist*.[40]

But most importantly, AFL leaders now energetically began pursuing legislation at the federal level. Gompers initiated a regular correspondence with congressmen, senators, and government officials. AFL leaders became leading spokesmen on such problems as the eight-hour day, immigration, the injunction, compulsory arbitration, the initiative and referendum, and seamen's rights.[41] The AFL legislative committee, headed by Andrew Furuseth of the Sailors' Union of the Pacific, began reporting on pending legislation and more generally acted as a lobbying force: It organized testimony before congressional and Senate committees, drafted bills and found sponsors for them, and worked to influence the content of other bills. When these limited efforts proved unsuccessful, the AFL leaders escalated their tactics in a way that foreshadowed their efforts a decade later. For example, they conferred with President McKinley in 1897 and requested his support for labor legislation, asked congressmen to state their position on a key issue and published the responses in the *American Federationist*, and instructed AFL members to petition their political representatives.[42]

---

[39] Samuel Gompers, "Organizers' 'Gritty' Resolves," *AF*, 4 (1), March 1897, 14–15. On the reorganization of the AFL, see also Stromquist, "Looking Both Ways."

[40] For example, see the following editorials by Gompers: "Labor's Friends (?) – Save Us From These," *AF*, 3 (1), March 1896, 33; "With Compliments to Would-Be Union Wreckers," *AF*, 3 (3), May 1896, 52; "When to Challenge Is Treachery," *AF*, 5 (1), March 1898, 10–11.

[41] For example, Congressman John B. Corliss to Samuel Gompers, April 16, 1896; Edward F. McSweeney, Secretary, U.S. Immigration Investigating Commission to Gompers, May 12, 1896; Gompers to Hilary Herbert, Secretary of the Navy, August 22, 1896. All in *AFL Records*, reel 59.

[42] Another sign of the AFL's new focus on politics can be seen in the content of the *American Federationist*: After 1895, it regularly carried articles about state and federal legislation. For examples, see Samuel Gompers, "Division and Defeat, or Unity and Success – Workers of the West, Which Shall it Be?" *AF*, 5 (2), April 1898, 34–6; idem, "The President and Labor," *AF*, 4 (3), May 1897, 41–2; AFL Executive Council to the President, Cabinet, and Congress of the U.S., April 21, 1897, *AF*, 4 (3), May 1897, 56; "Senators and Congressmen on the Eight-Hour Workday," *AF*, 5 (1), March 1898, 1–3; Andrew Furuseth and George Chance to Samuel Gompers and the AFL Executive Council, July 12, 1898, *AF*, 5 (6), August 1898, 120–1. At this time, the AFL Executive Council consisted of P. J. McGuire (Carpenters), James Duncan (Granite Cutters), James O'Connell (IAM), M. M. Garland (Iron and Steel Workers), Frank Morrison (ITU), and John Lennon (Tailors).

While the AFL leaders experimented with political tactics, they developed arguments regarding the proper relationship between labor and politics. At the center stood two tightly linked concepts: first, pure and simple unionism, which placed the trade unions at the center of the labor movement; and, second, anti-partyism, a theory that accepted the need for political activity while rejecting partisanship as the road to success.

The conservative trade unionists who headed the AFL perceived their trade union federation as a sort of embryonic government or state, and this notion underpinned pure and simple politics. As a poem published in the *American Federationist* in 1898 declared:

> Sail on, good ship, the future State!
> Sail on, O Federation, strong and great!

Trade unionists frequently relied on such imagery. In 1896, George McNeill compared trade unions to the monopolies, and concluded: "It is the function of the trade unions to create a democratic monopoly of labor. They must be the banking houses, as well as the army and navy . . . the AFL must step forward out of its present loose form of federation into a compact government. . . ." Likewise, as Gompers declared, the AFL represented "the germ of a future state which all will hail with glad acclaim."[43] However, as a future state, the AFL should be beholden to no greater authority. From this idea derived the AFL leaders' emphasis on autonomy and their rejection of state or political party intervention in AFL affairs.

Gompers repeatedly stressed his commitment to political action during the late 1890s. He wrote in 1898, for example: "No one having any knowledge of . . . the labor movement ever conceived the notion to advise or request the working people to abstain from the use of their political power."[44] Gompers celebrated workers' political achievements at the municipal level and justified them as necessary due to a corrupt political system that ignored workers' needs. In fact, Gompers even sought to give the AFL credit as a central influence in the emergence of working-class political activism at the local level.[45]

In Gompers's mind, however, successful political action must be linked solidly to a revolt against the party system. The biggest political problem in the United States, he argued, was the role played by the political boss and the party. Because of them, Americans could not freely register their opinion on issues.

---

[43] Samuel Gompers, "Our Hopes are All With Thee," *AF*, 5 (4), June 1898, 71–3; Gompers, "Trade Unions – Their Philosophy," January 1899, *AFL Records*, reel 110; George E. McNeill, "The Trade Unions and the Monopolies," *AF* 3 (10), December 1896, 208–9; see also Tomlins, *The State and the Unions*, 57.

[44] Samuel Gompers, "The AF of L and Political Action," *AF*, 5 (4), June 1898, 73–4.

[45] Samuel Gompers, "Trade Unionists in Municipal Affairs," *AF*, 9 (8), August 1902, 433–4. Gompers celebrated the election of these trade unionists as Mayors: John T. McMillan, Ashtabula, Ohio; John P. Studley, New Haven, Connecticut; Bernard Bell, Masillon, Ohio; Ignatius Sullivan, Hartford, Connecticut; Stephen Charters, Ansonia, Connecticut; and Samuel Jones, Toledo, Ohio. See *AF*, 8 (9), September 1902, 645.

Indeed, according to Gompers, "It is party slavery which has done more to prevent political advancement than all other things combined." Invoking the concept of slavery, Gompers sought to demonstrate the threat party politics posed to workers' liberty. Unions presented the only tool workers could use to sever the chains binding them to the parties: "the organization of a union . . . is the beginning of the movement to alienate the workers from party domination. . . ." Gompers conceded that this was a complicated approach to political struggle. Some of our friends, he said, have trouble distinguishing between "political action of the trade union movement and political partisanship." Struggling to make his point clear, Gompers declared: "The American labor movement is as much above party as the heavens are from the earth; and it is safest and the best for the workers that they be kept wide apart."[46]

This approach proved popular and enabled Gompers to unite many trade unionists behind him. Although Socialists continued to play an important role in the Federation after the defeat of the Morgan program and Gompers's return to office, for the moment, their ascendancy had ended. At the same time, however, antiparty-ism should not be seen as merely an antisocialist weapon. Its contribution was far more complex than that. Antipartyism motivated trade unionists to follow Gompers and his allies on political as well as economic matters. And with time, as Gompers's approach to politics increasingly rejected statist legislation, it helped consolidate AFL members' support for a narrow and exclusivist political strategy.

Why did antipartyism appeal to so many AFL members? Several factors encouraged trade unionists to embrace an antiparty approach to politics. For one thing, American trade unionists perceived the British labor movement as a model to be followed, and in this period, the key to British trade union politics was independence from the major parties. In 1894, British trade unionist Tom Mann reported to Americans that the Independent Labor Party would probably run twenty candidates for office, and he stressed that Americans must remain free of the major "plutocratic" parties: "Let the Democratic and Republican parties seek you, . . . and when they seek you beware of compromise." Of course, in Britain, the revolt against party slavery contributed to the rise of a labor party rather than merely nonpartisan tactics. Nonetheless Gompers and likeminded leaders depended on such sentiments to corroborate their political positions.[47]

One did not need to look to Britain to see the influence of antipartyism. A distrust of parties and partisanship had been an integral element in American republicanism since the late eighteenth century. Civic virtue and partisan conflict in this view were incompatible. Thomas Paine wrote, for example, that

---

[46] Gompers, "The AF of L and Political Action," 73–4. On the meanings of slavery in American political culture, see Roediger, *Wages of Whiteness: Race and the Making of the American Working Class* (New York: Verso Books, 1991), 20, 27–31.

[47] Tom Mann, "Tactics Present and Future," *AF* 1 (4), June 1894, 65–6. William Dick notes that Gompers relied on the British example to bolster his nonpartisan position: See his *Labor and Socialism*, 123.

republicanism "does not admit of an interest distinct from that of the nation." In his farewell address to the nation, George Washington likewise warned against the damage that could be done by "the party spirit." Numerous historians have documented republicanism's impact on the nineteenth-century labor movement. Workers often employed the symbols and concepts of republican ideology to argue for their demands and to defend their central role in American society. Even after the Civil War, institutions like the Knights and the AFL were steeped in a republican tradition. Thus, in decrying party tyranny as a threat to workers' liberty, Sam Gompers was merely reaching to a vocabulary often relied on by workers.[48]

Antiparty sentiment has waxed and waned throughout the history of the United States. Often it appeals most intensely to Americans at times when the party system is being transformed. During the 1850s, for example, the Democratic Party fragmented as antipartyism facilitated the emergence of a coalition that evolved ultimately into the Republican Party. Another example might come from our own times: in the 1990s, antiparty sentiment pervades American political culture and has helped fuel the political career of Ross Perot. Similarly, the years between 1880 and 1915 experienced dramatic challenges to partisan politics, the emergence of a new party system, and a spreading cynicism toward partisan attachments. Even before the AFL, groups like the Greenback and Prohibition parties adopted antiparty rhetoric to argue for their goals.[49]

---

[48] On republicanism, see Joyce Appleby, *Capitalism and a New Social Order: The Republican Vision of the 1790s* (New York: New York University Press, 1984); Robert Shalhope, "Republicanism in Early America," *William and Mary Quarterly* 38, 1982, 334–56; Joyce Appleby, *Liberalism and Republicanism in the Historical Imagination* (Cambridge: Harvard University Press, 1992), esp. chaps. four, eleven, and thirteen; Drew R. McCoy, *The Elusive Republic: Political Economy in Jeffersonian America* (Chapel Hill: University of North Carolina Press, 1980). For the quotes from Paine and Washington, see Eric Foner, *Tom Paine and Revolutionary America* (New York: Oxford University Press, 1976), 89; and Ronald Formisano, *The Birth of Mass Political Parties, Michigan, 1827–1861* (Princeton: Princeton University Press, 1971), 56. For more on working-class interpretations of republicanism, see also Sean Wilentz, *Chants Democratic: New York City and the Rise of the American Working Class, 1788–1850* (New York: Oxford University Press, 1984); and Bruce Laurie, *Artisans into Workers*. It might be thought that Gompers's emphasis on "party slavery" suggests a racial component to his antipartyism. Certainly, labor republicanism was shaped by a racial consciousness. Yet David Roediger notes that in the aftermath of emancipation, blackness could no longer be equated easily with either servility or slavery. Research conducted for this study found no occasion where notions of "party slavery" were matched with racial references. Thus, my interpretation links the concept of party slavery with traditions of republicanism rather than seeing it as a code for attitudes regarding whiteness versus blackness. See David Roediger, *Wages of Whiteness*, 167–84.

[49] Michael F. Holt, "The Politics of Impatience: The Origins of Know-Nothingism," *Journal of American History*, 60, September 1973, 309–31; Ronald Formisano, "Political Character, Antipartyism, and the Second Party System," *American Quarterly*, 21, Winter 1969, 685–8; Paul Kleppner, *The Third Electoral System, 1853–1892: Parties, Voters, and Political Cultures* (Chapel Hill: University of North Carolina Press, 1979).

The late nineteenth century witnessed the heyday of partisan political culture. So unwavering was the prevailing partisanship that the major parties could mobilize their "troops" in a campaign with speed and efficacy. Around the turn of the twentieth century, however, dynamics emerged that transformed partisanship and the parties' role in American politics. Voting turnout began a sharp decline in 1904 that was never fully reversed; at the same time, independent voting and ticket splitting increased dramatically. As a result, the parties lost the ability to control and mobilize their mass membership. According to Richard McCormick, the decline in party loyalties may be attributed to three main causes: the demise of competitiveness between the parties associated with the realignment of the 1890s; the emergence of "reform" measures (such as registration requirements) that limited party machines' capacity for discipline; and the rise of extra-party organizations, or interest groups, that competed with the parties for Americans' loyalties.[50]

The demise of partisan culture McCormick described is typified by the American Federation of Labor. The antipartyism it stressed during the 1890s constituted the AFL's first serious effort to break workers' ties to the mainstream and oppositional parties. In the next decades other groups, many of them the AFL's bitter enemies, would join in the revolt against partisan culture. A reaction against the parties' high incidence of corruption would provide an important element in this revolt. In the 1890s, however, the AFL leaders simply tapped this hostility toward the parties that workers shared with other Americans in order to consolidate their political control over the labor movement and to forestall any number of alliances between workers and political parties that they considered disastrous.[51]

---

[50] Richard L. McCormick, "The Party Period and Public Policy," in his *The Party Period and Public Policy: American Politics from the Age of Jackson to the Progressive Era* (New York: Oxford University Press, 1986), 222–3. On the decline of partisanship, see also Walter Dean Burnham, "The Changing Shape of the American Political Universe," in his *The Current Crisis in American Politics* (New York: Oxford University Press, 1982).

The rising significance of interest groups is discussed by Samuel P. Hays, "Political Parties and the Community-Society Continuum," in William Nisbet Chambers and Walter Dean Burnham, eds., *The American Party Systems: Stages of Political Development* (New York: Oxford University Press, 1975), 152–81. To compare the politics of the AFL with that of other extra-party organizations, see Peter Odegard, *Pressure Politics: The Story of the Anti-Saloon League* (New York: Columbia University Press, 1928). For a contrast between the AFL and British labor, see Ross M. Martin, *TUC: The Growth of a Pressure Group, 1868–1976* (New York: Oxford University Press, 1980).

[51] For more information on Americans' revolt against the party system, see Michael E. McGerr, *The Decline of Popular Politics: The American North, 1865–1928* (Oxford: Oxford University Press, 1986); Richard L. McCormick, *From Realignment to Reform: Political Change in New York State, 1893–1910* (Ithaca, NY: Cornell University Press, 1981); idem, "Political Parties in American History," and "The Discovery that Business Corrupts Politics: A Reappraisal of the Origins of Progressivism," both in his *The Party Period and Public Policy*, 143–96 and 311–56; and David P. Thelen, *The New Citizenship: Origins of Progressivism in Wisconsin, 1885–1900* (Columbia: University of Missouri Press, 1972).

Nonpartisanship also served the needs of groups within the AFL. Federation leaders found it attractive because it kept members from wholesale involvement in a political movement independent of their control – such as a Socialist or Labor Party. Many locally based trade unionists favored nonpartisanship because it allowed them to support whichever party they wished – an important virtue in an age of urban bosses and political machines – and to make their own decisions about alliances. In an organization like the AFL, which was highly centralized on political matters (as we saw in Chapter One), the nonpartisan strategy provided one of the only sources of local political autonomy.[52]

By the end of the nineteenth century, the key elements of pure and simple politics had emerged and eclipsed rival approaches within the AFL. Conservative unionists articulated a vision in which the trade unions stood at the center of labor's political as well as its economic universe. Rather than rejecting all political activity, they eschewed partisan ties of any kind and stressed that the trade unions must stand triumphantly alone. On a tactical level, they engaged in nonpartisan lobbying. This approach helped Gompers and other conservative unionists to consolidate their control over the institution, uniting a broad coalition of AFL members behind them and pushing the Socialists to the margins of the organization. In stressing antipartyism, conservative leaders drew on a rich tradition in American political culture, and the notion allowed them to tap workers' longtime cynicism toward the political system. Yet Gompers also employed antipartyism for new ends, casting doubt not only on Republicans and Democrats, but also on new radical parties seeking to create an alternative to traditional politics.

Once the AFL committed to this approach, however, new dynamics came into play. Gompers needed to deliver some degree of political efficacy to AFL members. Nonpartisanship emerged as a useful tool for solidifying conservative unionists' power within the Federation, but it had only limited potential as a means to achieving the Federation's political goals. In the next years, labor's grievances would increase as the American state bureaucracy expanded and grew more interventionist. Even as Gompers established his political dominance within the AFL, pressures grew on him to change course.

---

[52] Michael Rogin makes a similar point in "Voluntarism: The Political Functions of an Antipolitical Doctrine," *Industrial and Labor Relations Review*, 15 (4), July 1962, 521–35.

CHAPTER THREE

Labor's New Century

After 1897, the great economic depression began to fade into Americans' memories. As recovery set in, a consolidation and centralization of power became visible across the United States. A flurry of statemaking activities began to restructure America's political economy, beginning in 1898 with the Spanish-American-Cuban-Filipino War, and continuing afterwards as state managers in the army, navy, civil service, and many other areas pushed to develop the size and capability of their own bureaucracies. The federal government's budget increased significantly during these years, making it a major employer of labor.[1] Military strength and commercial enterprise received new emphasis as the federal government's twin goals, leading the state into interventionist adventures around the globe.

Perhaps the Panama Canal provided the best symbol of this new climate, a project heralded by President Theodore Roosevelt as "the colossal engineering feat of all the ages." For years, American government and business leaders had dreamed of a canal that could strengthen the navy's strategic capabilities while enhancing the flow of commerce. After negotiations with Colombia proved fruitless, construction of the canal became possible in 1901 when the United States gave its support to a revolution engineered by a group that included representatives of the New Panama Canal Company. Construction finally began in 1906; before its completion in 1914, the canal would require the labor of more than 45,000 men, women, and children, who excavated more than 230 million cubic yards of earth.[2]

---

[1] The federal budget nearly doubled between 1880 and 1900, then rose another 30 percent by 1910 to a total of $693,617,000. See *Historical Statistics of the United States: Colonial Times to 1970* (Washington, DC: U.S. Government Printing Office, 1975), 1104.

[2] Roosevelt's comment can be found in his letter to James E. Watson, August 18, 1906, in Elting E. Morison, ed., *The Letters of Theodore Roosevelt*, Vol. 5 (Cambridge: Harvard University Press, 1952). On the expanding state, see Emily Rosenberg, *Spreading the American Dream: American Economic and Cultural Expansion, 1890–1945* (New York: Hill and Wang, 1982); Stephen Skowronek, *Building a New American State: The Expansion of National Administrative Capacities, 1877–1920* (Cambridge: Cambridge University Press, 1982); Gerald

Although the Panama Canal vividly illustrated politicians' determination to expand the central state bureaucracy, it formed just one part of a broader movement toward the centralization of power in American life. Private citizens played equally vital roles in this process. Corporate leaders, for example, moved quickly to stabilize their position through organization as soon as recovery returned. Their merger movement from 1898 to 1904 swallowed well over 2,000 companies to create some 200 trusts.[3] Among businessmen lacking the resources to play a role in trustification, a new movement grew popular. Known as the open-shop drive, it united employers around a single principle: opposition to trade unions. Beginning as an economic movement, the open-shop drive at first focused its efforts on shop floor battles with union activists. Yet the employers leading this movement grew increasingly politicized during the first years of the twentieth century. Seeking allies in their war against organized labor, open shop employers turned skillfully to the judiciary and to congress.

Other citizens similarly reinvented their relationship to the state and to each other by forming organizations that could represent their interests at the local, state, and national level. Associations emerged for doctors, historians, consumers, and a myriad of other groups. These years became, in the phrase coined long ago by Robert Wiebe, the "age of organization."[4] Amidst this context of an expanding state bureaucracy and energized organizing among diverse social groups, national-level political relationships became more important. In the nineteenth century, the states typically exerted more influence than the federal government in shaping Americans' daily lives. But by the early twentieth century, national-level politics became a key terrain of power as the state bureaucracy expanded and as the presidency widened its scope of activity. Citizens seeking to defend their interests increasingly looked beyond their state legislatures and pressed their claims at the federal government's doorstep.[5]

The changes wrought by America's "age of organization" greatly shaped the trade union movement. Unions leaped ahead in size and strength as the American

O'Gara, *Theodore Roosevelt and the Rise of the Modern Navy* (Princeton: Princeton University Press, 1943); Harold and Margaret Sproat, *The Rise of American Naval Power, 1776–1918* (Princeton: Princeton University Press, 1939). On the Panama Canal, see Walter LaFeber, *The Panama Canal: The Crisis in Historical Perspective* (New York: Oxford University Press, 1979), and David McCullough, *The Path Between the Seas: The Creation of the Panama Canal, 1870–1914* (New York: Simon & Schuster, 1977), 472 and 611.

[3] Selig Perlman, "Upheaval and Reorganisation," in John Commons et al., eds., *History of Labour in the United States* (New York: Macmillan, 1918), 2:522; Alfred Chandler, *The Visible Hand: The Managerial Revolution in American Business* (Cambridge: Belknap Press, 1977), 332; Naomi R. Lamoreaux, *The Great Merger Movement in American Business, 1895–1904* (New York: Cambridge University Press, 1985).

[4] On "the age of organization," see Robert Wiebe, *The Search for Order, 1877–1920* (New York: Hill and Wang, 1967), 199 and passim; see also idem, *Businessmen and Reform: A Study of the Progressive Movement* (Cambridge: Harvard University Press, 1962).

[5] Wiebe, *Search for Order*, passim; Martin Sklar, "Studying American Political Development in the Progressive Era, 1890s–1916," in his *The U.S. as a Developing Country* (Cambridge: Cambridge University Press, 1992), 37–77.

Federation of Labor saw its membership soar from 280,000 workers in 1898 to more than 1.6 million by 1904. This represented the most dramatic period of sustained growth in labor's history to that time. The conflicts of the 1890s had shorn labor of its more inclusive organizations: the Knights and the American Railway Union virtually disappeared. The business unions that remained, largely organized into the AFL, now dominated the labor movement. With these changes came a new confidence, often a new militancy, among American skilled workers, whereas most unskilled and semiskilled workers languished without organizational representatives.[6]

Although the leaders of the AFL enjoyed the growing strength of their organization, corporate consolidation, the open shop drive, and the expanding state bureaucracy made it imperative that they develop a coherent political strategy. Facing AFL members' demands that they establish a coherent political program, leaders like Samuel Gompers also found themselves aiming at a moving target as the federal government assumed new powers. And, increasingly, union leaders confronted a new political adversary in the form of the National Association of Manufacturers (NAM), a virulent anti-union organization and the leader in America's open shop drive. While workers and employers continued to clash on shop floors across the country, their rivalry entered a new sphere as both the AFL and the NAM asked Congress for friendly legislation. The bitter struggle that ensued pushed AFL leaders and members to reassess their attitudes toward electoral politics.

The Federation's Political Agenda

By the first years of the twentieth century, the American Federation of Labor stood triumphantly as the dominant trade union organization in the United States. Workers belonging to the AFL continued to disagree about many issues during these years, debating politics, the principles of craft versus industrial unionism, and whether to expand organizationally to include the unskilled. For the most part, though, the uneasy truce forged during the 1890s held sway and gave dominance to a coalition around Gompers that favored craft unionism and rejected socialism in favor of nonpartisan politics. Although leaders like John Mitchell were included in Gompers's inner circle, the industrial unionism represented by his own UMW made little headway during these years. After the chastening experience of the 1890s depression, craft autonomy and business unionism dominated AFL affiliates. AFL organizers made little effort to organize unskilled workers, and hence the Federation became less friendly than ever to African-Americans, women, and immigrants. Thus, the AFL leadership represented primarily the viewpoint of skilled craftsmen. As we saw in previous chapters, their world view focused on protecting their position from outsiders and working to prevent a deterioration in working conditions, skill level, and wages.

[6] For membership statistics, see Selig Perlman, "Upheaval and Reorganisation," in Commons, *History of Labour*, 2:522.

The small group of men allied with Gompers at the AFL's helm typified this skilled craftsman's world view. Formally, leadership in the AFL fell to Gompers and his two top aides: AFL Treasurer John Lennon and Secretary Frank Morrison. Both men worked with Gompers for decades and exhibited persistent loyalty to him and his goals for the AFL.

Born in 1850 to the family of a Wisconsin tailor, John Lennon became president of the Journeymen Tailor's Union in 1884, and served as general secretary of the union from 1886 until 1910. AFL delegates elected him treasurer in 1890 and continued to support him in that office until 1917. Lennon was a conservative in union matters and a supporter of craft principles. Politically a loyal Democrat, Lennon supported the Populist movement during the 1890s. Amidst the Democratic Party's many factions, Lennon positioned himself as a "Bryan man." In 1900, he requested permission from Gompers to campaign for Bryan, but Gompers refused. In the next years, Lennon's advice was sought more often as Gompers moved closer to the Democrats.[7]

Gompers possessed no more loyal and dedicated lieutenant than his secretary, the printer Frank Morrison, who served as the only full-time salaried official in the AFL besides President Gompers. Morrison possessed no independent base of power. Instead, he owed his rise within the labor movement completely to Gompers. His ascendancy resulted from a controversy caused when the previous secretary accused President Gompers of engaging inappropriately in partisan politics. August McCraith, like Morrison a printer but a philosophical anarchist, served as secretary of the AFL during the tumultuous years from 1893 until 1897. His tenure ended when he charged Gompers with violating the AFL's nonpartisan policy by supporting the Democrats during the 1896 presidential campaign. The AFL Executive Council evaluated McCraith's charges, but voted its "fullest confidence" in Gompers. Nobody presented McCraith's name to the 1897 convention as a candidate for reelection. Instead, Frank Morrison replaced him as AFL secretary, a position he would hold for more than four decades, stepping down in 1939.[8]

Morrison had little in common with his predecessor. Loath to stake out a position independent of Gompers, Morrison worked as a quiet and respectful aide. Born in 1859 in Ontario, Canada, the son of a Scots-Irish immigrant who worked as a farmer and a sawyer, Morrison left high school to learn the printing trade and in 1886, living in Chicago, joined Local 16 of the International Typographers' Union. In the early 1890s, Morrison attended Lake Forest University Law School and later gained admittance to the Illinois bar. A founder

---

[7] On Lennon's interest in populism, see J. F. Finn, "A. F. of L. Leaders and the Question of Politics in the Early 1890s," *Journal of American Studies*, 7 (3), December 1973, 254–5. Philip Taft, *The A. F. of L. in the Time of Gompers* (New York: Harper, 1957), 292; Gary Fink, ed., *Biographical Dictionary of American Labor Leaders* (Westport, CT: Greenwood Press, 1974).

[8] Taft, *The AFL in the Time of Gompers*, 130–1; Samuel Gompers, *Seventy Years of Life and Labor: An Autobiography* (New York: E. P. Dutton, 1925), 1:378–9.

of the Chicago Federation of Labor, Morrison held no high union position when he was elected secretary of the AFL in 1897. Thus, his loyalties lay first and foremost with the AFL.[9]

In addition to Lennon and Morrison, Gompers certainly paid attention to the opinions of powerful union leaders like International Association of Machinists (IAM) President James O'Connell, a key figure among the conservative craft unionists; United Brotherhood of Carpenters and Joiners of America (UBCJA) President William Huber, a ringleader in the group that pushed P. J. McGuire out of his union's leadership and led the carpenters' down the path of efficient business unionism; and conservative granite cutter James Duncan, close friend and ally to Gompers. All these men sat on the Executive Council for many years, and in some cases, their position of power within the AFL bureaucracy was not derived from any position they held in their own union. O'Connell, for example, began serving as AFL vice president and Executive Council member in 1895 and continued until 1918, even though his union rejected him as president in 1912 and replaced him with socialist William Johnston. Mitchell served as AFL vice-president from 1898 until 1914, though Tom Lewis succeeded him as UMW President in 1908.[10]

Yet although the conservative business unionists had established dominance over the AFL, their leadership did not go unchallenged. Socialism remained a vital tradition within the AFL, especially among rank-and-file workers and among local- and state-level leaders. The Socialist Party of America, founded in 1901, united a diverse group of American leftists. The party officially favored working within the trade union movement – that is, the AFL – and in 1901, the party adopted a policy of "non-interference" in the affairs of trade unions. Between 1901 and 1906, the Socialist Party developed a sizeable base in trade unions. By 1904, 1,200 party locals existed in thirty-five states; its membership had risen from 15,975 in 1903 to 20,768. By 1908, that membership would double again, to more than 41,000 members organized into more than 3,000 locals. According to a canvass of members conducted by the party in 1908 (to which one-sixth of its members responded), two-thirds categorized themselves as workers; of those, 60 percent categorized themselves as skilled craft workers. Thus, as Nick Salvatore notes, the Socialist Party, although dominated by middle-class professionals in its leadership, "had a solid and vital working-class core."[11]

---

[9] See Taft, *The AFL in the Time of Gompers*; Lewis Lorwin, *The American Federation of Labor, History, Policies, and Prospects* (Washington, DC: The Brookings Institution, 1933); and Fink, *Biographical Dictionary*. Interestingly John Lennon, like Morrison, possessed no strong base in his union: both were Federation men above all.

[10] See Julia M. Greene, "The Strike at the Ballot Box: Politics and Partisanship in the American Federation of Labor, 1881–1916," Ph.D. diss., Yale University, 1990; and Fink, *Biographical Dictionary*.

[11] Philip Foner, *History of the Labor Movement in the United States*, Vol. 3, *The Policies and Practices of the American Federation of Labor, 1900–1909* (New York: International, 1964), 390; Nick Salvatore, *Eugene V. Debs: Citizen and Socialist* (Urbana: University of Illinois Press, 1982), 221. Other useful sources on socialism in the early twentieth century include

Socialism had declined in the AFL since the early 1890s, but its influence began to rise during the first years of the twentieth century. It peaked in 1912, when Socialist Max Hayes ran for the AFL presidency against Sam Gompers and received the votes of approximately one-third of the AFL delegates. Unions with a strong contingent of Socialists among their members included the United Mine Workers, Brewery Workers, Machinists, Cigarmakers, Tailors, Hat and Cap Makers, Painters, and Boot and Shoe Workers.[12] Socialists within the AFL formed a highly vocal minority that exerted significant pressure on the AFL leaders. During this period, the Socialist Party's arsenal included journals and newspapers such as the *International Socialist Review*, the *Appeal to Reason*, and influential urban newspapers such as the *Social-Democratic Herald* and the Chicago *Socialist*.[13] Together, these forces offered a constant critique of conservative craft unionism and in particular they impelled the AFL leaders to achieve some degree of political success.

Yet the AFL leadership remained very much a stronghold of conservative unionism. Though prominent as a group within the AFL, no socialist sat on the AFL Executive Council during these years or won inclusion in Gompers's inner circle. In fact, during the early years of the twentieth century, AFL leaders launched a fierce attack on socialist principles. Debates at AFL conventions demonstrate the degree to which antisocialism became a central tactic in Gompers's campaign to consolidate his power in the Federation.

The best example of this process occurred at the 1902 convention, when socialist Max Hayes of Cleveland proposed a resolution calling for workers to "overthrow the wage system" and establish "an industrial co-operative democracy." Although this measure's success would have indicated AFL delegates'

John H. M. Laslett, *Labor and the Left: A Study of Socialist and Radical Influences in the American Labor Movement, 1881–1924* (New York: Basic Books, 1970); Michael Nash, *Conflict and Accommodation: Coal Miners, Steel Workers, and Socialism, 1890–1920* (Westport, CT: Greenwood Press, 1982); Henry F. Bedford, *Socialism and the Workers in Massachusetts, 1886–1912* (Amherst: University of Massachusetts Press, 1966); Charles Leinenweber, "The Class and Ethnic Bases of New York City Socialism, 1904–1915," *Labor History*, 22 (1), Winter 1981, 31–56; Melvyn Dubofsky, "Success and Failure of Socialism in New York City, 1900–1918: A Case Study," *Labor History*, 9 (4), Fall 1968, 361–75; Ira Kipnis, *The American Socialist Movement, 1897–1912* (New York: Columbia University Press, 1952); James Weinstein, *The Decline of Socialism in America, 1912–1925* (New York: Monthly Review Press, 1967); James Green, *Grass-roots Socialism: Radical Movements in the Southwest, 1895–1943* (Baton Rouge: Louisiana State University Press, 1978); Sally M. Miller, *Victor Berger and the Promise of Constructive Socialism, 1910–1920* (Westport, CT: Greenwood Press, 1973); and Richard Judd, *Socialist Cities: Municipal Politics and the Grass Roots of American Socialism* (Albany: State University of New York Press, 1989).

[12] Marc Karson, *American Labor Unions and Politics: 1900–1918* (Carbondale: Southern Illinois University Press, 1958), 131; James Weinstein, "The Problems of the Socialist Party, Before the First World War," in Seymour Martin Lipset and John H. M. Laslett, eds., *Failure of a Dream? Essays in the History of American Socialism* (Garden City, NY: Anchor Press, 1974), 302.

[13] Foner, *History of the Labor Movement*, 3:390. In 1903, the *Appeal to Reason* had a weekly circulation of 50,000.

support for socialist principles, it was clearly too radical for most delegates. Toning down the resolution made possible a coalition between socialists and other delegates who favored political action. William B. Wilson, a miner associated politically with the Democratic Party, proposed an amendment to the resolution so that it advised workers to "organize their economic and political power to secure for labor the full equivalent of its toil." Here was precisely the sort of formulation that could cut across ideological factions to unite delegates in a coalition broader than the reigning Gompersism. In fact, the vote provides a rare glimpse of support within the Federation for political activity. Delegates only narrowly defeated the resolution, by 4,897 to 4,171 votes (387 abstained). Unions supporting the resolution included the miners, the carpenters, and the brewers. Although leftists like Max Hayes used this vote to proclaim that Socialists accounted for nearly half the AFL's members, Victor Berger more accurately noted that many delegates perceived the resolution as favoring the Democratic Party. He concluded that Socialists could realistically count on the votes of only some 2,000 delegates.[14]

The next year, delegates reintroduced the resolution, but this time the vote took place amidst an aggressive antisocialist campaign led by President Gompers. Although Gompers had opposed Socialists for years in the pages of the *American Federationist*, until 1903 his attacks focused on a specific Socialist leader or tactic. Speaking against the resolution, Gompers now launched a full-scale attack on the Socialist Party and its principles and theories. Gompers's voice thundered through the convention hall as he proclaimed: "Economically, you are unsound; socially, you are wrong; industrially, you are an impossibility." Defending his vision of change achieved through nonpartisan politics centered in the trade unions, President Gompers rejected Socialist arguments that the strategy had failed: "I venture to say that there are more trade unionists in Congress, and in our state legislatures holding clear cards than there are elsewhere in similar positions the world over." In his speech, Gompers placed socialism and trade unionism in opposition, claiming that the two fundamentally conflicted with one another.[15]

---

[14] Victor Berger, "The American Federation of Labor and Socialism," *Social Democratic Herald*, December 6, 1902; see Foner, *History of the Labor Movement*, 3:383–4 and 3:390.

[15] Gompers reprinted this speech in the *American Federationist* (hereafter cited as *AF*) and gave it a telling title: "Trade Unionism vs. Socialism" (*AF* 11 [1], January 1904, 44–5). In future years, Gompers stressed that trade unionism and socialism inherently conflicted with one another, thus nimbly defining the Socialist movement as fundamentally outside of, and hostile to, the movement of organized labor. For examples of Gompers's attack on socialists during the 1890s, see Gompers, "Labor's Friends (?) – Save Us From Them," *AF*, 3 (1), March 1896, 33; idem, "With Compliments to Would-Be Union Wreckers," *AF*, 3 (3), May 1896, 52. For a Socialist account of this debate, see Max Hayes, "The World of Labor," *International Socialist Review*, 4 (6), December 1903, 376–7. The IAM held a referendum to instruct its delegates how to vote on this resolution. By a large margin, the machinists voted to endorse socialism, but their delegates nonetheless opposed the resolution at the AFL Convention. See Max Hayes, "The World of Labor," *International Socialist Review*, 4 (7), January 1904, 433–6.

Gompers's antisocialism allowed him to rally the majority of delegates to his side to defeat the resolution overwhelmingly: 11,282 opposed the measure versus 2,147 in favor of it. In the next years, conservative unionists would make regular use of antisocialism much as they had in 1903. Gompers himself portrayed this vote as a tremendous victory for trade unionism. The decision facing the AFL delegates, as Gompers described it, had been "whether the trade union movement was to continue upon a clear course, untrammeled by political partisanship, or whether it would be committed to speculative theories of political economy, and also be made a tail to a political party kite."[16]

Gompers had humbled the Socialists, but his victory would be costly for the Federation. In the long run the AFL's antisocialism, combined with its unwillingness to organize unskilled workers, encouraged the formation of a radical rival, the Industrial Workers of the World. More immediately, Gompers's antisocialism painted him into a small corner of political options. His antipartyism, marshalled against Socialists and non-Socialists alike, limited AFL strategies to lobbying, and his programmatic critique of socialism pushed him to reject any political strategy based on a positive conception of the state.

Furthermore, Socialists were not the only ones who could raise questions about the wisdom of the AFL's limited political program. The potential always existed for a coalition within the Federation that would unite Socialists with Populists and others favoring a more aggressive political strategy. Precisely this sort of coalition had nearly voted in Max Hayes's 1902 resolution calling on workers to organize their full political power. In the first years of the twentieth century, and continuing throughout the Progressive era, workers in cities across the country engaged in a diverse range of political activities. Workers' political vision, one broadly influenced by traditions of working-class republicanism, could be observed in action throughout the United States as they fought to improve the basic conditions of daily life. In these struggles, issues like municipal ownership (of streetcars, for example), tax reform, and improved city services appear repeatedly in labor's programs.[17]

The form and shape of workers' political battles varied widely. In rare cases, a powerful movement could build and sustain an independent labor party, as in the closed-shop city of San Francisco. There the Union Labor Party, created by a handful of union activists, swept into power in 1901 by electing a mayor and three supervisors. This success followed on the heels of a citywide strike

---

[16] Samuel Gompers, " 'Twas a Great Convention," *AF*, 11 (1), January 1904, 32–5. See also Foner, *History of the Labor Movement*, 3:383–6; and Kipnis, *American Socialist Movement*, 145–51.

[17] See generally the important work in progress of Shelton Stromquist, "The Politics of Class: Urban Reform and Working Class Mobilization in Cleveland and Milwaukee, 1890–1910," paper presented to the Organization of American Historians, Reno, 1988; and idem, "Working-Class Republicanism and the Social Crisis of the 1890s," unpublished paper; for examples of the prevalence of issues like municipal ownership, see labor newspapers of the period, e.g., the Birmingham (Alabama) *Labor Advocate*, January 24, 1908.

involving machinists, teamsters, and ultimately waterfront workers, and the city's use of police power in that strike dominated the campaign. For more than a decade in San Francisco, labor ruled and fought for measures like public works programs and social health insurance.[18]

The socialist movement could also bring workers significant political power, as the case of Milwaukee demonstrates. Its Social Democratic Party stood as America's most successful urban socialist party. Built on the support of Milwaukee's large German-American working class, the Social Democrats offered a comprehensive program of urban reform, focusing on issues like municipal ownership and free medical services and textbooks. At its height in 1910, the party's mayoral candidate received more than 38 percent of the vote, and voters elected many Social Democratic candidates in these years to lesser offices (alderman, state senate, school board, etc.).[19]

Less dramatic, perhaps, but equally significant, were labor's alliances with reform movements, usually linked to one of the major parties at the municipal level. In some cities, entrenched machines held a lock on voters' loyalties and effectively prevented working-class communities from exercising much influence. But more often, as Shelton Stromquist has shown, reform factions (most often in the Democratic Party) looked to working-class communities and often adopted much of labor's program, at least temporarily, in an effort to build a successful electoral base. Stromquist expands on the earlier work on urban progressivism by Joseph Huthmacher and John Buenker to argue that class visions *and* class tensions lay at the heart of urban progressivism. This phenomenon seems clearest in the industrial heartland of the Midwest. In Cleveland, for example, working-class politics helped revive the fortunes of the Democratic Party and carried single taxer Tom Johnson to four terms as mayor. Johnson built his reputation by championing municipal ownership of the railways, tax reform, an expanded park system, and improved sanitation. He benefited from working-class support and borrowed from the legacy of workers' political activism, though he was never completely at ease with the politics of class. By 1909, after Johnson angered many workers through his actions in a streetcar strike, the coalition disintegrated.[20]

The shifting and often temporary nature of these coalitions makes workers' political contributions at the local level difficult to uncover in any detail, which helps explain why scholars have rarely focused attention on them. Yet the

[18] Michael Kazin, *Barons of Labor: The San Francisco Building Trades and Union Power in the Progressive Era* (Urbana: University of Illinois Press, 1987), 51–8 and 152.

[19] Consult Sally Miller, *Victor Berger and the Promise of Constructive Socialism, 1910–1920* (Westport, CT: Greenwood Press, 1973), 35–9; Stromquist, "Politics of Class"; Marvin Wachman, *History of the Social-Democratic Party of Milwaukee, 1897–1910* (Urbana: University of Illinois Press, 1945); and Judd, *Socialist Cities*.

[20] Besides Stromquist, see also the earlier works on urban progressivism: J. Joseph Huthmacher, "Urban Liberalism and the Age of Reform," *Mississippi Valley Historical Review*, 44, September 1962, 231–41; and John D. Buenker, *Urban Liberalism and Progressive Reform* (New York: Charles Scribner's Sons, 1973).

character of local working-class political mobilization is important for understanding the AFL's political evolution at the national level. The studies by Kazin
and Stromquist build on the earlier work of Gary Fink, who demonstrated two
decades ago in his study of Missouri labor politics that urban workers engaged
more aggressively in political action than did their national union officials,
and in particular they rejected antistatism and supported a wide range of social
legislation.[21]

Workers' political contributions at the local level thus played a double
role, presenting leaders like Samuel Gompers with an example and a threat. The
diverse achievements of working-class activists in cities across the United States
sustained the national AFL leaders' awareness of the possibilities inherent in
political activity. Yet the cauldron of local-level politics also threatened to disrupt the plans of pure and simple trade union leaders. Gompers, of course, had
endeavored since the early 1890s to keep AFL members from forming partisan
attachments. Political activity of any kind endangered his vision of a labor community wherein the trade union (and particularly the AFL) stood at the forefront,
leading workers onward. Whether Socialist or non-Socialist, local working-class
political activity placed a constant pressure on AFL leaders to achieve political
efficacy, while raising the specter of potential alliances and mobilizations outside of their control. With time, workers at the local level helped push the AFL
leadership into electoral politics, as the latter sought both to contain and direct
the political passions of the American working class.

Between 1898 and 1906, AFL leaders tried to reconcile these varied tensions
by pursuing a limited lobbying campaign. Subordinating politics to economic
strategy, they sought to win through political action only such demands as would
allow craft unionism an unfettered chance at success. And during an age of state
expansion and heightened interventionism, the AFL leaders refused to envision
a positive role for the state bureaucracy. Fearful of government intervention in
workers' affairs, Gompers believed organized labor should seek through legislation only those goals that it could not otherwise achieve. As Gompers proclaimed: "Our movement stands for the wage-earners doing for themselves what
they can toward working out their own salvation. But those things that they can
not do for themselves the Government should do."[22]

---

[21] For more on local-level, working-class politics, consult Gary Fink, *Labor's Search for Po-
litical Order: The Political Behavior of the Missouri Labor Movement, 1890–1940* (Columbia:
University of Missouri Press, 1973); idem, "The Rejection of Voluntarism," *Industrial and
Labor Relations Review*, 26 1973, 605–819; Irwin Yellowitz, *Labor and the Progressive
Movement in New York State, 1897–1916* (Ithaca, NY: Cornell University Press, 1965);
Barbara Musselman, "The Quest for Collective Improvement: Cincinnati Workers, 1893–
1920," Ph.D. diss., University of Cincinnati, 1975; Bedford, *Socialism and the Workers*;
and John H. Keiser, "John Fitzpatrick and Progressive Unionism, 1915–1925," Ph.D. diss.,
Northwestern University, 1965. In using the term "antistatism," I mean an approach to politics that opposes most forms of state intervention and perceives government as a negative
influence that should remain as limited as possible.

[22] Gompers, "Eight Hour Constitutional Amendment," *AF*, 5 (6), June 1898, 110–13.

AFL leaders like Gompers married this antistatist approach to a tactical focus on the *national* political sphere, and made little coordinated effort to influence legislation at the state or city level during this period. Many state-level activists actively pursued legislative goals, but they did so on their own. The AFL's emphasis on federal legislation derived from trade unionists' experience during the 1890s, when they learned that legislative gains won at the state level were often nullified as employers sought intervention from federal courts. As a result, the AFL made legislation at the federal level a top priority, seeking at the very least to back up the efforts of state federations, and at most to make Congress a vanguard in prolabor legislation.[23]

Indeed, when assessing the antistatism of the national AFL leaders, it is important to keep in mind that their chosen terrain was the federal government, and they developed strategies precisely for that national level. Although Gompers would ask little of the federal government, he favored a somewhat more aggressive approach in the individual states. In 1898, for example, the Utah state legislature passed eight-hour legislation for workers in certain industries, and the U.S. Supreme Court lent its blessing to the law. Gompers enthusiastically applauded the move, making it clear that he would like to see hours legislation passed in every state.[24] Gompers continued to see state legislatures as a central locus of power in American politics, as indeed they were.

The narrow political universe inhabited by AFL leaders meant they would seek to achieve only extremely limited goals by lobbying Congress. Political divisions within the AFL (not only socialism, but also Republican or Democratic affiliations divided skilled workers), the antisocialism and antistatism of the AFL leadership, the leaders' subordination to powerful affiliated international unions (each with its own political makeup, and many of them opposing direct political action), and the federal realm in which the national AFL leaders operated: All these factors influenced which political goals the Federation would fight for, and together they resulted in a modest list of legislative demands.

AFL leaders focused their political agenda on four major goals. First, they sought to free labor organizations from any state activity that limited the rights of trade unions. This involved work to eliminate judicial discrimination against the labor movement (through injunctions or persecution under the Sherman Anti-Trust Act), and to establish a union's right to make use of such tactics as the strike, picketing, and boycotts. Second, the AFL strove to free labor organizations from (what its leaders considered) unfair competition with cheaper labor sources. To this end, the AFL attempted to restrict immigration, convict labor, and child labor, because each of these made it more difficult for trade unionists to win a fair wage through their economic organization. Third, the AFL sought

---

[23] Selig Perlman, "Upheaval and Reorganisation," in Commons, *History of Labour*, 531.

[24] See Samuel Gompers, "Utah's Eight Hour Law: Which State Will Follow," *AF*, 5 (2), April 1898, 36; P. J. Maas, "An Eight Hour Day Legal as Well as Moral," *AF*, 5 (2), May 1898, 23–5.

to make American politics more democratic, working for demands such as the initiative and referendum, in order to help their members achieve the first two goals. Last but increasingly important in an age of state expansion, the AFL worked to make the federal government a model employer. This would set a standard for other employers and aid the Federation's economic struggle to win goals such as the eight-hour day.[25]

A complete catalogue of the AFL's legislative goals during the early twentieth century would include the eight-hour day on government work, an anti-injunction bill, a Chinese exclusion bill, restrictions on immigration, a bill prohibiting child labor, a prison labor bill, various seamen's rights issues, and the initiative and referendum. These were for the most part trade union issues, generated by the organizational needs of the early twentieth-century AFL, and reflecting the outlook of its constituency, primarily skilled craft workers. Many AFL demands sought to protect its skilled members from competition with workers outside of the Federation: This was the case with the bills regarding immigration, Chinese exclusion, and child and prison labor.[26]

Of all the workers whose competition worried AFL leaders, immigrants – and especially Asians – clearly ranked the highest. Chinese immigrants aroused the greatest anger among western workers, as Alexander Saxton has explored, yet agitation in favor of Chinese exclusion was widespread throughout the East and Midwest as well. AFL leaders, especially Samuel Gompers, emerged as leading spokesmen in favor of legislation that would eliminate Chinese workers from American shores or harass those already here. At its founding convention, the AFL called for strict enforcement of the Chinese Exclusion Act. In following years AFL leaders cautiously watched over bills affecting the status of Chinese workers, fighting for extension of the 1882 act and for bills requiring those Chinese workers already present to register with the U.S. government. Nor

[25] Louis Reed, *The Labor Philosophy of Samuel Gompers* (Port Washington, NY: Kennikat Press, 1966); Fred Greenbaum, "The Social Ideas of Samuel Gompers," *Labor History*, 7 (1), Winter 1966, 35–61. For more on the thinking of Samuel Gompers, see also George B. Cotkin, "The Spencerian and Comtian Nexus in Gompers' Labor Philosophy: The Impact of Non-Marxian Evolutionary Thought," *Labor History*, 20 (4), Fall 1979, 510–23. An important contribution of authors such as Gary Fink and Michael Kazin has been their demonstration that local-level leaders were more willing to work for statist goals than was the national-level AFL. See Fink, *Labor's Search for Political Order*; and Kazin, *Barons of Labor*.

[26] For more information on these issues, consult Gwendolyn Mink, *Old Labor and New Immigrants in American Political Development: Union, Party, and State, 1875–1920* (Ithaca, NY: Cornell University Press, 1986); Alexander Saxton, *The Indispensable Enemy: Labor and the Anti-Chinese Movement in California* (Berkeley: University of California Press, 1971); Lucy Salyer, "Captives of Law: Judicial Enforcement of the Chinese Exclusion Laws, 1891–1905," *Journal of American History*, 76 (1), June 1989, 91–117; Roger W. Walker, "The AFL and Child-Labor Legislation: An Exercise in Frustration," *Labor History*, 11 (3), Summer 1970, 323–40; Jerold S. Auerbach, "Progressives at Sea: The La Follette Act of 1915," *Labor History*, 2 (3), Fall 1961, 344–66; and Hyman Weintraub, *Andrew Furuseth: Emancipator of the Seamen* (Berkeley: University of California Press, 1959).

were Chinese immigrants the only ones to face the wrath of the AFL. In 1908, an article in the *American Federationist* called attention to the Hindus and Sikhs settling in the Pacific Northwest: "They are but the advance guard of the starving ... hundreds of thousands of East Indians who will swarm across the Pacific and rival the Chinese invasion unless means are taken to exclude them." The AFL also worked strenuously to restrict European immigration through such means as literacy tests and taxation.[27]

As important as restricting or eliminating immigration was to AFL leaders, however, the issue did not dominate American labor politics nor did it prove as significant as the injunction and the eight-hour day when it came to shaping the AFL's agenda. As late as 1900, for example, AFL convention delegates refused to pass a resolution that called for immigration restriction. Time and again when deciding which party or candidate to support over the following years, AFL leaders and members made it clear their standard was *not* immigration restriction.[28] How and why, then, did the injunction and the eight-hour day so dominate the AFL's political program?

Numerous scholars have demonstrated the ways judicial hostility impeded working-class organization by the late nineteenth century. Using the injunction, judges could prohibit a wide range of behaviors – from picketing and striking to the use of certain words. If someone violated the injunction, they were in contempt of court and could be sent to prison. Passage of the Interstate Commerce Act in 1887 and the Sherman Anti-Trust Act in 1890 greatly spurred use of this judicial tool. The former act made it illegal to interfere with interstate commerce and the Sherman Act stated that any contract or combination that restrains trade or commerce is illegal. Although legislators designed the Sherman Act to apply only to large combinations of capital, in 1893 a number of lower courts decided that this included labor organizations as well. The Sherman and Commerce acts allowed a greater use of injunctions by causing many labor actions otherwise considered legal to fall within the "unlawful" confines of equity law. The Sherman Act also provided a new means to punish labor organizations, independent of the injunction: Violators could be sued for

---

[27] "Trades Union Convention," *New York Tribune*, December 8, 1886, in Stuart Kaufman et al., eds., *The Samuel Gompers Papers*, Vol. 1 (Urbana: University of Illinois Press, 1986), 454–5; Samuel Gompers to Adlai Stevenson, April 4, 1894, in Kaufman, *Gompers Papers*, (Urbana: University of Illinois Press, 1989), 3:488–90; Samuel Gompers, "Talks on Labor," *AF*, 13 (2), February 1906, 97–9; Earle William Gage, "Hindu Immigration," *AF*, 15 (1), January 1908, 23–4; A. A. Graham, "The Un-Americanization of America," *AF*, 17 (4), April 1910, 302–4; Samuel Gompers, "Immigration, General and Asiatic," *AF*, 18 (4), April 1911, 296–7.

[28] For a different interpretation of immigration and AFL politics, see Mink, *Old Labor*. Mink argues (p. 197) that labor's entrance into electoral politics in 1906 resulted from a split between the AFL and big business over the issue of immigration. The evidence I have seen does not suppport this proposition. For a critique of Mink's argument and methodology, see Julia Greene, "Review of *Old Labor and New Immigrants*," *International Labor and Working-Class History*, 34, Fall 1988, 122–6.

damages. This would become a major weapon against labor, second only to the injunction itself.[29]

More immediately, the Sherman and Interstate Commerce acts encouraged courts to rely more heavily on injunctions. William Forbath estimates that the courts issued 2,095 injunctions – both state and federal – between 1890 and 1920. Furthermore, he notes, injunctions became particularly widespread in the case of large strikes, sympathetic strikes, and conflicts involving industrial unions. As Felix Frankfurter and Nathan Greene described it: "the extraordinary remedy of injunction has become the ordinary legal remedy, almost the sole remedy. . . . The injunction is America's distinctive contribution in the application of law to industrial strife."[30]

Soon after an injunction helped defeat the Pullman boycott and sent its leader Eugene Debs to prison for contempt, the AFL began to focus its energies on fighting this particular manifestation of judicial hostility. By the late 1890s, AFL leaders carefully followed all developments in injunction law, repeatedly encouraged a testing of the injunction, and worked for federal anti-injunction legislation.[31] In two cases, the Federation leaders believed they had successfully tested and triumphed over the labor injunction. In 1897, a federal judge handed down an injunction against a strike led by the United Mine Workers (UMW) in West Virginia. Gompers called this "the most . . . sweeping injunction in the history of the country and perhaps the world." Under its provisions, strikers could not

---

[29] The Sherman Anti-Trust Act declares that "Every contract, combination in the form of trust or otherwise, or conspiracy, in restraint of trade or commerce among the several States, or with foreign nations, is hereby declared to be illegal." Felix Frankfurter and Nathan Greene, *The Labor Injunction* (New York: Macmillan, 1930), 6–10 and 23; Arnold Paul, *Conservative Crisis and the Rule of Law: Attitudes of Bar and Bench, 1887–1895* (Ithaca, NY: Cornell University Press, 1960), 107. For more information on the long and troubled relationship between the American labor movement and the courts, see also William Forbath, *Law and the Shaping of the American Labor Movement* (Cambridge: Harvard University Press, 1991); Daniel Ernst, *Lawyers Against Labor: From Individual Rights to Corporate Liberalism* (Urbana: University of Illinois Press, 1995); and Victoria C. Hattam, *Labor Visions and State Power: The Origins of Business Unionism in the United States* (Princeton: Princeton University Press, 1993).

[30] Frankfurter and Greene, *Labor Injunction*, 52–3; they also state (p. 49) that between 1901 and 1930, there had been 118 applications to federal courts for injunctive relief, of which 100 were successful. These statistics included only injunctions issued by federal courts. Furthermore, even at the federal level, only injunctions that were appealed were reported. Thus, the actual number of injunctions must have been much higher. William Forbath's estimates include both temporary and permanent injunctions, though he counts only one injunction in those cases where a permanent injunction followed a temporary injunction. His estimates, he argues, are conservative. See William E. Forbath, *Law and the Shaping of the American Labor Movement*, 60–3 and 193–8.

[31] In August 1895, during Gompers's forced sabbatical away from the AFL, President John McBride listed as key bills that Congress should pass: a more clear definition and a limitation of the injunction; and a repeal or amending of both the Sherman Anti-Trust Act and the Interstate Commerce Act, so as to exclude labor organizations. Later that year, McBride added to the list a bill to restrict the jurisdiction of courts in contempt proceedings. John McBride, "Legislation Needed," *AF*, 2 (6), August 1895, 109; and idem, "Crimes Against Judges," *AF*, 2 (10), December 1895, 171–2.

urge scabs to quit their jobs, nor could they hold public meetings. Visiting the area, Gompers and UMW President Blatchford held open meetings and exhorted miners to stop working in order to test the injunction. The courts backed down and police made no arrests. When the union won the strike, Gompers attributed the victory to this fight against the injunction.[32] Again in 1900, striking New York cigarmakers, most of them *not* unionized, faced an injunction issued by the New York State Supreme Court that forbade the union and its officers from contributing financially to the support of the strikers. The Cigarmakers' Union refused to comply with the injunction and again the police made no arrests.[33]

Many other strikes, however, met with defeat through injunctions handed down by state and federal courts, and the AFL's limited efforts to win reforms during the 1890s accomplished nothing.[34] Thus in early 1900, the AFL escalated its anti-injunction work by drafting a bill with the help of lawyers. Its congressional allies introduced the bill into the House of Representatives in February 1900. For the next 14 years, until Congress passed the Clayton Act in 1914, the AFL worked constantly to pass anti-injunction legislation. During most of this period, AFL strategy targetted the conceptual underpinnings of injunction law, seeking to define conspiracy so as to exclude from it any legal actions. In this way, leaders hoped to exempt from the injunction actions that, if undertaken by individuals or by nonworkers, would be considered legal.[35]

In 1912, the AFL changed its strategy and attacked a different premise of injunction law. This new bill, which led directly to the Clayton Act of 1914, attempted to slip workers out of the injunction net by declaring that labor is not a commodity, and thus the Sherman Act should not be used on labor or agricultural organizations. Although hailed as a great victory, the Clayton Act allowed courts to continue using the injunction by simply redefining their conceptual bases. Thus, the AFL worked nearly two decades to pass only a weak antidote to the injunction. The contrast with Britain is informative: There a much stronger and more effective approach succeeded earlier. In 1906, the Trade Disputes Act exempted labor unions from liability for wrongful acts committed by their members. The American labor movement never attempted this strategy.[36]

---

[32] Samuel Gompers, "Injunctions Unrespected," *AF*, 4 (7), September 1897, 155–60; an idealized account of the battle can be found in idem, *Seventy Years*, 2:198–205.

[33] Samuel Gompers, "Judge Freedman's Notorious Injunction," *AF*, 7 (6), June 1900, 162–4; idem, "The Happiness Not to Know," *AF*, 7 (7), July 1900, 212–14.

[34] For example, see Samuel Gompers, "Conflicting Judicial Decisions," *AF*, 9 (5), May 1902, 234–5.

[35] See "President Gompers' Report to the 26th Annual Convention of the AFL," reprinted in *AF*, 13 (12), December 1906, 978–9.

[36] Although the Clayton Act was modeled in part on the Trade Disputes Act, it did not attempt to exempt workers from liability for tortious actions. On both bills, see Frankfurter and Greene, *Labor Injunction*, 135–57. On the Clayton Act, see Forbath, *Law and the Shaping of the American Labor Movement*; Stanley Kutler, "Labor, the Clayton Act, and the Supreme Court," *Labor History*, 19 (3), Winter 1962, 19–38; Dallas L. Jones, "The Enigma of the Clayton Act," *Industrial and Labor Relations Review*, 10 (2), January 1957, 201–21; and Martin J. Sklar, *The Corporate Reconstruction of American Capitalism, 1890–1916* (New York: Cambridge University Press, 1988).

Although judicial hostility emerged as a new threat during the late nineteenth century, one that prodded the AFL into political engagement, the goal of shorter hours possessed long and venerable roots in American labor history. From the call for ten hours in the 1840s to the eight-hour demand that galvanized workers during the 1880s, the shorter hours movement, as David Roediger and Philip Foner noted, could uniquely unite workers across potential barriers based on gender, race, skill, or craft.[37] The AFL spearheaded major drives for the eight-hour day repeatedly during its history, most notably in the nationwide strike wave of May 1886. The Gilded Age shorter hours movement blended political, social, and industrial tactics: Activists worked toward legislation, but they also organized mass demonstrations and strikes.

Yet Gompers and his allies profoundly transformed the politics of shorter hours after 1890. They urged affiliated unions to fight for the eight-hour day using economic tactics, but they focused their own efforts on a new lobbying campaign at the federal level. In this new legislative push, the AFL abandoned its commitment to shorter hours for *all* workers and demanded only an eight-hour day for government employees. Here was the apogee of Gompersian anti-statism: Collapsing the state so that it became just another employer (albeit an unusually influential one), the AFL merely requested that the federal government be beyond reproach in its own employment practices. Gompers hoped if the government became a model employer on this issue, it would contribute to the achievement of the eight-hour day across the country.[38]

The AFL leaders' new focus on winning the eight-hour day only for government employees indicates the rising significance of the state in these years. As the federal government expanded and undertook more ambitious military and foreign policy adventures at the turn of the century, it became an important shaper of the U.S. political economy. Nowhere does this phenomenon appear more clearly than in shipbuilding. Between 1880 and 1910, the budget of the Navy Department increased by 30 percent, and shipbuilding composed a leading part of this budget. Between 1898 and 1913, the number of U.S. battleships rose from 11 to 36, and each year in this period, congress authorized an

---

[37] David Roediger and Philip Foner, *Our Own Time: A History of American Labor and the Working Day* (New York: Verso Books, 1989), vii. On the nineteenth-century history of the shorter hours movement, see also David Montgomery, *Beyond Equality: Labor and the Radical Republicans, 1862–1872* (New York: Alfred Knopf, 1967); Philip Foner, *History of the Labor Movement*, Vol. 2, *From the Founding of the AFL to the Emergence of American Imperialism* (New York: International Publishers, 1955); and Thomas Dublin, *Women at Work: The Transformation of Work and Community in Lowell, Massachusetts, 1826–1860* (New York: Columbia University Press, 1979).

[38] In congressional hearings in 1904, for example, Gompers was asked about the claim made by the bill's opponents that it would encourage industries across the country to begin the eight-hour day. Gompers responded: "That is one of the primary features and purposes that we have in view. We know that the enactment of this bill by Congress will have a tendency to extend the eight hour day." See "Eight Hour Bill Considered. Argument of President Gompers Before The House Committee on Labor," *AF*, 11 (5), May 1904, 407–11.

average of two new battleships. These massive shipbuilding projects greatly increased the number of men who would be affected by an eight-hour law for government employees. In any case, and despite the limitations of their eight-hour strategy, Federation leaders consistently stressed the goal and it would become a vivid symbol of the AFL's political capabilities – or lack thereof – during the Progressive era.[39]

Beginning in the 1860s, several state legislatures had passed eight-hour laws, and in 1868, Congress passed an eight-hour law for all government employees. The U.S. Supreme Court rendered this law ineffective in 1876 when it decided that any special agreement between employers and workers would take precedence. If workers consented to do a certain job, they must be understood to have agreed to the terms of more than eight hours' work per day.[40]

In 1897, the AFL began working for passage of a new bill to provide government employees with an eight-hour day. It sought to extend the 1868 bill by making it applicable to contractors and subcontractors doing government work. During hearings on this bill, Congressman J. J. Gardner of New Jersey worked closely with the AFL. Believing the AFL's bill would be declared unconstitutional and would be unenforceable, Gardner proposed that the government incorporate into all its contracts a clause mandating that eight hours be the maximum work day. The AFL adopted this as its eight-hour strategy for the next decade and Gardner became a crucial ally for many years, working to shepherd the bill through Congress.[41]

The eight-hour day and injunction reform became the key issues by which conservative trade unionists leading the Federation measured their political success during the early twentieth century. Whereas local-level activists pressed the AFL hierarchy to construct an effective political program, national leaders increasingly relied on antisocialist tactics to consolidate their control over a politically diverse membership. Yet as organized labor grew stronger in the years after 1897 both numerically and financially, its accomplishments galvanized employers opposed to the union movement. They began agitating in the late nineteenth century, building powerful associations and skillfully opposing unionists on the shop floor. By 1903, they would enter the political realm as well.

[39] Taft, *The AFL in the Time of Gompers*. For a slightly different interpretation of the AFL's fight for eight hours during this period, see Roediger and Foner, *Our Own Time*, 145–208. On shipbuilding and the budget of the Navy Department, see United States Bureau of the Census, *Historical Statistics of the United States: Colonial Times to 1970* (Washington, DC: The Bureau of the Census, 1976), 1114; and Allan R. Millett and Peter Maslowski, *For the Common Defense: A Military History of the United States of America* (New York: The Free Press, 1984), 302–3.

[40] As Montgomery wrote of this decision in *Beyond Equality*, 320–3, the Supreme Court had "first inferred into [the law] . . . a free-contract clause, then held that government officials need not obey its provisions if they found them undesirable." See also Foner, *History of the Labor Movement*, 2:98–9.

[41] Gompers, *Seventy Years*, 2:230–7; "Extracts from Argument of President Gompers" (before the House Committee on Labor), *AF*, 11 (7), July 1904, 594–5.

Unbeknownst to the AFL leaders, these employers would soon recast the economic and political conditions in which labor operated, forcing the unions to develop new strategies and tactics.

The Open-Shop Drive

For many businessmen, America's turn-of-the-century merger movement brought either great wealth or bankruptcy. But those firms in the middle, those that survived the wave of trustification yet did not benefit from it, confronted a mixed economic picture during these years. A growing economy brought increased opportunity for most American businesses, not merely for the trusts. Yet the mergers created an environment in which businesses required more capital in order to survive. This raised the stakes for businessmen at a time when the threat of bankruptcy or takeover by another corporation constantly loomed.[42] Thus, well-to-do businessmen independent of the trusts responded with their own version of a merger movement, rapidly creating a spectrum of employers' associations across the country. Like trustification, this movement rested on innovative efforts of a decade or more before, but only in the years after 1897 did the new employers' associations spread rapidly across the United States. Trade associations, industry-specific organizations, and chambers of commerce all flourished after 1897.[43]

The new organizational strengths of workers and employers overlapped with intensified conflict on shop floors across the country, as the two groups fought for control over their shared environment. Strikes became endemic between 1898 and 1904, more than doubling in number during that period as compared to the previous five years. The number of workers involved in strike activity saw a comparable rise.[44] Particularly in industries such as the metal and building trades, militant workers saw economic recovery as a chance to win back what they had lost (in wages, limitation of working hours, or basic conditions) during the depression. For a brief moment, trade agreements between employers and labor seemed to promise industrial harmony: United Mine Workers President John Mitchell indicated their potential during the 1902 anthracite strike when he suppressed a movement among bituminous miners to violate their own trade agreement and initiate a sympathy strike. Yet a more common trend could be seen

---

[42] Thomas C. Cochran, *The American Business System: A Historical Perspective, 1900–1955* (Cambridge: Harvard University Press, 1957), 58–61.

[43] Wiebe, *Businessmen and Reform*, 16–41.

[44] Between 1893 and 1898, 7,029 strikes occurred; between 1899 and 1904, the number rose to 15,463. Similarly, the number of workers involved jumped from 1,684,249 in the earlier period, to 2,564,782 in the later period. Lorwin, *The American Federation of Labor*, 58–63; see also Paul Douglas, "An Analysis of Strike Statistics, 1881–1921," *Journal of the American Statistical Association*, 18, September 1923, 866–77; and Leo Wolman, *The Growth of American Trade Unions, 1880–1923* (New York: National Bureau of Economic Research, 1924).

in the metal trades. The Murray Hill agreement of 1900 between the National Metal Trades Association and the International Association of Machinists, proudly supported by the National Civic Federation (NCF), broke down within a year to mutual recrimination.[45]

Between 1900 and 1903, the young employers' associations emerged as representatives of a different approach to industrial relations, one characterized by unbending hostility to trade unionism. Quickly the strategy flowered into a widespread social movement among American employers, supplanting the harmonious tactics favored by the NCF to become the most popular solution to workplace conflict. The open shop drive first emerged in Dayton, Ohio, in 1900, when thirty-eight firms agreed to challenge labor's power. They broke a machinists' strike, defeated for reelection a judge and a sheriff considered partial to labor, and created an anti-union organization for workers (the Modern Order of the Bees).[46]

In the next years, the open shop drive spread throughout the United States, with employers in Chicago, Denver, Indianapolis, Pittsburgh, and Detroit building the most influential movements. Although lacking in national leadership at first, the local movements shared certain characteristics. Anti-union employers tended to stress principles of Americanism, liberty, and independence. Their rhetoric focused on the unions' "tyranny" over innocent working men. As one journalist noted: "Without the aid of non-union men . . . the employers would fight without troops. The ease with which they enlist non-union workmen is eloquent proof of the unpopularity of many unions in their own field."[47] Because the AFL excluded most unskilled working people, the employers found this to be an effective criticism.

---

[45] David Montgomery, *The Fall of the House of Labor: The Workplace, the State, and American Labor Activism, 1865–1925* (New York: Cambridge University Press, 1987), 259–69; Selig Perlman, *History of Trade Unionism in the United States* (New York: Macmillan, 1922), 163–88.

[46] John Keith, "The New Unions of Employers," *Harpers' Weekly*, 38, (2457), January 23, 1904, 130–4.

[47] Isaac Marcosson, "The Fight for the 'Open Shop,'" *World's Work*, 11 (11), December 1905, 6956–65; Keith, "The New Unions," 130–4. *American Industries* is an excellent source for tracing the spread of the open-shop drive: for example, "Freedom in Kansas City," *American Industries*, 1 (23), July 15, 1903, 15; J. West Goodwin, "Sedalia's Citizens' Alliance and Others," *American Industries*, 1 (24), August 1, 1903, 13–14; and James C. Craig, "How Colorado Had to Fight, and Fought and Won," *American Industries*, 2 (19), May 16, 1904, 5–6; "The Open Shop – Its Success," *American Industries*, 9 (7), May 15, 1908, 6–7, and 9 (12), August 1, 1908, 18–19. The contemporary press generally portrayed the open shop drive in a favorable light. See, for example, Charles W. Eliot, "Employers' Policies in the Industrial Strife," *Harper's Monthly Magazine*, 110 (658), March 1905, 527–33; Walter Page, "The Open Shop and New Labor Leadership," *The World's Work*, 11 (11), December 1905; Harrison Gray Otis, "A Long, Winning Fight Against the 'Closed Shop,'" *The World's Work*, 15 (2), December 1907, 9675–9. On Americanism, consult also Andrew Neather, "Popular Republicanism, Americanism, and the Roots of Anti-Communism, 1890–1925," Ph.D. diss., Duke University, 1994.

The employers' associations also relied on a common group of tactics. They initiated lockouts to preempt workers' strikes, and organized non-union workers into protective societies, providing them with housing and safe travel to work when necessary. Like unions, the power of employers' associations rested on an ability to enlist as many employers as possible: Thus they used pressure tactics to persuade business concerns to affiliate. In addition, many employers' associations actively worked to shape their local labor markets.

In Detroit, for example, metal trades businessmen formed the Employers' Association of Detroit in late 1902 and began an aggressive fight against unions in the following year. As Thomas Klug has shown, they introduced machinery to simplify labor, and brought in less skilled and unapprenticed workers from the external labor market to compete with union workers. They devised new guidelines for assessing work performance and for the hiring, dismissal, and disciplining of workers. Detroit employers also established a labor bureau to extend their control over the local labor market and to provide a mechanism for blacklisting and strikebreaking.[48] Such devices were not confined to Detroit. Investigating in 1904, William English Walling found labor bureaus in use throughout the country. In Cincinnati, for example, "Men out of a job are learning to go ... [to the employers' bureau] for work, instead of tramping about the suburbs or waiting at the shop door." He also found that employers' labor bureaus routinely kept detailed files on any worker they hired or discharged.[49]

Meanwhile the open-shop drive leaped beyond the local level and recruited several powerful adherents among the national associations. By 1905, the National Metal Trades Association, the United Typothetae, the National Founders' Association, and the National Erectors' Association had all adopted a hostile, anti-union approach to industrial relations.[50] More important, during these years, three organizations with broader goals joined forces. In 1902, the American Anti-Boycott Association was formed, a stridently anti-union organization that focused on fighting the labor movement through litigation (mostly using labor injunctions and suits against union leaders for contempt of court). In 1903 David Parry, a militant open-shop activist and a carriage manufacturer from Indianapolis, created the Citizens' Industrial Alliance (CIA). The CIA served as a broad umbrella group (it accepted as members businesses, individual employers, and

---

[48] Thomas A. Klug, "Employers' Strategies in the Detroit Labor Market, 1900–1929," in Nelson Lichtenstein and Stephen Meyer, eds., *On the Line: Essays in the History of Auto Work* (Urbana: University of Illinois Press, 1989), 42–72. The quotation is on p. 49. See also idem, "The Roots of the Open Shop: Employers, Trade Unions, and Craft Labor Markets in Detroit, 1859–1907," Ph.D. diss., Wayne State University, 1993.

[49] William English Walling, "Can Labor Unions Be Destroyed?" *The World's Work*, 8 (1), May 1904, 4755–8.

[50] Clarence Bonnett, *Employers' Associations in the United States* (New York: Macmillan, 1922), 24; Foner, *History of the Labor Movement*, 3:39–40; Sidney Fine, "*Without Blare of Trumpets": Walter Drew, The National Erectors' Association, and the Open Shop Movement, 1903–1957* (Ann Arbor: University of Michigan Press, 1995).

other citizens – as long as they did not belong to a union) to aid and assist the employers' associations. The CIA existed throughout the country, with its strongest branches in the western states. In Los Angeles alone, the CIA counted 6,000 members; in the state of Colorado, it claimed 30,000 members.[51] The third and greatest victory of the burgeoning open-shop drive by far, however, lay in winning over the National Association of Manufacturers in 1902.

Founded in Cincinnati in 1895, the NAM spent its early years quietly advocating increased foreign trade. Three members of the NAM, all open shop leaders in their respective communities of Indianapolis, Dayton, and St. Louis, sought to transform the association into the national representative of the employers' anti-union movement. In 1902, this faction elected its man, David Parry of Indianapolis, to the presidency. The foreign trade faction attempted to regain control over the association in 1903 and again in 1905, but failed both times. In the next years, members favoring a conciliatory approach to labor relations drifted out of the NAM, whereas employers attracted to its anti-union focus flooded into the organization.[52]

David Parry rapidly refocused the young NAM. At the next convention he formalized the association's hostility toward labor in a fiery speech, describing the union movement as "a mob-power, knowing no master except its own will." After this speech, NAM delegates unanimously adopted a "Declaration of Principles" that established the association's position on labor issues. It opposed any acts interfering with the personal liberty of employers or employees. Under Parry's leadership the NAM journal, *American Industries*, became the open shop's leading voice.[53]

Thus, by 1904, the NAM emerged as the central leader of the anti-union movement, and "Parryism" became a common synonym for the open shop drive. As a contemporary put it, Parry was "rapidly becoming one of the most important personages of the day, for he is at the forefront of a movement which has more social significance than any other at the present time."[54] In addition to

---

[51] Bonnett, *Employers' Associations*, 24; Foner, *History of the Labor Movement*, 3:39–40; "For Free Industrial Conditions: Through the Citizens' Industrial Association," *American Industries*, 2 (7), November 16, 1903, 3–4; George G. Suggs, Jr., *Colorado's War on Militant Unionism: James H. Peabody and the Western Federation of Miners* (Detroit: Wayne State University Press, 1972); Ernst, *Lawyers Against Labor*. For a fine study of antilabor movements in one city, see Robert P. Ingalls, *Urban Vigilantes in the New South: Tampa, 1882–1896* (Knoxville: University of Tennessee Press, 1988).

[52] Parry's fellow activists were John Kirby (pioneer of Dayton's open-shop movement) and James Van Cleave (owner of Bucks' Stove and Range Co. and a St. Louis anti-union activist). Wiebe, *Businessmen and Reform*, 27–9; Bonnett, *Employers' Associations*, 301–2.

[53] Albert Steigerwalt, *The National Association of Manufacturers, 1895–1914: A Study in Business Leadership* (Ann Arbor: Graduate School of Business Administration, University of Michigan, 1964), 109–15.

[54] Keith, "The New Unions of Employers," 131; see also Ray Stannard Baker, "Organized Capital Challenges Organized Labor," *McClure's Magazine*, 23 (3), July 1904, 282.

running the NAM between 1903 and 1907, Parry created one more open shop organization: the National Council for Industrial Defense, affiliated with the NAM but responsible for its work on legislation. Under Parry and his successors, the NAM developed a triple focus: fighting unions on the shop floor, in the courts, and in politics. By 1908, the NAM had 3,000 members nationwide.[55]

The open shop strategy proved so useful for uniting employers that NAM leaders gradually began to feel somewhat captured by it. Basing cooperation on the labor issue, NAM leaders could build a broader coalition of employers than would be possible otherwise. In the midst of divisive tariff conflicts in 1909, the NAM secretary wrote:

It is surprising how many of our members take issue with us on everything except the labor question. This tariff situation should be a warning to our leaders to never undertake anything that is not directly connected with the labor question. On that the manufacturers are a unit. The minute you get away from it there is no unity.[56]

It was precisely the opposition to organized labor, in short, that molded American employers into an effective social movement. At a time when businessmen were divided by such characteristics as region, size of business, and type of concern, opposition to labor made possible a common outlook. Some employers rejected the militant anti-unionism of the open shop movement, preferring a conciliatory approach. Other employers favored a campaign against labor in principle, but disapproved of NAM's provocative militancy. Nonetheless, among most employers, from small businessmen to trusts, the anti-union strategy grew increasingly popular during the early Progressive era.

The employers most active in the open-shop drive, including those in the NAM, were typically large, locally based manufacturers; as Robert Wiebe described the movement, its adherents were wealthy businessmen one significant step below the trusts.[57] Parry himself, an Indianapolis carriage maker employing 1,000 workers, personifies this trend. At the same time, the open-shop drive attracted a diverse group of employers. As an Omaha trade unionist described the movement in 1904, "every bank, every retail store, every wholesale house, every railroad official, and every contractor is in the wreckers' association. There are, no doubt, seven hundred men in it." The NAM featured U.S. Steel in its

---

[55] Albion G. Taylor, *Labor Policies of the National Association of Manufacturers* (Urbana: University of Illinois Press, 1928), 18; "For Free Industrial Conditions: Through the Citizens' Industrial Association," *American Industries*, 2 (7), November 16, 1903, 3–4.

[56] Frederick Schwedtman to James Emery, February 5, 1909, in U.S. Senate, *Maintenance of a Lobby to Influence Legislation: Hearings Before a Subcommittee of the Committee on the Judiciary*, 63rd Cong., 1st sess., 1913 (hereafter cited as *Maintenance*), Vol. 3, pt. 2, 2635. Similarly, President James Van Cleave wrote to David Parry in 1908: "the labor question is by far the most important issue with which the NAM has dealt in the past, and must deal in the future. This question interests more members than all other questions together." James Van Cleave to David Parry, October 16, 1908, *Maintenance*, Vol. 2, pt. 2, 2223.

[57] Wiebe, *Businessmen and Reform*, 13–14.

journal as the ideal open shop employer, and it worked efficiently for legislation with such magnates as Adolphus Busch of St. Louis.[58]

By 1903, the ascendancy of anti-unionism could be seen even in the activities of the National Civic Federation, the group that worked to promote a more harmonious approach to industrial relations. In that year, the NCF organized a convention to discuss the open-shop drive, but the gathering failed miserably. Reformer William English Walling attended and described the session in this way: "Instead of the peace talk of the previous conferences, every employer favored the open shop, and every union man opposed it." In following years, the NCF avoided the issue of the open shop as strenuously as the NAM emphasized it.[59]

Lobbying and Class Conflict

As organized labor and the open shop employers searched for any possible advantage in their battle against each other, and in a period of dramatic state expansion, both groups increasingly focused their attention on the political sphere. By the first years of the twentieth century, both the AFL and the NAM had launched aggressive campaigns to influence federal legislation, and their efforts shared remarkable similarities. Both groups focused their efforts on the anti-injunction bill and the eight-hour day for government employees, though with opposing goals in mind. Similarly, both the employers and labor attempted to pursue a nonpartisan strategy, yet found themselves pushed toward partisan alliances. Their contest over federal legislation deeply influenced each organization and ultimately encouraged them to go beyond lobbying and enter electoral politics.

The AFL began its lobbying effort in 1895, many years before the NAM launched its own campaign. Immediately on winning reelection to the AFL presidency that year, Gompers moved Federation headquarters from Indianapolis to Washington, D.C., and established a permanent legislative committee. By 1900, the AFL engaged in a wide spectrum of lobbying activities at the federal level, often working closely with Hugh Fuller, the legislative representative for the railroad brotherhoods.[60] Between 1898 and 1903, the AFL inched closer to a position of influence with Congress. Federation leaders successfully opposed efforts to expand antitrust legislation and to double the penalties for violating

---

[58] F. A. Kennedy to Gompers (n.d.), *AF*, 11 (6), June 1904, 507–8; Bonnett, *Employers' Associations*, 341.

[59] William English Walling, "Can Labor Unions Be Destroyed?" *The World's Work*, 8 (1), May 1904, 4755–8. For more on the social character of the NAM and its rival, the NCF, see James Weinstein, *The Corporate Ideal in the Liberal State, 1900–1918* (Boston: Beacon Press, 1968); and Montgomery, *The Fall of the House of Labor*, 272–5.

[60] Frank Valesh, "Alleged Anti-Trust Laws," *AF*, 4 (2), April 1897, 25–6; Andrew Furuseth et al., AFL Legislative Committee to the AFL Executive Council, *AF*, 7 (7), July 1900, 193–200. On the assistance given to the AFL by Fuller of the railroad brotherhoods, see Andrew Furuseth et al., AFL Legislative Committee, "National Legislation Report," in *AF*, 9 (3), March 1902, 127.

the Sherman Act in 1900, and they won from Congress a more stringent Chinese exclusion bill.[61]

More importantly, Federation leaders came tantalizingly close to victory on the two issues they most cared about. Three years in a row, the House of Representatives passed the anti-injunction and eight-hour bills desired by the AFL, though each year the bills died in the Senate. Also during this period, the AFL saw Congressman John Gardner of New Jersey, considered one of labor's best friends in Congress, appointed to the critical chairmanship of the Labor Committee. The AFL leaders had specifically asked Speaker of the House Thomas Reed to appoint Gardner to the chairmanship, and they rejoiced when he agreed in 1898.[62]

Confident by the first years of the twentieth century that the House would favorably consider its requests, the AFL leaders began to focus on winning over senators. The U.S. Senate presented a greater challenge for the AFL because its members were not popularly elected at that time. Yet by 1901, Gompers felt optimistic that a major success was at hand. The eight-hour bill had passed the House once again, and had been reported favorably by the Senate committee. Allies of the AFL introduced the bill on the Senate floor, and worked hard for its passage. Many Senators assured the AFL leaders that the bill would pass. But in the final moments of that session of Congress, another bill displaced the eight-hour bill, and it never came up for a vote. Gompers was present in the gallery, hoping to witness the AFL's first great victory, when the "legislative tragedy" occurred. As Gompers described it: "Never in my life have I been more disappointed than when just as I felt that victory was within our grasp, the work of years became as nothing. I was heart-sick over the disappointment."[63]

Unbeknownst to Federation lobbyists, their fortunes had begun a change for the worse. Under the NAM's leadership, the open shop drive aggressively entered the political sphere beginning in 1902. NAM Secretary Marshall Cushing centered himself in Washington, D.C., and began agitating against the eight-hour bill in the autumn of that year, and NAM political agent Martin Mulhall worked extensively in the field. To rally employers around its agenda, the NAM sent a letter and a pamphlet giving "Thirty Three Reasons" against the eight-hour bill to nearly 9,000 manufacturers and government contractors. In one letter, David Parry noted that so far the eight-hour bill had been blocked by "the efforts of

---

[61] Samuel Gompers, "Relative to Trust Legislation," *AF*, 7 (5), May 1900, 134–5; Andrew Furuseth et al. to Gompers and the AFL Executive Council, June 11, 1900, *AF*, 7 (7), July 1900, 193–210. For other AFL victories during this period, see Furuseth to Gompers, "The Seamen's Bill Passed," *AF*, 5 (11), January 1899, 217; Samuel Gompers, "An Effective Chinese Exclusion Measure," *AF*, 9 (2), February 1902, 69–70; Furuseth and Thomas Tracy, "The New Chinese Exclusion Law," *AF*, 9 (6), June 1902, 275–96. As part of this campaign, the AFL circulated its well-known pamphlet entitled *Some Reasons for Chinese Exclusion: Meat vs. Rice, American Manhood vs. Asiatic Coolieism, Which Shall Survive?*

[62] Charles Nelson and James Grimes, "AFL Legislative Report," *AF*, 11 (4), April 1904 314–15; Samuel Gompers' testimony before the House Committee on Labor, *AF*, 11 (7), July 1904, 589–601; Gompers, *Seventy Years*, 2:232–3.

[63] Gompers, *Seventy Years*, 2:233–5.

Cramps and Carnegie people" (i.e., shipbuilding interests). But "organized labor does not propose any longer that this scheme shall be worked on them and it is now proposed to force the bill through the next session of Congress."

The NAM asked employers to write their congressmen and senators and oppose the bill's passage. Secretary Cushing proudly wrote Parry that Senator Louis McComas – a close ally of the AFL's who had introduced the eight-hour bill in the Senate – had received more than 600 letters from employers about the bill. The employers' effort seemed to influence many senators. The Senate committees considering the anti-injunction and eight-hour bills amended each one in a way that dramatically altered its meaning and greatly displeased the AFL. For example, the Senate Judiciary Committee added an amendment to the anti-injunction bill that effectively reversed the latter's meaning. Rather than limiting injunctions, the bill would actually authorize the issuance of injunctions.[64]

After winning these amendments, Cushing visited Sam Gompers to give him the news. As Cushing later reported, Gompers "fairly trembled with indignation. He would not at once submit to any kind of interview but called Morrison . . . into a private room . . . and they began to send telegrams right and left." Confronted with defeat, the AFL leaders had no trouble divining its cause. Gompers wrote that "a new source of opposition has manifested itself from the NAM. . . ."[65]

Next, NAM leaders expanded their operations from the Senate to labor's stronghold in the House of Representatives. At the center of this new relationship between employers and congressional Republicans stood the Speaker of the House, Joseph Cannon. This powerful "standpatter" looked kindly on an alliance with antilabor employers. Representatives of the NAM moved first to influence Cannon's appointments to the House Committee on Labor.[66] Once the speaker selected committee members, NAM leaders mobilized to control as many of them as possible. The NAM contacted employers in each congressman's home state in search of ways to influence them.

[64] Cushing to Parry, December 20, 1902, *Maintenance*, Vol. 1 appendix, pt. I, 50–7. Cushing's comment about Cramps and Carnegie having halted the bill for the last three years refers to William Cramps and Sons Ship and Engine Building Company and the Andrew Carnegie Steel Works. Other sources back up this claim: Before 1902, almost all opposition to the eight-hour bill came from these two sources, both being firms that had many contracts with the government. See also James Bennett to Cushing, December 28, 1903, *Maintenance*, Vol. 1 appendix, pt. I, 167; D. M. Parry to H. L. Roberts, October 8, 1902, *Maintenance*, Vol. 1 appendix, pt. I, 38. On the amendment to the anti-injunction bill, see also the President's Report, *Report of the Proceedings of the Twenty-Second Annual Convention of the AFL* (Bloomington, IL: Pantagraph, 1902), 18–19.

[65] Cushing to Parry, December 20, 1902, *Maintenance*, Vol. 1 appendix, pt. I, 50–7; and President's Report, *Report of the Proceedings of the Twenty-Second Annual Convention*, 18–19.

[66] Cushing to N. W. Kendall, New Haven, December 7, 1903, *Maintenance*, Vol. 1, pt. 2, 144–5; J. D. Spreckles to Cannon, December 2, 1903, *Maintenance*, Vol. 1, pt. 2, 136–7. On Joseph Cannon's political orientation, see Blair Bolles, *Tyrant from Illinois: Uncle Joe Cannon's Experiment with Personal Power* (New York: W. W. Norton, 1951); and William Rea Gwinn, *Uncle Joe Cannon, Archfoe of Insurgency: A History of the Rise and Fall of Cannonism* (New York: Bookman Associates, 1957).

Richard Bartholdt, a St. Louis congressman and a member of the Labor Committee, exemplified how this approach could work. In November 1903, James Van Cleave of St. Louis wrote Cushing with information that Adolphus Busch, the prominent St. Louis brewer, "practically holds Mr. Bartholdt in the hollow of his hand . . . [and Bartholdt] dances like a jumping jack whenever Mr. Busch pulls the string." Cushing soon moved to confirm the information, writing the Anheuser-Busch Brewing Company to discuss the House Labor Committee and the need for congressmen who were not "afraid of the labor vote." Within a few months, the NAM had, through Busch, an indirect line of communication with Congressman Bartholdt.

This relationship proved fruitful for anti-union employers during hearings on the eight-hour bill held by the Labor Committee in 1904. The NAM sought to draw out the hearings as long as possible, so the bill could not come up for a vote. Thus, Cushing wired Busch, asking him to instruct Bartholdt to extend the eight-hour hearings for three or four more weeks. Busch immediately wired Bartholdt, then wired back to Cushing that same day to transmit Bartholdt's response: The hearings would be extended.[67]

The employers and their congressional friends believed labor's bills must never be allowed out of committee. Congressman Littlefield of Maine, a top NAM ally, once remarked that if during this period the bills desired by labor had been reported by the Judiciary Committee, the House of Representatives would certainly have passed them by a large majority. Thus, as Secretary Cushing described his tactics in an internal memo to NAM field workers, "A week ago we demanded hearings and got them and now the game is to string them out indefinitely. . . . We get the witnesses to come, put other organizations to the front, . . . canvass the Committee secretly, bring pressure to bear secretly. . . ."[68]

As a result of the NAM's political campaign, the AFL abruptly ceased to enjoy any political success even as its leaders intensified their efforts. The House Judiciary Committee held hearings on the anti-injunction bill in 1903, 1904, and again in 1905, but the bill never left committee. Introducing the bill in 1904, Congressman Grosvenor of Ohio described the impact of the employers' political campaign. The same bill had been before Congress for years, Grosvenor noted, and had repeatedly passed the House almost unanimously. Yet now "a frantic, senseless, hysterical outcry goes up from all over the country that this bill, if passed, is to strike down some great principle of law that the country depends upon for its salvation."[69]

[67] Van Cleave to Cushing, November 25, 1903, 128–9; Cushing to Dear Sir at Anheuser-Busch, December 7, 1903, 145; Cushing to Adolphus Busch, March 5, 1904, 269; Busch to Cushing, March 5, 1904, 270. All documents are from *Maintenance*, Vol. 1, pt. 2.

[68] Cushing to "The Boys on the Firing Line," March 8, 1904, *Maintenance*, Vol. 1, pt. 2, 274–5; Bonnett, *Employers' Associations*, 324.

[69] Quoted by Gompers in his testimony on the bill before the House Judiciary Committee, *AF*, 11 (7a), July 15, 1904, 6–7. For the NAM's gleeful celebration of these events, see Junior Junius, "Popular Uprisings Too Much for 'Labor' Bills," *American Industries*, 2 (18), May 2, 1904, 1–2.

The AFL's eight-hour bill met with the same fate. In 1904, the AFL stepped up its efforts to see the bill passed, and the House committee conducted another series of lengthy hearings. However, opponents of the bill dominated the hearings and for the first time in several years the House Committee on Labor refused to report the bill favorably. Instead, it referred the bill to the Department of Commerce and Labor for an investigation of the extent to which the bill would harm U.S. manufacturing. Gompers charged that the committee sought to bury the bill and he refused to participate in the resulting investigation. The AFL legislative committee gloomily described this defeat as the most unfavorable action taken by the House Committee on Labor in eight years.[70] Nor was it a temporary setback. The AFL would achieve no more lobbying victories until the Republicans lost control of Congress in 1910.

Beyond Lobbying

In 1904, the war between the AFL and the NAM escalated as each organization stepped tentatively beyond lobbying and into the world of electoral politics. Each organization continued to focus on the federal level of government, seeking to influence congressional elections. The AFL bureaucracy began for the first time to mobilize rank-and-file trade union members, whereas NAM's electoral activism involved not its own constituency – employers – but members of the working class. NAM leaders relied on secretive and often deceptive tactics – or what the NAM liked to call "gumshoe work." Each effort paved the way for more extensive political programs in 1906.

Although NAM leaders had enjoyed great success in their congressional lobbying project, they set out in 1904 to punish a few politicians who had loyally assisted organized labor. Their most strenuous campaign targeted Congressman William Hughes of New Jersey, one of the AFL's most faithful allies. NAM fieldworker Martin Mulhall hired six trade unionists who employed a range of nefarious tactics against Hughes. Their campaign relied on no public speeches or literature. Instead, they "organized" quietly among the working men, as Mulhall put it. Translated, this probably means they relied on money to persuade voters to vote against Hughes. Sometimes their work involved more ambitious tactics, as in this example provided by Mulhall: When the AFL sent 75,000 circulars into Hughes's district to assist his bid for reelection, Mulhall's workers managed to receive the circulars and destroy them. William Hughes lost his bid for reelection in 1904.[71]

---

[70] Samuel Gompers, "Juggling with the Eight Hour Bill," *AF*, 11 (5), May 1904, 396–7; James Grimes and Charles Nelson, AFL Legislative Report, April 16, 1904, *AF*, 11 (5), May 1904, 404–5; "President Gompers' Report," *Report of the Proceedings of the Twenty-Fourth Annual Convention of the AFL* (New York: Graphic Acts Printing, 1904), 28–9.

[71] Mulhall's testimony in *Maintenance*, Vol. 3, 2480–1 and 2486–92. The NAM also opposed Republican Senator Louis McComas of Maryland. Like Hughes, McComas lost his reelection battle in 1904.

The AFL's 1904 strategy, on the other hand, involved a modest effort to educate AFL members and mobilize them behind prolabor candidates. Federation leaders urged rank-and-file trade unionists to question candidates on three issues: an anti-injunction bill, an eight-hour bill, and the initiative and referendum. Unionists asked candidates not only to state their opinion, but to pledge themselves to support labor's position on each issue. The AFL bureaucracy took few concrete steps to interest workers in this strategy, however, other than mailing out a special issue of the *American Federationist* instructing workers on how the system should work.

This campaign document was filled with the stirring rhetoric that had justified the AFL's political activity for the last decade. The labor movement must secure legislation – but by following a trade union policy rather than a partisan one. As Gompers wrote:

One of the great ills from which the political morale of our country suffers is the party domination, which in turn is usually dominated by a political boss. We find our people arrayed in parties against each other, when, in truth, many find themselves in sympathy with measures for which the opposite party is the sponsor.[72]

In relying on the tactic of questioning candidates, the AFL employed a political procedure with some history at the local level. In 1899 a student of the labor movement, William Burke, wrote that on the local level, trade unionists regularly engaged in electoral politics through a nonpartisan questioning of candidates and support for those who supported labor's demands.[73] In 1902, the AFL published a special issue of the *American Federationist* describing the system of questioning candidates. A number of towns adopted it with successful results in their municipal elections. That same year, Missouri trade unionists applied the approach to national affairs, questioning candidates for the U.S. Senate and House of Representatives: Would they vote to give the people more power at once through the initiative and referendum? Missouri activists pledged nine of the sixteen elected congressmen to their political agenda.[74]

Despite this strategy's potential, the AFL's first effort to influence its members' voting behavior in 1904 achieved little. The AFL later noted that results would have been better if trade unionists had borrowed the "zealous" questioning tactics adopted by Missouri activists.[75] It would require more strenuous efforts to steer AFL workers off the path of limited political action pursued by the Federation since 1894. AFL leaders thus faced a quandary. Their efforts had

[72] *AF*, 11 (7a), July 15, 1904, 3 and 13.
[73] William Maxwell Burke, "History and Functions of Central Labor Unions," in *Studies in History, Economics, and Public Law*, 12 (1), edited by the faculty of political science at Columbia University (New York: Macmillan, 1899). See also George H. Sibley, "Questioning of Candidates," *AF*, 13 (5), May 1906, 316–17.
[74] *AF*, 11 (7a), July 15, 1904, 15–16.
[75] *Report of the Proceedings of the Twenty-Fifth Annual Convention of the AFL* (Washington, DC: The Law Reporting Company, 1905), 78.

proved ineffective so far, but they hesitated to embark on a more aggressive strategy. However, events after 1904 finally pushed the AFL leaders to break with tradition and launch an electoral strategy.

In 1905, the founding of the Industrial Workers of the World (IWW) threatened the AFL's dominance in the economic sphere. The IWW united groups existing outside of the AFL (in particular, the Western Federation of Miners and Daniel DeLeon's Socialist Trade and Labor Alliance) with a number of Socialist Party leaders – all of whom opposed the AFL's narrow craft unionism. At the IWW's first convention, in June 1905, delegates representing 60,000 workers and 43 unions attended. IWW members blended principles of industrial unionism with beliefs in socialism, anarchism, and/or syndicalism. Although many Socialists condemned the IWW as a "dual union" wrongly competing with the AFL, others, especially those associated with the Socialist Party's left wing, enthusiastically began to work with the new organization. The latter included Eugene Debs, William Trautman (editor of the Brewery workers' journal), and Algie M. Simons (editor of the *International Socialist Review*). After 1908 the IWW rejected political activity in favor of syndicalism, but until that time, Socialists played an important role in the organization and made strenuous appeals for political engagement.[76]

The IWW challenged the very nature of the AFL's trade unionism, calling into question its exclusivism and its craft basis of organization. From the moment the AFL leaders learned that plans were being made to create the new radical federation, they launched an attack. Gompers derided the IWW leaders for "treason" and compared their critiques of the AFL to those made by leaders of the National Association of Manufacturers. John Lennon appealed to workers to ignore the IWW and stick with the AFL, noting that just as American employers had united in their fight against workers, so the labor movement must eschew the Wobblies' attempt to divide the working class.[77]

The Wobblies turned this charge on its head and accused the AFL with dividing workers from one another. Or as their poignant name for the AFL put it, Gompers stood at the helm of the American *Separation* of Labor. One Wobbly writer described conditions in a western city: "There are good men in the separated unions in Spokane. . . . But could a good man armed with a bow and arrow hope to conquer the man with the rifle? It is the fault of the wrong

---

[76] The split between the Socialists and the IWW became even more final in 1913 when IWW leader William Haywood was recalled from the Socialist Party's National Executive Council. On the IWW, see Melvyn Dubofsky, *We Shall Be All: A History of the Industrial Workers of the World* (New York: Quadrangle Books, 1969); and Paul Brissenden, *The I.W.W.: A Study of American Syndicalism* (New York: Columbia University Press, 1957).

[77] For a sample of AFL leaders' attack on the IWW, see Samuel Gompers, "Mr. Hayes, Socialist of Cleveland – And Others," *AF*, 12 (5), May 1905, 280–2; Hugh McGregor, "Words of Warning," *AF*, 12 (6), June 1905, 354–5; Samuel Gompers, " 'Tis Treason, Gentlemen," *AF*, 12 (6), June 1905, 358–61; John Lennon, "That Stab at Labor," *AF*, 12 (8), August 1905, 511; Luke Grant, John Lennon, et al., "Labor Day: Harbinger of the Better Time," 12 (9), September 1905, 606–10.

disorganization of the craft unions that they are not able to fight the employer.
. . ." While the Socialist party continued to accuse Federation leaders of poor
political judgement, the Wobblies attacked the conservative alliance dominating
the AFL for its limited economic and organizational strategies. In this way, they
intensified the pressures facing the AFL from the left.[78]

Months later, in early 1906, Samuel Gompers learned of the British labor
movement's great triumph in electing scores of trade unionists to the House of
Commons. American labor activists had followed British labor politics since the
1880s. The British workers' victory now resonated loudly in American union
halls: Fifty-four trade unionists won election, and of those, twenty-nine had been
endorsed by the Labour Representation Committee. The remainder of the new
M.P.'s had been endorsed by either the miners or the Liberal Laborites. British
unionist Thomas Reece reported the event in the *American Federationist* and
commented that the reliance on the labor vote should not be seen as indicating
any "disbelief in the efficiency of the trade union as a great economic worker."
Rather, he said, workers were suddenly convinced that Parliament would be the
quickest way to remedy certain troubles in Britain.[79]

As Gompers compared the political environment around him to these happy
successes in Britain, the former must have seemed gloomy indeed. During this
same period, Congress dealt the AFL a defeat – one of its most devastating,
Gompers thought – that would shape the Federation's political strategy for years
to come. This fight concerned construction of the Panama Canal, and it took the
AFL squarely into issues regarding the prerogatives of an expansionist state.

In the spring of 1906, Congress busily prepared the groundwork for beginning construction on the canal. Many Americans perceived the canal as a splendid engineering challenge that would show their country at its best. Labor
approached the matter cautiously, supporting the project while insisting on two
main demands: Americans rather than "foreigners" must build the canal, and
they must build it while working an eight-hour day.

As Sam Gompers put it, the canal should be built with "American enterprise,
American genius, and American labor."[80] AFL leaders first attempted to prevent the government from employing Chinese laborers to build the canal. Chief
Engineer John Stevens wanted to import Chinese laborers for the job because
he liked their work on U.S. railroads under his supervision. Despite labor's criticisms that the Chinese Exclusion Act should apply to this project, Theodore
Roosevelt approved Stevens's plan to employ Chinese workers. However, Secretary

---

[78] See, for example, "Pillar of the Law in Farce-Comedy," March 18, 1909; and "Craft
Scabbery," April 15, 1909: both in the IWW newspaper, *Industrial Worker*.

[79] See Thomas Reece, "British Labor Notes," *AF*, 13 (3), March 1906, 155; James Wignall,
"Labor in the Recent British Parliamentary Election," *AF*, 13 (4), April 1906, 225–7; James
Hinton, *Labour and Socialism: A History of the British Labour Movement, 1867–1974*
(Amherst: University of Massachusetts Press, 1983), 74–5.

[80] "President Gompers' Report," *Report of the Proceedings of the Twenty-Fifth Annual Convention*, 33–4.

of War William Taft, who had direct supervision of the canal, vetoed the idea. He argued that the peonage basis of Chinese workers' labor too closely approached enslavement and hence violated the U.S. Constitution. By late 1906, Stevens had given up his hopes of importing Chinese workers, but he turned quickly to other sources. For a while, Stevens attempted to bring in southern Europeans, primarily Spaniards. But he rejected them in favor of West Indians, believing Europeans did not work as hard and too often organized or struck for better pay and conditions.

Canal engineers employed American citizens for supervisory and highly skilled jobs, but the Americans pleased them little more than had the Spanish. American workers brought unions with them, or started them when they arrived; with the help of their unions, they demanded local negotiations and went on strike. Back home, their union leaders lobbied Washington to improve their poor living and working conditions. Meanwhile, West Indians began migrating in large numbers to Panama. Michael Conniff has estimated that during the construction of the canal – 1904 to 1914 – between 150,000 and 200,000 men and women migrated to Panama from the West Indies, constituting a "demographic tidal wave" in a country of only 400,000 inhabitants.[81]

Having failed to prevent the employment of "foreigners" on the canal, AFL leaders next attempted to validate the eight-hour day on government work. In 1906, AFL leaders fought to defeat a measure that would exempt alien labor on the Panama Canal construction from the existing eight-hour bill. A congressional debate over this issue broke down largely on party lines, with the Democrats supporting the AFL's position. Republican congressmen argued that exempting foreign workers from the eight-hour day would ensure a speedy and less expensive completion of the project, thereby limiting the tax burden on Americans; further, they claimed that West Indians were inferior workers incapable of accomplishing much in eight hours, and that their tolerance for tropical climates made it possible to work them longer hours. To these claims, the AFL leaders and their congressional supporters raised humanitarian concerns: More than eight hours' labor in the tropical zone of Panama would endanger workers' health. Democratic Congressman Champ Clark charged that the exemption constituted "an effort to break down the eight-hour law. . . ." Another congressman proclaimed that "The merest laborer in the world ought to have time and opportunity to do something else besides working at this job to pile one dirty dollar on the top of another. . . ." Nonetheless, both houses of Congress passed the provision. American supervisors and skilled workers would continue to work an eight-hour day, but West Indians and other foreigners typically worked upwards of ten hours daily. Gompers demanded that President Roosevelt veto the bill, arguing that "To enact . . . a provision applying to alien workmen that is deemed

[81] Michael L. Conniff, *Black Labor on a White Canal: Panama, 1904–1981* (Pittsburgh: University of Pittsburgh Press, 1985), 25–9. This discussion is based primarily on Conniff's study. See also Raymond Allan Davis, "West Indian Workers on the Panama Canal: A Split Labor Market Interpretation," Ph.D. diss., Stanford University, 1981.

unwise and inhuman for Americans, is an exhibition of total disregard of human life."[82] Roosevelt signed the bill, apparently unmoved by labor's complaint.

The politics of the canal became symbolic of the AFL's failure to influence the federal government effectively in a new age of state expansion and imperialism. Perhaps most problematic was this congressional vote to nullify the eight-hour day. Although the AFL had accustomed itself to political defeat, its problems previously could be attributed to Speaker Cannon's tyrannical control over committees, and his ability to prevent bills from coming up for a vote. This time, however, a bill *had* come up for a vote and the vast majority of congressmen and senators willfully opposed organized labor's wishes. Gompers called the vote "one of the severest blows that could be given by those who are unfriendly to our movement."[83] As we will see in the next chapter, the AFL would soon allow this defeat to dominate its political strategy, using the vote on the canal's eight-hour day as its major litmus test for congressional candidates in the elections of 1906.

Finally, just as labor confronted defeat on the Panama Canal issue, it faced another crisis that demonstrated the open-shop drive's impact and, in particular, the relationship between employers' anti-union activities in the workplaces, in the courts, and in the legislative halls. The crisis involved an injunction that crippled a major trade union's strike for the eight-hour day.

The International Typographical Union decided at its 1905 convention to demand enforcement of the eight-hour day beginning January 1,1906, and instructed its leaders to meet with the United Typothetae of America (UTA) – the employers' association in the printing industry – to negotiate their demand. Workers and employers in the printing industry had clashed over the hours of work for decades. The UTA owed its origin to Chicago printers' demands for the nine-hour day in 1887; it successfully resisted the printers' demand for eleven years until it submitted and granted nine hours throughout the industry. With this victory, the printers immediately began working toward the eight-hour day, and employers fiercely resisted their efforts.[84] Now, in 1905, when the ITU pledged with new vigor to win eight hours, the employers' association refused to negotiate. In September, the ITU began strikes in cities across the country for the eight-hour day.[85]

---

[82] "Eight Hour Law and the Panama Canal: Congress Nullifies an Economic Principle – Without Even a Hearing by Those Vitally Interested – Our Protest," *AF*, 13 (3), March 1906, 163–4; and *Congressional Record: The Proceedings and Debates of the Fifty–Ninth Congress, First Session, Also Special Session of the Senate*, Vol. XI (Washington, DC: U.S. Government Printing Office, 1906), 1603–11.

[83] Gompers to Elmer Ellis, Litchfield, Illinois, August 14, 1906, *American Federation of Labor Records: The Samuel Gompers Era* (Microfilming Corporation of America, 1979), reel 61.

[84] Bonnett, *Employers' Associations*, 226–88, esp. 232–4; Samuel Gompers, "Printers' Eight Hour Movement," *AF*, 12 (10), October 1905, 750.

[85] Samuel Gompers, "Printers' Progress in Eight Hour Movement," *AF*, 12 (11), November 1905, 834–8; "President Gompers' Report to the 26th Annual Convention of the AFL," November 12, 1906, *AF*, 13 (12), December 1906, 976–7.

In November, Gompers reported that employers in many towns had applied for injunctions against the striking printers, and in January 1906, Judge Jesse Holdom of Chicago handed down the injunction that broke the printers' strike – although it did not kill their drive for the eight-hour day. In Gompers's words, the injunction "violated every fundamental right of citizenship. It prohibited not only peaceable picketing, but any moral suasion whatever, and even any lawful attempt by the printers to induce non-union printers to join the union." Furthermore, Holdom sentenced the union's leaders to jail and fined the union $1,500 for violating the injunction. The printers' strike had been unusually peaceful. Thus, the incident proved wrong those who said that if only workers respected the law, and struck peacefully and without intimidating others, there would be no injunctions.[86]

Gompers visited Chicago with ITU President James Lynch and proclaimed the injunction to be contemptible: "If I had to choose between the exercise of my constitutional rights as an American citizen and obeying such an injunction order, I do not hesitate to say that I would choose going to jail."[87] For Gompers, a man who yearned for respectability, these were fighting words.

The Holdom injunction proved an important blow because of the importance of the eight-hour day in the AFL's political agenda. The NAM blocked the AFL's efforts to win anti-injunction legislation from Congress; it contributed to a climate of judicial hostility that resulted in the Holdom injunction, and in doing so it helped defeat another trade union fight for the eight-hour day. The printers' fight and the Holdom injunction dramatically demonstrated to Gompers the interrelated nature of the AFL's political and industrial battles and the damaging impact of the employers' open-shop drive. In this way, the printers' strike helped push the AFL toward a more ambitious political strategy.[88]

Years later, Gompers wrote that the employers' initiatives against labor, and the increasing use of the injunction and the Sherman Anti-Trust Act, forced workers to seek legislation from Congress to provide relief. And to secure this legislation, he wrote, "it was necessary to break the strangle-hold which enabled organized employers to control legislation. In order to get action by Congress, I knew we had to make an appeal to congressmen and that no appeal would be stronger than a threat of action at the ballot box."[89]

To Gompers's reflections written twenty years after the fact, we may add evidence provided by NAM fieldworker Mulhall. In 1905, he had an extraordinary

---

[86] Samuel Gompers, "Judge Holdom's Injunction Frenzy," *AF*, 13 (3), March 1906, 156–8. One might also consult Samuel Gompers, "Printers Will Win," *AF*, 13 (2), February 1906, 88–9.

[87] "Prefer Prison to Obeying Injunction," *AF*, 13 (3), March 1906, 168 (reprinted from the Chicago *Interocean*, January 29, 1906). Despite the damage caused by this injunction, the printers' drive for the eight-hour day continued, and in 1909, the employers gave in to their demand. See Bonnett, *Employers' Associations*, 234.

[88] For more on this injunction, see Karson, *American Labor Unions and Politics*, 37–41; and Greene, "The Strike at the Ballot Box," chapter 2.

[89] Gompers, *Seventy Years*, 2:241–2.

discussion with George Squires, a bookkeeper employed at the AFL headquarters. Just months after the 1904 elections, Squires told Mulhall that the AFL had decided to work hard for all pro-labor congressional candidates, like William Hughes of New Jersey, who had lost in the recent elections. The AFL, Mulhall reported, "intended to go into politics for all it was worth." According to Mulhall, the AFL leaders had learned a lesson from the NAM. Gompers and the members of the Executive Council now believed, Mulhall reported, that "the only way they could successfully combat the Manufacturers' Association was to do as they did, actively enter politics and defeat the men who were against labor legislation and support those who were in favor of it."[90]

By March 1906, Gompers and his allies in the AFL were about to embark on their most ambitious bid yet for political influence, initiating a full-scale effort to elect only those congressional candidates who would support labor's demands. A lobbying campaign pursued by the AFL leaders for more than a decade had resulted in precious few gains. At the same time, judicial hostility had begun to pose a major threat to the labor movement.

In the minds of AFL leaders, the irritation caused by injunctions and antitrust suits represented not the capriciousness of a neutral judiciary, but a growing intimacy between employers and the state bureaucracy. The employers' open-shop drive successfully challenged labor in workplaces, in the courts, and ultimately in legislative halls. As early as 1901, the effects of the open-shop drive could be seen in workplaces around the country. When, in 1903 and 1904, the NAM became a highly effective lobbying force in Washington, D.C., the AFL must have felt it was losing a high-stakes game of chess. In these years, the Federation's limited successes in Congress rapidly melted away. By alienating the U.S. Congress from organized labor, the NAM removed legislative work as a fruitful path to political efficacy for the AFL.

Furthermore, in the early stages of the AFL's fight for federal legislation, it had been possible to ignore partisan distinctions and to work with representatives of both major parties. Thanks to the NAM, by 1903 this was becoming difficult, and by early 1906, impossible. Less shy of partisan attachments, the NAM linked itself closely to the Republicans – especially through politicians like Speaker of the House Joseph Cannon. The NAM's success in attaching itself to the dominant party and in thwarting the AFL's hopes for federal legislation began to make labor's fight a partisan one. During the next years, the AFL leaders gradually began to take note of party affiliations and to favor the Democratic Party. Although the open-shop drive began as a workplace-centered strategy in the late 1890s by 1906 ambitious NAM activists had forced organized labor to rethink its relationship to the party system.

---

[90] Mulhall to Cushing, February 5, 1905, *Maintenance*, Vol. 1 appendix, pt. I, 474–5; and Vol. 3, 2501.

PART TWO

The Strike at the Ballot Box

In a powerful strike we'll soon engage
    Where Judge and injunction can not prevail;
Striking men of every craft,
    Be sure that you strike upon the right nail;
Don't be this or don't be that
    Because you inherited it of your kin;
God and home pleads for just action,
    If you have never thought it's time to begin.

Let it be a peaceful strike
    Of men in line from sea to sea,
O' blistered hands and sweaty brow;
    Do present conditions satisfy thee?
No matter where our fathers fought
    Let us be men as they;
Let us vote without party pride
    When the strike comes on election day.

Come, ye striking sons of toil
    Don't sell that vote on election day;
Get in line with the rank and file,
    And strike for yourself without delay.
Remember he who buys the vote
    Would grind you flesh and bone;
The man who sells this liberty
    Would sell his wife, his child, his home.

Russell R. Doty, *American Federationist*,
15 (10), October 1908, 876.

CHAPTER FOUR

A Popular Uprising of
Honest Men

In 1906, Samuel Gompers and Frank Morrison broke with tradition and took the American Federation of Labor directly into electoral politics. Harassed by injunctions, menaced by anti-union employers, scorned by Congress, and inspired by British unionists, the AFL leaders decided to transcend the lobbying campaign they had followed for a decade and attempt instead a program of mass mobilization. Gompers and Morrison created a Labor Representation Committee that designed the AFL's new campaign program and controlled decisions of strategy and tactics. Through this committee the AFL leaders hoped to mobilize the entire Federation hierarchy, from the Executive Council to the leaders of the state federations and central labor unions, and on down to rank-and-file trade unionists across the country. The campaign program pragmatically declared its goal: Organized labor would "reward our friends and punish our enemies," particularly when it came to congressional elections. In more grandiose terms, Gompers called on rank-and-file workers to create "a popular uprising of honest men."[1]

Workers across the United States at this time already participated in diverse political activities, as we saw in the preceding chapter, and many had urged their national leaders for years to initiate a more aggressive political strategy. The centralization that occurred in the American labor movement after the 1880s, when local-level unions lost power to the international affiliates and the national bureaucracy of the AFL, made it more difficult for local activists to exercise political independence. The central labor unions, historically the political heart of organized labor, had long ago been stripped of their political and economic autonomy by the national organizations. Labor's national leaders, in short, had acted as a brake on independent labor politics for some time. Now their decision to enter the electoral sphere would have important ramifications for American workers.

The AFL campaign program of 1906 confronted American workers simultaneously with an opportunity and a danger. Although initiated from the top

---

[1] The call to create a popular uprising comes from the AFL Executive Council, "A.F. of L. Campaign Programme," *American Federationist* (hereafter cited as *AF*), 13 (8), August 1906, 531.

down, the strategy nonetheless exhorted American unionists to become politically engaged, to organize conventions, nominate candidates, and form political committees or labor parties. As such, it promised to revitalize labor's political vision, encourage grassroots activism, and even, potentially, generate a more democratic Federation of Labor. But the campaign program also constituted an unprecedented effort by the national bureaucracy of the AFL to take command over American working-class politics, to guide workers' political passions into channels believed safe and effective. How would rank-and-file trade unionists respond to this initiative? Would their political vision mesh with that of their leaders? These and similar questions awaited the members and leaders of the AFL as they began testing the waters of mass electoral politics.

Labor's Program

Having decided by early 1906 to embark on a more ambitious political program, the men leading the AFL needed a strategy that would not violate their pure and simple principles. Because of the variety of political alliances at the local level, they required an approach that could work with Democratic Party or Republican Party loyalties. Theoretically, Socialist loyalties also must be taken into account, though the leaders agreed they should undertake no strategies that might encourage the growth of socialism among AFL members. Given the history of political tensions within the Federation, these leaders wanted a nonpartisan strategy, one that would not introduce "party slavery" into trade unionists' affairs. The strategy should focus on congressional elections, because for AFL leaders like Gompers and Morrison, teaching Congress a lesson constituted a major goal. Last but hardly least, any strategy must meet the AFL's manly requirements: it must be a program for proud, independent, and self-respecting men. Trades unionists' gendered self-conception influenced the creation and the reception of the Federation's program.

In the early months of 1906, the leaders began laying the groundwork for the new electoral program. At a February meeting of the AFL Executive Council, Gompers related his frustration with Congress, saying, "There seems to exist an utter disregard of either the interests, the requests or the protests of labor." Gompers proposed that they invite the heads of all affiliated unions to convene and discuss the congressional stalemate at a Protest Conference on March 21, and the Executive Council agreed. In the interim, Gompers and Andrew Furuseth, president of the International Seamen's Union and longtime lobbying representative for the AFL, met to determine the issues that would shape their campaign.[2] They composed a document, the "Bill of Grievances," itemizing ten

---

[2] Andrew Furuseth served as president of the International Seamen's Union for 52 years. In 1895, he headed the AFL's first legislative committee and continued in that position for several years. Furuseth, who shared Gompers's antistatism, clearly influenced the evolution of AFL legislative priorities – as seen in its emphasis on seamen's rights. He helped Gompers devise the 1906 campaign program, though typically his role was limited to lobbying for

issues on which the AFL had serious complaints: the eight-hour law for government employees, convict labor, immigration, Chinese exclusion, seamen's rights, ship subsidy, the Sherman Anti-trust and Interstate Commerce laws, the labor injunction, the anti-labor bias of the House Committee on Labor, and the right of petition for government employees.[3] All these issues had been present on the AFL's agenda for years. Now, however, labor leaders highlighted Congress's anti-labor bias. Workmen feel these grievances, they proclaimed, because Congress responded to their concerns with hostility and indifference. Labor has waited long and patiently, and it firmly asks Congress to redress these grievances. "But if, perchance, you may not heed us, we shall appeal to the conscience and the support of our fellow citizens."[4]

In March, approximately fifty unions – almost half of those affiliated – sent delegates to the AFL's protest conference, as did the central labor unions of Washington, D.C., and Chicago.[5] However, the national leaders seem to have designed the conference not as a forum for open discussion about the Federation's political future, but simply as a dramatic way to initiate the new policy. Although the conference was devoted entirely to political problems, the affiliates most concerned with politics, the state federations of labor and the central labor unions, were excluded from the proceedings.[6] According to the AFL leaders' plans, the local political affiliates would not be involved in deciding campaign strategy, even though implementation would depend heavily on those same bodies.[7]

---

labor's bills. See Samuel Gompers, *Seventy Years of Life and Labor* (New York: E. P. Dutton, 1925), 1:347–8; Philip Foner, *History of the Labor Movement in the U.S.*, Vol. 3, *Policies and Practices of the American Federation of Labor, 1900–1909* (New York: International, 1964), 157; Paul S. Taylor, *The Sailor's Union of the Pacific* (New York: Arno Press, 1971), 110–33 and 174–83; Hyman Weintraub, *Andrew Furuseth: Emancipator of the Seamen* (Berkeley: University of California Press, 1959); and Jerold S. Auerbach, "Progressives at Sea: The La Follette Act of 1915," *Labor History*, 2 (4), Fall 1961, 344–66.

[3] For a discussion of these issues and their place in labor's political strategy, see Chapter Two. Despite the continuity between the AFL's 1906 agenda and that of the preceding decade, Gompers and Furuseth dropped one key demand from their Bill of Grievances, the initiative and referendum, which had been an important labor priority for years. See "Labor's Bill of Grievances," *AF*, 13 (5), May 1906, 293–7.

[4] Gompers, *Seventy Years*, 2:242–3; "Labor's Bill of Grievances," 293–7.

[5] For a sample letter from Gompers to a union president, inviting him to attend the AFL Conference, see Gompers to Frederick Stingle, president, United Gold Beaters' National Protective Union, March 5, 1906, *American Federation of Labor Records: The Samuel Gompers Era*, microfilm ed. (Microfilming Corporation of America, 1979), (hereafter cited as *AFL Records*), reel 60.

[6] The two local labor organizations that attended the conference, the Washington, D.C., Central Labor Union and the Chicago Federation of Labor, were each a special case: the former because it was the local central labor union and closely affiliated with the AFL national headquarters; and the latter because it was one of the strongest local labor organizations in the country *and* because it was headed by a salaried AFL organizer (John Fitzpatrick).

[7] "President Gompers' Report," *Report of the Proceedings of the Twenty-Sixth Annual Convention of the American Federation of Labor* (Washington DC: Graphic Arts Printing, 1906), 14.

As the protest conference came to a close, a group of AFL leaders visited
President Theodore Roosevelt, Speaker of the House Joseph Cannon, and pro-
tempore President of the Senate, William Frye and read their grievances aloud
to each one. Roosevelt and Frye both appeared indifferent during the presenta-
tion, but Cannon, grasping that the labor leaders intended their complaint as an
indictment of his leadership, responded vehemently. Gompers recalled that he
"delivered us a rather patronizing lecture" on the "fair and liberal" processes by
which congressmen received appointments to House committees. When Gompers
took issue with Cannon's portrayal, the speaker retaliated: "You are not the
whole thing. You are not the only pebble on the beach." Gompers answered
that "We are just a few pebbles whom you ought to consider and whether we
are small or large, influential or impotent, at least our earnest requests ought to
be given favorable consideration."[8]

In the next months, the AFL leaders made a last push to achieve their legislative goals, imploring Congress to pass their anti-injunction and eight-hour bills,
and again they failed. In a delaying tactic, members of the Judiciary Committee
postponed action on the Federation's anti-injunction bill until they could investigate the meaning of "property rights."[9] Meanwhile, Chairman John Gardner of
the Labor Committee, one of the AFL's oldest and best friends in Congress,
abruptly lost interest in the eight-hour bill in 1906. Although the committee
voted in favor of the bill, Gardner himself abstained from the vote and then
delayed reporting it to the larger House until insufficient time existed for a vote.
Indeed, though the AFL leaders would not be cognizant of this fact for some
time to come, Gardner had just been converted from the AFL's ally to one of
its most prominent congressional enemies. After years of effort, Speaker Cannon
had finally won Chairman Gardner over to his side.[10] This incident reinforced
Gompers's belief that unless his Federation could humble Speaker Cannon and
the other conservatives in Congress, its desired reforms would not succeed.

After these defeats at the hands of Cannon and his allies, the AFL finally
launched its new mobilization strategy, aggressively broadcasting to trade unionists through pamphlets and the *American Federationist* the procedures they
should follow. Though based on the principle of questioning candidates used

[8] Gompers, *Seventy Years*, 2:243–4.
[9] Samuel Gompers, Frank Morrison, and Thomas Spelling, "A Letter to President Roosevelt,"
May 12, 1906, in *AF*, 13 (6), June 1906, 377–80; Gompers, "Men of Labor, Be Up and
Doing," *AF*, 13 (7), July 1906, 464–7.
[10] For more information on Gardner's relationship with the AFL, see Julia Greene, "The Strike
at the Ballot Box: Politics and Partisanship in the American Federation of Labor, 1881–
1916," Ph.D. diss., Yale University, 1990, 194–7. On Gardner's earlier alliance with the
AFL, see Chapter Three above. Gompers knew Gardner had turned against the AFL, and he
believed Cannon was responsible. He simply did not realize – until later – the permanency
of Gardner's conversion. See Gompers, *Seventy Years*, 2:232–7; Gompers to Denis Hayes,
October 5, 1906, Samuel Gompers Letterbooks, Library of Congress, Washington, D.C.;
for details on AFL legislation in this period, see Gompers's Report on Legislation to the
AFL Executive Council, June 18, 1906, *AFL Records*, reel 61.

previously, the AFL's campaign program represented a dramatic escalation of politics within the labor movement. The AFL now urged all affiliated bodies, and especially central labor unions, local unions, and state federations, to intervene in the earliest stages of the political process. Federation leaders advised trade unionists to influence the *nomination* of candidates rather than merely questioning those already nominated. Union activists should appoint special committees, hold conventions, or in some other way coordinate political activities throughout their congressional district, and find someone to nominate who would support labor and progressive measures. Though the program focused on Congress, unionists could tackle state legislatures or other offices as they desired.

When it came to choosing candidates to support, the AFL national leadership laid out its objectives clearly. AFL members should seek above all to defeat those who had been hostile to labor in the past, and they should energetically support congressmen or state legislators friendly to labor. Whenever possible, workingmen should elect trade unionists: "Send trade unionists to your legislature and to Congress with clean-cut union cards in their pockets and then you will be represented."[11]

Nonpartisan principles continued to dominate the campaign strategy: Workingmen should pay attention not to candidates' party affiliations, but their record on labor issues. The AFL hoped trade unionists could get their candidates nominated by one of the major parties, undoubtedly knowing that success would be difficult otherwise. But if both the Democrats and the Republicans disregarded workers' demands, an independent labor candidate should be nominated, "so that honest men may have the opportunity . . . to vote according to their conscience. . . ." In that case, workers should collaborate with minority parties or other progressive elements.[12]

To make their mobilization strategy effective, Federation leaders demanded that unionists at every level of the movement engage in energetic political work. Gompers received a commitment from all members of the AFL Executive Council that they would help campaign around the country. He turned the *American Federationist* into an effective propaganda organ for the duration of the campaign. And most importantly, Gompers expected and worked hard to encourage an unprecedented level of activity at local and state levels. Only aggressive action by local activists would allow the Federation program to reach rank-and-file workers. AFL leaders urged local and state workers to engage in a broad range of activities, from forming committees and organizing conventions, to questioning, nominating, and ultimately campaigning for candidates.

[11] Executive Council of the AFL, "The AFL Campaign Programme," *AF*, 13 (8), August 1906, 529–31; Samuel Gompers, "Talks on Labor," given in Providence, Rhode Island, *AF*, 13 (7), July 1906, 473.

[12] Executive Council of the AFL, "The AFL Campaign Programme," *AF*, 13 (8), August 1906, 531. This document provides the most succinct statement of the AFL leadership's political recommendations, and the AFL distributed it to local unions, central labor unions, and state federations across the country.

Although this program appeared simple and pure enough on paper, in reality it would engender tensions between different levels of the AFL and raise a number of complexities for the national leaders. Because of the new strategy, AFL leaders began committing vastly more resources to political work. The program rested at heart on a mobilization of local workers, so it brought national leaders into close contact with the state and local arms of the organization as they sought to encourage in trade unionists a greater political awareness and activity. Furthermore, by unlocking the Pandora's box of politics, AFL leaders risked losing control over trade unionists' political energies. Exploring this dilemma requires a close look at the roles played by members and leaders throughout the Federation hierarchy.

Resources at the Top

Because the national AFL leaders had initiated labor's 1906 campaign program, they naturally played an important role, distributing money or literature to campaigns around the country, providing information and guidance to local workers, and supervising organizers whom they assigned to political duties. Gompers, Morrison, and the Machinists' President James O'Connell constituted the Labor Representation Committee, which oversaw all campaign matters. In practice Gompers and Morrison took responsibility for most political duties, with some assistance from Andrew Furuseth and John Lennon.

They began in July by sending out a pamphlet to every local union, central labor union, and state federation across the country detailing the nature and structure of the new campaign and calling on workers to mobilize. At the same time, they asked affiliated labor organizations as well as individual trade unionists to contribute money to the campaign. One appeal declared that "The hostile press of the country and all the resources of trust and corporate power are arrayed against us in a desperate effort to prejudice the people of the country against the justice of our cause. . . ." By requesting voluntary contributions, the Labor Representation Committee raised a total of $8,225.94 for the 1906 campaign.[13]

This modest sum was not nearly enough money to pay all the organizers and speakers assigned to the campaign, and to print all the political literature ultimately distributed by AFL headquarters. AFL leaders supplemented their campaign finances by taking money out of the AFL's General Fund to pay many or most of their organizers. Morrison reported on finances after the AFL campaigned in Maine, for example, and commented that "If we had charged the expenses of all the organizers who were in the Second Congressional Maine District against the fund, it would have been more heavily taxed." The AFL's

---

[13] Frank Morrison, "To the members of the Executive Council, AFL," September 17, 1906; Morrison to Max Morris, August 17, 1906: both from the Frank Morrison Letterbooks, Manuscript Department at William R. Perkins Library, Duke University (hereafter cited as Morrison Letterbooks); and the AFL Executive Council to "Organized Labor and its Friends," September 24, 1906, *AF*, 13 (10), October 1906, 819–20.

financial report, published in March 1907 to list its campaign expenditures, includes the salary for only a fraction of the total number of organizers assigned to political duties. The unlisted organizers must have received their salary and expenses as always from the Federation's General Fund. Thus, we can expect that the actual campaign expenses for the AFL were at least double their asserted figure of $8,000.[14]

The AFL also brought to its campaign a great many resources that cannot be measured easily. For example, activists affiliated with the AFL's network of national, state, and local organizations across the country could be counted on to work for little or no pay: Gompers hoped to mobilize the leaders and members of the AFL's 119 affiliated international and national unions, its 37 state federations of labor, 571 city central bodies, and 925 local unions affiliated directly with the AFL.[15] In addition, AFL headquarters itself added a remarkable set of resources. The AFL staff – ranging from 32 to 40 stenographers – could be used for political work; they printed and distributed among AFL members some 90,000 copies of AFL pamphlets such as the *Bill of Grievances* and the *Textbook of Labor's Political Demands*.[16] Executive Council members and other prominent labor leaders would assist with speechmaking; and above all, the AFL could count on its network of volunteer and salaried organizers spread throughout the country.

These organizers constituted the most important innovation in the Federation's political campaign. By 1906, the AFL included 1,300 volunteer organizers across the country in addition to nearly 50 full-time salaried organizers. Although the AFL relied heavily on both kinds of organizers for its new strategy, the salaried organizers more effectively represented the national leadership's wishes: they had fewer ties to any one locale because they traveled around the country, going where Gompers and Morrison sent them. As we saw in Chapter One, the AFL had only begun hiring organizers on a permanent basis as recently as 1899; yet by 1908, the Federation spent more than $59,000 annually to hire organizers. The national leaders saw salaried organizers as central to organized labor's future expansion.[17]

The organizers played a central role in the AFL's new political program. Gompers and Morrison shifted most of the salaried organizers off their regular

---

[14] American Federation of Labor, *Financial Report of the American Federation of Labor Political Campaign of 1906: Being a True Account of All Moneys Received and Expended for that Campaign* (Washington, DC: AFL, 1907).

[15] Frank Morrison to Isaac Mitchell, August 29, 1902, Morrison Letterbooks; "Composition of AF of L," AFL Executive Council, *Text Book of Labor's Political Demands* (Washington, DC: AFL, 1906), 7.

[16] AFL, *Financial Report of the AFL Political Campaign of 1906*, 15–16.

[17] Philip Taft, *The A.F. of L. in the Time of Gompers* (New York: Harper & Row, 1957), 99; on the number of organizers in 1908, see "Secretary Morrison's Report," *Report of the Proceedings of the Twenty-Eighth Annual Convention of the American Federation of Labor* (Washington, DC: National Tribune, 1908), 42; Frank Morrison to W. C. Hahn, September 16, 1908, Morrison Letterbooks.

industrial work, and transformed them into political functionaries – an unprecedented application of union organizers' energies. Handpicked by national
leaders rather than elected by convention delegates, organizers answered only to
those leaders, and hence they served as personal emissaries for the highest union
officials. In the case of the AFL, for example, the organizers took orders only
from Gompers or Morrison. In now giving to these emissaries a *political* function, Gompers and Morrison made a powerful move to establish the dominance
of the AFL on political as well as economic matters. The political organizers
extended the reach of national leaders into towns and cities across the country.
This structural innovation allowed the AFL leaders to implement their long-held
political philosophy: The trade union must enter politics, rather than letting politics into the union.

More than forty salaried organizers worked at political tasks during the 1906
campaign, with efforts ranging from a minimum of only a few speeches to a
maximum of nearly four months of continuous political work. The core group
consisted of eight permanent AFL organizers: M. Grant Hamilton, Sam DeNedry,
Thomas Flynn, Stuart Reid, Cal Wyatt, Hugh Frayne, Jacob Tazelaar, and Jeff
Pierce. These men, the cream of the AFL's organizing force, worked almost
constantly for the AFL campaign from around September 1 until the election
on November 6. Some devoted even more time. Stuart Reid, for example, headed
to Maine and devoted himself to full-time political organizing from late July
onwards.[18]

Most other organizers took charge of one or two campaigns and worked on
them from one to four weeks. This group included John Frey of the Iron Molders,
Edwin Wright of the Illinois Federation of Labor, E. E. Greenawalt of the
Pennsylvania Federation of Labor, and E. N. Nockels of the Chicago Federation
of Labor. Typically these men entered a crucial district, maneuvered aggressively for a few days or weeks to mobilize and organize the local activists, then
moved on to another campaign. Nockels, for example, participated in the AFL's
nine-day blitz into Joseph Cannon's district around Danville, Illinois, and then
returned home to focus on conditions back in Chicago.[19]

Besides the salaried organizers, Gompers expected his Executive Council
members would play the most vital role in the campaign. But he failed to anticipate the political divisions the campaign would create. Among top officials,
only Gompers and Morrison engaged in extensive political activity. Gompers,
of course, edited the *American Federationist* and wrote many of its articles, the
bulk of which focused on politics during the six months preceding the campaign. Both leaders, but especially Morrison, supervised the salaried organizers,
and through them exerted a far-reaching influence on the direction of campaigns
across the United States. The two officials corresponded directly with scores of
local leaders, responding to requests for advice about whom to support or how

[18] D. J. McGillicuddy to Gompers, July 28, 1906, Gompers Letterbooks.
[19] For a complete list of the AFL's political workers, see Greene, "Strike at the Ballot Box," 219.

to run a campaign, and they also produced the Federation's campaign literature. Last of all, Gompers and Morrison traveled extensively to give speeches for or against specific congressmen, knowing their presence would contribute greatly to energizing the local troops. Gompers traveled the most, conducting two major campaign trips. From August 18 until September 8, Gompers spent most of his time in Charles Littlefield's congressional district in southwestern Maine; a second campaign trip in mid-October reached from New York and Baltimore to Chicago and Kankakee, Illinois; Lafayette, Indiana; and Scranton, Pennsylvania. Besides these tours, Gompers made a long visit to New York and Chicago in late September to lead negotiations between rival political organizations among the workers in each city.[20]

The rest of the Executive Council did little to meet their obligations in the campaign. Most members made a few speeches on behalf of some candidate, but this fell far below the level of activity expected by Gompers and Morrison. John Lennon served as troubleshooter during conflicts among Chicago trade unionists, and also worked on Joseph Cannon's district in central Illinois. James O'Connell (IAM) served as the third member of the Labor Representation Committee, along with Morrison and Gompers, although his influence on the committee appears to have been slight.[21] Max Morris of Denver (Retail Clerks) and Denis Hayes of Philadelphia (Glass Bottle Blowers) made speeches and oversaw trade unionists' activity in their regions.

The remaining AFL officials assumed virtually no political duties, which caused great resentment among more active leaders. Furthermore, the inactivity of William Huber (Carpenters), James Duncan (Granite Cutters), John Mitchell (Miners), and Daniel Keefe (Longshoremen) suggested more serious political disagreements. Although apparently all Executive Council members had agreed to the campaign program, these four never supported it wholeheartedly. All were conservative business unionists distrustful of mixing politics with trade unionism, and some, like Mitchell and Keefe, possessed strong partisan ties that made them uncomfortable with the AFL campaign.

The problem grew most acute in the Maine campaign. There the AFL fought to defeat Charles Littlefield, one of its most effective and determined enemies in the House of Representatives. Gompers wrote each member of the Executive Council, reminding them of the commitment to help and asking them to go to Maine. But no one went. Gompers became especially incensed by John Mitchell's unwillingness to visit the district, perhaps because his popularity among workers would have been politically advantageous. Gompers wrote Mitchell repeatedly, pleading with him to come to Maine or at least to indicate his support and thereby squelch the rumors circulating that he opposed the AFL program. Mitchell took so long to respond that Gompers could not publish his answer in local

[20] AFL, *Financial Report*, 1907; Morrison to W. E. Kennedy, September 29, 1906, Morrison Letterbooks; Gompers to the AFL Executive Council, October 4, 1906, Gompers Letterbooks.
[21] Despite O'Connell's presence on the Labor Representation Committee, no evidence has emerged suggesting that he played an influential role during the 1906 campaign.

newspapers before election day.[22] After Maine, the rumors continued. The New York press reported that AFL officials divided over political strategy and named Mitchell and Duncan as opponents of Gompers's strategy.[23]

Even had all the Executive Council members participated enthusiastically, the AFL's national headquarters did not possess sufficient resources to float an entire nationwide campaign. After all, the strength of the AFL, politically as well as economically, lay in its network of organizations across the country. Because the AFL's campaign program sought above all to get its rank-and-file members out voting, and for the right candidate, it became necessary to mobilize local leaders – and through them, the rank and file – to the greatest extent possible. Maybe Gompers realized that by allowing people at the local level to manage their own affairs, he would help generate the greatest amount of enthusiasm. Or, perhaps he saw it as the most expedient tactic: These were congressional races, and people living in the district would best know whom to support.

As a result, local autonomy emerged as a central and carefully enunciated principle of the new AFL strategy. The AFL national leadership almost always refused to support someone seeking a candidacy, including AFL members, until they saw that the local movement had endorsed the individual. For example, Frank Buchanan, a leader of the Bridge and Structural Iron Workers in Chicago, knew the AFL leaders and wrote regarding his desire to run for Congress. Gompers expressed pleasure that Buchanan planned to run. However, he warned, "you understand that if there is any movement inaugurated by the trade unionists of Chicago in conformity with the AFL political campaign program, it would be wisest for all of us to turn in and do the best we can along that line."[24]

---

[22] Executive Council members Lennon, Morris, O'Connell, and Huber sent other officials from their unions to help Gompers in Maine. In addition, James Golden (president of the United Textile Workers) went to Maine, as did representatives of the International Seamen's Union and the International Brotherhood of Blacksmiths and Helpers. See James Kline to Gompers, August 13, 1906; Lennon to Gompers, August 15, 1906; Max Morris to Gompers, August 16, 1906; William Huber to Gompers, August 18, 1906; W. H. Frazier to Gompers, August 20, 1906; H. J. Conway to Gompers, August 21, 1906; Joseph Valentine to Gompers, August 21, 1906; John Golden to Gompers, August 22, 1906; Gompers to Mitchell, August 26, 1906, Gompers Letterbooks; James O'Connell to Gompers, August 27, 1906; Lennon to Gompers, August 28, 1906; Walter Ames to Gompers, August 30, 1906; Denis Hayes to Gompers, August 30, 1906; E. C. Morrison to Gompers, September 4, 1906; Gompers to Frank Morrison, September 8, 1906, Gompers Letterbooks; Mitchell to Gompers, September 8, 1906. Except where noted otherwise, all the preceding are from AFL Records, reels 61 and 62.
[23] Gompers and Morrison, "Statements to the Press," responding to an article in the New York Sun, September 21, 1906, AFL Records, reel 62.
[24] Gompers to Frank Buchanan, August 6, 1906, AFL Records, reel 61. For other examples, see Gompers to D. B. Keith, Selma, Alabama, July 2, 1906, AFL Records, reel 61; Gompers to E. B. Kennedy, New York City, August 24, 1906, Gompers Letterbooks; Gompers to Charles Wolf, Waverly, New York, August 8, 1906, AFL Records, reel 61; Gompers to G. W. Johnson, Chicago, September 6, 1906, AFL Records, reel 62; Gompers to Michael Goldsmith, Cleveland, September 6, 1906, Gompers Letterbooks; Gompers to J. J. Mack, Dubois, Pennsylvania, September 25, 1906, Gompers Letterbooks.

Similarly, Gompers and Morrison chose to begin an active campaign only in areas where local workers appeared ready to join in. Once the national leaders had announced the campaign program, they waited to see which local movements would seize the opportunity. Unless local activists responded enthusiastically to the AFL program, as Morrison put it, ". . . any action that might be taken by the Labor Representation Committee, would meet with weak and ungracious support. We will probably center our forces in localities where there is an opportunity to achieve success."[25]

Thus, the AFL organizers geared their activities to helping local leaders establish a competent campaign organization. The campaign documents focused on energizing and politicizing local and state leaders of the AFL. A steady stream of printed matter headed out from AFL headquarters to towns across the country. Leaflets and pamphlets as well as articles in the *American Federationist* exhorted workers regularly to "Be Up and Doing!" Indeed, the AFL began explicitly to redefine trade unionists' duties so as to include political activity. Political work, the AFL instructed, had become a *necessary* component of trade unionism. By working to elect honest men to Congress and state legislatures, the AFL leaders told workers, "you will more completely and fully carry out your obligations as union men. . . . Labor demands a distinctive and larger share in the governmental affairs of our country; it demands justice; it will be satisfied with nothing less."[26]

The AFL leaders also assisted local campaign fights by turning their headquarters into a clearinghouse of information about congressmen. The AFL collected and distributed information about congressmen's voting records and their reaction to the Bill of Grievances. In April, the AFL sent a copy of the Bill of Grievances to each congressman and asked for his response; if the congressman replied with a vague commentary, the AFL made a second request for clarification. The *American Federationist* published all responses, accompanied by Gompers's editorial commentary, taking up nearly fifty pages in its September issue. In addition, the AFL responded directly to workers' requests for information. Trade unionists wrote the AFL headquarters by the hundreds for congressmen's records or for advice on political strategy. Responding to these requests became an extremely time-consuming job for the AFL staff.[27]

---

[25] Frank Morrison to J. L. Rodier, October 19, 1906, Morrison Letterbooks.

[26] Samuel Gompers, "Editorial," *AF*, 13 (5), May 1906, 318; AFL Executive Council, "A.F. of L. Campaign Programme," *AF*, 13 (8), August 1906, 531.

[27] Gompers to Dear Sir (requesting a response to the Bill of Grievances), April 26, 1906, *AFL Records*, reel 61; Gompers to Dear Sir (asking for more specific comments), August 1, 1906, *AFL Records*, reel 61; "Queries and Answers: Members of Congress Give Their Opinion of Labor's Bill of Grievances," *AF*, 13 (9), September 1906, 643–88. Gompers considered forty-seven responses from Democratic congressmen acceptable, out of a total of fifty, whereas he considered only twenty-three of the seventy-three responses from Republican congressmen favorable.

Tactics at the Bottom

The AFL campaign program immediately elicited significant enthusiasm among workers throughout the AFL hierarchy. Local and state labor officials across the country began working on congressional and state legislative contests.[28] As early as mid-July, activists in Ogden, Utah, had organized several political conferences with the Salt Lake City labor movement, but they feared that opposition from Socialists and from Mormons would hinder their efforts. An organizer from Los Angeles reported that AFL affiliates there had formed a Public Ownership League with branches in most wards. "Trade union questions and politics mix well at these meetings," he concluded. Dubois, Pennsylvania, trade unionists held a convention of workers that included representatives for the Farmers, Miners, Painters, Clerks, and Trainmen, and nominated several trade unionists for the state assembly. "Never before have the men taken so much interest in politics," reported the Camden, New Jersey, central labor union.[29]

The impact of their own mobilization impressed many labor activists. "Already candidates for the Legislature who heretofore have been either indifferent or hostile are coming out with identical platforms. The effect has been electrical," the secretary of the Minnesota State Federation of Labor wrote after his federation passed its political program. A Cincinnati trade unionist wrote Morrison in the same vein: "Labor within this city is gaining ground every day as you can see by the way all the candidates on different tickets are declaring that they have the support of Labor in the coming election."[30]

Based on correspondence between AFL headquarters and local labor movements, we can estimate workers' responses to the campaign program. In 121 congressional districts, or in 30 percent of all districts (404), AFL members

---

[28] According to Frank Morrison, workers were very active in state legislative contests: He believed that would be the site of labor's greatest gains. For example, see Frank Morrison to Charles Stelzle, September 28, 1906, Morrison Letterbooks; Morrison to Richard Braunschweig, September 28, 1906, Morrison Letterbooks; Morrison to Cal Wyatt, November 8, 1906, Morrison Letterbooks. In June 1906, the AFL checked with its state federations of labor and found that there were fifty-one trade unionists in eighteen state legislatures across the country: "President's Report" to the AFL Executive Council, June 18, 1906, *AFL Records*, reel 61. Unfortunately, despite Morrison's hopes for state legislatures, the AFL did not assess the number of trade unionists elected in 1906. The only mention of results in state legislative contests comes from Morrison in a letter to Cal Wyatt. Five men had been nominated for the legislature from the Scranton, Pennsylvania, area, he said, and all were elected: November 8, 1906, Morrison Letterbooks. More research is needed on this aspect of AFL politics.

[29] H. L. Gant, Odgen, Utah, Trades and Labor Assembly, to no one, n.d. (received July 12, 1906), *AFL Records*, reel 61; L. D. Biddle, Los Angeles, to Gompers, July 2, 1906, *AFL Records*, reel 61; J. B. Mack, Dubois, Pennsylvania, to Gompers, August 10, 1906, *AFL Records*, reel 61; Charles Kontnier, president, Division 52, American Association of Street and Electric Railway Employees, East Liverpool, Ohio, to Gompers, August 2, 1906, *AFL Records*, reel 61; James Grau to Gompers, July 25, 1906, *AFL Records*, reel 61.

[30] W. E. McEwen, secretary-treasurer, Minnesota Federation of Labor, June 18, 1906, *AFL Records*, reel 61; Joseph J. Barnett, secretary, Common Club, Cincinnati, to Morrison, September 26, 1906, *AFL Records*, reel 62.

demonstrated some degree of political activism. Their involvement ranged widely, from mere requests for congressmen's records, to more extensive measures such as establishing a special committee, or fighting an aggressive, full-scale campaign. These active districts fell into twenty-seven different states, though most were in industrialized areas where organized labor enjoyed its greatest strength: Ohio, Indiana, Illinois, Pennsylvania, California, and New York. However, trade unionists in most regions of the country showed some interest in the AFL program. For example, in seven southeastern states (Alabama, Georgia, Virginia, North Carolina, Tennessee, Kentucky, and Missouri), AFL members grew more politically active.

Meanwhile, labor organizations in approximately sixty towns across the country displayed a heartier response to the AFL's new strategy and established some form of campaign structure such as a special committee, a convention, or a labor party. These new institutions questioned and nominated candidates. Workers in Wichita, Kansas, for example, established an Independent Voters' Labor League; St. Joseph, Missouri, organized a Local Gompers Legislative Club; and in at least seven areas, workers mobilized through labor parties.[31] National leaders did not urge local activists to create labor parties or similar political organizations, but neither did they oppose them. The incidence of such organizations suggests a strong interest in political activism at the local level.[32]

For all their diversity, local movements almost always lacked money, and they pleaded with the national leadership for organizers, speakers, funds, and campaign literature.[33] With few funds, local workers relied heavily on labor-intensive

[31] W. E. Bryan to Gompers, September 30, 1906; Alfred G. Roberts to Gompers, October 6, 1906. Labor parties existed in Pittsburgh; Baltimore; Danville, Illinois (only temporarily); Atlantic City; Jersey City; Alameda County, California; Altoona, Pennsylvania; and New York City. See Harry F. Vollmer to Gompers, October 3, 1906; Cal Wyatt to Frank Morrison, August 22, 1906; Clifford Reed to Gompers, July 30, 1906; William Riddle to Gurden Levake, October 23, 1906; Joseph Rooney to Gompers, October 24, 1906; Charles Boynton to Gompers, September 26, 1906; Maurice J. Holland to Gompers, September 22, 1906; and Central Federated Union of New York to Members of Organized Labor, August 5, 1906: all *AFL Records*, reels 61–3.

[32] When the secretary of the Danville, Illinois, Trades and Labor Council wrote Gompers that it had formed an Independent Labor Party, he responded: "I am gratified to know that the AFL campaign program has been so promptly acted upon by the Trades and Labor Council of Danville. . . ." Clifford Reed to Gompers, July 30, 1906, *AFL Records*, reel 61; Gompers to Reed, August 1, 1906, Gompers Letterbooks.

[33] John Keyes of the Connecticut Federation of Labor wrote Morrison to say it had established a political committee of 15, but please send "all the political labor reading you can as there is considerable socialists here and anyone know[s] they have no love for President Gompers," August 12, 1906, *AFL Records*, reel 61. More often, workers requested organizers and speakers. See, for example: H. E. Gubrandsen, secretary-treasurer, International Photo-Engravers' Union, Minneapolis, to Gompers, September 10, 1906, *AFL Records*, reel 62; Robert S. Maloney, Lawrence, Massachusetts, Central Labor Union, to Gompers, October 24, 1906, *AFL Records*, reel 63; Charles B. Reese, Martinsville, Virginia, to Gompers, September 19, 1906, *AFL Records*, reel 62; Elmer L. Morlette, member, metal polishers' union, to Gompers, October 4, 1906, *AFL Records*, reel 62.

tactics. Frank Barr, an active trade unionist from the small industrial city of Marion, Indiana, sent Gompers his account of the workers' campaign there against Congressman Fred Landis. It suggests the problems faced by a typical local campaign.

Writing after the election, when Landis had won a narrow victory, Barr described their tactics. "Our Legislative Committee, which was appointed as per your request, fell down on us, as so many of our recent committees have done, and as a consequence what we did against Landis had to be done quickly and in a few days." They began by calling a special meeting of the Marion Trades' Council just days before the election. There they adopted resolutions condemning Landis for his vote on the eight-hour law, and asking all union men to vote against him. They also printed 10,000 anti-Landis bills, and sent an organizer through the district to distribute the bills and mobilize local trade union leaders. When this organizer reached the town of Peru, however, he found that another trade unionist named O. P. Smith had begun organizing *in favor of* Landis. Smith, editor of a local labor paper, was running for state representative on the same ticket – Republican – as Landis. As part of his efforts on behalf of Landis, Smith threatened the secretary of the Peru Trades Assembly that his organization "would be severely punished by [Gompers], if they had anything to do with political affairs." Smith had employed this tactic in several other towns as well, and Barr believed it greatly damaged their campaign against Landis.[34] Fighting with few resources and sometimes, as in Peru, opposed by other trade unionists, those loyal to Gompers found it difficult to apply AFL campaign strategy effectively.

In Baltimore, the Federation of Labor attempted to elect Conductor George Smith and defeat Congressman Sidney Mudd by relying on two main strategies. First, activists made a house-to-house canvass of all voters. Second, they worked to mobilize the thousands of machinists at the Baltimore and Ohio Railroad workshops in their congressional district. Baltimore leaders managed to get Gompers and James O'Connell of the International Association of Machinists to come and give speeches for Smith.[35] Local unionists relied often on personal networks for maximum efficiency, as the campaign of trade unionist Charles Young of south Chicago shows. He and his campaign workers analyzed their district, a heavily Republican one, to assess how many votes they needed to win and from whom. Then they appointed a trade unionist to each of eighty-nine precincts and instructed them to win at least forty-five Republican voters in their precincts over to Young's side.[36]

These examples suggest that the resources and abilities of local leaders differed significantly from those of the national leaders. The national AFL leaders

[34] Frank Barr, secretary-treasurer, Marion Central Trades' Council, to Gompers, November 7, 1906, *AFL Records*, reel 64.

[35] Ed Hirsch, Baltimore Federation of Labor, to Gompers, October 20, 1906; R. Lee Guard to Ed Hirsch, October 23, 1906: both *AFL Records*, reel 63.

[36] Charles Young to Frank Morrison, September 18, 1906, *AFL Records*, reel 62.

controlled the finances, and so they decided which districts would receive organizers and printed material. Local activists possessed more knowledge about
local conditions as well as broad networks of personal acquaintances, and they
could accomplish labor-intensive tasks. Because of these differences, local and
national leaders needed each other. Local leaders required the resources that only
national leaders in control of union budgets could afford, and their ability to
decide where to send organizers and speakers gave the national leaders a great
deal of control over the campaigns. However, the program could not succeed
without energetic work at the local and state levels, so national leaders remained
indebted to the local movements as well.

Local and national leaders differed in more than just their resources and tactics, however. An analysis of the campaigns across the country indicates that
national and local leaders also made different decisions about how to run the
campaigns and about which candidates to support. The AFL's role in the congressional contests fell into two distinct patterns.

The first pattern involved races in which the national AFL leadership dominated while participation by local- and state-level leaders usually constituted only
a minor influence. The AFL's national leaders focused on attacking well-known
and powerful congressmen who had opposed the AFL's legislation. Gompers
and Morrison consistently stated this core principle of their campaign program:
They aimed to attack labor's enemies. Gompers expressed his priorities, for
example, when he wrote that AFL organizers, "while sent in the districts in
opposition to Congressmen who are unfavorable to our legislation, invariably
have a kind word to say for the candidates on the local ticket, who are friendly
to us." And Morrison coldly scolded an organizer who made the mistake of
endorsing a candidate: "I was not aware that we endorsed candidates. I thought
we opposed those who were unfriendly to us." Because of this orientation, AFL
leaders normally remained indifferent about whom they supported in the election. AFL organizers often attacked the opponent in their speeches with barely
a mention of the candidate they supported.[37] As the *American Federationist*
instructed workers, "Defeat labor's known enemies, even if you have to elect
those who are not straight labor men. If we can not use the 'other man' as a
staff to lean upon, for temporary purposes he may be just good enough to use
as a stick to beat the enemy."[38]

The AFL national leaders put most of their time, money, and energy into
these races, catapulting them into the national spotlight. Gompers and Morrison
fought their most aggressive battle against Speaker Joseph Cannon of the House
of Representatives, but they also targeted many of his top allies, including John
Dalzell of Pennsylvania (the chairman of the House Committee on Rules) and

[37] Gompers to W. J. Campbell, secretary of the UMWA Local No. 2297, Brookwayville,
Pennsylvania, October 12, 1906, Gompers Letterbooks; Morrison to Stuart Reid, September
28, 1906, Morrison Letterbooks; Gompers to M. Grant Hamilton, October 8, 1906, *AFL
Records*, reel 63.
[38] *AF*, 13 (8), August 1906, 322.

Charles Littlefield (the chairman of the House Judiciary Committee).[39] These races usually focused on Republican candidates and took place in strongly Republican districts or states. This plus the fact that the AFL targeted the most powerful men in Congress left only a small chance for victory. Though the AFL leaders dueled with many of the top congressional conservatives in 1906, they achieved not a single success.

Local and state labor movements rather than the AFL's national leaders dominated in the second pattern of races. These races were typically positive campaigns, in active support of new or incumbent candidates. Significantly, campaigns of this sort often supported a candidate who was a trade unionist or, at least, a "friend of labor." Such campaigns received little national attention, and did not generate the voluminous documentation that the nationally dominated campaigns did. Therefore, although these campaigns were more common than the other type, they have for the most part been lost to history.

National leaders' dominance over the campaign program was at its most extreme in the congressional district around Lewiston, Maine, when the AFL fought its famed battle against Charles Littlefield in 1906. The AFL flooded the district with top leaders such as Gompers himself, organizers from outside of Maine, and nationally known labor figures from around the country. The AFL sent at least fourteen people into the district at one time or another, most of them organizers who spent anywhere from a week to two months.[40] Local labor activists played almost no role in this campaign. Similarly, in Pittsburgh, the AFL national leadership built a pugnacious campaign against John Dalzell. Nine organizers entered the district at the behest of national leaders. Two of these visited for only a few days to give speeches or try to reconcile competing groups; three worked on a short-term basis, for two weeks

---

[39] Others of Cannon's allies targeted by the AFL included James Watson (Indiana), James Kennedy (Ohio), James Sherman (New York), George Foss (Illinois), George Lilley (Connecticut), Zeno Rives (Illinois), Richard Bartholdt (Missouri), William Humphrey (WA), R. Wayne Parker (New Jersey), Samuel McCall (Massachusetts), Sidney Mudd (MD), and Nicholas Longworth (Ohio). Longworth, Bartholdt, and McCall were on the Labor Committee; Parker was a well-known opponent of the AFL's anti-injunction bill; and Watson served as majority whip and as Speaker Cannon's right-hand man. Undoubtedly, the AFL would have targeted James Gardner, the chairman of the House Labor Committee, as well, except that Gompers believed (mistakenly, it turned out) that his sudden opposition to labor's bills would prove only temporary.

[40] Gompers to Stuart Reid, July 31, 1906, Gompers Letterbooks; James Kline to Gompers, August 13, 1906; Morrison to Gompers, August 17, 1906; William Huber to Gompers, August 18, 1906; W. H. Frazier to Gompers, August 20, 1906; H. J. Conway to Gompers, August 21, 1906; James Fitzgerald to Gompers, August 22, 1906; John Golden to Gompers, August 22, 1906; Stuart Reid to Gompers, August 28, 1906; Walter Ames to Gompers, August 30, 1906; Frank Morrison to J. J. Sullivan, September 5, 1906, Morrison Letterbooks; Frank Morrison to Jacob Tazelaar, September 6, 1906, Morrison Letterbooks; Gompers to Collis Lovely, October 4, 1906, Gompers Letterbooks. Except where noted otherwise, all the preceding are from *AFL Records*, reels 61–2.

or less; but the other four organizers stayed in Pittsburgh long-term, for up to 10 weeks.[41]

Workers had created a Union Labor Party in Pittsburgh about a year before. The AFL organizers, upon visiting, did not like what they found. A prominent leader of the party belonged to the Knights of Labor and, according to AFL organizers, he discouraged workers from becoming active. The organizers studied the situation to determine whether they could take over the organization or would have to create a new one. Organizer Cal Wyatt speculated that about one-half the political committee "are men who we can influence and are representatives of affiliated AFL bodies."[42] Yet, ultimately, the AFL leaders decided they could more easily create a new organization to supersede the Union Labor Party. Significantly, AFL organizers ran this new body. A local union activist served as chairman, but his position was nominal and no one expected him to do any work. Three of Gompers's allies actually managed the campaign, two of them paid AFL organizers, and all of them sent into Pittsburgh from outside by the AFL leadership.[43]

The AFL organizers' influence over this campaign extended even to tactical details. Organizer M. Grant Hamilton reported that at a campaign meeting, a speaker had "violently" attacked the Republican Party with hardly a mention of Congressman Dalzell. After the meeting ended, Hamilton called all union men together and lectured them on campaign tactics. In such a strong Republican state, he warned, assaults on that party could only result in defeat. According to Hamilton, the men reacted favorably to his comments.[44] However, local activists undoubtedly had misgivings about the AFL's strong-arm tactics, from superseding their party with a new organization to lecturing them on strategy.

[41] On Pittsburgh, see Cal Wyatt to Frank Morrison, August 20, 1906, *AFL Records*, reel 61; T. H. Flynn to Thomas Tracy, October 1, 1906, *AFL Records*, reel 62; Frank Morrison to Cal Wyatt, September 27, 1906, Morrison Letterbooks; M. Grant Hamilton to Thomas Tracy, October 5, 1906, *AFL Records*, reel 62; Gompers to Clarence V. Tiers, October 15, 1906, *AFL Records*, reel 63; D. A. Hayes to Gompers, October 15, 1906, *AFL Records*, reel 63; Frank Morrison to Cal Wyatt, October 16, 1906, Morrison Letterbooks; Gompers to John Frey, October 23, 1906, Gompers Letterbooks; Gompers to E. E. Greenawalt, October 23, 1906, Gompers Letterbooks; Frank Morrison to Thomas Flynn, October 22, 1906, Morrison Letterbooks.

[42] Wyatt to Morrison, August 22, 1906, *AFL Records*, reel 61.

[43] John Frey to Gompers, October 24, 1906, *AFL Records*, reel 63. See also Wyatt to Morrison, August 20 and 22, 1906, *AFL Records*, reel 61; Morrison to Wyatt, September 15, 1906, Morrison Letterbooks; M. F. Tighe of the Union Labor Party of Pittsburgh to Gompers, September 21, 1906, *AFL Records*, reel 62; Morrison to D. A. Hayes, October 4, 1906, Morrison Letterbooks; Frey to Gompers, October 16 and 18, 1906, *AFL Records*, reel 63; Gompers to Frey, October 19, 1906, Gompers Letterbooks; Frey to Gompers, October 21, 1906, *AFL Records*, reel 63; Gompers to Frey, October 23, 1906, Gompers Letterbooks; Morrison to Thomas Flynn, October 22, 1906, Morrison Letterbooks; Morrison to Hayes, October 22, 1906, Morrison Letterbooks; Morrison to William Terry, October 23, 1906, Morrison Letterbooks; and E. E. Greenawalt to Gompers, October 27, 1906, *AFL Records*, reel 63.

[44] Hamilton to T. Tracy, October 5, 1906, *AFL Records*, reel 62.

Even with the new organization, an AFL organizer in Pittsburgh complained to
Gompers and Morrison that "there is an apparant lack of enthusiasm among the
members of organized labor" regarding the campaign.[45]

Not all cases were this one-sided, but usually when the AFL intervened in
a congressional district, it played a central role. The fight against John Kennedy
of Youngstown, Ohio, is one case where both local and national people actively
participated, yet even here the AFL national leaders played a critical role. The
AFL allowed the political organization created by AFL members, the United
Labor Congress, to continue to exist, and its leadership remained unchanged.
But AFL national representatives worked closely with people there. Although
local workers had been inclined to support Kennedy's bid for reelection, the AFL
organizers convinced them to oppose him. In addition, AFL representatives –
primarily Sam Gompers – mediated relations between Democrats and the labor
activists at the local level.[46]

Although his actions indicated that opposing labor's enemies formed his top
priority, Gompers often talked about his other goal: electing trade unionists to
political office. Gompers highlighted the possibility of electing union workers
almost any time he communicated with rank-and-file AFL members, hinting that
to him it was the most important part of the campaign strategy.[47] Gompers seems
to have realized that this would be most appealing and thus most energizing to
workers. However, the AFL leaders' emphasis on trade unionists was by no
means only rhetorical. True to their strictures in the "Campaign Programme,"
Gompers and Morrison did desire to see trade unionists in the next Congress,
and in their letters to workers, they regularly sought to persuade unionists to
run. When a Terre Haute friend wanted Gompers to support someone for Congress who was not a unionist, the labor chieftain responded negatively: "I am
free to say that I should like to see a bona fide labor man, that is, a man in the
ranks of labor, . . . nominated and elected to Congress. There is no reason why
such a man could not be found."[48]

Furthermore, although trade unionists running for Congress did not receive
the same attention from AFL headquarters as did hostile congressmen, most

---

[45] E. E. Greenawalt to Gompers, October 27, 1906, *AFL Records*, reel 63.

[46] Cal Wyatt to Morrison, August 22, 1906; Morrison to Flynn, October 16, 1906, Morrison
Letterbooks; T. H. Flynn to Thomas Tracy, October 1, 1906; M. Grant Hamilton to Thomas
Tracy, October 5, 1906; Gompers to J. A. Robinson, October 15, 1906; J. A. Robinson to
Gompers, October 15, 1906; John C. Welty to Gompers, October 15, 1906; Morrison to
Wyatt, October 16, 1906, Morrison Letterbooks; Gompers to John C. Welty, October 18,
1906; Morrison to Samuel DeNedry, October 22, 1906, Morrison Letterbooks; Samuel
DeNedry to Gompers, October 24, 1906; Gompers to Peter McArdle, November 1, 1906;
M. Grant Hamilton to Gompers, November 1, 1906: except where noted otherwise, all are
from *AFL Records*, reels 61–4. See also *The Cleveland Citizen*, October 6, 1906.

[47] For example, see a trio of speeches Gompers made in June in Erie, Pennsylvania;
Providence, Rhode Islands; and Poughkeepsie, New York, in "Talks on Labor," *AF*, 13 (7),
July 1906, 472–4.

[48] Gompers to John Lamb, Terre Haute, Indiana, June 30, 1906, *AFL Records*, reel 61.

received some assistance. Often, the national leaders sent an organizer or two into the district, and perhaps a few speakers. Gompers himself made speeches for numerous trade union candidates. For example, when Charles Donahue, president of the Connecticut Federation of Labor, ran for Congress, Gompers visited Bridgeport to speak in his favor and sent an organizer to help with the campaign.[49]

In most cases, though, AFL activists at the local and state levels led the campaigns in support of trade unionists. These campaigns provided a more productive arena for labor politics than the attacks on labor's enemies carried out by the national AFL. Activists attempted in at least twenty-five districts to nominate trade unionists to Congress in 1906. Of those efforts, thirteen trade unionists won a nomination and four won election to the U.S. Congress: Thomas Nicholls and William Wilson, mine workers from Scranton and Williamsport, Pennsylvania; William Cary, a telegrapher from Milwaukee; and John McDermott, a telegrapher from Chicago.[50] Most trade unionists ran on the Democratic ticket. One union man ran as an independent, one as a Socialist, and two as Republicans, but the remaining nine ran as Democrats. Joining together with allies of the labor movement, the new labor congressmen would form a small but unprecedented Labor Group in the House. When the Democrats took over control of the House in 1910, a leading member of that Group, William B. Wilson, would become the chairman of the Committee on Labor.

Of all the trades represented among the labor candidates for Congress, miners demonstrated the most skill at nominating and electing congressmen. Three miners stood among the twelve trade unionists nominated for Congress, with two of those three (Wilson and Nicholls) victorious on election day. The AFL

---

[49] Gompers to P. H. Connolly, secretary, Connecticut Federation of Labor, October 5, 1906, *AFL Records*, reel 62; Gompers to Charles Donahue, October 6, 1906, *AFL Records*, reel 62; Gompers to William E. Terry, organizer, Providence, Rhode Island, October 6, 1906, *AFL Records*, reel 62; Gompers to Charles Donahue, October 8, 1906, *AFL Records*, reel 63; Gompers to James Duncan, Quincy, Massachusetts, October 8, 1906, *AFL Records*, reel 63; Gompers to Duncan, October 11, 1906, Gompers Letterbooks.

[50] Some scholars list additional trade unionists as winning election in 1906, mentioning in particular Isaac Sherwood of Ohio and William Hughes of New Jersey. For example, Philip Foner lists Hughes as an "active trade unionist"; Foner, *History of the Labor Movement*, 3:330. Hughes loyally and energetically supported the AFL in his political activities, and he held honorary membership in the Steam Shovel and Dredge Engineers' Union. But the twenty-sixth president of the United States deserved the label of trade unionist as much as did Hughes. William "Injunction Judge" Taft, a politician despised by organized labor during this period, was declared an honorary member of the Steam Shovel and Dredge Engineers' Union. See T. J. Dolan, secretary-treasurer, International Brotherhood of Steam Shovel and Dredge Men, to Gompers, July 31, 1908, *AFL Records*, reel 61.

The other trade unionists nominated for Congress were Charles Young (printer, Chicago), Frank Buchanan (structural ironworker, Chicago), John Walker (miner, Danville, Illinois), Congressman William Hunt (stonecutter, St. Louis), James O'Connor (printer, Utica, New York), Timothy Healy (international president, Stationary Firemen, Yonkers, New York), Charles Donahue (president, Connecticut Federation of Labor, Derby, Connecticut), Henry Gottlob (printer, Newark, New Jersey), and George Smith (conductor, Baltimore).

sent out two organizers to help the candidates, and Gompers and John Mitchell visited each district to give a speech (this was Mitchell's only activity for the campaign).[51] In Danville, Illinois, another miner stood as the Socialist Party's candidate against Speaker of the House Joseph Cannon, and this case illustrates both the complexities of local–national relationships during the campaign, as well as the challenges facing labor when it tackled a powerful enemy.

Speaker Cannon's congressional district, the 18th of Illinois, stood as a Republican stronghold in a Republican state. It contained six primarily rural counties: Kankakee, Iroquois, Vermilion, Edgar, Clark, and Cumberland counties. The district hugged a long and narrow stretch of land along the Indiana border, beginning in the north with Kankakee County, only some forty miles from Chicago. It then stretched southward about 125 miles, through dusty flat farmland and small mining towns. At its widest spot, the district was no more than fifty miles across. Danville was its only city – and a small one at that, with fewer than 28,000 people in 1910. The only other sizable town was Kankakee with a population of nearly 14,000.[52]

Labor's hopes in this district rested in the Danville area, an important center for manufacturing. Mining, railroad shops, brick production, and brewing dominated the town, and other leading industries included farm implements production, foundry and machine works, harness making, and cigarmaking.[53] Four major railroads intersected at Danville, employing between them some 2,000 workers. The mining industry of central Illinois had entered into a decline by 1906, but it remained a potent economic force. Whereas in 1907 the region contained fifty-nine working mines, by 1908 this number had decreased to only forty-three. They employed 2,796 miners; when combined with workers in related jobs, both underground and on the surface, the total work force in the mining industry came to nearly 4,000.[54]

[51] Morrison to E. C. Patterson, August 23, 1906; Morrison to Hugh Frayne, October 16, 1906; Morrison to J. L. Rodier, October 19, 1906: all Morrison Letterbooks.

[52] After Danville and Kankakee came some very small towns: the largest were Paris and Hoopeston with 6,100 and 3,800 inhabitants respectively, five towns with between 1,500 and 2,500 people, and a score of villages ranging from 100 to 1,500 people. United States Department of Commerce, Bureau of the Census, *Thirteenth Census of the United States, Taken in the Year 1910*, Vol. 9: *Manufactures* (Washington, DC: U.S. Government Printing Office, 1912), 264; and Danville City Council, *Danville, 1906* (Danville: n.p., 1906).

[53] The largest producer of paving bricks in the United States in the early twentieth century was the Western Brick Company in Danville. It began production in 1900; in 1904, the United Brick and Clay Workers signed their first contract with the company. There were at least four brewing companies in Danville by 1906. See Danville City Council, *Danville 1906*; "Western Brick," *The Heritage of Vermilion County*, Autumn 1974, 12–13; Danville *Commercial-News*, October 13 and November 6, 1906; Jack Moore Williams, *History of Vermilion County, Illinois*, Vol. 1 (Topeka, KS: Historical Publishing, 1930), 415–20.

[54] Williams, *History of Vermilion County*, 437–40; Robert Shanks, "Railroads: Danville Junction," *The Heritage of Vermilion County*, Spring 1966, 10–12; Danville *Commercial-News*, 29, 1908; author's discussion with Richard Cannon, Fithian, Illinois, October 11, 1988; "Vermilion County Coal," *The Heritage of Vermilion County*, Autumn 1981, 4–5, and Winter 1981–2, 3 and 15–16.

The Republican inclination of voters in this district, its predominantly rural character, as well as Cannon's fame and prestige nationwide, all made the House speaker an extremely difficult target for labor activists. But the ace in Cannon's hand was an institution he had won for his region, the Danville Soldiers' Home.

The National Home for Disabled Volunteer Soldiers sat peacefully on 324 beautiful acres at the eastern edge of Danville. Its attractiveness and economic contribution to the city (some one million dollars per year) made the home the pride of many Danville citizens. Congress established the Soldiers' Home in 1897 at a cost of $1,321,690, as one of nine national soldiers' homes placed throughout the United States during the 1890s. It had been a sign of Cannon's growing power in Congress that he managed to secure one for his home town.

As one commentator expressed it, the Soldiers' Home provided Danville with "one of its most noted beauty spots, which is visited by practically everyone who comes to this city." The home constituted a veritable town unto itself. It contained more than two dozen buildings, including several barracks, a bakery, kitchen, laundry, mess hall, mortuary, chapel, administration buildings, residences for top officials of the home, a power house, its own dam, bandstand, theater, restaurant, social hall, amusement hall, and a street car depot to connect the inhabitants conveniently with downtown Danville. The icing on the cake was a beautiful Carnegie library, situated near the center of the complex. Each year, Congress appropriated $400,000 to maintain the home. Intended for veterans of the Civil War, the home included also some who fought in the Spanish-American war. During the first decades of the century, 2,243 veterans lived there, representing every state in the nation and every regiment in the Civil War.

Speaker Cannon, of course, cared most about that last statistic. The twenty-two hundred veterans represented guaranteed votes for the speaker. They owed their home to him, and he visited regularly. Indeed, according to stories passed down in Danville, at election time the veterans marched in delegations from the Soldiers' Home to the ballot box to vote en masse for the Republicans and receive a gift of whiskey. Anyone who opposed Cannon knew they must reckon with the votes of the old soldiers.[55] And, in fact, labor's fight against Cannon in 1906 stood little chance of succeeding for all the preceding reasons. Speaker

---

[55] *National Home for Disabled Volunteer Soldiers. Danville Branch* (souvenir pamphlet) (Danville: Frederick W. Studdiford, Member Home Company D, 1903), Vermilion County Historical Museum; Williams, *History of Vermilion County*, 483–6; *Photo Album of Old Soldiers' Home* (Illinois Historical Survey, University of Illinois); author's discussion with Richard Cannon, Fithian, Illinois, October 11, 1988. See also Judith Gladys Cetina, "A History of Veterans' Homes in the United States, 1811–1930," Ph.D. diss., Case Western Reserve University, 1977. The Danville Soldiers' Home still stands, and it is a remarkable sight. Today, the large complex serves as both a veterans' hospital and a community college. For a rich exploration of veterans and American politics, see Theda Skocpol, *Protecting Soldiers and Mothers: The Political Origins of Social Policy in the United States* (Cambridge: Harvard University Press, 1992).

Cannon won his reelection battle, and with a margin of victory virtually unchanged since the last off-year contest.[56]

Despite this outcome, the dynamics in his district made for a fascinating race. In July 1906, Danville workers created a labor party to nominate an independent candidate against Speaker of the House Cannon. Soon after that, when the Socialists nominated John Walker, the popular district president of the United Mine Workers, the labor party immediately dissolved and workers moved into full support of Walker's candidacy. Based on a broad labor coalition but led by the Socialist Party, a strong campaign began for John Walker. The Socialists of Illinois focused most of their attention and resources in 1906 on this race, and in Walker, they had a strong candidate. As the Socialist newspaper of Chicago expressed it, "He is a man well known and greatly admired by his thousands of friends among the miners. John can make a speech, too. Cannon will have to get up very early to beat our John as an orator." The strong support for Walker among trade unionists increased Socialist enthusiasm for the campaign: As their newspaper argued, it provided the opportunity "to present the Socialist argument to thousands of people who otherwise would not listen to it. . . ."[57]

By mid-October, the Socialist campaign was moving at full force. The party arranged speakers and campaign literature for the district and set up a rigorous speaking schedule for the candidate. At least six organizers worked in the district, and the national executive committee contributed resources as well. Organizers blanketed the district with literature; according to one activist, they distributed an average of 8,000 to 10,000 leaflets throughout the district during each week of the campaign. During the last two weeks before election day, the party covered billboards in Danville and nearby mining towns with "theater size" bills "proclaiming the socialist message," and pasted smaller posters on telegraph and lampposts. Last but not least, Socialist leader Mother Jones visited to campaign for Walker. She began with a rousing speech at Danville's public square on October 10 and then toured through the congressional district with Walker.[58]

The Socialist campaign for Walker occasionally emphasized radical themes, such as the leaflet that proclaimed "A VOTE FOR SOCIALISM is a declaration

---

[56] In 1906, Cannon's vote and his margin of victory were both almost identical to his returns in 1902. He received 22,941 votes in 1902 and 22,804 in 1906; Democratic candidates received 15,254 in 1902 and 12,777 in 1906, and Prohibition candidates received 1,177 and 1,897 votes, respectively. The Socialist Party did not exist in 1902, but in 1904, its candidate received 1,099 votes, and in 1906, Walker received 1,551 votes. Thus, no one seriously threatened Cannon's power in any of the early twentieth-century elections. See William Rea Gwinn, *Uncle Joe Cannon: Archfoe of Insurgency: A History of the Rise and Fall of Cannonism* (New York: Bookman Associates, 1957), 275–7.

[57] Chicago *Daily Socialist*, September 15, 1906, p. 1; "Socialist Party State Campaign," Chicago *Daily Socialist*, September 22, 1906, p. 1; "The Situation in the 18th District," Chicago *Daily Socialist*, October 13, 1906, p. 3.

[58] "The Situation in the 18th District," Chicago *Daily Socialist*, October 13, 1906, p. 3; "Walker vs. Cannon," Chicago *Daily Socialist*, October 27, 1906, p. 3.

for Industrial Liberty. Working Class Domination. The Full Product of Your Labor. End of all Exploitation." Another leaflet testified to the significance of the Soldiers' Home, addressing itself to "the old Soldiers" whom, it said, typically vote Republican to support the party of Lincoln. However, the Republican Party had changed, transformed into a representative of corporate privilege: ". . . while you old soldiers have gone forth in battle and freed the blacks, the capitalists of this country have enslaved both whites and blacks. . . . Old soldiers, several years ago a new revolutionary party has sprung up in the United States, a party whose mission is even grander than that of the old abolitionist party; a party that contemplates the emancipation of all mankind . . . the Socialist Party."[59]

Most of the time, however, the Socialist campaign downplayed radicalism to stress the same issues that ranked high in the AFL's Bill of Grievances. Walker, like other AFL strategists, focused his campaign on Joseph Cannon's record, and this led him to emphasize the response of Congress to AFL demands. A typical leaflet asked:

> Who Fought the Anti-Injunction bill?
> Who Fought to Let the Chinese In?
> Who Forced the Working People of this Country to Go Into Competition with 9¢ an hour Cheap Coolie Labor?
> Who Helped Annul the 8-Hour Law?
> Who Fought Every Request of the Working People to Congress?
> Who Spurned with Contempt the Representatives of Labor?
> WORKINGMEN
> Ask Joseph G. Cannon these questions, and then ask him how he can have the GALL to ask a workingman to vote for him.

Here was a leaflet that Gompers himself might have sponsored.[60]

This raises a question: Where were the AFL leaders amidst the busy commotion in Danville? Gompers and Morrison had planned a comprehensive campaign against "Uncle Joe," whom they considered their top congressional enemy. But once workers there began mobilizing behind a Socialist Party candidate, Federation leaders demonstrated profound ambivalence. Although the national leaders knew and liked Walker, they hesitated to become involved. Their main fear seemed to be not simply supporting a Socialist, though that was a part of it. But more importantly, as the treasurer of the AFL, John Lennon, put it: "for us to go in there and make the fight and have it turn out a fizzle, it seems to me would be worse than to keep our hands off."[61] The AFL did not think a Socialist could beat powerful Joe Cannon, especially when competing against a

---

[59] "To the Old Soldiers," political leaflet held in the Illinois State Historical Society Broadside Collection, Springfield, Illinois.

[60] These political campaign leaflets are held in the Illinois State Historical Society's Broadside Collection, Springfield.

[61] John Lennon to Gompers, August 6, 1906, *AFL Records*, reel 61.

Democratic candidate as well. So local labor fought the battle on its own, relying on door-to-door canvassing, rallies among the miners, talks at the railroad
shops, and political literature paid for by the Socialist Party.

Meanwhile, workers in the Danville area waited nervously to see what
Gompers would do, whether he would at least give verbal support to a Socialist
miner for Congress. They wrote, asking him to endorse Walker, to send organizers and speakers, and to come out himself. A leader of the typographers in
Danville wrote Gompers saying that some men would soon visit to get his
endorsement of Cannon's Democratic opponent: ". . . you can do organized labor
here no small favor by turning them down strong, should they reach you. The
Trades and Labor Council have unanimously endorsed John Walker, and not
one union man has uttered a word against him." Similarly the secretary of the
Labor Council reported to Gompers that every local union affiliated with the
AFL had welcomed the Walker campaign.[62] At first, Gompers refused to come,
or to send organizers, although when a trade unionist wrote asking whether he
should support the Socialist Walker, Gompers implied that he should do so.
Finally, in the last ten days of the campaign, the AFL significantly shifted its
position and decided to send in a "flying wedge" of six organizers to tour the
district and rally opposition to Cannon.[63] Thus by the end of the 1906 election
season, the AFL leaders had committed themselves to supporting a Socialist's
candidacy in one of the nation's most visible races. This suggests that, occasionally, pressure from local activists could exert a profound influence on the
national leaders.

Yet national leaders and their organizers could be problematic allies for local
activists. Although assistance from an AFL organizer greatly aided a campaign,
and local labor officials clamored for direct assistance, those same organizers
commonly controlled campaign decisions regardless of local workers' wishes.[64]
Tellingly, the districts where AFL leaders poured the most resources typically
suffered from little participation by local activists. Local workers perhaps felt
uninterested in tackling well-known congressmen who could not be beaten easily. However, the dominance of national AFL officials in these campaigns also
must have discouraged many workers from active involvement.

---

[62] T. K. Heath to Gompers, September 25, 1906; Reed to Gompers, October 1, 1906: both
   AFL Records, reel 62.
[63] Lennon to Gompers, August 17, 1906; Morrison to Gompers, August 23, 1906; William
   Taylor to Gompers, September 2, 1906; Gompers to Taylor, September 6, 1906; George
   Kuemmerle to Gompers, September 30, 1906; P. H. Strawhan to Gompers, October 7, 1906;
   Gompers to M. Grant Hamilton, October 8, 1906, Gompers Letterbooks; Morrison to Henry
   Walker, October 20, 1906, Morrison Letterbooks; G. W. Perkins to Gompers, October 30,
   1906; J. D. Pierce to Gompers, October 30 and 31, 1906; Morrison to Pierce, November 1,
   1906, Morrison Letterbooks. Except where noted otherwise, all *AFL Records*, reels 61–3.
   For a more detailed discussion of the Walker campaign, see Greene, "The Strike at the
   Ballot Box," chapter 5.
[64] William Mahon to Gompers, September 14, 1908; T. K. Heath to Gompers, September 25,
   1906; John Welty to Gompers, October 24, 1906: all *AFL Records*, reel 62.

Local activists succeeded in running their own campaigns only when one of two conditions prevailed. Where organized labor enjoyed great strength (such as New York City or Chicago) or when the AFL leaders felt relatively indifferent about a campaign's outcome (i.e., normally a "positive campaign" where labor fought for a trade unionist or a close ally of the labor movement), AFL national headquarters offered its services, but essentially left the important decisions to local people. One or both of these conditions existed in a great many cases, because the AFL leaders focused their resources and attention on six to eight crucial districts.

Political Conflict in the AFL

Although the majority of trade unionists greeted the AFL's campaign program with enthusiasm, the strategy generated diverse tensions and political quarrels at every level of the AFL hierarchy. These disagreements shed light on the barriers that prevented trade unionists from uniting and exercising influence in the political sphere. We previously saw that considerable differences separated local activists from their national leaders over what kinds of campaigns to run and whom to nominate for office. Disagreements also emerged over which issues mattered in the campaign, the degree of freedom allowed to local workers, which political party would best represent workers' interests, and even the future of labor politics in America. The new campaign program also heightened tensions within the AFL between Socialists and the pure and simple trade unionists who dominated Federation affairs. And ultimately, amidst these disagreements, AFL workers began to question their relationship to the party system: If nonpartisanship had failed, and if party alliances enslaved the working class, what path into the political arena would bring success?

The issues making up the AFL agenda in 1906 provided one lightning rod for disagreement. National leaders chose to focus on issues that grew out of their battle for federal legislation, but these often seemed like distant concerns to local activists. When a worker in Eureka, California, asked Gompers for literature discussing the issues relevant to his area, he received only a copy of the Bill of Grievances and a letter from Gompers saying the Federation would produce no literature regarding local issues. Local organizations, Gompers urged, must generate such documents themselves.[65] The AFL national leaders stressed the injunction and the eight-hour bill for government employees in their campaign activities. These were leading trade union concerns at the time, to be sure, but they poorly suited the day-to-day needs of workers across the United States. As such, they would not likely provide the basis for a grassroots social movement.

In fact, AFL workers faced a much richer spectrum of political issues from which to choose than that suggested by the Bill of Grievances. In September 1906,

[65] Gompers to W. H. Jewett, October 1, 1906, Gompers Letterbooks.

as the campaign began to heat up, the Birmingham, Alabama, *Labor Advocate* published prominently on its front page what it called the "AFL Program." This program shared little in common with the goals of Gompers or Furuseth. The Birmingham workers' agenda included an eight-hour law for *all* workers; the abolition of sweatshops; municipal ownership of streetcars, waterworks, and gas and electric plants; nationalization of telegraph, telephone, railroads and mines, and abolition of the monopoly system of landholding.[66] This agenda was nearly identical to the proposal made by Thomas Morgan and debated by AFL convention delegates back in 1894. Birmingham's trade unionists, mostly non-Socialists, still adhered to the vision of working-class collectivism represented by Morgan's program.

Across the country, as we saw in Chapter Three, trade unionists pursued political goals such as municipal ownership, improved city services, and tax reform. And during this same period, William Randolph Hearst began to enjoy his greatest political popularity among workers. He built his appeal on the broadest possible agenda, all of which, he said, added up to "Americanism." Hearst's Independence League spread into working-class communities across the country, stressing goals like regulation of trusts, public ownership of streetcars, popular election of senators, and the eight-hour day.[67]

Typically, local activists pushed these broader reform goals aside to focus on the goals itemized in the Bill of Grievances once they began participating in the AFL campaign program. Focusing their efforts on congressional campaigns, most unionists stressed the injunction and the eight-hour bill for government employees. Some independent labor movements created a more ambitious list of goals. The Central Federated Union of New York City, for example, called for municipal ownership of public utilities; abolition of the electoral college; direct election of president, vice-president, judges, and senators; and the initiative and referendum. More typical was the path chosen by Chicago activists: For decades, unionists there had pursued a broad range of social welfare goals, yet now in 1906 those activists participating in the AFL campaign program relied primarily on the Bill of Grievances for setting their agenda.[68]

Thus the AFL's campaign program tended to push labor activists into an unusually narrow arena of politics. Other problems existed with the AFL's choice of issues as well. Gompers and Morrison advised workers to decide their opinion of candidates by interrogating congressmen's records, especially in the most

[66] Birmingham *Labor Advocate*, September 15, 1906, "The AFL Program."

[67] See Greene, "The Strike at the Ballot Box"; and Birmingham *Labor Advocate*, September 15, 1906, "Hearst Named for Governor."

[68] Executive Committee, Central Federated Union, to the Members of Organized Labor of the City of New York, August 5, 1906, *AFL Records*, reel 61. For an example of a local movement virtually repeating the issues in the Bill of Grievances, see the United Labor Congress, Mahoning County, Ohio, to the Congressional Candidates of the 18th Congressional District, September 21, 1906, *AFL Records*, reel 62. For more on Chicago politics, see Greene, "The Strike at the Ballot Box," chapter 5.

recent session of Congress. This not only focused the campaign on incumbents, it also limited labor's strategy to measures Speaker Cannon allowed onto the main congressional floor.

In the 1905–6 session of Congress, Cannon and his allies so firmly controlled the House of Representatives that virtually no bills of interest to the AFL came up for a vote. Measures to reform injunction law or to enforce the eight-hour bill died in committee. Only one vote, AFL leaders believed, could measure whether a candidate deserved their support: The one exempting alien labor on the Panama Canal from the eight-hour law for government employees. It would be difficult to imagine an issue more poorly suited to serving as a central plank in labor's campaign. It placed the AFL in an extremely unpopular position. The Panama Canal touched a patriotic chord among Americans of all classes. Few native-born white Americans would support endangering the success of this engineering project because of the discomfort caused to unskilled and foreign-born laborers. A majority of congressmen had voted to exempt the canal from the eight-hour bill, and most Americans appeared to support them in this decision.[69]

Many AFL members found the Panama Canal a difficult issue on which to base their campaign work. Only an international union, however, openly opposed Gompers on this point. T. J. Dolan, the secretary-treasurer of the International Brotherhood of Steam Shovel and Dredge Men, perhaps the major union involved in constructing the canal, asked Gompers not to blacklist Congressman Boutell of Chicago because he voted to exempt alien labor. Dolan argued that the congressman had always supported the eight-hour day before. Furthermore, Dolan himself believed the canal should be exempted from the eight-hour law. His own union members constructing the canal either worked eight-hour days or received extra pay for overtime. According to them, ". . . it is utterly impossible to get any work out of Jamaica negroes which are furnished to do the laborious work down there. The U.S. is not in a position to furnish the common labor for that work. This I know to be a fact."

Yet Gompers refused to back down, ironically relying on racist language to defend workers of color: "Every dollar expended in that canal will be paid for by the American people and they have never yet shown themselves to be too niggardly to pay a fair American standard of wages." While standing up for foreign laborers, Gompers seemed more concerned about the impact on his own skilled American craftsmen: "if the alien laborers are compelled to work twelve, fourteen or more hours a day, . . . American workmen [cannot] limit their hours of daily labor to eight." Whether the Americans received overtime pay missed the point: "it is not for overtime that the Eight Hour Law was enacted, it was to secure a limit of the working day to eight hours. . . ."

[69] The vote on this measure was 146 in favor, 102 against, with 138 abstaining. See *The Congressional Record: The Proceedings and Debates of the Fifty-Ninth Congress, First Session, Also Special Session of the Senate*, Vol. 40 (Washington, DC: U.S. Government Printing Office, 1906), 1608.

Gompers rejected any notion that the congressman deserved the AFL's support, and he continued to urge defeat for anyone who voted to exempt the Canal from the eight-hour day. Congressman Boutell, Gompers stressed, "is no doubt 'quite friendly to labor,' just about this time, when he seeks the votes of the working people and the friends to labor in order to re-elect him." The Steam Shovel and Dredge Men's union continued to differ with Gompers. Soon thereafter, its leaders made Boutell an honorary member of the union and strongly supported his bid for reelection. A number of other congressmen argued strenuously to their working-class constituencies that the Canal Vote should not be seen as representative of their position on labor issues.[70]

The question of disciplining AFL members, or, as the national leaders referred to it, of "enforcing" the AFL program, emerged repeatedly during this campaign. Dissent and disagreement would grow into a more crippling issue by 1908, but the AFL leaders first developed their strategy for combatting it in 1906. Gompers and Morrison did not anticipate complete acceptance of their political strategy. As Gompers confided to a friend, ". . . we cannot expect to attain absolute discipline in every place. Not even the old political parties with their machinery and their unlimited funds and men are capable of doing that."[71] Nonetheless, the AFL leaders did attempt to carry as much of the labor movement behind them as possible. As Morrison put their strategy, "We will do everything we can to protect our programme before all conventions."[72]

In fact, the national leaders' response varied according to the source of dissent. With a high-ranking international official like Dolan of the Steam Shovel and Dredge Men, little could be done. More strenuous efforts could be chanced to win cooperation from central labor unions or local activists. Some locals rejected the entire AFL program on the grounds that unions should not mix politics with union affairs. And, in a few cases, workers argued that labor should not engage in politics except through a labor party. Establishing its own party, the Central Federated Union of New York declared in its manifesto: "There is room for all union men in this party, and there is no excuse for labor men accepting nominations from the old political party machines, who only use them as strike breakers." Similarly the secretary of the Ashland, Wisconsin, Central Labor Council complained that the AFL campaign program was built on the flimsy basis of candidates' personal promises: "Campaign promises are easily made and . . . quickly broken. Until Labor can put in the field and support a strictly Labor ticket we elect to engage in politics merely as individuals."[73]

---

[70] T. J. Dolan to Gompers, August 15, 1906, *AFL Records*, reel 61; Gompers to Dolan, August 20, 1906, *AFL Records*, reel 61; Dolan to Gompers, September 6, 1906, *AFL Records*, reel 62; Gompers to Dolan, October 6, 1906, Gompers Letterbooks; Dolan to Gompers, October 9, 1906, *AFL Records*, reel 63. For another example of workers finding the Panama issue to be unworkable, see E. M. Roszelli to Gompers, October 10, 1906, *AFL Records*, reel 63.

[71] Gompers to Edgar A. Perkins, August 4, 1906, *AFL Records*, reel 61.

[72] Morrison to Adam Menche, Kewanee, Illinois, September 27, 1906, Morrison Letterbooks.

[73] Central Federated Union of New York City to Members of Organized Labor, August 5, 1906; Grant Childs, secretary, Central Labor Council, Ashland, Wisconsin, to Gompers, August 24, 1906: both *AFL Records*, reel 61.

Socialists criticized the Federation program in harsher tones. Whereas many non-Socialist unionists applauded the AFL leaders for finally embarking on a more aggressive political program, Socialists rightly felt threatened and slighted. The narrow trade union demands included in the Bill of Grievances disgusted many radical workers, as did Gompers's flirting with the Democratic Party while he avoided the Socialists. One radical union interrogated Gompers about his recent political practices. When Debs ran for the presidency in 1900 and 1904, the union asked, "Did you, Mr. Gompers, work for . . . the election of this man? Or did you advise organized labor to scab at the ballot box and vote for the candidates of the parties from which you have for years been begging 'in vain.' "[74]

AFL national leaders acted aggressively in several cities to silence Socialist critics and prevent them from defeating the Federation's program. From August through October, organizers traveled out to battle with Socialists. Morrison, for example, congratulated an organizer in early September on "the throwdown of the Socialists in Pawtucket, Rhode Island." The campaign program may have even provided pure and simple leaders with the excuse to attack Socialists in local unions where their presence was strong. As Morrison noted, "It seems to me that the Socialists are being defeated in nearly all the Central Bodies where they had had a standing. They have been completely knocked out in St. Louis."[75]

The most extensive battle occurred over control of the Cleveland's United Trades and Labor Council and its organ, the Cleveland *Citizen*. Following orders from the AFL leadership, organizer Thomas Flynn began working in late August to ensure that a "trade unionist" (the leadership's common term for a non-Socialist AFL member) win election as delegate to the AFL convention from the Cleveland Labor Council. This required defeating, for the position the prominent Cleveland union activist Max Hayes, a typographer, Socialist, and longtime editor of the Cleveland Labor Council's official organ, the *Citizen*. By late September, the battle had escalated to one of control over the Cleveland Labor Council. Morrison alerted Flynn that the Socialists m··· . have been aware of his actions. "Not possible for a campaign to be carried along lines that you

---

[74] Robert Matteson et al. of the National Park Lodge, No. 168, in Livingston, Montana, to Gompers, May 15, 1906. For other examples of Socialist criticism of the strategy, see R. D. Mitchell, secretary, Phoenix Miners' Union, Western Federation of Miners Local No. 8, to Gompers, August 4, 1906; M. M. Gradeo, secretary, Tailors' Union No. 402, to Gompers, August 23, 1906; Garnett Riley, president, Minnesota District Union No. 11, Western Federation of Miners, to Gompers, August 11, 1906; F. Ludwig, secretary, Cigarmakers Local No. 10, Providence, Rhode Island, to Gompers, August 9, 1906; B. Weckstein, secretary, Bakery and Confectionery Workers No. 167, Newark, New Jersey, to Gompers, August 6, 1906; William Prince, secretary, Western Federation of Miners No. 44, Randsberg, CA, to Morrison, July 30, 1906; Cigarmakers Local No. 245, Ashland, Wisconsin, to Gompers, August 18, 1906; W. U. Ewing, Musicians' Protective Union No. 302, Haverhill, Massachusetts, to Gompers, August 16, 1906; all *AFL Records*, reel 61.

[75] Similar fights broke out between Socialists and pure and simple trade unionists in this period in Providence, Rhode Island; Kewanee, Illinois; and New Castle, Pennsylvania. See Morrison to William E. Terry, Providence, Rhode Island September 1, 1906; Morrison to Adam Menche, September 27, 1906; Morrison to Stuart Reid, October 20, 1906: all Morrison Letterbooks.

mention without it getting to their attention. You can gamble upon the fact that they . . . took as much action as they could to offset your efforts."

Those unionists in Cleveland allied with Gompers managed to pass resolutions ensuring their control over both the Labor Council and the *Citizen* (leading one Gompersite delegate to exult: "We've put the Socialists down and out. . . ."), but a second vote returned the Socialists to power. At the next meeting of the Labor Council, a bitter battle broke out between Socialists and Gompers's pure and simple allies. When some workers cheered on hearing Gompers's name, another delegate bitterly cried out: "All right, follow on if you want to become the tail to somebody's political kite." The Socialists certainly saw AFL organizer Flynn – and by extension, Samuel Gompers himself – as the cause of their troubles. The Cleveland *Citizen* noted bitterly: "Until Mr. Flynn arrived in Cleveland the labor movement was progressing on a high plane, but since the gentleman's advent secret meetings have been held, schemes concocted, enmities aroused and a generally bad feeling engendered that promises anything but good to the toilers who work and live here." Amidst such tensions, the AFL leaders decided to retreat. Ordering Flynn to leave Cleveland, Morrison noted that otherwise, workers there "may feel that the AFL is the directing force in this protest against the [domination] of the Socialists, which, of course, you know is not true."[76]

Enforcement, however, could work both ways. In fact, local workers often demanded that the AFL national leaders respect their prerogatives. The principle of "local autonomy" constituted more than a gift from national leaders: It was a precondition for workers' active involvement in the campaign program. Regularly, local activists wrote Gompers demanding that he not endorse anyone until they decided what to do, or upbraiding him for endorsing the wrong person. St. Louis workers wrote Gompers in September, for example, to say that the Democratic nominee against Congressman Richard Bartholdt was on his way to Washington to get Gompers's endorsement. They instructed Gompers not to give it, as they hoped to nominate a straight labor candidate.[77] We saw the same thing when Illinois workers told Gompers not to back the Democratic candidate, as they supported

---

[76] See Morrison to Thomas Flynn on these dates: August 27, 1906, September 29, 1906, and October 23, 1906; Morrison to Max Morris, October 12, 1906; Morrison to the AFL Executive Council, October 13 and 20, 1906; Morrison to James Duncan, October 24, 1906. For the AFL's battle against Socialists in New Castle, see Morrison to Stuart Reid, October 20 and 24, 1906. Morrison wrote Reid in the midst of his work in New Castle: "I am satisfied that you are now in your seventh heaven. A real fight with real Socialists, and victory perched on your banner in the first round. What I am looking for is the sequel – remember Cleveland." For all the preceding, see Morrison Letterbooks. The quote from the *Cleveland Citizen* appeared on October 20, 1906, but for a full report, see also the issues for October 13 and 27.

Occasionally, the AFL enforced its program before non-Socialist challengers. When Gompers saw an article in the *Washington Post* about Cincinnati workers opposing the eight-hour bill, he immediately instructed organizers to investigate as it would be of great use to the AFL's opponents. Gompers to Frank Rist, October 13, 1906, Gompers Letterbooks.

[77] Nat Eaton, first vice-president, International Association of Car Workers, St. Louis, to Gompers, September 21, 1906, *AFL Records*, reel 62.

Socialist John Walker. Similarly, when reports circulated that Gompers had endorsed the incumbent Congressman Buckman of St. Cloud, Minnesota, area trade unionists met en masse and endorsed him as well. The editor of the St. Cloud labor newspaper criticized the AFL leaders' endorsement, saying he could never vote for Buckman, that no union voter should, and Gompers must correct his error "if organized labor here wishes to hold the respect of the public at large." Morrison responded that they had not endorsed the congressman, and hoped, if conditions were as this unionist described them, that no labor man would.[78]

Just as the AFL's campaign program raised questions about the relationship between local and national leaders and the degree of freedom allowed to the former on political questions, so it also initiated debate about the meaning of party politics. Formally, this campaign strategy continued the nonpartisan focus emphasized by national leaders for more than a decade. The AFL leaders urged their members to escape party tyranny, ignore their party loyalties, and vote for the best man, whether Republican, Democrat, Socialist, or independent. Success depended on enfranchised workers taking their class consciousness into the ballot box while abandoning their partisan ties. Yet, by embarking on an electoral campaign, AFL leaders and members in effect began experimenting with their relationship to the party system. Unionists throughout the Federation hierarchy asked themselves: How could a class organization operate effectively within the party system? What sort of alliances would sustain their independence and manliness while affording political success? And how closely could the AFL move toward the existing parties without slipping into the abyss of partisanship?

When he took the Federation into politics, Gompers hoped to avoid partisan attachments. The times urgently required that the unions escalate their political activities, he argued, but labor must cautiously approach its new responsibilities: "We must remain in the middle of the road so far as the interests and principles of labor are concerned but every element should be used to further those interests and principles."[79] Yet in the context of America's political structure, partisanship constituted an integral part of that middle road.

Speculation flourished that with their campaign program, AFL workers had taken a first step toward a labor party. Many outside of the labor movement criticized the Federation for precisely this. As one newspaper editor said, ". . . it will not mend matters to turn the labor union into a political party." And socialist unionists such as Max Hayes saw in the program the beginning of a labor party similar to Great Britain's.[80]

---

[78] Charles Allen, editor and publisher of the St. Cloud (Minnesota) *Union Herald*, to Morrison, August 30, 1906; Morrison to Allen, September 6, 1906: both *AFL Records*, reel 62.

[79] Gompers to James H. Hatch, October 3, 1906, Gompers Letterbooks.

[80] Samuel Gompers, "The Solicitude of Our Friend – the Enemy," *AF*, 13 (8), August 1906, 536–8. William Dick, *Labor and Socialism in America: The Gompers Era* (Port Washington, NY: Kennikat Press, 1972), 123. For an example of Max Hayes's reaction to the AFL campaign program, see his column titled "World of Labor" in *International Socialist Review*, April 1906, 6 (10), p. 628.

Gompers and Morrison strenuously contested the idea that they had moved toward forming a labor party, and they repeatedly described their program as identical to that undertaken by British labor. In fact, by the summer of 1906, British unionists had gone beyond their Labor Representation Committee to create the Labour Party. Yet in a speech to New York City cigarmakers, Gompers hotly denied that a labor party existed in Britain. Similarly, Morrison also argued that the AFL had established the same policy as had the British Trades Union Congress: Both the AFL and the TUC, he said, had *centralized* their political activity – by forming a Labor Representation Committee that determined policy for the entire labor movement instead of letting each union create a separate approach.[81]

The Federation leaders stood between a rock and a hard place. They abhorred the idea of a labor party nearly as much as they despised Socialism: Both would dramatically lessen the power and control possessed by men like Gompers and Morrison, Furuseth, and Lennon. Yet in a system dominated by the parties, nonpartisanship provided no passport to political influence. Reconciliation with a major party, on the other hand, beckoned to AFL leaders and promised an end to their political stalemate.

We saw in Chapter Three that the NAM's success at forming a close relationship with conservative Republicans forced the AFL leaders to go beyond lobbying and think more carefully about how the major parties might be useful. Thus during 1906, although Federation leaders remained committed to nonpartisanship in their rhetoric, in fact they and unionists across the country moved closer to the Democratic Party. Most trade unionists who ran for Congress did so as Democrats; and AFL members most often supported Democratic congressmen for reelection. More importantly, during its campaigns in this year, the AFL began for the first time to share political strategy and finances with Democrats in some locations, establishing a precedent for a much stronger alliance that was soon to come. The Republican Party, meanwhile, became increasingly estranged from labor. Joseph Cannon's criticism of the AFL grew so shrill that President Roosevelt himself urged Cannon to stop attacking Gompers, as it would only alienate the public and win sympathy for labor's cause.[82]

These changes in AFL political policy confused and sometimes bewildered rank-and-file trade unionists. The secretary of the Arkansas State Federation of Labor expressed his perplexity to the AFL leaders in July 1906. While some of his members had begun mobilizing politically as Gompers suggested, there were problems: "it will be some time before the majority will understand the difference between partisanship and politics."[83] In Progressive America, the two were indeed difficult to disentangle.

---

[81] Samuel Gompers, "Talks on Labor: Trade Unions and Politics," *AF*, 13 (8), August 1906, 541–5; Morrison to J. D. Pierce, Chicago, September 13, 1906, Morrison Letterbooks.

[82] For Roosevelt's advice to Cannon, see the letter dated September 17, 1906, Joseph G. Cannon Papers, Illinois State Historical Society, Springfield. For more information on the AFL's evolving relationship to the Democratic Party, see chapter 6, below.

[83] L. H. Moore to Gompers, July 16, 1906, *AFL Records*, reel 61.

The vocabulary AFL members used to express their political opinions provides one indication of how deeply these issues resonated. The political perspectives of AFL workers were shaped profoundly by the legacy of republicanism, an ideology that placed great value on notions like independence, bravery, equality, and pride. Workers, according to this perspective, must carry themselves in the political sphere in a dignified way at all times and avoid actions that would make them appear servile or deferential.

AFL unionists linked these notions closely to qualities of manliness. Male workers had debated the "manly" or "unmanly" consequences of political strategies since before the AFL's founding. References to masculinity seemed especially common at times of political crisis. During the 1894 debate over Thomas Morgan's program, for example, one of its opponents declared: "I hope we are men enough, that we have manhood enough to settle the question here."[84]

In 1906 and again in 1908, the Federation's political debates repeatedly touched on issues of masculinity. The poem that most poignantly expressed the AFL's goals, entitled "The Strike at the Ballot Box," included the following stanza: "No matter where our fathers fought, Let us be men as they. . . ." Candidates like Milwaukee telegrapher William Cary commonly employed such concepts in their campaign literature. Arguing that trade unionists should be elected to Congress so labor would have friends "inside," a poster for Cary noted that "The real man should not have to stand on the outside with his hat in his hand and humbly knock at the door."[85] Conversely, Gompers's critics regularly chastised the campaign program for its unmanly characteristics. Montana Socialists felt disgusted by the Bill of Grievances and complained to Gompers, "As a specimen of the abject, servile, unmanly attitude to which honest workingmen can descend, it is a gem. From beginning to end there is not a single demand in it . . . there is nothing but the whine of the coward and the supplication of the slave to his master. . . . No one has any respect for a beggar."[86]

For AFL workers, manliness thus became not only central to their political culture, but a shorthand way to evoke other values a republican citizen should possess. Back in 1898, Gompers had justified the AFL's lobbying work: "Some say that we cringingly supplicate Congress for laws. This is positively untrue. On the contrary, we ask the members of Congress, in a plain, honest, manly fashion, to enact legislation in the interests of labor agreed upon at our conventions." A few years later, Gompers explicitly linked masculinity with republican citizenship: "Sturdy, virile manhood" was "essential to the maintenance and perpetuation of free institutions and a republican form of government." Nor

---

[84] American Federation of Labor, *A Verbatum Report of the Discussion on the Political Programme, At the Denver Convention of the American Federation of Labor, December 14, 15, 1894* (sic) (New York: The Freytag Press, 1895), 46.

[85] Russell R. Doty, "The Strike at the Ballot Box," *AF*, 15 (10), October 1908, 876; William Cary's campaign poster, July 1906, *AFL Records*, reel 61.

[86] Robert Matteson and other officials of the National Park Lodge No. 168 in Livingston, Montana, to Gompers, May 15, 1906, *AFL Records*, reel 61.

was Gompers the only unionist to make this connection. As an Indianapolis carpenter in 1908 described the meaning of the AFL's campaign program, "The trade union has stood these many years as a policeman, with club in hand, beating back the robber; but the robber has now got the Government at his back, and now the American workingman must use the weapon of a free man – the ballot – and through that weapon become master."[87]

Thus the questions facing AFL workers touched on more than politics. At stake was the proud independence of male trade unionists. Nonpartisanship seemed a failed strategy, but flirting with the party system risked working-class enslavement. In 1903, Gompers had railed against the Socialist Party by inquiring of trade unionists whether they desired to be the "tail to somebody's political kite." Now, in 1906, during the battle to control the Cleveland Central Labor Union, a trade unionist responded to cheers for Gompers by saying: "All right, follow on if you want to become the tail to somebody's political kite." Suddenly, under Gompers's leadership, even pure and simple politics seemed to threaten workers' independence.

As an effort to mobilize trade unionists on behalf of class-conscious political behavior, the AFL campaign program of 1906 achieved significant success. The national leaders ably used the resources of the AFL for political ends, turning the *American Federationist* into a propaganda tool and assigning their salaried organizers to political tasks. Trade unionists across the country acted energetically on the AFL program. Yet, as an effort to influence the makeup of Congress, the campaign's achievements remained limited. The AFL failed to defeat any of its top enemies in the Republican Party, such as Joseph Cannon or Charles Littlefield. But AFL members and leaders could celebrate the election of four trade unionists to Congress.

---

[87] Samuel Gompers, "Division and Defeat ... or Unity and Success?" *AF*, 5 (2), April 1898, 34–6; on labor republicanism and manliness generally as well as Gompers's quote in 1902, see R. Todd Laugen, "Racial Americanisms: Labor Anti-Imperialism, 1897–1902," unpublished manuscript; David Kennedy speaking in the Indianapolis *Union*, October 17, 1908, p. 1. For more on manliness, see Andrew Neather, "Popular Republicanism, Americanism, and The Roots of Anti-Communism, 1890–1925," Ph.D. diss., Duke University, 1993; Mary H. Blewett, "Manhood and the Market: The Politics of Gender and Class among the Textile Workers of Fall River, Massachusetts, 1870–1880," in Ava Baron, ed., *Work Engendered: Toward a New History of American Labor* (Ithaca, NY: Cornell University Press, 1991), 92–113; E. Anthony Rotundo, *American Manhood: Transformations in Masculinity from the Revolution to the Modern Era* (New York: Basic Books, 1993); Steven Maynard, "Rough Work and Rugged Men: The Social Construction of Masculinity in Working-Class History," *Labour/Le Travail*, 23, Spring 1989, 159–69; Gerda W. Ray, "From Cossack to Trooper: Manliness, Police Reform, and the State," *Journal of Social History*, 28 (3), Spring 1995, 565–86; Gail Bederman, *Manliness and Civilization: A Cultural History of Gender and Race in the United States, 1880–1917* (Chicago: University of Chicago Press, 1995). On race and concepts of slavery, see David Roediger, *The Wages of Whiteness: Race and the Making of the American Working Class* (London: Verso Press, 1991).

Historians such as Gary Fink, Michael Rogin, and Michael Kazin have argued that state and local leaders followed a different political agenda than did their national counterparts.[88] The character of the AFL's 1906 campaign reinforces their findings. Local and national leaders sharply diverged in the political choices they made. Their diverse activities suggest that political debate within the AFL was richer and more complex than a focus on divisions over socialism might indicate. Local labor leaders fought their campaigns less like a pressure group and more like a labor party. Theirs were more positive campaigns, and more often they supported trade unionist candidates for office.

Yet the AFL campaign program also involved a new activism by the national organization, carried out primarily by the AFL's paid organizers. The strategy brought national and local labor officials into direct contact, a new phenomenon for labor politics. This interaction was a complicated and often troubled one. One rarely sees direct evidence of local people criticizing the activities of AFL organizers in their town (as it is rare in general to see criticism of Gompers's machine, except by Socialist Party leaders). Yet the differing political approaches, combined with the greater resources and control held by the national representatives, often created tensions at the heart of the AFL political program. Although disagreements remained limited in 1906 by the AFL's principle of local autonomy, the national leaders inconsistently applied that principle. On several occasions, Gompers and Morrison felt compelled to enforce their program, particularly when they faced dissent from Socialists. All these problems would grow dramatically in 1908, when the Federation added to its political activities by participating in a presidential campaign.

---

[88] Gary M. Fink, *Labor's Search for Political Order: The Political Behavior of the Missouri Labor Movement, 1890–1940* (Columbia: University of Missouri Press, 1973), 161–82; Michael Rogin, "Voluntarism: The Political Functions of an Antipolitical Doctrine," *Industrial and Labor Relations Review* 15 (4), July 1962, 521–35; Michael Kazin, *Barons of Labor: The San Francisco Building Trades and Union Power in the Progressive Era* (Urbana: University of Illinois Press, 1983).

CHAPTER FIVE

Delivering the Labor Vote

In February 1908, the open-shop drive achieved its greatest victory when the U.S. Supreme Court declared, in *Loewe v. Lawlor*, that labor organizations could be prosecuted as trusts under the Sherman Act. On hearing of the decision, Samuel Gompers proclaimed: "the most grave and momentous crisis ever faced by the wage-workers of our country is now upon us. Our industrial rights have been shorn from us and our liberties are threatened."[1] Earlier events had demonstrated the open-shop activists' profitable political alliance with the Republican Party and especially its congressional leaders, but now *Loewe v. Lawlor* showed that the nation's highest court had enlisted in the antilabor campaign. Labor felt a noose tightening around its neck.

More than ever before, by 1908, trade unionists saw politics as providing the solution to their deepening crisis. Judicial harassment, they concluded, could be eliminated only by winning legislation that would exempt unions from the Sherman Act and limit injunctions, or that would allow citizens to elect federal judges. J. C. Skemp, secretary-treasurer of the Painters' Union, for example, argued that workers must proceed by electing their friends to state legislatures and to Congress: "We must sink all racial, religious, and political differences and stand shoulder to shoulder as one man. We must carry our unionism to the ballot box. Too long we have left it in the shop and on the job."[2]

Thus, the American Federation of Labor leaders escalated their political strategy again in 1908, fighting with renewed vigor and determination to elect their friends and defeat their enemies. At the heart of this new strategy stood a formal

---

[1] "Address to Workers," issued by the AFL's Conference of Protest, March 18, 1908, *American Federationist* (hereafter cited as *AF*), 15 (4), April 1908, 269.

[2] J. C. Skemp in "Amend the Sherman Anti-Trust Law – Labor Must Exercise its Political Power. A Symposium by Men of Affairs," *AF*, 15 (5), May 1908, 359–60. See also Owen Miller (secretary, American Federation of Musicians), Daniel Keefe (president, International Longshoremen, Marine, and Transportworkers' Association), George L. Berry (president, International Printing Pressmen's Union), *AF*, 15 (3), March 1908, 168, 178, and 172, respectively; J. H. Kaefer (Stove Mounters' International Union), and J. B. Grout (International Metal Polishers' Union), *AF*, 15 (5), May 1908, 360–1.

partnership between the AFL and the Democratic Party in support of William Jennings Bryan's presidential bid. The two organizations shared finances and consulted together to shape the substance and tactics of the campaign. As organized labor's most ambitious effort yet to influence the course of national politics, this alliance pushed the AFL into vastly different circumstances. The national limelight, the arena of presidential politics, and partisan loyalties all began to influence labor's political capabilities in ways Gompers scarcely could have anticipated.

At the same time, the AFL's political visibility in 1908 gave ordinary trade unionists a new means of influencing the major parties. Workers, their needs and interests, and the political role played by their dominant institutions all became leading issues in national politics during 1908, helping to recast partisan relationships and alliances along the way. The major parties, along with other influential players like William Randolph Hearst and the Socialists, competed amongst themselves to attract working-class voters. How did the AFL's new role affect the political process, the parties, the mechanics and discourse of their campaigns, and even the AFL itself? Those questions will concern this and the following chapter.

Partisan Culture and the Working Class

In 1893, James Bryce wrote in *The American Commonwealth* about the dominant role parties played in American political life, especially as compared to their counterparts in Europe. In the United States, he wrote, "party association and organization are to the organs of government almost what the motor nerves are to the muscles, sinews, and bones of the human body. They transmit the motive power, they determine the directions in which the organs act."[3] Fifteen years later, party politicians faced a more complex political environment. The nineteenth-century world of partisan politics faded after 1896 as closely contested elections, unwavering party loyalties, and campaign politics based on mass entertainment all declined. The party ruled over American politics during the Gilded Age, but by the Progressive era both party structures and traditions began to decompose in discernible ways. Citizen participation in electoral politics fell, while split-ticket voting and other measures of independent thinking soared. Factionalism divided the Republican Party and Democratic Party organizations during this period, as progressive and conservative wings battled for ascendancy. Last but not least, the parties faced challenges from new sectors as the presidency and independent state bureaucracies grew more influential and as organizations like the NAM and the AFL emerged to contest the parties' power. The presence of these and many other organizations on the political stage meant that

---

[3] James Bryce, *The American Commonwealth* (New York: Macmillan, 1920, originally 1893), 2:3.

a new level of political rivalry became influential, as groups jockeyed against each other and against the political parties for status and power.[4]

Yet, although no longer at the height of their power, the parties still dominated the body politic much as Bryce had written a decade before. At least three factors helped the partisan culture withstand its challengers. First, the new extra-party organizations, although often innovative and politically aggressive, lacked the parties' experience and range, particularly at electoral maneuvers. They needed the parties' resources to achieve political success. Similarly, the state bureaucracies remained nascent and vulnerable to party pressure throughout the Progressive era. Second, as Walter Dean Burnham has noted, the party system now "pivoted on a bifurcated, increasingly entrenched structure of one-party hegemony." The former Confederate states and some border areas remained loyally Democratic, whereas the Republicans dominated through much of the Northeast and Middle West, particularly in urban-industrial areas.[5] Third, although the parties could not stave off key political reforms during the Progressive era, they did control the shape those reforms assumed. When passing laws that shaped the electorate, or the ease with which alternative parties could compete electorally, the major parties managed to lose little. Even as the electorate shrank in size and as the major parties grew less attractive to Americans, alternatives to those parties (independent and Socialist parties) were ironically being closed down.[6] These factors sustained the structure and culture of the party system and made the AFL's nonpartisanship increasingly untenable.

Because the major parties became vulnerable to attack during these years and began losing many of their traditional supporters, they scrambled to reinvent themselves and adapt to changing political circumstances. Elites in both parties cast an eye across American society, searching for allies, and both groups trained

---

[4] The best introduction to these changes in American politics is Walter Dean Burnham, "The System of 1896: An Analysis," in Paul Kleppner et al., eds., *The Evolution of American Electoral Systems* (Westport, CT: Greenwood Press, 1981), 147–202. See also Samuel Hays, "Political Parties and the Community-Society Continuum," in William N. Chambers and Walter Dean Burnham, eds., *The American Party Systems: Stages in Political Development*, 2nd ed. (New York: Oxford University Press, 1979), 152–81; Michael McGerr, *The Decline of Popular Politics: The American North, 1865–1928* (Oxford and New York, 1986); Richard McCormick, *From Realignment to Reform: Political Change in New York State, 1893–1910* (Ithaca, NY: Cornell University Press, 1981); and *idem, The Party Period and Public Policy: American Politics from the Age of Jackson to the Progressive Era* (New York: Oxford University Press, 1986). For a useful analysis of Progressive era political historiography, see Daniel Rodgers, "In Search of Progressivism," *Reviews in American History*, 10 (4), December 1982, 113–32.

[5] See Burnham, "System of 1896," 181.

[6] On changes in election laws and their impact, see Peter H. Argersinger, "'A Place on the Ballot': Fusion Politics and Antifusion Laws," *American Historical Review*, 85, 1980, 287–306; Paul Kleppner and Stephen C. Baker, "The Impact of Voter Registration Requirements on Electoral Turnout, 1900–16," *Journal of Political and Military Sociology*, 8, 1980, 205–26; and Charles Edward Merriam and Louise Overacker, *Primary Elections* (Chicago: University of Chicago Press, 1928).

their sight carefully on those American workers who could vote. Two factors complicated the parties' effort to court workers' support. First, both the Democrats and Republicans needed to decide *which* workers they wished to recruit, and in particular whether they would appeal to workers en masse, or, working through the leaders of organized labor, to American trade unionists. Second, both parties sought not to alienate employers, and factions within each party remained hostile to labor and its demands.

Historically, the Democratic Party stood for local autonomy, a weak central government, and a commitment to individual liberty. As David Sarasohn recently demonstrated, however, from 1896 onwards the party remade itself into the major representative of reform in America, rejected its old affection for laissez-faire policies, and accepted the need for governmental activism.[7] In 1896, the Democratic Party split apart as conservative Cleveland Democrats and businessmen jumped ship while William Jennings Bryan built a reformist campaign around the issue of free silver. Party leaders spent the next decade locked in a struggle for control. In 1904, eastern conservatives regained dominance over the party, but failed to elect their presidential candidate, Alton Parker. Although Roosevelt campaigned in that year as the enemy of the trusts, the Democrats' conservative gold standard candidate still could not win significant business support. After the 1904 returns came in, Bryan and his supporters returned to power within the party. By 1906, Democratic unity was increasing around a program that firmly embraced reform and governmental activism.

Bryan himself was a complex personality. A charismatic demigod to thousands of adoring Americans, to his many opponents (particularly easterners), he was no more than a Prairie buffoon, a hick lacking proper manners. One Lincoln woman described him decades later to her daughter as "simply the most handsome man I ever saw. He was spellbinding." Teddy Roosevelt, on the other hand, felt that although Bryan was "a kindly, well-meaning man, he is both shallow and a demagogue."[8] Yet whatever his personal strengths or weaknesses, Bryan dominated the Democrats in the period after 1896, shaping the party into a reform organization capable of winning the White House. The turning point in the Democrats' long struggle toward political success appears now to have been the years around 1906 and 1908. Despite continued defeats in those years, the Democrats began to gain in popularity and momentum, gradually building up a wave of support that would finally bring victory in 1912.[9]

[7] David Sarasohn, *The Party of Reform: Democrats in the Progressive Era* (Jackson: University Press of Mississippi, 1989). See also Robert Cherny, "The Democratic Party in the Era of William Jennings Bryan," in Peter B. Kovler, ed., *Democrats and the American Idea: A Bicentennial Appraisal* (Washington, DC: Center for National Policy Press, 1992), 171–201.

[8] Interview with Helen K. Greene, regarding her mother's descriptions of Bryan, February 22, 1994; Theodore Roosevelt to Elihu Root, September 4, 1906, in Elting E. Morison, ed., *The Letters of Theodore Roosevelt*, Vol. 5 (Cambridge: Harvard University Press, 1952).

[9] On 1906 as a turning point in the Democrats' fortunes, see Sarasohn, *Party of Reform*, 26–7; and Samuel P. Hays, "The Social Analysis of American Political History," *Political Science Quarterly*, 80 (3), September 1965, 386.

Historians have often portrayed Bryan as indifferent to political victory, stressing that to him principles mattered more than success. Yet, although he certainly opposed the crude opportunism resorted to by many politicians, some contemporaries saw another side of Bryan. Teaching Sunday school in Normal, Nebraska, in 1907, Bryan announced one day that the topic of discussion would be "Success." One clever little boy, "thinking of Mr. Bryan's having twice run in vain for the Presidency of the United States" proposed that "one's success should be judged by the effort put forth." But Bryan sharply corrected the boy, declaring that the only measure of success lay in achieving one's goal.[10] Although Bryan never occupied the White House, he did win his larger ambition: He defeated the conservatives in his party and remade the Democratic Party into a vehicle for reform.

Bryan's political philosophy evolved during the early Progressive era to embrace a broad range of reforms. Immediately after the 1904 campaign, Bryan wrote that Democrats must abandon their laissez-faire philosophy and accept the need for a stronger and more activist federal government. A year and a half later, returning from an extended trip abroad that enhanced his reputation at home, Bryan spelled out his intentions in a riveting speech: "Plutocracy is abhorrent to a republic. . . . The time is ripe for the overthrow of this giant wrong." Stressing the "Jeffersonian doctrine of equal rights to all and special privileges to none," Bryan called for the elimination of monopolies, direct election of senators, an income tax, injunction reform, and, most provocatively, government ownership of all railroads. Here was a program that could generate enthusiasm among American workers, one bearing great similarity to the proposals made by Hearst's Independence League at this time.[11]

Yet on hearing of this program, moderate Democrats throughout the country excoriated Bryan for what they considered his bow toward socialism. One New York publisher wrote in dismay, "I have been flattering Bryan – to help shut off the Hearst boom – and I have indulged in hopes that he would develop into a real leader. But that railroad program simply stuns me. I believe it will land Bryan again in the ditch, and it should land him there before our convention." Joseph Pulitzer's *New York World*, a leading voice among Democrats, expressed its disgust more openly: "Within six hours after he had landed at the Battery he had split his party wide open again. That was indeed peerless

---

[10] Theodore A. Kiesselbach, "What's In a Life?" unpublished autobiographical manuscript. The view that Bryan cared little for success originally came from the memoirs of Arthur W. Dunn, *From Harrison to Harding: A Personal Narrative, Covering a Third of a Century, 1888–1921* (New York: G. P. Putnam's Sons, 1922), 2:47–9. Dunn quotes the Nebraskan as responding, when a politician criticized him for choosing "impossible" issues that would meet with defeat: "Win! Win! That's it! You want to win! You would sacrifice principle for success. I would not."

[11] Bryan's 1904 statement supporting a more active central government is discussed in Paolo E. Coletta, *William Jennings Bryan*, Vol. 1, *Political Evangelist, 1860–1908* (Lincoln: University of Nebraska Press, 1964), 353; Bryan's 1906 speech is published in *The Commoner*, September 7, 1906.

leadership."[12] Although Bryan dropped government ownership from his program to soothe the worries of moderate Democrats, which undoubtedly weakened his appeal among workers, many easterners remained hostile toward him and conservative party papers like the *New York Times* refused to support his nomination. Thus, while the Democrats demonstrated unusual unity as the 1908 campaign approached, some critics refused to climb on Bryan's wagon. Not until Woodrow Wilson emerged four years later did a complete reconciliation between the Cleveland and Bryan wings take place.[13]

Bryan's leadership elevated a select group of men to leading positions within the Democratic Party. The most important player was Charles W. Bryan, who lacked his older brother's charm but perhaps outdid him in political sagacity. Charles ran the Bryan machine back in Nebraska, put out the *Commoner*, and advised his brother on all political matters.[14] After Charles, William Bryan counted newspapermen among his closest allies. Josephus Daniels of North Carolina had been a strong "Bryan man" since 1896, and in 1908 would head the party's Publicity Bureau. Louis F. Post, a single taxer, municipal ownership activist, and publisher of Chicago's *Public*, anchored Bryan on his left. Bryan declared to Post during this period that "I count you among the soundest as well as among the most discreet of my political advisors...."[15] And though their relationship could easily grow cold, Bryan also looked to Henry Watterson of the *Louisville Courier-Journal* for advice on political matters. Watterson, a leader of the Gold Democrats who bolted the party in 1896, spoke with a more influential voice than most other Democrats. As a moderate, his support for Bryan counted a great deal. Bryan knew the power of Watterson's editorial commentary, telling him once that "You are in a position to answer those New York fellows as none of the rest of our papers can." Accordingly, Bryan sought Watterson's advice on most key decisions, including his choice for vice-president and for National Chairman of the party.[16]

Under Bryan's leadership, the Democratic Party shaped itself, as Sarasohn has noted, into a coalition of outsiders: southerners, westerners, farmers, immigrants,

---

[12] G. H. Benedict to Alton Parker, September 1, 1906, Alton Parker Papers, Library of Congress Manuscripts Division; the *World* is quoted in Sarasohn, *Party of Reform*, 23.

[13] Unlike the *New York Times*, many newspapers that had previously opposed Bryan now supported his candidacy: These included, for example, the *New York Staats Zeitung*, the *Buffalo Courier*, the *Boston Globe*, and the *Charleston News and Courier*. See *The Commoner*, July 24, 1908. Yet reformist magazines like *The World's Work*, which had been boosting Bryan, soured on him after this speech and ultimately supported Taft for the presidency in 1908. Compare the magazine's position immediately before and after Bryan's speech by consulting "The March of Events," *The World's Work*, 12 (4), August 1906, and 12 (6), October 1906.

[14] On Charles Bryan, see Larry G. Osnes, "Charles W. Bryan, 'His Brother's Keeper'," *Nebraska History*, 48 (1), Spring 1967, 45–67.

[15] Bryan to Post, November 12, 1904, Louis F. Post Papers, Library of Congress, Manuscripts Division.

[16] For a view of their relationship, see Bryan to Henry Watterson, May 26, June 5, and June 23, 1908, Henry Watterson Papers, Library of Congress, Manuscripts Division.

and, Bryan hoped, workers. Having alienated most businessmen, the Democrats had no choice but to build a program of reform that would appeal to enfranchised workers on the farms and in the factories. And that is precisely what they did. The South, where the legacy of populism and the absence of powerful corporations produced strong support for reform, provided the party's greatest strength. Yet Southern progressivism was limited to whites: Regional leaders like Josephus Daniels, the influential publisher of the *Raleigh* (N.C.) *News and Observer*, combined a reform spirit with fierce racism. The "Jim Crow Progressivism" practiced by southern Democrats alienated many northerners, but the approach was certainly not limited to the South. William Jennings Bryan's racial outlook, according to historian William Smith, would have been acceptable to any southern segregationist; as party leader, the views of "The Peerless One" reinforced and propagated the Democracy's racism.[17]

If the party's current strength lay with farmers and white southerners, its future potential rested in the votes of American workers. Since the debacle of 1896, Bryan had become enamored of a singular dream: Democratic victory would be achieved through a political marriage of workers and farmers. That year, the party won farmers' support but failed to convince northern workers of its virtues. Without strong support from the working class, Democrats would possess little foothold in the country's industrial centers because business so firmly opposed them.[18] Bryan dutifully supported organized labor's goals beginning with his first race against McKinley, but his own penchant to build single-issue campaigns limited his appeal among workers. In 1896, for example, he preached for silver incessantly – even though the Democratic platform included other issues that might appeal more successfully to working-class voters nervous

[17]   See Sarasohn, *Party of Reform*, 20 and *passim*; William H. Smith, "William Jennings Bryan and Racism," *Journal of Negro History*, 54 (2), April 1969: 127–49; Jack T. Kirby, *Darkness at the Dawning: Race and Reform in the Progressive South* (Philadelphia: Lippincott, 1972); Arthur S. Link, "The Progressive Movement in the South, 1870–1914," *North Carolina Historical Review*, 23, October 1946, 483–94; Dewey Grantham, *The Democratic South* (New York: W. W. Norton, 1965); and *idem, Southern Progressivism: The Reconciliation of Progress and Tradition* (Knoxville: University of Tennessee Press, 1983). Similarly to Sarasohn's image of Democrats as "outsiders," some scholars see the party as representing America's "periphery" in opposition to the Republican-dominated "metropole." See, for example, Elizabeth Sanders, "Farmers, Workers, and State Expansion in the Progressive Era," CSSC, *The Working Papers Series*, 72, July 1988; and Paul Kleppner, *Continuity and Change in Electoral Politics, 1893–1928* (Westport, CT: Greenwood Press, 1987).

The links between the Democratic Party and populism extended well beyond the South. In 1904, for example, Bryan received reports that he should not visit New York to campaign for Parker, because all the Bryan men were supporting the *Populist* ticket instead of the Democratic. See Durbin Van Vleck to Bryan, August 25, 1904, William Jennings Bryan Papers, Library of Congress, Manuscripts Division.

[18]   Sarasohn, *Party of Reform*; also on the Democratic Party's evolution during this period, see J. Rogers Hollingsworth, *The Whirligig of Politics: The Democracy of Cleveland and Bryan* (Chicago: University of Chicago Press, 1963); on business support for the Republicans, see Herbert Croly, *Marcus Alonzo Hanna: His Life and Work* (New York: Macmillan, 1912).

about inflation. In 1900, Bryan's campaign focused on imperialism: again, an issue that at best failed to address workers' problems, and at worst alienated workingmen influenced by the nationalism and jingoism of the day.

Other barriers also loomed over the Democracy's project to recruit workers behind the party's banner. Workers' race, ethnicity, and religion, and the region or city in which they lived all shaped their political preferences. Since the 1896 contest between Bryan and McKinley, the Republican Party had strengthened its hold over the industrialized sections of the North and Middle West, whereas the Democrats gained in the South. Nonsouthern urban workers had provided the Republicans with important gains. Yet in many northern cities, Democratic machines continued to claim workers' loyalties, and throughout the region many workers, particularly recent immigrants and workers of German or Irish descent, remained tied to the Democrats. Protestant workers born to native-born parents were most likely to vote Republican.[19]

Even for those workers inclined to favor the Democrats, the party's history included several troubling episodes. The worst depression in history up to that time began in 1893 under Democratic President Cleveland, and voters possess exceptionally long memories when it comes to an economic crisis. In 1894, Cleveland deployed an injunction and federal troops to break the Pullman boycott. Furthermore, the rural and southern roots of the Democratic Party repelled many workers. Although the populist movement appealed to some industrial workers, aspects of the farmers' movement – such as the cry for silver – failed to excite many others. Building unity between farmers and workers would require gradual change and work at the grassroots level. Some workers likewise resented the visible role southerners played within the Democratic Party because of the region's harsh treatment of workers and unions, and, in some cases, because of its racist caste structure.[20]

Furthermore, enfranchised workers inhabited a complex political universe by 1908, one in which diverse groups competed for their support. Many trade unionists, following decades of advice from pure and simple leaders, disdained party politics. Left-wing syndicalists argued that workers should reject politics altogether, and after 1905, this position found new strength in the Industrial Workers of the World, most of whose leaders embraced an antipolitical syndicalism. Though strongest organizationally among unskilled workers like northwestern lumbermen, the IWW's ideas appealed to many more workers than those it counted as

[19] See Burnham, "System of 1896."

[20] On labor and populism, see Lawrence Goodwyn, *The Populist Moment: A Short History of the Agrarian Revolt in America* (New York: Oxford University Press, 1978); and Charles McArthur Destler, *American Radicalism, 1865–1900* (Chicago: Quadrangle Books, 1966); on labor and the Democratic Party, see Gwendolyn Mink, *Old Labor and New Immigrants in American Political Development: Union, Party, and State, 1875–1920* (Ithaca, NY: Cornell University Press, 1986); on Cleveland's administration and the Pullman boycott consult Hollingsworth, *Whirligig of Politics*, and Nick Salvatore, *Eugene V. Debs: Citizen and Socialist* (Urbana: University of Illinois Press, 1982).

members, especially in the West.[21] The Socialist Party of America, on the other hand, embraced political struggle as an important route to power for the working class. For many years, Gompers had used nonpartisanism and his concept of "party slavery" to attack the Socialists. Now that trade unionists appeared ready to jettison their nonpartisan principles, radicals within the AFL insisted vociferously that only *one* party, the Socialist, deserved workers' loyalties. Once again running Eugene Debs for the presidency but also innumerable candidates at the state and municipal levels, the Socialists would make a mighty appeal for working-class support. Debs was never a more effective speaker than in 1908 and, as Nick Salvatore has noted, his speeches "crystallized opposition to corporate capitalism and legitimized for untold numbers of Americans their individual anger that grew out of their daily work experiences."[22]

William Randolph Hearst further complicated the political decisions facing American workers in 1908. Since 1902, the charismatic publisher had worked to build an organization, the Independence League, that appealed especially to workingpeople. Hearst possessed important resources: an influential chain of newspapers across the country, his own personal ambition for political success, and an approach to social reform that attracted many workers. Hearst's papers celebrated issues like regulation of trusts; public ownership of streetcars, railroads, and mines; a graduated income tax; popular election of senators, and the eight-hour day for all wage-earning workers. In 1906, Hearst won the Democratic nomination for governor of New York. His campaign spoke directly to the needs of workers and generated great enthusiasm among the lower classes. William Jennings Bryan hailed his campaign, whereas President Roosevelt, horrified at the thought of a Governor Hearst, mobilized against him.[23]

Hearst lost narrowly in 1906, blaming his defeat on the lackluster support given him by New York's Democratic machine. Feeling betrayed, the publisher began openly opposing the major parties – and especially the Democrats. While declining in popularity, his Independence League continued trying to recruit working-class support for its nominees. In 1908 its campaign focused on attacking traditional party politics, especially as embodied in the Democratic Party. In July, Hearst reported that Gompers had asked him to support Bryan and the Democrats in the name of patriotism. Hearst published his curt refusal: "I do not think the path of patriotism lies in supporting a discredited and decadent old party, which has neither conscientious conviction nor honest intention, nor endorsing chameleon candidates who change the color of their political opinions

---

[21] See Melvyn Dubofsky, *We Shall Be All: A History of the Industrial Workers of the World* (New York: Quadrangle Books, 1969), 138–41.

[22] Salvatore, *Eugene V. Debs*, 224; see also Charles Lapworth, "The Tour of the Red Special," *International Socialist Review*, 9 (6), December 1908, 401–15.

[23] Roosevelt described Hearst to a friend as "the most potent single influence for evil we have in our life." See Theodore Roosevelt to John Strachey, October 25, 1906, Elting E. Morison, ed., *The Letters of Theodore Roosevelt*, Vol. 5 (Cambridge: Harvard University Press, 1952). For Bryan's view, see *The Commoner*, November 16, 1906.

with every varying hue of opportunism." While in power, Hearst charged, the Democrats "did more to injure labor than all the injunctions ever issued before or since. I have lost faith in the emphatic protestations of an unregenerate democracy."[24] Because of Hearst's popularity among American workers, his hostility seriously threatened Democratic hopes of attracting working-class votes.

The Republican Party also suffered from factionalism in this period, torn between a progressive and a conservative wing. The difference, as Woodrow Wilson would quip a few years later, was that "in the Republican party the reactionaries are in the majority, whereas in the Democratic party they are in the minority."[25] The dominant position occupied by conservative leaders palpably heightened the tensions between Republican workers and their party at a time when organized labor was growing more politically aggressive. This pushed reformist Republicans to try a double-fisted strategy, reining in their antilabor colleagues while seeking to assuage Republican workers' worries. On neither score did the Republicans enjoy significant success.

Theodore Roosevelt typifies the dilemmas faced by progressive Republicans. To many workers, Roosevelt stood as a hopeful beacon of reform. The 1902 anthracite strike, in which Roosevelt threatened that federal troops would take over the mines if coal operators did not agree to arbitration, enhanced his popularity among workers. His support for limitations on injunctions and for restrictions on immigration likewise heartened many trade unionists. In 1904, Roosevelt wrote privately that "We must not only do justice, but be able to show the wage workers that we are doing justice."[26] Yet the president's record on labor was far from unblemished. He sanctioned the use of armed force against striking silver miners in the West, and in 1903, his stand in a union dispute at the Government Printing Office led the NAM to proclaim him "the father of the open shop drive."[27] These incidents provided just one sign of the deep ties between the Republican Party and business, ties that since 1896 had been the key to the party's power. After Roosevelt, the party's leaders all came from its conservative wing. Senator Nelson Aldrich and Congressman Joseph Cannon, the leaders of the Senate and House of Representatives, respectively, valued their friendly relationship with the National Association of Manufacturers. Roosevelt's

---

[24] Gompers denied having asked Hearst to support the Democrats. See *The Commoner*, July 24, 1908; Gompers, "Mr. Hearst's Political Toy," *AF*, 15 (9), September 1908, 734–6.

[25] Cited in Sarasohn, *Party of Reform*, xi.

[26] George Mowry, *The Era of Theodore Roosevelt, 1900–1912* (New York: Harper, 1958), 141–2; *idem, Theodore Roosevelt and the Progressive Movement* (New York: Hill and Wang, 1946), 18–19; Horace Samuel Merrill and Helen Galbraith Merrill, *The Republican Command, 1897–1913* (Lexington: University Press of Kentucky, 1971), 270; "From the President's Message," *AF*, 15 (1), January 1908, 36–8.

[27] See Foner, *History of the Labor Movement in the United States*, Vol. 3: *The Policies and Practices of the American Federation of Labor, 1900–1909* (New York: International, 1964), 51; A. M. Simons, "Crisis in the Trade Unions," *International Socialist Review*, 4 (4), October 1903, 238–42; and Max Hayes, "The World of Labor," *International Socialist Review*, 5 (2), August 1905, 111–14.

chosen successor in 1908, William H. Taft, possessed few of his mentor's sympathies toward labor. To the contrary, Taft was known in labor circles as the "Injunction Judge" for the precedent-setting injunction he issued in 1893.[28]

Roosevelt felt deeply shaken by labor's opposition to Republican candidates in 1906. He wrote repeatedly to friends about his concern over American workers' new political activism, and he believed the congressional leaders' treatment of the AFL had been unwise: "It is a bad business to solidify labor against us." During the 1906 campaigns, he demanded that conservatives within his party curtail their attacks on labor, telling Speaker Cannon, for example, "I want very much that our people shall quit attacking Gompers," because it could only unite workingmen against the Republican Party.[29] Yet when conservatives like Cannon and Sherman began fighting labor and forced Roosevelt to choose between his prolabor principles and stalwart party loyalty, the president sided easily with the latter. Letters he wrote for public distribution called firmly for reelection of all Republicans, including prominent antilabor conservatives like Cannon: "This administration has had no stouter friend than the Speaker of the House . . . it is a simple absurdity to portray him as an enemy of labor."[30] During the 1908 campaign, Roosevelt would follow much the same strategy: He pushed the party to make concessions to labor, but when defeated by conservatives closely linked to the NAM, he closed ranks and attacked labor and its demands for all he was worth.

The Birth of Labor's Democracy

In these years, the defeats unionists suffered at the hands of hostile employers continued to mount. Open-shop businessmen united to eliminate unionism in industries like steel, electrical machinery, and meatpacking. Acting on their own,

[28] Merrill and Merrill, *Republican Command*, 244 and 272; Nathaniel Stephenson, *Nelson W. Aldrich* (Port Washington, NY: Kennikat Press, 1971); Mowry, *Era of Theodore Roosevelt*, 235; White Busbey, *Uncle Joe Cannon. The Story of a Pioneer American* (New York: Henry Holt, 1927); William Rea Gwinn, *Uncle Joe Cannon, Archfoe of Insurgency: A History of the Rise and Fall of Cannonism* (New York: Bookman Associates, 1957); James Holt, *Congressional Insurgents and the Party System, 1909–1916* (Cambridge: Harvard University Press, 1967). On Aldrich's ties with the NAM, see Marshall Cushing to Aldrich, October 5, 1904, U.S. Senate, *Maintenance of a Lobby to Influence Legislation: Hearings Before a Subcommittee of the Committee on the Judiciary* (hereafter cited as *Maintenance*), 63rd Congress, 1st Session, 1913, Vol. 1 appendix, p. 1, p. 421; and testimony of Martin Mulhall, *Maintenance*, 3:2478. On Judge Taft's 1893 injunction, see Felix Frankfurter and Nathan Greene, *The Labor Injunction* (New York: Macmillan, 1930), 6–7.

[29] Roosevelt to James Wilson, September 11, 1906; Roosevelt to Henry Cabot Lodge, October 2, 1906; Roosevelt to Cannon, September 17, 1906: all in Morison, *Letters of Theodore Roosevelt*, Vol. 5.

[30] Privately, Roosevelt described with some glee his plans to make a partisan appeal: "I shall convulse the goo-goos and the mug-wumps with horror by . . . making as strong a plea as I know how for the election of a Republican Congress. It will be done, of course, on the most excellent nonpartisan grounds." Roosevelt to Henry Cabot Lodge, August 9, 1906; and Roosevelt to Edgar E. Clark, September 5, 1906: in Morison, *Letters of Theodore Roosevelt*, Vol. 5.

the great trusts also took action to eradicate the unions and these forces together halted the growth of trade unionism. Until 1911, AFL membership remained lower than the high point reached in 1904, before the employers' activism had begun to hinder labor organizing. Even when growth returned in 1911, the proportion of the work force represented by the AFL continued to decline. Coal mining and construction grew in importance within the AFL during these years. By 1910, with the singular exception of the Bridge and Structural Ironworkers, the trustified industries had all eliminated unionism.[31]

Adding to workers' troubles, the American economy underwent a brief but severe depression during late 1907 and early 1908. The depression resulted from a financial panic precipitated in late October 1907, when the Knickerbocker Trust Company shut down to prevent a run on the bank. Americans felt the depression's impact primarily during the first half of 1908, and especially in basic industry: Iron production during the first six months of 1908, for example, fell by 50 percent. Workers suffered the worst consequences of the downturn: Unemployment increased by at least 5 percent and wages fell both in real and monetary terms. Industrial production declined by nearly 16 percent during 1907 and 1908. Although conditions began to improve by mid summer of 1908, the 1907 panic adversely affected business until the European war began to strengthen the economy in 1915.[32]

Together, these circumstances depleted union treasuries and left labor activists with a sullen outlook. So far, and much to the chagrin of AFL leaders, years of lobbying and the electoral mobilizations of 1906 had done nothing to relieve their political problems. Judges continued to hand down injunctions and prosecute trade unions under the Sherman Anti-Trust Act as they had for decades. Now in early 1908, labor's legal problems crescendoed to a climax in two cases, each of them instigated and prosecuted by leaders of the open-shop drive. These cases demonstrated to trade unionists not only the influence of anti-union employers, but also the assistance given them by Republican Party leaders.

The first case pitted AFL leaders against James Van Cleave, president of the National Association of Manufacturers. In 1906, the AFL placed Buck's Stove and Range Company, owned by Van Cleave, on its list of boycotted companies. The Metal Polishers' Union, then striking against the firm, had asked AFL leaders to do this. In response, Van Cleave successfully requested an injunction prohibiting the AFL and its Executive Council from conspiring to boycott. Hoping to test the constitutional issues involved in the labor injunction (and

[31] Philip Taft, *The AFL in the Time of Gompers* (New York: Harper, 1957), 233; Helen Marot, *American Labor Unions* (New York: Henry Holt, 1914); Lewis Lorwin, *The American Federation of Labor: History, Policies, and Prospects* (Washington, DC: The Brookings Institution, 1933), 124–7; and John Commons, *History of Labour in the United States* (New York: Macmillan, 1918), 2:522–7.

[32] Stanley Lebergott, *The Americans: An Economic Record* (New York: W. W. Norton, 1984), 395–7; Harold U. Faulkner, *The Decline of Laissez Faire, 1897–1917* (New York: Rinehart, 1951), 30–1; Harold U. Faulkner, *American Economic History*, 7th ed. (New York: Harper, 1954).

against the advice of AFL attorneys), Gompers continued to discuss the case in editorials. The AFL's defense rested on freedom of speech: As Gompers wrote in the *American Federationist*, the injunction "is an invasion of the liberty of the press and the right of free speech."[33]

In July 1908, Buck's petitioned the Supreme Court of the District of Columbia to judge Gompers, Frank Morrison, and John Mitchell in contempt of court for violating the injunction. The D.C. Supreme Court delayed its decision on the contempt charge until after the November elections so as not to damage the Republican Party's political fortunes, but during the autumn months – the heart of the busy campaign season – the Court conducted hearings on the contempt charge, thereby harassing the AFL leaders. Gompers testified at times for days and nights in succession during this period and he confided to a friend: "The strain under which I am laboring now is tremendous."[34]

On December 23, 1908, Justice Daniel Wright of the D.C. Supreme Court judged Gompers, Mitchell, and Morrison guilty of contempt and sentenced them to prison terms of 12, 9, and 6 months, respectively. Rejecting their appeal to freedom of speech, Wright declared that the AFL forced society to choose between "the supremacy of law over the rabble or its prostration under the feet of the disordered throng." AFL leaders appealed the decision and ultimately the courts dismissed all charges due to technicalities – but it took seven long years to resolve the case. Furthermore, though the AFL officials escaped prison terms, the open-shop movement had won an important victory.[35]

The U.S. Supreme Court's decision in *Loewe v. Lawlor*, handed down in February 1908, constituted a greater threat to organized labor. In July 1902, the United Hatters of North America went on strike and proclaimed a boycott against Dietrich Loewe and Company of Danbury, Connecticut. With its sales reduced by the boycott, Loewe sued the members of the union in 1903, claiming violation

---

[33] Samuel Gompers, "Free Press and Free Speech Invaded by Injunction against the AF of L – A Review and Protest," *AF*, 15 (2), 98–105. A leading AFL attorney in this case was Alton Parker, the Democratic Party's presidential nominee in the 1904 election.

[34] R. Lee Guard to H. S. McCartney, September 21, 1908; Gompers to Frederick Pierce, September 26, 1908; Morrison to M. Grant Hamilton, September 23, 1908; on September 26, 1908, a "Union Man" wrote perceptively to Gompers during this same period: "Don't you think this trial brought on at the present, is a scheme of the 'Administration' to keep you here in Washington and prevent you going on the stump." All of the preceding can be found in *American Federation of Labor Records: The Samuel Gompers Era* (Microfilming Corporation of America, 1979) (hereafter cited as *AFL Records*) reel 67. On the delay of the decision so as not to hurt the Republicans' electoral fate, see Barry F. Helfand, "Labor and the Courts: The Common-Law Doctrine of Criminal Conspiracy and Its Application in the Buck's Stove Case," *Labor History*, 18 (1), Winter 1977, 100.

[35] This discussion of the Buck's case is based primarily on Bernard Mandel, *Samuel Gompers: A Biography* (Yellow Springs, OH: Antioch Press, 1963), 263–83; other useful sources include Helfand, "Labor and the Courts"; Taft, *AFL in the Time of Gompers*; and for Judge Wright's quote, see Christopher Tomlins, *The State and the Unions: Labor Relations, Law and the Organized Labor Movement in America, 1880–1960* (New York: Cambridge University Press, 1985), 67.

of the Sherman Anti-Trust Act. Passed in 1890, the Sherman Act declared any contract or combination restraining trade or commerce to be illegal, allowed violators to be sued for damages, and required that violators pay *triple* the amount of damages. Dietrich Loewe had co-founded the American Anti-Boycott Association and this organization now planned and funded his suit against the hatters as a test case of the boycott. The suit requested $240,000 in damages, and attorney Daniel Davenport argued successfully that individual members of the United Hatters should be held liable for those damages.[36]

When Congress passed the Sherman Act in 1890, leading politicians reassured AFL leaders it would be used only against large combinations of capital. Yet from 1893 onwards, unions faced prosecution under the Sherman Act much more frequently than did corporations. Labor leaders impatiently waited during these years for the courts to confirm what they already knew: that anti-trust actions should not be used against unions. Now, by including unions within the purview of the Sherman Act, the U.S. Supreme Court legitimized one of the most powerful weapons against the labor movement, to the horror of trade unionists across the country.[37]

Labor activists recognized the threat the Court's action represented, and a hail of denunciations followed in the next months.[38] Repeatedly, labor leaders called for a new political battle to combat judicial hostility. Some, for example, contrasted *Loewe v. Lawlor* to Britain's Taff Vale decision, which had made trade unions liable for the actions of their members, and thus had spurred many union workers to send labor representatives to Parliament. As E. Lewis Evans, the secretary-treasurer of the Tobacco Workers' Union, asked: "Have we not the same ability and brains as the trade unions across the sea? It is time for us to be up and doing and to waste no further time. Let us send men to Congress who will support the interests we represent. . . ."[39]

[36] David Bensman, *The Practice of Solidarity: American Hat Finishers in the Nineteenth Century* (Urbana: University of Illinois Press, 1985), xi–xiii and 201–8.

[37] For the Supreme Court's decision, see *Dietrich Loewe et al. v. Martin Lawlor et al.*, U.S. 389, 1908. A jury trial awarded the company the full amount of damages claimed, $252,130.90, and the U.S. Supreme Court upheld the award. The union's members were to pay the damages: Their homes and bank accounts had been attached to the suit. To save them, the AFL's 1915 convention called on all American workers to donate one hour of pay on January 27, 1916, for meeting the verdict. The money collected from this, in addition to funds donated by the United Hatters of America, paid for the damages. See Taft, *AFL in the Time of Gompers*, 266–8; Mandel, *Samuel Gompers*, 289–91; Bensman, *Practice of Solidarity*, 201–8; and William Forbath, *Law and the Shaping of the Labor Movement* (Cambridge: Harvard University Press, 1991).

[38] Denis Hayes, "Supreme Court Decision in the Hatters' Case," *AF*, 15 (3), March 1908, 167; "Address to Workers," issued by the AFL's Conference of Protest, March 18, 1908, *AF*, 15 (4), April 1908, 269.

[39] E. Lewis Evans, in "Amend the Sherman Anti-Trust Law – Labor Must Exercise Its Political Power. A Symposium by Men of Affairs," *AF*, 15 (5), May 1908, 354–5; for similar comments, see John Commons, ibid., 354; John Golden, President of the United Textile Workers, in *AF*, 15 (3), March 1908, 171–2.

While publicly AFL leaders stressed the dangers judicial hostility posed to workers' constitutional rights and liberties, in private they worried more about the economic impact of the recent court decisions. The hatters' case and the Buck's suit drained precious finances out of trade union treasuries. Thus, Frank Morrison declared that although injunctions had become a serious problem, "Suits are in my opinion going to be general and the organization will be compelled to defeat them." Politics could provide the most expedient solution: "If we can elect a sufficient number of Congressmen to capture the House of Representatives, adopt an Anti-injunction bill and secure a law taking us out from under the Sherman Anti-Trust law we may be able to save the organization hundreds of thousands of dollars. . . ." In fact, before the Danbury hatters' case ended, the AFL spent nearly $100,000 defending them. The Federation assessed its affiliated unions and appealed for voluntary contributions to raise money for the hatters and to defend Gompers, Morrison, and Mitchell against the contempt charge linked to the Buck's Stove case.[40]

Facing these economic and political pressures, the AFL called its affiliates together for a special conference just as it had in 1906. Representatives of 118 national and international unions attended the two-day meeting, joined by representatives of a farmers' organization and the railroad brotherhoods. Again, the AFL leaders excluded state federations of labor and the central labor unions from this special conference, even though those organizations typically focused on political tasks. This conference produced a document, "Labor's Protest to Congress," which attacked the antilabor bias of the judiciary and Congress. The AFL demanded that Congress pass two amendments to the Sherman Anti-Trust Act during the current session: one would exempt from the Act all organizations (and their members) not operating for profit nor having capital stock; a second amendment exempted arrangements among people engaged in agriculture or horticulture. "Labor's Protest" only briefly mentioned three other issues that, it charged, Congress had ignored for years: a bill to regulate and limit injunctions; an employers' liability law; and an extension of the eight-hour law for all government employees.

While denouncing Congress, "Labor's Protest" also attacked the role played by the Republican Party. Labor emphatically protests, it began, "against the indifference, if not actual hostility, which Congress has shown towards the reasonable and righteous measures proposed by the workers for the safeguarding of their rights and interests." Trade unionists would hold congressmen responsible if they did not pass satisfactory legislation. In particular, "we aver that the party in power must and will by labor and its sympathizers be held primarily responsible. . . ." for failure to pass the requested amendments.[41]

[40] Morrison to W. C. Hahn, September 16, 1908, Frank Morrison Letterbooks, Perkins Library, Dake University (hereafter cited as Morrison Letterbooks). See also Morrison to Andrew Furuseth, October 29, 1908, and Morrison to Max Morris, October 28, 1908, Morrison Letterbooks.

[41] "Labor's Protest to Congress," *AF*, 15 (4), April 1908, 261–6.

In the months that followed, Federation leaders launched an intensive campaign to pressure Congress into meeting its demands. Morrison mailed three million circulars to secretaries of local unions, central labor unions, and state federations, ultimately reaching some 25,000 unions. The missives explained the AFL's concern with judicial hostility, appealed for funds to cover the AFL's long-term campaign costs, and spelled out precisely what workers should do to assist the AFL strategy.[42] Their guidelines focused on traditional pressure-group tactics. The AFL simply asked local unions, central labor unions, and state federations to organize mass meetings for April 19 or 20, at which workers should protest the Supreme Court decision and send a resolution to Congress urging it to pass the AFL's amendments. In addition, the AFL made an early call for unity and discipline: It asked local unionists to follow closely the strategy outlined by the conference, and such further plans as suggested by the Executive Council or future conferences, "so that our strength and influence shall not be frittered away by different lines of action."[43]

Meanwhile, AFL leaders began an energetic lobbying campaign. Gompers ordered seven AFL organizers back to headquarters to serve as legislative committeemen. Focusing on the demands listed in the "Protest to Congress," the AFL's Legislative Committee made an extensive canvass of the members of the House of Representatives, asking each one to declare himself for or against the legislative demands of labor. The committee gathered pledges of support from more than 250 congressmen.[44] By late spring, Gompers and Morrison seemed confident that Congress would pass the legislation they desired. Mass meetings in cities throughout the country produced "thousands and thousands" of resolutions from local unions, central labor unions, and state federations. Morrison wrote in early May that "We have the members of Congress thoroughly aroused through the literature that is coming in. I think the bills are going to be adopted, though they will not give the full relief that we desire."[45] Yet when Republican members of Congress met in late May to consider labor's demands, and despite pressure from an insurgent minority, the congressmen voted overwhelmingly in the negative. This ended any hope that the AFL's bills would pass during the current session of Congress.[46]

---

[42] Morrison to M. Grant Hamilton, September 28, 1908;, Morrison to Arthur A. Hay, April 11, 1908; Morrison to Stuart Reid, April 24, 1908; [Morrison and Gompers] to Organized Labor and Friends, n.d. [April 1908]; letter of instruction and sample resolution, *AFL Records*, reel 65, 547–9; Morrison to W. J. French, April 29, 1908: except where noted, all documents are from the Morrison Letterbooks.

[43] Representatives of National and International Unions and Farmers' Organizations, "Address to Workers," March 18, 1908, *AF*, 15 (4), April 1908, 267–9.

[44] Morrison to James Duncan, April 8, 1908, Morrison Letterbooks; Editorial Note, *AF*, 15 (8), August 1908, 610; "Congress and Labor" (AFL Legislative Committee's Official Report), *AF*, 15 (8), August 1908, 589–95.

[45] AFL Legislative Committee, "Congress and Labor. AF of L Legislative Committee's Official Report," *AF*, 15 (8), August 1908, 590; Frank Morrison to William E. Terry, May 2, 1908, Morrison Letterbooks; Morrison to Will J. French, April 29, 1908, Morrison Letterbooks.

[46] AFL Legislative Committee, "Congress and Labor," 589–95.

Gompers and Morrison attributed their legislative defeats to the dominance of Republican leaders such as Joseph Cannon, John Dalzell, and John Sherman, who controlled the House agenda by burying undesirable bills in committee. Democratic congressmen demanded angrily that the full House be allowed to entertain the AFL's bills. In May, Gompers emphasized publicly that "Labor will hold the *failure to legislate* by this session of Congress – no matter for what reason – as the *refusal to legislate*." The AFL legislative committee informed Republican members of Congress that this message applied to them in particular. When Republican congressmen pleaded that the blame lay with Speaker Cannon, Gompers pointed to the Republican support that repeatedly elected Cannon as Speaker: "Labor holds those members of the House responsible who allowed Congress to be delivered bound hand and foot, as they say, until it is impossible to secure legislation except at the permission of this one man."[47]

Although reform-minded Republicans like Theodore Roosevelt disapproved of Congress's treatment of labor, conservative House leaders flaunted their opposition. Congressman John Sherman of New York, soon to become his party's nominee for the vice-presidency, proclaimed that "The Republican party in this House, the Republican party in this nation, is prepared today to accept full responsibility, not only for everything that is done, but for that which is not done in the way of legislation and administration." Charles Littlefield, head of the subcommittee considering the AFL's anti-injunction bill, bragged that he had the bill "in his pocket and he intended to keep it there and never let it see the light of day."[48]

As the warfare between organized labor and the Republican Party intensified in these months, President Roosevelt again tried to intervene and repair the damage. A meeting between his protégé, William Howard Taft, and AFL leaders led to the drafting of a plank on injunction reform for the Republican platform. Roosevelt and Taft both pleaded with the convention delegates to pass the injunction plank. In July, Republican members of the AFL Executive Council (Daniel Keefe and James Duncan) attended the Republican Convention along with Gompers. Party leaders treated the Federation derisively. Their Platform Committee refused to meet with the AFL and offered instead only a ten-minute meeting with a subcommittee. As they walked into the meeting, the AFL officials were shocked to see Republican Party leaders flanked by James Emery, James Van Cleave, and Martin Mulhall of the National Association of Manufacturers.[49]

---

[47] Samuel Gompers, "Congress Will Be Held Responsible," *AF*, 15 (6), June 1908, 453; AFL Legislative Committee, "Congress and Labor," 591.

[48] Sherman is quoted in Samuel Gompers, "Congressional Perfidy – The Responsibility – Labor's Duty," *AF*, 15 (7), July 1908, 526. See also the AFL Legislative Committee's Report, "Congress and Labor," 589–95; the paraphrase of Littlefield's quote comes from Morrison to M. F. Tighe, October 28, 1908, Morrison Letterbooks.

[49] This account relies primarily on Gompers, *Seventy Years of Life and Labor: An Autobiography* (New York: E. P. Dutton, 1925), 2:260–3; see also Gompers, "Both Parties Have Spoken – Choose Between Them," *AF*, 15 (8), August 1908, 598–606.

Federation officials asked the Republicans for support on issues ranging from an eight-hour day for government employees to woman suffrage, but they gave priority to injunction reform and an amendment to the Sherman Act.[50] Conservative Republicans easily controlled the convention proceedings, however, and the AFL's concerns mattered little to them. Headed by Senator Aldrich and NAM President James Van Cleave, the Platform Committee passed an injunction plank that supported existing judicial practices, rather than calling for a limitation on injunctions as Roosevelt, Taft, and the AFL leaders desired. As George Mowry put it, the feeling at the time "was that the President and his friend had won the nomination and had lost everything else."[51]

Weeks later, the Democrats graciously welcomed AFL representatives to their Denver convention as friends and allies. Federation leaders met with the entire Platform Committee, of which Alton Parker (an AFL attorney in the Buck's case) was the chairman. After a lengthy discussion, the Democrats included most of the AFL's requests in its platform, and Gompers declared himself well satisfied with the planks on the Sherman Act and the injunction. The platform criticized the Republicans for raising "a false issue regarding the judiciary"; it stated that "injunctions should not be issued in any cases in which injunctions would not issue if no industrial disputes were involved"; and it proclaimed that labor organizations should not be regarded as illegal combinations in restraint of trade. These points were central to the AFL's position on injunctions and the Sherman Act. The platform also endorsed several of labor's lesser demands, such as extension of the eight-hour day, a general employers' liability law, and creation of a Department of Labor.[52]

The Democrats' actions behind the scenes demonstrated how carefully they considered labor's desires. Over the course of 1908, William Jennings Bryan began a regular correspondence with Samuel Gompers that laid the groundwork for their alliance. Soon after the Supreme Court handed down its Danbury hatters' decision, for example, Bryan sent Gompers an editorial he had written that demonstrated how labor organizations differed from trusts. Through their correspondence, Gompers ultimately influenced the Democratic platform for the state of Nebraska, which in turn provided the basis for the national party platform. That summer, when Bryan began writing the platforms regarding anti-trust and

---

[50] The AFL also requested that the Republican and Democratic parties support: a general employers' liability law; creation of a Department of Labor; creation of a federal bureau of mines and mining, and the appropriation of funds to investigate mine disasters; and establishment of a postal savings bank. See Gompers, "Both Parties Have Spoken," 598–606.

[51] Mowry, *Era of Theodore Roosevelt*, 229. Another major defeat for Roosevelt and Taft came over the tariff. They had wanted the platform to promise a downward revision of the tariff. Instead, the plank merely promised to revise the tariff, carefully neglecting to mention whether the revision would move upward or downward.

[52] Gompers, "Both Parties Have Spoken," 598–606. The only AFL demands that received no mention by the platform were woman suffrage and a postal savings bank.

injunction reforms in preparation for the national convention, he and Gompers again discussed their formulation.[53]

During the Democratic Convention William Bryan stayed in Lincoln, communicating by telegram with his brother Charles, who managed their concerns on the spot in Denver. Together they made the major decisions about the party platform. Alton Parker of New York submitted a plank on injunction reform that he had worked out with the AFL leaders. Bryan and his brother feared the plank failed to protect workers' rights, because it did not allow for a trial nor provide a notice before issuance of a temporary injunction. The railroad brotherhoods specifically asked Bryan to fight for the latter. Bryan seemed surprised that labor would accept Parker's plank, but after receiving the AFL leaders' written approval, he agreed to it. He declared to Charles, "As New York is the center of wealth and business, it is well enough to have that state take the responsibility for the injunction plank, if the plank is satisfactory to the laboring men. But on the other questions . . . I would rather run on a Nebraska platform than on a New York platform."[54] Labor's own limited demands in this case narrowed the Democratic platform.

After the party conventions, Gompers publicly endorsed the Democratic Party platform and its presidential candidate. In an *American Federationist* editorial, Gompers rehearsed the AFL's requests, its appearance at the two party conventions, and its treatment by each party. The facts added up naturally to one conclusion: Labor must support the Democrats. Gompers attacked the Republican plank on injunctions as "a flimsy, tricky evasion of the issue . . . an endorsement of the very abuse against which labor justly protests." And he condemned the Republicans in harsh terms: "The Republican party . . . lines up with the corporate interests of the country and defies the people to help themselves." The Democrats, on the other hand, endorsed the principles Gompers and his colleagues had struggled toward for years. The masses of workers, Gompers declared, "will rise in sympathy to the Democratic party in the coming elections."[55]

In the following weeks, the AFL and the Democratic Party transformed their relationship to create an unprecedented and far-reaching alliance. Democratic leaders initiated the idea of a partnership, and John Lennon of the AFL acted

[53] In the next months, Bryan and Gompers met at least twice more to plan the Democratic campaign's strategy for appealing to workers. See the correspondence between W. J. Bryan and Gompers in the *AFL Records* on these dates during 1908: January 21; February 3, 27; March 11; June 27, 30; July 24; August 1, 6, 14, 28 (reels 65 and 66). Coletta, *William Jennings Bryan*, notes that the platform that Bryan submitted to the Democratic Convention – and that was, for the most part, approved – was a combination of the Nebraska state platform, the AFL program, and the Oklahoma constitution. Labor had also exerted a great influence on Oklahoma's constitution. See Coletta, *William Jennings Bryan*, 405; and Keith Bryant, "Labor in Politics: The Oklahoma State Federation of Labor during the Age of Reform," *Labor History*, 10 (3), Summer 1970, 259–84.

[54] See the telegrams between William Jennings and Charles Bryan in the Bryan Papers, Library of Congress, Manuscripts Division, Box 48, Convention Subject Files.

[55] Gompers, "Both Parties Have Spoken," 598–606.

as a mediator between the two groups.[56] Lennon, as we saw in earlier chapters, had urged Gompers for years to move closer to the Democrats. Now Lennon began regular discussions with leading Democrats (including William and Charles Bryan, Democratic National Chairman Norman Mack, and Labor Bureau Chief Martin Wade) to negotiate the details of their alliance. Meanwhile, he also worked to win Gompers's approval of the plan, which would revolve around placing a "first class labor man at headquarters" in Chicago to run the Democrats' Labor Bureau. Lennon insisted that the AFL needed to have one of its own at the heart of Democratic Party operations, "to stop them from stupidity" and to keep them from undertaking strategies that would not be successful with workers.[57]

According to Lennon, a partnership with the Democratic Party would also help the AFL achieve its key goal: defeating Speaker of the House Joe Cannon in his bid for reelection to Congress. The cost of mounting a campaign in Cannon's district would easily exceed $2,500, which organized labor could certainly not afford. But if the AFL joined forces with the Democratic Party, the latter would assign men to districts where labor most desired to elect or defeat chosen candidates. Lennon also assured Gompers that any labor man appointed to the Democrats' Labor Bureau would consult regularly with the AFL leadership.[58]

By August 25, Gompers had agreed the AFL should enter a formal political relationship with the Democratic Party. Accompanied by James O'Connell, Frank Morrison, and organizer Grant Hamilton, Gompers met with Norman Mack, the chairman of the Democratic National Committee. Together they wrote a formal agreement establishing the basis for cooperation between the Democratic Party and the AFL over three major areas: finances, campaign literature, and organizers. Finances featured most prominently. The two organizations agreed that "the AFL and its officers, neither directly or indirectly, are to receive from you or anyone else any financial contributions or financial assistance for this campaign, either before or after."

Secondly, Mack and Gompers agreed that the Democratic Party would print and distribute whatever literature the AFL's Labor Representation Committee deemed necessary for communicating its political goals to working people. For example, the AFL leadership planned to write two pamphlets immediately, and the Democrats agreed to print one and a half million copies of each one and distribute them. Similar quantities of future pamphlets would be printed on the AFL's request. In addition, the Democratic National Committee (DNC) guaranteed that the Illinois Democratic Party would print whatever literature Joseph Cannon's opponent needed for his battle. All of this literature, the two groups agreed, would naturally carry a union label.

---

[56] M. J. Wall, Chair, Labor Committee, Democratic National Committee, to Gompers, August 10, 1908; Gompers to Norman Mack, August 17, 1908; Norman Mack to Gompers, August 17, 1908: all *AFL Records*, reel 66.

[57] Lennon to Gompers, August 19 and 21, 1908, *AFL Records*, reel 66.

[58] Lennon to Gompers, August 19, 23, and 24, 1908; Lennon to M. Grant Hamilton, August 20, 1908: all *AFL Records*, reel 66.

The third area of agreement concerned the AFL organizers who would personally represent the AFL within the bowels of Democratic Party bureaucracy. The AFL agreed to appoint its most able men to party headquarters around the country: Grant Hamilton would work at headquarters in Chicago, with regular assistance from John Lennon; AFL organizer Harry J. Skeffington received appointment to the Democratic offices in New York City; and John J. Keegan and Edgar A. Perkins to offices in Indianapolis. These organizers would work closely with Democratic Party officials, helping to plan campaign strategy. In addition the AFL would suggest several other labor men whom the DNC could send around the country on campaign assignments. Most importantly, the agreement noted that all organizers would be supervised by Gompers, not by the Democrats. And in particular, "in any disputed question the matter shall be determined by the [AFL's] Labor Representation Committee," a body in turn constituted by Gompers, O'Connell, and Morrison.[59]

By the time the presidential campaign began in September 1908, then, the Federation leaders had publicly endorsed the Democratic Party platform and its presidential candidate and had established a comprehensive alliance with the Democratic National Committee. Connections between trade unions and party politicians were certainly not new in 1908. Labor activists had often played a role in partisan campaigns, whether advising party elites or carrying out laborious chores. But a formal partnership between organized labor and a major political party such as this agreement represented had never been seen before, and its consequences were likewise unknown. In describing the agreement he had reached with DNC Chairman Norman Mack, Gompers declared that the AFL would work for the success of the Democratic ticket in the campaign, because both the AFL and the Democrats have "a common interest in the attainment of that purpose." The truth of that statement would be tested rigorously in the months to come.[60]

Shall the People Rule?

William Jennings Bryan centered the Democratic campaign of 1908 around one question: "whether the government shall remain a mere business asset of favor-seeking corporations, or be an instrument in the hands of the people for the advancement of the common weal."[61] Capping their campaign with the slogan "Shall the People Rule?" Democrats hoped to evoke a Jeffersonian program of

---

[59] Gompers to Norman E. Mack, August 28, 1908, *AFL Records*, reel 66. See also Samuel Gompers, "Congressional Responsibility and Labor's Duty," *AF*, 15 (10), October 1908, 864–8. In one additional area of negotiation, the DNC agreed to put men in Maine to run the campaign there. The AFL still smarted from its failed effort to defeat Charles Littlefield of Maine for Congress in 1906. By this time, Littlefield had announced that he would not seek reelection, but the AFL continued to work to replace him with a Democrat.
[60] Gompers to Norman Mack, August 28, 1908, *AFL Records*, reel 66.
[61] Quoted in Coletta, *William Jennings Bryan*, 416.

political and economic reform. More specifically, Democrats targeted the corrupt use of money in politics, and especially politicians' reliance on money from special interests for winning elections; the indirect election of U.S. senators as a limitation of democracy; the rules in the U.S. House of Representatives that allowed the speaker to dominate the House agenda and thus prevent reform; the need for regulation of the trusts; and the rights of labor.

The Democrats' support for workers' rights anchored their new image as the party of reform. Their labor campaign focused almost entirely on two issues: labor's legal rights (the need for an anti-injunction law and an amendment to the Sherman Anti-Trust Act), and the hostility shown labor by Congress and in particular by Speaker Joseph Cannon. A letter to American workers, written by Gompers but published and distributed by the Democrats, stated well the central concerns of their joint campaign: "The facts are that the Judiciary, induced by corporations and trusts and protected by the Republican party, is, step by step, destroying government by law and substituting therefor a government by Judges. . . . It is sought to make of the judges irresponsible despots, and by controlling them using this despotism in the interest of corporate power."[62] Bryan also took pains to support other AFL demands, such as a Department of Labor with full cabinet powers.[63]

AFL and Democratic leaders worked closely together to hammer out the campaign's basic character. Gompers or Morrison communicated often with Norman Mack, the Chairman of the Democratic National Committee (DNC). Teams of AFL organizers occupied offices at the DNC's headquarters in Chicago and at regional centers in New York City, Indianapolis, and later Buffalo, New York. These organizers linked the AFL with Democratic Party leaders on a daily basis. And, as in 1906, the Federation again assigned scores of organizers to work with local labor activists throughout the United States in building labor's political campaign.

Grant Hamilton, an articulate organizer and Typographers' Union member with close ties to Gompers, represented the AFL at the Democrats' Chicago headquarters. Hamilton seems to have been responsible for most day-to-day decisions regarding the nature of the labor campaign, although he worked with the AFL and Democratic leaders to make more important decisions. He corresponded on almost a daily basis with Gompers and Morrison, and John Lennon visited headquarters at least weekly to assist him.[64] As for campaign literature, Frank

[62] See, for example, Hamilton to Gompers, September 18, 1908, *AFL Records*, reel 67; and "How Speaker Cannon Has Abused Labor," campaign leaflet, Joseph G. Cannon papers; Gompers's quote comes from his letter to "Men of Labor, Lovers of Human Liberty," October 12, 1908, *AFL Records*, reel 68.

[63] See, for example, "Democracy's Appeal to the Country," *The Commoner*, November 6, 1908.

[64] For examples of the close contact Hamilton maintained with Morrison and Gompers, see: Morrison to Hamilton, September 1, 1908, Morrison Letterbooks; Morrison to Hamilton, September 4, 1908, Morrison Letterbooks; Gompers to Hamilton, September 9, 1908; Gompers to Hamilton, September 10, 1908; Hamilton to Gompers, September 10, 1908; Hamilton to Gompers, September 11, 1908; Hamilton to Gompers, September 13, 1908; Hamilton to

Morrison wrote to a friend that Hamilton "has control to a great measure of the literature that will be sent out to the labor press and to the press generally." In addition, Hamilton oversaw the other labor bureaus around the country. The formal agreement between the AFL and the DNC stated that all organizers used in the campaign would answer to AFL officials and that any conflicts would be resolved by the AFL, not by the DNC. These factors indicate that Hamilton and his superiors at AFL national headquarters were largely responsible for determining the nature of the Democratic Party's labor campaign.[65]

Gompers wrote most of the campaign literature the Democrats distributed among workers, often sending reprints of letters or editorials he'd written to Democratic headquarters. And while Democratic leaders decided where they would focus their campaign activities without consulting their labor allies, the AFL leaders chose which organizers to hire and the two groups decided together where to send them. Once assigned, the labor organizers answered only to AFL leaders: usually Morrison, Hamilton, or the Federation representatives in charge of the regional labor bureaus.[66]

Gompers, September 14, 1908; Morrison to Hamilton, September 16, 1908, Morrison Letterbooks; Gompers to Hamilton, September 17, 1908; and Hamilton to Gompers, September 18, 1908; on Lennon visiting headquarters once or twice a week, see Lennon to Gompers, September 21, 1908. Except where noted otherwise, all preceding documents can be found in *AFL Records*, reel 67.

[65] Gompers to Norman E. Mack, August 28, 1908, *AFL Records*, reel 66; Morrison to Ed Stephenson, September 16, 1908, Morrison Letterbooks. For examples of Hamilton conferring with Mack, see Gompers to Hamilton, September 9, 1908, *AFL Records*, reel 67; Gompers to Hamilton, September 10, 1908, *AFL Records*, reel 67; Gompers to Hamilton, September 24, 1908, *AFL Records*, reel 67; Hamilton to Gompers, September 24, 1908, *AFL Records*, reel 67; Hamilton to Gompers, September 26, 1908, *AFL Records*, reel 67. On Hamilton overseeing the other labor bureaus, see Hamilton to Gompers, September 14, 1908, *AFL Records*, reel 67; for Morrison's comment that Hamilton was "in charge of the labor bureau," see Morrison to Max Morris, September 15, 1908, Morrison Letterbooks. A further indication of the AFL's proprietary sentiment toward the labor campaign is Morrison's tendency to refer to the DNC labor bureaus as "*our* committees." See Frank Morrison to Jacob Tazelaar, October 17, 1908, Morrison Letterbooks.

[66] On the nature and distribution of campaign literature, see Hamilton to Gompers, September 10, 1908; Gompers to Hamilton, September 22, 1908; Hamilton to Gompers, September 18, 1908; Morrison to Hamilton, September 16, 1908, Morrison Letterbooks; Gompers to "Men of Labor, Lovers of Human Liberty," October 12, 1908; Morrison to Hamilton, September 4, 1908, Morrison Letterbooks; Morrison to Hamilton, September 16, 1908, Morrison Letterbooks; Hamilton to Thomas Tracy, September 19, 1908; Hamilton to the *Labor Journal*, Zanesville, Ohio, September 21, 1908; Hamilton to Gompers, September 22, 1908; Hamilton to Gompers, September 30, 1908; on the two organizations' decision-making procedures regarding organizers, see Gompers to Hamilton, September 17, 1908; Hamilton to Morrison, September 30, 1908; Hamilton to Gompers, September 13, 1908; John Morrison (in charge of the New York Democratic Labor Bureau) to Gompers, September 19, 1908; Morrison to Hamilton, October 4, 8, and 14, 1908, Morrison Letterbooks; Gompers to Hamilton, September 26, 1908; Hamilton to Morrison, October 4, 1908; Hamilton to Gompers, October 9, 1908; Gompers to Hamilton, October 22, 1908. Except where noted otherwise, all are from the *AFL Records*, reels 67 and 68.

Money for the AFL's campaign came from three financial sources. As in 1906, Federation leaders asked local unions, central labor unions, and state federations of labor to contribute to the campaign fund, and this raised approximately $8,000 – the same disappointing amount as in 1906. Because the Democrats funded the AFL's campaign literature, the AFL spent its campaign fund on organizers and on campaign tours undertaken by leaders such as Gompers and Morrison.[67] The national and international unions provided a second source of funds for the AFL campaign. Although most contributed very little, in a few cases – and more often than in 1906 – they assisted the AFL program generously. The International Typographers' Union provided exemplary assistance, funding an entire operation in California to carry the state for Bryan. Similarly, the Printing Pressmen offered to put as many as fourteen organizers into the field to work on the AFL program. Other unions that contributed organizers included the Retail Clerks, the United Mine Workers, and the Iron Molders.[68]

But the AFL relied most heavily on its third source of financial assistance, the Democratic Party. Most AFL organizers doing campaign work received their salaries from the Democrats, not from the AFL. The number of organizers assigned to political work in 1908 more than doubled compared to the number in 1906 – reaching more than 100 – and the AFL could not have funded more than half of these. In some cases state, county, or local Democratic organizations paid AFL organizers to assist them, but more typically, as Hamilton described it, the arrangement, "wherever necessary men were to go on the payroll of the [Democratic] National Committee when you [Gompers] suggested them."[69] The financial ties between labor and the Democrats grew more complex as the campaign wore on, because party leaders frequently asked that the AFL pay the organizers and then receive reimbursement from them. The reason? When hired by the Democrats, organizers tended to demand more money

[67] AFL circular, "To Organized Labor and Friends in the U.S.," August 1, 1908, *AFL Records*, reel 66; Morrison to James O'Connell, September 28, 1908, Morrison Letterbooks. The AFL raised exactly $8,469.98 through these appeals: Foner, *History of the Labor Movement*, 3:357. On the AFL hiring some organizers with money from its campaign fund, see Morrison to Hamilton, October 4, 1908, *AFL Records*, reel 68.

[68] See Hamilton to Gompers, September 24, 1908; Gompers to Hamilton, September 26, 1908; Arthur A. Hay to Gompers, August 26, 1908; Hay to Gompers, September 8, 1908; Gompers to Hamilton, September 10, 1908; George L. Berry, president, Printing Pressmen, Cincinnati, to Gompers, September 28, 1908: all from *AFL Records*-reels 67 and 68. Ultimately, Berry seems to have contributed many fewer organizers than fourteen, perhaps as few as four or five.

[69] Hamilton to Gompers, September 24, 1908, *AFL Records*, reel 67. For financial negotiations in specific cases, see Gompers to Hamilton, September 26, 1908, *AFL Records*, reel 67; Hamilton to Morrison, September 25, 1908, *AFL Records*, reel 67; Morrison to Hamilton, October 8, 1908, Morrison Letterbooks. For an example of a local Democratic organization funding AFL organizers, see Morrison to J. A. Noecker, chairman, Democratic Headquarters, Pottsville, Pennsylvania, October 13, 1908, Morrison Letterbooks.

than the party felt able to pay. Organizers working for the Federation would accept significantly lower wages.[70]

Its alliance with the Democratic Party allowed the AFL to launch a much more ambitious campaign than in 1906. Based on explicit references to campaign literature made by labor and party leaders, we can estimate that they distributed at least 5 million pieces.[71] At the center of labor's campaign stood imagery of the American Revolution. Hamilton sent postcards to individual workers, asking them to enlist as "Minute Men of Labor." Interested trade unionists filled in their names and addresses and answered questions regarding how many pieces of campaign literature they could use (either foreign- or English-language), then mailed the card back to Hamilton. He would then respond with a package of literature and a personal letter thanking the worker for his or her loyalty to the AFL program.

Within half a week of mailing the first postcards, Hamilton had collected responses from 100,000 individual workers and from 13,000 secretaries of local unions. A week later, the returns remained impressive, as some 200 responses flowed into headquarters each day.[72] The Democrats and the AFL relied on other tactics as well – sending campaign literature and cartoons to labor newspapers,

[70] The Democrats paid labor organizers $8 per day, and some trade unionists rejected that as too low. From the AFL, organizers received between $5 and $7.50 per day. Hamilton to Morrison, September 30, 1908, *AFL Records*, reel 68; H. Lloyd to H. J. Skeffington, September 30, 1908, *AFL Records*, reel 68. For more examples of the Democratic National Committee funding AFL organizers, see: Gompers to Norman Mack, September 11, 1908, *AFL Records*, reel 67; Morrison to Hamilton, September 23, 1908, Morrison Letterbooks; Morrison to Hamilton, October 4, 14, and 17, 1908, Morrison Letterbooks; Morrison to Herman Robinson, October 30, 1908, Morrison Letterbooks. Because of its appeal to local unions for campaign funds, the AFL did have an independent source of money: At times it used this fund to cover costs for which the DNC would not spend money. For example, Morrison wanted an assistant to help Hamilton at DNC headquarters, and learned with surprise that the Democrats would not cover such an expense. Thus, Morrison sent a man to help him and said: "we will carry him for you, so that you will have this extra assistance. . . ." Morrison to Hamilton, October 2 13, 1908, Morrison Letterbooks.

[71] This figure contrasts dramatically with the AFL's output of literature in 1906, when running a campaign on its own. Then the AFL distributed at most only 100,000 pieces of literature. This is a highly conservative estimate of the number of labor-related leaflets; the actual number may have been much greater than 5 million. Hamilton to Gompers, September 10, 1908; Morrison to T. T. O'Malley, September 16, 1908, Morrison Letterbooks; Hamilton to Gompers, September 18, 1908; John Morrison to Gompers, September 19, 1908; Hamilton to Thomas Tracy, September 19, 1908; Gompers to John Morrison, September 19, 1908; John Morrison to Gompers, September 21, 1908; Hamilton to Gompers, September 22, 1908; Hamilton to Gompers, September 26, 1908; James Duncan to Gompers, September 29, 1908; John Morrison to Gompers, October 2, 1908; Hamilton to R. Lee Guard, October 3, 1908; Hamilton to Gompers, October 3, 1908; Harry Eichelberger to Gompers, October 9, 1908; Morrison to James Noecker, October 7, 1908; Hamilton to Gompers, October 24, 1908. Except where noted otherwise, all are from *AFL Records*, reels 67–9.

[72] John Morrison to Gompers, September 19, 1908; Hamilton to T. Tracy, September 19, 1908; Hamilton to Gompers, September 22, 1908; Hamilton to Gompers, September 26, 1908; Hamilton to Gompers, September 30, 1908: all *AFL Records*, reels 67 and 68.

and mailing out 21,000 copies of the *American Federationist* to barber shops in eleven crucial states, for example – but the "Minute Man" campaign represented their most aggressive attempt to reach local workers through literature.[73]

As in 1906, the AFL leaders relied heavily on organizers to communicate and enforce their strategy. With help from international affiliates and the Democratic Party, the number of political organizers sent out by the AFL more than doubled from only 42 in 1906 to more than 100 men in 1908.[74] The length of time devoted by these organizers varied greatly, from one week to two months or more. Most organizers, or more than fifty, worked for three to four weeks during the height of the campaign season. Twenty-one organizers worked for a longer period, ranging from five to ten weeks, and more than thirty worked only for one to three weeks.[75] The campaign focused on twenty-two states across the country, sending labor literature regularly to each one, but salaried labor organizers were doled out more selectively. Morrison wrote in late October that "we have massed our forces" in New York, Ohio, Indiana, and Illinois, with "a few detachments also in Rhode Island, Connecticut, Maryland, and West Virginia." The New York City bureau, in charge of seven eastern states, placed almost all its resources into winning New York State for Bryan. The national headquarters of the Democratic Labor Bureau in Chicago coordinated activities for the entire country, but it focused its resources on Illinois and Ohio in particular.[76]

---

[73] Hamilton to the *Labor Journal*, Zanesville, Ohio, September 21, 1908, *AFL Records*, reel 67. Mack asked Gompers to send out 21,000 copies of the *American Federationist* to barber shops in these states: New York, New Jersey, Connecticut, Rhode Island, Ohio, Indiana, West Virginia, Delaware, Maryland, Colorado, and Nebraska. John Morrison to Gompers, September 21, 1908, *AFL Records*, reel 67.

[74] This is again a conservative estimate, based on explicit references to organizers in the AFL documents. There may have been many more. The Democratic National Committee apparently appointed some labor organizers without seeking the AFL's recommendation. For example, Max Morris mentioned to Gompers that the DNC had appointed labor people to do work in Utah and Montana: Morris to Gompers, October 13, 1908, *AFL Records*, reel 68. Furthermore, organizers usually answered to Hamilton at the DNC in Chicago, and few documents from his work there have survived. The AFL leaders also lost almost all contact with one of their three labor bureaus: The Indiana bureau was active, and in contact with Hamilton, but not with Gompers and Morrison. This bureau undoubtedly managed numerous political workers. See Morrison to J. Tazelaar, October 17, 1908, Morrison Letterbooks.

[75] Of those organizers we know about, affiliates of the AFL contributed approximately thirteen, and the Democrats and the AFL itself paid for the approximately one hundred that remained. On the ITU's campaign in California, see Arthur Hay to Gompers, August 26, 1908, *AFL Records*, reel 66; Hay to Gompers, September 17, 1908, *AFL Records*, reel 67; political circular, Anti-Otis Clubs, [n.d.], *AFL Records*, reel 67, 563; the retail clerks contributed an organizer for six weeks to help UMW leader W. B. Wilson win reelection to Congress: Max Morris to Gompers, September 22, 1908, *AFL Records*, reel 67.

[76] The campaign targeted the following twenty-two states: Connecticut, Rhode Island, New York, New Jersey, Delaware, Maryland, West Virginia, Ohio, Indiana, Illinois, Kentucky, Kansas, Wisconsin, North Dakota, South Dakota, Minnesota, Nebraska, Nevada, Colorado, California, Washington, and Oregon: See Morrison to Max Morris, September 15, 1908, Morrison Letterbooks; and Morrison to E. M. Howard, October 28, 1908, Morrison Letterbooks.

Although their alliance with the Democratic Party vastly expanded the Federation's resources and allowed its leaders to launch a more ambitious campaign, the new partnership had other and more complex consequences. Most importantly, the AFL leaders' strategy became more centralized than ever in 1908, and they no longer emphasized a mass mobilization of American workers.

In 1906, the AFL leaders repeatedly gave local workers concrete and detailed instructions to form political committees, hold conventions, and to question and nominate candidates. Now, in 1908, the advice changed: The AFL urged workers to scan candidates' records before voting, to vote for the Democratic Party, to hold a mass meeting one or two times, to write their congressmen, and to endorse formally the AFL campaign program. Although Gompers and Morrison repeatedly mentioned their motto to "elect our friends and defeat our enemies," they no longer discussed concrete mechanisms for accomplishing that – except for the suggestion to walk into a ballot box and vote Democratic. The leaders no longer focused on the desirability of electing trade unionists to office, and no one called, as they had in 1906, for a "popular uprising of honest men."[77]

Similarly, AFL organizers' goals and activities shifted dramatically in 1908. In 1906, organizers focused on mobilizing local workers and encouraged them to start their own political campaign structures. Organizers in 1908, on the other hand, were content to manage the local-level campaigns themselves. They usually made no pretense of creating an indigenous campaign structure, but got the work done by themselves as quickly and easily as possible.[78] A new tactic devoured organizers' time in 1908, one previously almost unknown: They fought to win endorsements for the AFL campaign program from local- and state-level labor organizations. Amongst themselves, AFL officers and organizers referred to this tactic as "enforcement." When Hatters' Union President John Moffit joined

[77] Contrast the AFL leaders' careful and explicit instructions to workers in the "A.F. of L. Campaign Programme," July 22, 1906, *AF*, 13 (8), August 1906, 529–32; with the absence of such in the comparable document "Address to Workers," March 18, 1908, *AF*, 15 (4), April 1908, 267–9. For 1908, see also: Gompers, "Both Parties Have Spoken," 598–606; idem, "Don't *Wabble*; Hit the Mark," *AF*, 15 (9), September 1908, 729–30; "Official Circular," AFL Executive Council to all Organized Labor, August 1, 1908, *AF*, 15 (9), September 1908, 744–7.

[78] In some cases, local campaign structures were established, but usually on the initiative of local workers. The bid of William Mahon, president of the Street and Electric Railway Employees, for a congressional seat in Detroit, provides an example of this: a "Mahon Non-Partisan Club" was created there, apparently by people working for Mahon's campaign. See Mahon to Gompers, September 24, 1908, *AFL Records*, reel 67. As in 1906, a number of local trade union organizations created some sort of political committee or convention, without direct prompting from a visiting organizer. For example, see W. J. Kenealy, Youngstown, Ohio, addressed to no one, August 1908, [no complete date given], *AFL Records*, reel 67; Daniel Kiefer, Cincinnati, to Gompers, September 21, 1908, *AFL Records*, reel 67; Harry S. Smith, New Brighton, Pennsylvania, to Gompers, March 12, 1908, *AFL Records*, reel 65; George Bennett, Edwardsville, Illinois, to Gompers, July 13, 1908, *AFL Records*, reel 66; M. J. Curry, Atlantic City, to Gompers, July 30, 1908, *AFL Records*, reel 66.

Gompers to tour through the Midwest, Morrison acknowledged the union's willingness to let Moffit "assist in enforcing the AFL political program."[79]

AFL leaders also kept an eye on potential sources of dissension, and sent organizers to troubleshoot at conventions of state federations, central labor unions, and international unions. For example, when Carpenters' president William Huber worried that his union would not endorse the Federation program, John Morrison, the AFL representative at the Democrats' New York Labor Bureau, provided extensive advice. If the Carpenters failed to endorse the AFL program, said Morrison, it "would be considered cowardly ... by the trade unionists of the country and at the same time construed by the opponents of labor, and probably heralded throughout the country by the newspapers. ..." To achieve the endorsement, Morrison suggested, "if you can draw ... [the Socialists'] fire and make them attack you because you are upholding the policy of the American Federation of Labor in this fight, you will solidify all the 'anti' Socialists against the Socialists and will unite all of the forces that are anti-Socialistic to your support."[80]

AFL leaders "enforced" their campaign program with more aggressive actions at the local level. When the Central Labor Union in Alton, Illinois, appeared unlikely to endorse the AFL program, Frank Morrison reacted immediately. He ordered AFL organizers, one based in Kansas City and the other at Democratic headquarters in Chicago, to agitate among the workers of Alton, and John Lennon, treasurer of the AFL, visited as well. With this cadre of pro-Gompers spokesmen, the AFL campaign program was successfully enforced in Alton.[81]

---

[79] Morrison to Martin Lawlor, secretary, United Hatters, September 28, 1908, Morrison Letterbooks.

[80] John Morrison to William D. Huber, August 29, 1908, *AFL Records*, reel 66; Huber to J. Morrison, September 2, 1908, *AFL Records*, reel 66; for another example of AFL action to enforce the political program at an international's convention, see Morrison to James Duncan, September 17, 1908, Morrison Letterbooks.

[81] Morrison to D. A. Hayes, October 18, 1908; Morrison to Hamilton, October 15, 1908; Morrison to Peter Duffy, October 18, 1908; Morrison to D. A. Hayes, October 26, 1908; Morrison to Peter Duffy, October 27, 1908; Peter Duffy to Morrison, October 23, 1908, *AFL Records*, reel 69. For other examples of the AFL national leaders' efforts to enforce their campaign program, see: Morrison to the AFL Executive Council, October 14, 1908; Morrison to Cal Wyatt, Louisville, KY, September 26, 1908; F. A. Kennedy, Omaha, to Gompers, October 5, 1908, *AFL Records*, reel 68; Morrison to John A. Moffitt, September 30, 1908; Morrison to John Morrison, September 29, 1908; Morrison to Frank L. Rist, September 28, 1908; John Kirchner, Philadelphia, to Gompers, September 5, 1908, *AFL Records*, reel 67; John Morrison to Morrison, September 26, 1908, *AFL Records*, reel 67; Gompers to John Lennon, September 4, 1908, *AFL Records*, reel 67; Hamilton to Morrison, August 3, 1908, *AFL Records*, reel 66; Morrison to Hamilton, September 26, 1908; Morrison to James Duncan, September 17, 1908; Morrison to John Morrison, September 29, 1908; Hamilton to Gompers, September 19, 1908, *AFL Records*, reel 67; Gompers to Theodore Perry, January 8, 1908, *AFL Records*, reel 65; Gompers to George Foster, January 23, 1908, *AFL Records*, reel 65; George Foster et al. to Gompers, January 31, 1908, *AFL Records*, reel 65. Except where otherwise noted, all are from the Morrison Letterbooks.

The dynamics of a presidential campaign help explain why Federation leaders centralized their campaign strategy in 1908. Gompers and his allies concentrated their resources on electing William Jennings Bryan to the presidency, and ignored most congressional campaigns.[82] The decentralized character of the 1906 campaign and its focus on local autonomy worked efficiently when the AFL battled in congressional districts across the country. But the nationwide arena of a presidential race increased the significance of the AFL's national leadership and made unity and discipline more essential. Furthermore, although the Democrats' financial support allowed the AFL to assign more organizers to political duties and distribute more literature, the link between the two organizations also raised the stakes for the AFL and made the leadership feel constrained to achieve at least the appearance of consensus. Gompers and Morrison needed to prove to the Democrats that the AFL was a worthwhile ally. They could prove this only by convincing the vast majority of AFL workers to support Bryan, which led them to deemphasize the popular aspects of their campaign program.

Prosperity Politics

At the height of the 1908 campaign, *Pearson's Magazine* noted the unusual prominence accorded labor by politicians: "How the orators of all parties praise the workingman in this year of political humility and expectation! How they thunder against his enemies and promise vague redress! How the presidential candidates and the myriad seekers for office smile and smirk, aye, and sometimes grovel in the dust, before the toiler who has a vote!"[83] The Democrats and the AFL leaders wanted to make labor a dominant theme in the 1908 elections, and they succeeded. But their strategy took place amidst a competitive world of national politics. Republicans, Socialists, Hearst's Independence League, and rival interest groups like the NAM all jockeyed to influence toilers' votes. In this context, the Democrats lost control over the meaning of "labor"

---

[82] The most important exceptions were the race against Joseph Cannon, the effort to elect a Democratic successor to Charles Littlefield in Maine, and a few districts where trade unionists ran energetic campaigns. On the continued belief among AFL leaders that congressional elections were important, see, for example: John Frey to Gompers, September 12, 1908, *AFL Records*, reel 67; William Huber to John Morrison, September 2, 1908, *AFL Records*, reel 67. The key races involving trade unionists that gained the interest of Gompers were those of miner William Wilson of Pennsylvania and Streetcar Employees President William Mahon of Detroit. On these and other congressional campaigns in which the national AFL leaders contributed resources, see: Morrison to Hamilton, September 9, 1908, Morrison Letterbooks; Stuart Reid to Gompers, September 15, 1908, *AFL Records*, reel 67; Max Morris to Gompers, September 22, 1908, *AFL Records*, reel 67; George Berry to Gompers, September 28, 1908, *AFL Records*, reel 68; Morrison to Hamilton, October 15, 1908, Morrison Letterbooks; Morrison to William Wilson, October 17, 1908, Morrison Letterbooks; Morrison to Hugh Frayne, October 27, 1908, Morrison Letterbooks; Morrison to Hahn, October 28, 1908, Morrison Letterbooks; Morrison to A. E. Ireland, October 7, 1908, Morrison Letterbooks.

[83] James Creelman, "Mr. Gompers and His Two Million Men," *Pearson's Magazine*, 20 (3), September 1908, 240.

as political discourse increasingly revolved around the AFL leaders' activity and their unprecedented relationship to the Democratic Party. What began as a crusade for the rights of labor turned sour as politicians challenged organized labor's right to speak for American workers.

The campaign in 1908 focused on one question: Which party best represented the future of reform in America? The progressive movement had gathered enough strength to make conservatism unpopular in most quarters; the rhetoric of the day emphasized issues like direct election of senators, trust regulation, and the rights of labor. The Democrats' struggle to represent reform was an embattled one, however, because the country's best-known progressive stood at the helm of the Republican Party. Theodore Roosevelt served as his party's spokesman, relying on his progressive image to bludgeon the Democratic Party's reform credentials.

Bryan's Jeffersonian program demanded a government of and for the people, and he claimed that under Republican leadership, special interests controlled the nation. Deriding the Republican reliance on corporate contributions, for example, Bryan pledged to raise his campaign fund through popular donations and to publicize his campaign contributions before the election. Later, Bryan charged that the U.S. Steel Corporation was contributing generously to the Republican war chest in return for immunity from prosecution.[84] But soon after this, Republican leaders, with help from Hearst, tied the Democrats to corrupt trust money. Hearst published letters he had found linking Governor Haskell of Oklahoma, the Democratic Party's Treasurer, to the Standard Oil Corporation. Roosevelt and Taft charged that Haskell's position as treasurer meant Standard Oil money for the Democratic Party. Haskell soon resigned, but not before the damage had been done: With this incident, the Republicans associated the Democrats with corporate corruption, thereby defusing many of their attacks on the Republicans.[85] With much of their planned strategy undermined, the Democrats began to emphasize their commitment to American workers more than ever.

Organized labor's new political prominence and its blossoming partnership with the Democratic Party deeply worried Republican leaders. As Joseph Cannon later described the situation, "None of us knew exactly how powerful Gompers and his crowd might prove."[86] Thus, party officials carefully created machinery of their own to recruit working-class votes, forming a Labor Bureau and organizing Republican clubs among various working-class constituencies. Railroad workers and miners provided important support for the Republican Party. Party officials reached beyond those groups, however, seeking endorsements from any prominent labor official in order to demonstrate the limits of Gompers's authority. A trade unionist from New Castle, Pennsylvania, described the party's new effort there: "Republicans are scouring the ranks of the Unions for men to

[84] Coletta, *William Jennings Bryan*, 413–18.

[85] Coletta, *William Jennings Bryan*; and Sarasohn, *Party of Reform*, 50–2.

[86] Joseph Cannon, autobiographical fragment, Joseph Cannon Papers, Illinois State Historical Society.

champion the cause of Taft." AFL leaders found that many of the activists who mobilized for their campaign in 1906 were no longer available. Frank Morrison worried about Ohio, for example, because "They have picked a number of the active men of two years ago and they have received appointments, thus ... silencing them from active work, no matter what their political view may be." One of the most active trade unionists in Youngstown during 1906 now served as oil inspector in a Republican administration, spending much of his time persuading workers to support Taft.[87]

The National Association of Manufacturers, closely tied to the Republican Party, also mobilized to line workers up behind Taft. Focusing on cities in New Jersey, New York, Pennsylvania, Ohio, Maryland, Missouri, and Indiana, the NAM influenced the selection of candidates and organized trade unionists into a conservative organization called the Workingmen's Protective Association. NAM organizers borrowed heavily from the campaign spectacles developed by the parties, for example, organizing torchlight parades and fife and drum corps, but they blended that culture with their traditional gumshoe arsenal, which involved tactics like bribery, coercion, and intimidation. Often the NAM targeted the same campaigns as the AFL, its organizers working, for example, to defeat the bid for reelection of congressman and ex-miner William B. Wilson, who would later become the first secretary of labor. NAM leaders also wanted to help Republican Presidential nominee Taft win workers' votes. Most of their time and resources, however, focused on helping conservative James Watson win the Indiana governor's election. The AFL leaders also focused great attention on this race, and their contribution to defeating Watson provided one of their few victories in 1908.[88]

More important than these activities, however, was the influence Republicans and NAM employers exercised on the language and rhetoric of the campaign. Both groups sidestepped the legal issues (most notably, the injunction) raised by the Democrats until quite late in the campaign, focusing instead on two quite different topics. They celebrated the Republican record on economic prosperity, a theme that had served the party well since 1896, while vociferously attacking the AFL for its role in the campaign and its ties to the Democratic Party.

[87] John Callahan of New Castle, Pennsylvania, to Gompers, July 24, 1908, *AFL Records*, reel 66; Morrison to Jere L. Sullivan, October 1, 1908, Morrison Letterbooks; Thomas H. Flynn to Gompers, July 17, 1908, *AFL Records*, reel 66. See also Julia Greene, "The Strike at the Ballot Box: Politics and Partisanship in the American Federation of Labor, 1881 to 1916," Ph.D. diss., Yale University, 1990, chapter 5.

[88] See Julie Greene, "Dinner-Pail Politics: Employers, Workers, and Partisan Culture in the Progressive Era," in Eric Arnesen, Julie Greene, and Bruce Laurie, eds., *Labor Histories: Class, Politics, and the Working-Class Experience* (forthcoming, University of Illinois Press); and Martin Mulhall to Henry Loudenslager, August 21, 1908, U.S. Senate, *Maintenance*, Vol. 2, pt. 2, 1915; Mulhall to Schwedtman, September 11 and October 23, 1908, *Maintenance*, Vol. 2, pt. 2, 2003–7 and 2,259; Schwedtman to H. B. Anthony, October 22, 1908, *Maintenance*, Vol. 2, pt. 2, 2,257; Mulhall's financial account, October 31, 1908, *Maintenance*, Vol. 2, pt. 2, 2,319; and his testimony in *Maintenance*, Vol. 2, pt. 1, 2,943–4.

During Bryan's first campaign for the presidency, Republicans had promised to bring prosperity back to America, and had threatened that a Democratic victory would only intensify the unemployment and low wages then bearing down on workers. In the next years, as economic conditions improved, Republicans sold themselves as the party of prosperity and the full dinner pail. They regularly reminded workers that the last Democratic president, Cleveland, had created the worst depression known to that time. Prosperity and the full dinner pail again dominated Republican discourse in 1908, particularly in industrial cities, even though the panic of 1907 had sparked a brief but acute depression that pushed thousands of workers out of their jobs and forced others to endure short time and reduced wages. Why then did Republicans continue to rely on their promise of full dinner pails?

The politics of prosperity allowed Republicans to stress their concern for workers at a time when they had rejected organized labor's demands for legal and other reforms. Whereas Democrats attacked plutocracy and the privileges accruing to special interests, Republicans spoke more consolingly of Americans' common interest in economic growth. This theme, premised on class harmony, assumed that workers and their employers shared a common political outlook: Both groups asked only that factories run strong. Thus, while Taft charged that Bryan's "election would mean a paralysis of business and . . . a recurrence of disastrous conditions of the last Democratic administration," Roosevelt added that it would bring calamity in particular to wageworkers.[89]

Some workers undoubtedly accepted that they shared with employers an interest in prosperity. For those who disagreed, Republican employers added a more coercive touch. Across the country, observers saw signs posted in factories that read: "Believing that the election of Taft and Sherman means a safe and progressive business administration the day following we shall start this plant on 'FULL TIME AND KEEP GOING.' "[90] Employers used these tactics of intimidation most blatantly in 1896, marching their workers dutifully in McKinley parades and forcing ardent Bryan men to carry Republican banners. So sharply was the connection drawn between job security and Republican victory that workers commonly feared showing any interest in the Democratic campaign, unless perhaps to a trusted friend. In Ohio, for example, an observer noted: "I know a great many of the working men. Many of them are wearing McKinley badges, but if they know you quite well, they will show you a Bryan badge on the inside of their vest and tell you that is the way they will vote."[91]

---

[89] Coletta, *William Jennings Bryan*, 420 and 422. For general information on Republican strategy in 1908, see Merrill and Merrill, *Republican Command*, 243–98; and Mowry, *Era of Theodore Roosevelt*, 226–43.

[90] See, for example, "Why is the 'Full Time and Keep Going' Plan not now in Operation," *The Commoner*, 8 (36), September 18, 1908.

[91] Braxton Davenport to William Oldham, October 22, 1896, William Jennings Bryan Papers, Library of Congress. For more on employers' tactics during 1896, see also Josephus Daniels, *Editor in Politics* (Chapel Hill: University of North Carolina Press, 1941), 196–201.

   Though the 1908 campaign involved less extreme tactics, employers still commonly marched their workers in Republican parades or put notices regarding the
dire consequences of a Bryan victory in employees' pay envelopes. The Thomas Bell
wrote in his novel of the steel industry that shopkeepers and workers in the
Pittsburgh region feared for their livelihood should they appear to waver in supporting Taft. The effects of the recent depression still could be seen in factories
partially shut down, but steel employers promised that if the Republicans won, "the
mill might resume full-time operations. . . ."[92] Perhaps prosperity politics worked
effectively in 1908, even as the country pulled out of a depression, because the
theme tapped into workers' vulnerabilities and their fears of layoffs and wage cuts.
   Occasionally, Democrats or their labor allies objected to the Republican
emphasis on prosperity. Gompers accused Republicans of exploiting the depression by "Dangling a dinner pail in the faces of honest workingmen. . . ." Taft
insulted workingmen, Gompers proclaimed, in assuming that the dinner pail could
represent workers' ideals. Furthermore, workers presently did not enjoy a full
dinner pail, nor had they for at least a year: "It is most unfeeling to tantalize,
and brutal to make such a reference to our hundreds and thousands of idle
men."[93] Like Gompers, some employers rejected this Republican ploy as coercive and refused to post the leaflets sent to them by the Republican National
Committee. One manufacturer angrily declared that McKinley had first promised
a full dinner pail in 1896: "Why then do we need more promises? Why after
twelve years of Republicans do we have so many idle mills and unused freight
cars?" Likewise Bryan used his newspaper, the *Commoner*, to attack Republican
myths about the full dinner pail. Yet such criticisms proved the exception.
Overall, the Republicans controlled the campaign's economic discussions and
used them to focus Americans' attention on their promise of prosperity. The
Democrats stuck with their emphasis on equal rights for labor, missing a grand
opportunity to address workers' concerns about their standard of living, their
fears of unemployment, or their low wages.[94]

[92] Thomas Bell, *Out of This Furnace: A Novel of Immigrant Labor in America* (Pittsburgh:
    University of Pittsburgh Press, 1974), 160–1. Bell adds that from a neighboring steel mill
    "came the usual reports of men fired for refusing to vote as the company wished."
[93] "Gompers in Indiana," *Indianapolis Star*, October 17, 1908, p. 5; " 'Full Dinner Pail Empty
    Says Bryan,' " *Indianapolis Star*, October 23, 1908, p. 2; Gompers, "Candidate Taft, Take
    Notice!" *AF*, 15 (11), November 1908, 960.
[94] O. Andrew Oswald, Cambridge, Nebraska, to Gompers, October 19, 1908, *AFL Records*,
    reel 68; P. C. Burns, president, American Electric Telephone Company, Chicago, to New York
    Leather Bolting Company, July 25, 1908, *AFL Records*, reel 66; Robert Baker, president,
    Austin Engine Company, to New York Leather Bolting Company, August 14, 1908, *AFL Re-
    cords*, reel 66. For more on employers and coercion, see Lennon to Gompers, November 2,
    1908, *AFL Records*, reel 69; J. G. Waterman, Louisville, KY, to Gompers, October 10, 1908,
    AFL Records, reel 68; "Employee at T. B. Clark and Company," Honisdale, Pennsylvania, to
    Gompers, September 21, 1908, *AFL Records*, reel 67. For *The Commoner*'s focus on
    the full dinner pail and the panic of 1907, see, for example, articles published on May 1
    and October 23, 1908. William Jennings Bryan wrote Gompers after the election that em-
    ployers' intimidating tactics had made it difficult for workers to support him. See Bryan to
    Gompers, November 10, 1908, *AFL Records*, reel 69.

The Republicans developed their second major issue for appealing to American workers immediately after the Democratic convention, as AFL leaders cozied close to Bryan and began exhorting trade unionists to support him as well. In the eyes of Republicans, Gompers had promised "to deliver the labor vote" to the Democratic Party. Gompers quickly labeled the charge absurd: "We recognize the absolute right of every citizen to cast his vote for any candidate and with any party that he pleases. Far be it from us to attempt to coerce the votes of the workers, nor are we so asinine as to promise to 'deliver the labor vote.' "[95]

But in the next weeks Republican speakers and newspapers tirelessly repeated this theme, charging Gompers and the AFL with "dictating" to workers, seeking to control their votes, and giving them no voice in deciding labor's political strategy. When Gompers addressed the Labor Day celebration in Danville, Illinois, for example, the local pro-Republican newspaper covered the event at length and praised workers profusely before focusing in on Gompers's "disappointing speech." Many workers expressed strong disapproval of Gompers, the reporter said: "His effort to turn a Labor Day celebration into an avowed Democratic meeting was resented." Furthermore, the newspaper reported, other labor men addressed the crowd and disagreed with Gompers. O. P. Smith of the Indiana Federation of Labor spoke and stressed organization rather than political activity. Said the reporter: "That indicated the feeling of a majority of the labor people present. They know that they advance their condition by organization, but when it comes to politics, they resent the intimation that they can be delivered body and soul by any man. Each man does his own voting and his own thinking."[96]

The accusation also allowed Republicans to taint the Democrats with the scandal of links to special interests. The *Denver Post*, for example, reprinted an article by open-shop activist C. W. Post that declared: "The only trust having the impudence to openly assert that it is going to elect its own trust representatives to public office is the *Labor Trust*. The election, therefore, will determine whether the Common Citizens retain control of public affairs, or allow the Labor Trust magnates to govern." Even an avowedly Democratic newspaper, the *New York Times*, picked up this charge. According to its editor, "Popular wrath might well be kindled by the complacent announcement of Mr. Gompers that he has saddled the Democratic donkey, and that it will do his will at the polls as it did at the convention when it adopted his plank. . . ."[97]

In their haste to delegitimize the AFL and its strategy, Republicans visited a host of other charges on Gompers, claiming he had always been partisan to the Democrats, for example, or that he was not a naturalized citizen and hence should not interfere in American politics. An "American Workingman" wrote

[95] Gompers, "Both Parties have Spoken," 603–4.
[96] In fact, O. P. Smith strongly favored political action and loyally followed Gompers's direction. Despite Gompers's focus on politics during 1908, like O. P. Smith, he continued to emphasize that organization remained more important than political work. See the Danville (Illinois) *Commercial-News*, September 8, 1908.
[97] C. W. Post, "A Dangerous Trust," *Denver Post*, October 1, 1908; New York *Times* editorial, n.d. [July 1908], *AFL Records*, reel 66.

in the Republican-affiliated Indianapolis *Star* of his humiliation at seeing the great AFL, an organization of native-born Americans, "being ruled and reigned by a foreigner," and a Jew at that. Such charges led Gompers regularly to exhibit his naturalization papers during political meetings, and to confess his personal political history: "I have never been . . . [a Democrat] and am not now. A long time ago I was a Republican, but I'm not guilty now."[98]

But, usually, Republicans remained focused on their charge that AFL leaders sought to dictate to workers and thereby "deliver the labor vote" to the Democrats. As Taft typically charged, "this thing of Mr. Gompers having the labor vote in his power and laboring men believing the lies he tells is something that I complain of."[99] When Hearst and the Socialists began hurling the same charge at AFL leaders, they reinforced its effectiveness. In his newspapers, Hearst charged that Gompers had received $40,000 from the Democrats and Republicans for his role in the campaign, and he publicized incidents in which local trade unionists opposed their national leaders. In Hearst's Chicago *Examiner*, for example, a headline blared: "REVOLT GROWING AGAINST GOMPERS. Louisville Federation on Verge of Disruption Over Steam Roller Tactics." Socialist organs adopted a similar refrain. As Max Hayes wrote in the *International Socialist Review*, "the working people are not taking very kindly to the idea that they can be bound, gagged, and delivered to Tom, Dick and Harry by Gompers or anybody else."[100]

The AFL leaders found that this charge of "delivering the labor vote" significantly damaged their campaign. Organizers repeatedly alerted AFL headquarters that local workers felt troubled by the accusations. While working between Danville, Illinois, and St. Louis, organizer Grant Hamilton commented to Morrison that "The opposition . . . endeavors to lend the impression that President Gompers assumes to control the labor vote, and this has found lodgement in the minds of some, but can be eradicated upon a proper representation of the subject."[101] As the AFL leaders braced themselves for a "vicious" last two weeks to the campaign, Morrison assessed the problems they faced: "The great effort of the Taft supporters will be . . . to impress upon the minds of the wage workers that their vote is being delivered and to try and create a resentment in their mind against the idea that they are not free agents."[102]

---

[98] An "American Workingman," to the Editor, *Indianapolis Star*, October 6, 1908, p. 6; "Democrats Sway State Federation," *Indianapolis Star*, October 1, 1908, p. 1. James Watson, campaigning as Republican candidate for governor of Indiana, repeatedly charged that Gompers was not a naturalized citizen and thus had no right to tell workers how to vote. See the transcript of a speech given by Watson on July 29, 1908, *AFL Records*, reel 66; and the Indianapolis *Union*, October 24, 1908. For the charge that Gompers had always been a Democrat, see the Danville *Commercial-News*, September 8, 1908.

[99] William Taft quoted in an editorial by Gompers: "Mr. Taft – Answer Before Election," *AF*, 15 (11), November 1908, 970.

[100] George Wellington, Louisville, Kentucky, to Gompers, September 9, 1908, *AFL Records*, reel 67; Max Hayes, "World of Labor," *International Socialist Review*, 9 (1), July 1908, 75–6.

[101] M. Grant Hamilton to Frank Morrison, July 25, 1908, *AFL Records*, reel 66.

[102] Morrison to Frank Kennedy, Omaha, October 2, 1908, Morrison Letterbooks.

AFL spokesmen, from the highest officials to the organizers in the field, finally found that responding to this charge could be a full-time job. Watching employers and Republican politicians attempt to manipulate workers' voting behavior in their interest, Gompers could barely contain his anger and frustration. Newspapers have criticized the AFL, he wrote, because its president "presumed to advise the workers as to how their interests could be best protected in this campaign. It now becomes clear that this was mostly a howl of rage on the part of those who had always arrogated to themselves the task of advising the toilers how to vote."[103]

The Republicans continued attacking labor on this front throughout the campaign, meanwhile avoiding substantive debate about the merits of the AFL's demands. But in the last two weeks of the campaign, they felt strong enough to make a frontal assault on Gompers and the AFL. The campaign reached its climax in an angry exchange of letters between President Roosevelt and Samuel Gompers regarding the AFL's demands and its role in electoral politics. Roosevelt had been active since the campaign's beginning, advising Taft privately and intervening publicly when necessary. Often, the president reserved his energies for issues related to the working class, and he headed a program within the party to attract labor to his party.[104]

In late October, Roosevelt launched his attack on the AFL. Writing to a senator who had criticized Bryan's stand on injunctions, Roosevelt made Gompers, the injunction, and the AFL's relationship with the Democratic Party into major campaign issues. He criticized the Democratic plank on the injunction as "vague and hazy," and ultimately devoid of legal meaning. Beyond that, Roosevelt portrayed Gompers's views on the courts as extremist and dangerous. The courts gave lawful businesses the right to carry on lawful activities; in Gompers's eyes, Roosevelt charged, this constituted "despotic power," and "the judges who exercise that power . . . [as] irresponsible despots." The Pearre anti-injunction bill that AFL leaders had asked Congress to pass would also legalize the blacklist and the sympathetic boycott, acts that even labor leaders had declared to be unjust and immoral. "Does Mr. Bryan believe that Mr. Gompers . . . and the part of the labor movement that agrees with him, has the right morally, and should be given the right legally, to paralyse or destroy with impunity the business of an innocent third person . . . ?" The blacklist and the secondary boycott Roosevelt called "two of the most cruel forms of oppression ever devised by the wit of man for the infliction of suffering on his weaker fellows. No court could possibly exercise any more brutal, unfeeling or despotic power than Mr. Gompers claims for himself and his followers. . . ."[105]

Newspapers across the country published Roosevelt's letter and, as one observer noted, it marked "the critical hour of the campaign."[106] In a lengthy

---

[103] Gompers, "Congressional Responsibility," 866.
[104] Foner, *History of the Labor Movement*, 3:356; Coletta, *William Jennings Bryan*, 426.
[105] Roosevelt to Senator Knox, October 21, 1908, *AFL Records*, reel 69; Coletta, *William Jennings Bryan*, 426.
[106] Edwin Pierce, lawyer, to Gompers, October 26, 1908, *AFL Records*, reel 69.

essay of his own, Gompers responded to what he called Roosevelt's "bitterly partisan" attack. Gompers quoted previous statements made by Roosevelt in which he called for injunction reforms and contended that the president had now changed his position out of party obligation: "It is the purpose of the opponents of Labor to vilify the labor movement through me and Mr. Roosevelt now joins the chorus upon the pretext that I have attacked the federal courts." Roosevelt's letter, Gompers concluded, resulted from his bitterness at having lost control over labor's vote: "seeing that the 'labor vote,' which so often has been corralled, diverted, and perverted by the politicians, is now aroused and determined to deliver its own vote," the president had grown into an angry demagogue, seeking to scare employers by charging that their property would be endangered if labor should receive equality before the law. Gompers described Roosevelt's letter as "an exhibition of impotent rage and disappointment, and an awful descent from the dignity of the high office of the president of the United States."[107]

The exchange did not stop there. Days before the election, Roosevelt penned another widely printed letter concerning labor, this one addressed to a trainman who requested his advice on which candidate best represented labor's interests. AFL leaders responded this time by putting out a *special edition issue* of the *American Federationist*. Again, the AFL Executive Council defended itself from the charge of partisanship, saying that in "performing a solemn duty . . . in support of a political party *Labor does not become partisan to a political party, but partisan to a principle.*"[108]

By November 1908, the AFL leaders seemed surrounded by criticism and controversy. Gompers's dramatic debate with the president, unprecedented in American campaign politics, helped rally some trade unionists around the AFL program. John Lennon declared after talking with rank-and-file workers in Illinois that whereas Roosevelt had been the most popular man in the United States six months ago, "Now they are ready to abuse his name at any . . . opportunity." Yet Roosevelt's considerable powers of persuasion undoubtedly helped many Republican trade unionists hew close to the party line. For his part, Gompers long remembered Roosevelt's antilabor role in this campaign. When Roosevelt bolted and formed his rival Progressive Party with a prolabor platform four years later, AFL leaders showed no interest but maintained their links to the Democratic Party. In his autobiography, Gompers stressed Roosevelt's role in 1908 as a primary reason why the Federation refused to consider supporting the Progressives in 1912.[109]

---

[107] "President Roosevelt's Attack on Labor, Answered by Samuel Gompers," *AF*, 15 (11), November 1908, 973–9.

[108] The special issue of the *AF* is not dated, but it is volume 15 (12), 1033–40; it probably came out in the last week or ten days before the election.

[109] Lennon to Gompers, October 27, 1908, *AFL Records*, reel 69. For Gompers's estimation of Roosevelt in 1912, see his *Seventy Years*, 2:276: "Because of Roosevelt's course in the 1908 campaign, I knew that if a candidate favorable to labor was to be nominated that candidate must be expected from the Democratic Party."

While facing charges from Roosevelt and other Republicans, Gompers also confronted what he called "personal attacks and violent abuse" from Hearst's newspapers across the United States, as well as from Socialists and other radicals.[110] All these critics shared a common criticism: The AFL "dictated" to workers, forcing certain political views on them, in an effort to "deliver the labor vote." These attacks heightened the pressure on AFL leaders to achieve unity on political matters, because any sign of dissent provided their critics with dramatic ammunition. At the same time, the charges highlighted the AFL's internal affairs and its growing centralization by vividly projecting an image of the Federation as undemocratic. Having thrown itself into national partisan politics, AFL leaders found events quickly spiraling beyond their control. Their political enemies made it more necessary for AFL leaders to discipline their troops in the name of Democratic victory, even as their criticisms made that strategy more politically dangerous.

We know how this story turned out. Taft won the election, giving the Republicans another four years in the White House. Yet the remarkable innovations of 1908 pointed to the future in important ways. The AFL's unprecedented partnership with the Democratic Party in 1908 had created a campaign centered around workingmen and their problems. By supporting and bolstering the most progressive wing of the Democratic Party, the American Federation of Labor helped its leader, William Jennings Bryan, defeat conservatives within his own party and win control over the Democracy's future. In that way, labor played an essential role in transforming the Democrats from the party of states' rights to the party of reform. In the following years, the Democratic Party's alliance with organized labor anchored its claim to represent the forces of progressivism. Ironically, the conservative and antistatist AFL had carved a sphere of influence within the party soon to become the architect of progressive statecraft. Although theoretically this created opportunities for some workingmen to shape their state and party system, in reality, the AFL bureaucracy mediated between that state and working Americans. Ultimately, trade unionists' political impact would reflect both their own desires and the organizational interests of their leaders in the AFL.

This raises important problems regarding the relationship between AFL members and their leaders. How and to what extent did these two groups shape one another's political activities and language? Indeed, even as the AFL leaders responded to the results of the 1908 election, feeling saddened to see Bryan defeated, a larger and more important question loomed for them: Had they succeeded in delivering the labor vote? Could labor's dominant institution convince trade unionists, and workers more generally, to support the Democratic candidate? We have seen that the AFL campaign changed its character in 1908, growing more centralized and less popular. Did this allow a greater efficiency

[110] Samuel Gompers, "Mr. Hearst's Political Toy," *AF*, 15 (9), September 1908, 734–6.

on the part of the leadership, or did the declining emphasis on the grass roots hurt the campaign? To these questions we now turn, with an exploration of how the AFL's 1908 campaign, and its alliance with the Democratic Party, influenced the labor movement's internal relationships and the political behavior of American trade unionists.

CHAPTER SIX

Party Politics and Workers' Discontent

Working-class voters experienced the campaign fever of 1908 in diverse ways. Some marched in Taft parades organized by the National Association of Manufacturers, while carrying banners that proclaimed "Prosperity First!" Others sat in barber shops reading the pro-Bryan literature sent there by the AFL, debating the Federation's program and the Democrats' virtues. In cities like Detroit, the talk centered not on Bryan or Taft, but on the congressional campaign of union activist William Mahon, in a race that pitted AFL members against nonunion workers at firms like the Ford Auto Company.

The 1908 elections highlighted the concerns of workingmen in unprecedented ways and thus presented workers with unusual opportunities. Yet they also took place amidst a rapidly changing political world. Scholars such as Paul Kleppner have shown that the ethnocultural and religious associations that so dominated Gilded Age politics faded rapidly after 1900. The decline in voting participation and the attacks on party domination from so many different corners, meanwhile, threatened to make politics less democratic, particularly for working-class voters. Because the parties remained the main institutions capable of attempting mass mobilizations, a decline in their power made it more difficult for nonelites to influence the American state. In this context, the AFL's campaign program was potentially quite important, providing a way to mobilize large numbers of voters who might otherwise fall into the great "party of nonvoters."[1]

Still, the AFL campaign program encountered a number of obstacles. Rank-and-file trade unionists often responded with enthusiasm, but their excitement did not always rebound to the benefit of the official AFL strategy. Workers had their own and often rivaling conceptions of effective political tactics and strategy. Furthermore, the AFL's plan stressed national-level elections, and especially the presidential candidacy of William Jennings Bryan. This focus potentially clashed with working-class agendas at the state and local levels. And last of all, the AFL and the Democratic Party were not the only groups seeking to

[1] Paul Kleppner, *Continuity and Change in Electoral Politics, 1893–1928* (Westport, CT: Greenwood Press, 1987), 224–5.

organize and mobilize the working-class vote. They found worthy opponents in the Republican Party and the open-shop employers in the National Association of Manufacturers, both of whom lavished special attention on workers during 1908, seeking to influence their political behavior.

Workers and the Campaign

For many trade unionists, supporting the AFL campaign program in 1908 became a proud responsibility, a way to demonstrate their commitment to the union cause. Although Federation leaders now focused their attention on the presidential campaign and stopped organizing at the local level, rank-and-file workers nonetheless created political committees, held conventions, and nominated and campaigned for candidates. Workers in such cities as Atlantic City, New Jersey, and Cleveland, Ohio, created Trade Union Political Leagues. The labor movement throughout Indiana, for example, actively opposed the gubernatorial bid of James Watson while also campaigning for Bryan.

The Minnesota State Federation of Labor buzzed with an unusual degree of activity during 1908, creating Bryan clubs in many towns and distributing tens of thousands of political leaflets. Significantly, the Minnesota officers reported to Gompers that they were moved by Hearst to begin an active campaign: They resented his efforts to cut into the labor vote in Minnesota, especially his hiring of several trade unionists at big salaries. The Republicans as well had hired prominent trade unionists to assist their campaign. In response, the Minnesota Federation sponsored a meeting of twenty-five union men in late September to plan a statewide campaign, hoping to establish political clubs in every town in which the labor movement possessed some foothold.[2]

Workers often structured their campaigns to show special support for Gompers and other AFL leaders in the face of Republican attacks. The Indiana Federation of Labor printed campaign stationery with bold letters proclaiming at the top of each sheet: **"GOMPERS IS RIGHT."** A Central Labor Council in upstate New York reported to Gompers on its successful Labor Day parade, in which members marched behind a large banner proclaiming "The Jamestown Unions

---

[2] Thomas Tracy to M. J. Curry, president, Trade Union Political League, Atlantic City, September 1, 1908; S. S. Stilwell, secretary, Labor's Political League, Cleveland, to Gompers, September 20, 1908; Persa Bell, Fort Wayne Federation of Labor, to Morrison, February 7, 1908; no signature to Gompers, February 17, 1908; E. H. Fessel, Anderson, Indiana, Trades Council, to Gompers, February 20, 1908; Theodore Perry, Indianapolis, ITU Local No. 1, to Morrison, February 20, 1908; William Huber to Gompers, April 3, 1908; H. D. Albers, secretary, Elkhart, Indiana, Non-Partisan Political Club, to Gompers, July 1, 1908; Hamilton to Morrison, August 15, 1908; W. E. McEwen, secretary-treasurer, Minnesota Federation of Labor, September 26, 1908; Sim A. Bramlette, president, Kansas Federation of Labor, August 15, 1908; Edwin R. Wright, president, Illinois Federation of Labor, May 22, 1908: all from the *American Federation of Labor Records: The Samuel Gompers Era* (Microfilming Corporation of America, 1979) (hereafter cited as *AFL Records*), reels 65–7.

Stand for Gompers." They continued: "The average intelligent laboring man has not been intimidated nor influenced to forsake [his] leader. . . ." The St. Louis Central Trades and Labor Union sent Gompers a resolution endorsing the AFL campaign program, and explained that it passed because "The local Republican press has been very vicious in its attacks upon you on account of your stand on political action. . . . [They are] trying to make the people believe that we have lost all confidence in you. . . ."[3]

Although in 1908 the AFL leaders no longer focused attention on the goal of electing trade unionists to Congress, union workers across the country continued to pursue this avenue to political power. As often as in 1906, labor activists attempted to nominate trade unionists for Congress – and this time, perhaps having learned something from their last experience, they enjoyed more success. Eighteen trade unionists won their party's nomination for Congress in districts stretching from Pennsylvania to California and from Wisconsin to Mississippi, and election day sent eight out of those eighteen triumphantly to Congress. The four trade unionists elected in 1906 all won their reelection campaigns: Thomas Nicholls and William Wilson (mine workers from Scranton and Williamsport, Pennsylvania), William Cary (a Milwaukee telegrapher), and John McDermott (a Chicago telegrapher). The 61st House of Representatives also included William Jamieson (a typographer from Iowa), John Martin (a lawyer and active member of the Brotherhood of Locomotive Firemen from Pueblo, Colorado), Arthur Murphy (a Mississippi member of the Railroad Trainmen), and Carl Anderson (an Ohio musician). Six of these eight trade unionists belonged to the Democratic Party, with only Cary of Wisconsin and Murphy of Mississippi winning as Republicans.[4]

Besides these victories, labor activists in several parts of the country conducted energetic, but ultimately unsuccessful, campaigns for labor candidates. In Youngstown, Ohio, steelworker Elias Jenkins ran on the Prohibition ticket against AFL enemy James Kennedy. Typographer George Tracy, president of

---

[3] O. P. Smith, Indiana Federation of Labor, to Gompers, August 25, 1908; E. George Lindstrom to Gompers, September 9, 1908; Owen Miller to Gompers, August 12, 1908: all *AFL Records*, reel 66.

[4] See Philip Foner, *History of the Labor Movement in the United States*, Vol. 3, *Policies and Practices of the American Federation of Labor, 1900–1909* (New York: International, 1964), 358. For more information on efforts to elect trade unionists, see these documents: W. J. Kenealy [to the AFL], August 1908; U. T. Webb to Gompers, September 17, 1908; P. J. McArdle, Pittsburgh, to Gompers, August 5, 1908; John Martin to Gompers, September 12, 1908; John Martin to Gompers, September 28, 1908; H. L. Eichelberger to Gompers, and Eichelberger to Joseph McGregor, both September 15, 1908; Gompers to J. W. Reynolds, September 19, 1908; Charles Miller [to Gompers], October 10, 1908; Robert E. Lee, Pottsville, Pennsylvania, to Gompers, October 14, 1908; James Hill, Peoria, Illinois, to Dear Sir, July 27, 1908; S. H. Thorne to Gompers, August 9, 1908; T. H. Flynn to Gompers, October 8, 1908; Gilbert Eagleson to Gompers, August 13, 1908; Gompers to Cal Wyatt, September 17, 1908; C. B. Crawford to Morrison, September 26, 1908; Morrison to C. B. Crawford, October 2, 1908; J. C. Shanessy to Gompers, July 31, 1908; Sim A. Bramlett to Gompers, June 4, 1908: all *AFL Records*, reels 65–8.

the California Federation of Labor, ran in San Francisco as the joint nominee of the Democrats, the Union Labor Party, and Hearst's Independent League.

Trade unionists conducted their most visible campaign on behalf of William D. Mahon of Detroit, International President of the Streetcar and Electric Railway Employees. A pragmatic ex-Socialist, Mahon enjoyed respect throughout the labor movement. Asked if he would run in August 1908, Mahon sought his executive board's approval before he would agree. They not only approved his candidacy, but created a "Mahon Independent Congressional Election Promotion Club," in order to mobilize union members behind him. Rank-and-file unionists created a Non-Partisan Railway Men's Club, with a membership of more than 2,000, which organized a network of supporters in each precinct and worked with other Detroit unions to ensure their strong support. The AFL exerted unusual efforts to assist Mahon: they funded at least three organizers for him, including a Polish worker, and they pressured Daniel Keefe, whose Longshoremen's Union had its headquarters in Detroit, to provide Mahon with support. In addition, Gompers and the presidents of the Retail Clerks and the Iron Molders visited Detroit to speak on Mahon's behalf.

Mahon and his supporters possessed little chance for victory in an open-shop city like Detroit, and the powerful employers' association launched its attack as soon as he announced his candidacy. Whereas Mahon attempted to focus his campaign on judicial hostility, the conservative employers' association directed attention to open-shop issues. Incumbent Congressman Edwin Denby proclaimed the closed shop "Un-American," saying, "I don't think it right for a union to keep me from getting a job if I don't belong to a union." In the end Mahon lost to Denby, but he ran far ahead of his ticket and union men supported him strongly. Unionists seeking an explanation for his defeat claimed that the Democratic Party refused to give Mahon anything but lackluster support, and more importantly, they pointed to the district's many nonunion workers. As the editor of the union's journal expressed this sentiment, "Mr. Denby owes his election to the vote of unorganized labor."[5] This phenomenon boded ill for the AFL's entire program.

Naturally, many labor organizations across the country endorsed the AFL's political program, and, as we saw in the previous chapter, more than 100,000 workers enrolled in the "Minute Men" campaign Grant Hamilton established at Democratic headquarters. Most labor leaders at the national level expressed

---

[5] William Mahon to Gompers, September 14, 1908, *AFL Records*, reel 67; Morrison to C. O. Pratt, September 16, 1908, Morrison Letterbooks; Morrison to Mahon, September 16 and 23 and October 2, 1908, Morrison Letterbooks; Mahon to Gompers, September 24 and October 1, 1908, *AFL Records*, reels 67 and 68; Morrison to Mahon, October 15, 1908, Morrison Letterbooks; Morrison to C. O. Pratt, October 16 and 19, 1908, Morrison Letterbooks; Morrison to H. F. DeGour, October 16, 1908, Morrison Letterbooks; Morrison to Hamilton, October 15, 1908, Morrison Letterbooks; see also *The Motorman*, official journal of the Streetcar and Electric Railway Employees, September through November 1908, passim.

support for the program as well.[6] For all this, however, workers' participation in the 1908 campaign remained remarkably subdued. The trade unionists running for Congress seem to have generated more excitement among AFL members than did William Jennings Bryan's Presidential campaign. The activities unionists engaged in so often during 1906, forming a political committee, holding a convention, or questioning candidates, occurred less often during 1908. Only thirty-one labor organizations reported to Gompers that they had built an active campaign in 1908, which suggests a striking decline in participation relative to 1906.[7] Because political mobilization typically intensifies dramatically during a Presidential campaign, workers' declining participation is particularly noteworthy.

Labor activists repeatedly complained of workers' indifference during the 1908 campaign. A Pennsylvania organizer noted that although most men would support the AFL program, "apathy . . . is one of the worst obstacles that we have to contend with." Edwin Wright, president of the Illinois Federation of Labor, similarly painted a grim picture of workers' activity in his region:

Politicians are tearing up and down the state in hot haste and prickly heat, the printing presses are working overtime, and, keep this private, the trade unionist candidates will (generally) get a fine drubbing. I have visited many towns, spoken before hundreds of unions, visited the men in shops and factories, but for all this they are not awake.[8]

Meanwhile, the AFL's support for Bryan and other Democrats generated political discord within the institution more intense than anything seen since the early 1890s, when unionists debated the Morgan program. After preaching for decades that labor must reject any partisan ties, Gompers and his allies among the national leadership had joined hands in a highly publicized alliance with a major party long identified with plutocracy. This alienated many factions of the AFL: Republicans and Socialists would obviously oppose the strategy, as would unionists who rejected all forms of party politics and those individuals favoring creation of a labor party. All Gompers's efforts could not hold together the diverse political tendencies within labor's union movement.

The AFL political program placed considerable pressure on leaders throughout the movement's hierarchy. In making their decisions, individual leaders

[6] For examples of efforts to have labor conventions endorse the AFL program, see Morrison to Frank L. Rist, September 28, 1908; Morrison to M. Grant Hamilton, October 15, 1908; Morrison to D. A. Hayes, October 18, 1908; and Morrison to Peter E. Duffy, October 18, 1908: all Morrison Letterbooks. The published endorsements can be found in "Labor Answers: Official Endorsement of American Federation of Labor Political Campaign," in the *American Federationist* (hereafter cited as *AF*), 15 (9), September 1908, 751–61; "Labor Makes Its Choice," *AF*, 15 (10), October 1908, 878–90; and "A.F. of L. Political Campaign," *AF*, 15 (11), November 1908, 985–90.

[7] Fifty-one labor organizations indicated such activity in 1906, as discussed in chapter 4.

[8] D. B. Hill, AFL Organizer, Jermyn, Pennsylvania, to Gompers, October 22, 1908; Edwin Wright to Morrison, July 31, 1908; H. G. Skeffington to Gompers, October 7, 1908; J. P. Reynolds, general secretary, Tile Layers and Helpers International Union, Allegheny, Pennsylvania, to Gompers, November 5, 1908; T. T. O'Malley, Canton, Ohio, to Gompers, November 11, 1908; Lennon to Gompers, November 4, 1908: all *AFL Records*, reels 68 and 69.

had to weigh not only their own preferences, but the sentiments of their union members. Workers in some unions, like the Carpenters or the Granite Cutters, seemed unfriendly to the program because they rejected the notion of participating in electoral politics on a class basis. In other unions, like the Miners or the Machinists, strong support for political activity existed among rank-and-file workers, but members divided sharply over which party or even which strategy to support. In these cases, where avid Socialists worked next to loyal Republicans and Democrats, the AFL leaders could find many of their strongest supporters as well as their most bitter opponents.[9]

For these reasons, some of the movement's most influential leaders distanced themselves from AFL politics during 1908. Although the AFL Executive Council had approved Gompers's strategy, several members of that body balked at his cozy friendship with the Democrats. In October, William Howard Taft happily declared in a speech that Gompers's own Executive Council refused to support his political policy. As examples he singled out James Duncan of the Granite Cutters, John Mitchell, ex-president of the Mine Workers, and Daniel Keefe of the Longshoremen.[10] Each of these men felt deeply ambivalent about the AFL's new direction, but Taft had not touched on the whole problem. Most of the Executive Council, and a number of leaders outside it, refused to commit themselves to the campaign. As Lennon complained to Gompers, "almost every day, because of the inactivity and silence of a number of members of the Council, their names are used to throw cold water on the effort we are making...." Morrison similarly observed that "when the smoke is cleared away it will appear as if President Gompers, Treasurer Lennon and Secretary Morrison were the only men who have gone right into the fray and addressed public meetings."[11]

John Mitchell, America's most popular labor leader, maintained ties to both major parties. Bryan considered him as a possible vice-presidential nominee, and

[9] For an excellent political portrayal of several unions, see John H. M. Laslett, *Labor and the Left: A Study of Socialist and Radical Influences in the American Labor Movement, 1881–1924* (New York: Basic Books, 1970).

[10] Duncan to Gompers, September 29, 1908; B. A. Larger to Gompers, September 29, 1908; Duncan to the Buffalo *Republican*, October 1, 1908; Duncan to Gompers, October 31, 1908; Duncan to Gompers, December 9, 1908; Simon Burns to Gompers, October 14, 1908: all *AFL Records*, reels 68–70.

[11] Three other Executive Council members, Max Morris of the Retail Clerks, Joseph Valentine of the Iron Molders, and Denis Hayes of the Glass Bottle Blowers, each contributed some time to the campaign. The remaining five members (Mitchell, Keefe, Duncan, Huber of the Carpenters, and O'Connell of the Machinists) seem to have done virtually nothing. Lennon to Gompers, October 17, 1908; Morrison to Lennon, October 18, 1908, Morrison Letterbooks. On Executive Council members refusing Gompers's request for assistance, see James O'Connell to Gompers, September 26, 1908; Joseph Valentine to Gompers, September 28, 1908; Daniel Keefe to Gompers, September 30, 1908; James Duncan to Gompers, October 1, 1908; John Mitchell to Gompers, August 3, 1908. To his credit, Keefe assisted Mahon in Detroit and addressed meetings in New York and Hoboken. It is difficult to imagine what he said, being so staunch a Republican. Keefe to Morrison, October 5, 1908. All the preceding are from *AFL Records*, reels 66–69, except where otherwise noted.

many called on him to run as a Democrat for governor of Illinois in 1908. Yet his friendship with Teddy Roosevelt, together with his desire to keep his political opinions private, led Mitchell to refuse to back Bryan. While he professed admiration for the Democrats' anti-injunction plank soon after the convention, in August he suddenly proclaimed that he would take no part in the Presidential campaign: "I will not say whether or not I am in sympathy with the stand taken by Mr. Gompers. I will not say what side I am on or make any predictions." This declaration sent shock waves through much of the labor movement. One worker wrote Gompers: "I hope it ain't so that Mitchell sold out Bryan...." Mitchell attempted to clear up things in September, stating in a newspaper interview that he supported Bryan's platform, not Taft's.[12]

In October, Grant Hamilton at Democratic headquarters took the liberty of mailing copies of Mitchell's interview, along with a picture of him, out to the secretaries of all local UMW unions. Furious, Mitchell complained to Gompers: "I am receiving numerous letters from our locals protesting against what they construe as an attempt upon my part to dictate for whom our members should vote...."[13] Days later Mitchell repudiated the campaign letter, writing the *United Mine Workers Journal* to announce that the letters were mailed without his knowledge and had caused him "serious embarrassment." Although he supported Gompers's program, he interpreted the program as eschewing ties to any political party and pushing instead for the election of trade unionists or other friends of labor. He would never, Mitchell insisted, dictate to workers on political matters. Many workers did resent the intrusion, and because of Mitchell's disclaimer, they blamed Gompers. A miner from Straight Creek, Kentucky, wrote Gompers that they had received the picture of John Mitchell. "Some of the boys were indignant about the matter. Samuel Gompers has been discussed and cussed and every name has been said about Samuel Gompers trying to lead the working man into the Democratic Party.... Send no more printed matter." This incident clearly damaged Gompers's struggle to portray the AFL as politically united.[14]

In contrast to Mitchell, Daniel Keefe, president of the Longshoremen, unabashedly and repeatedly proclaimed his support for William Howard Taft during the campaign. When asked whether he endorsed the AFL political program, Keefe firmly assented. Like others who opposed Bryan's candidacy, however, Keefe stressed that it was a nonpartisan strategy that depended on workers making their own political decisions. Keefe then reaffirmed his plan to vote for

---

[12] Mitchell is quoted in favor of the Democrats on the cover of *The Motorman*, August 1908. See also the Baltimore *Evening News*, n.d., *AFL Records*, reel 66, p. 373; "A Bryan Man" to Gompers, August 2, 1908, *AFL Records*, reel 66; Mitchell to the Buffalo *Republic*, September 15, 1908, *AFL Records*, reel 67.

[13] Mitchell to Gompers, October 12, 1908, *AFL Records*, reel 68.

[14] Mitchell's letter to the editor can be found in the *United Mine Workers Journal*, October 22, 1908; see also Mitchell to Gompers, October 17, 1908; M. J. Cullen to Gompers, October 19, 1908; Mitchell to Gompers, October 31, 1908: all *AFL Records*, reel 69.

Taft.[15] Keefe's conspicuous allegiance to the Republican Party angered many Federation leaders, and by the end of the campaign, relations within labor's highest councils had grown tense. Rumors flew that in return for supporting Taft, Keefe would receive an appointment as the next Commissioner-General of Immigration.[16]

The repercussions of Keefe's actions reached well beyond the 1908 campaign. Soon after the election, delegates to the AFL convention passed a resolution, initiated by Gompers, calling for any Executive Council members who could not support the AFL's political policies to resign. As a result, Keefe refused to stand for reelection to the Executive Council: "I have voted the Republican ticket in National affairs for thirty years and will continue to vote the Republican ticket." Soon after that, in December 1908, Roosevelt confirmed the earlier rumors by appointing Keefe Commissioner-General of Immigration. Keefe's Republicanism dealt the AFL campaign program one of its most damaging blows.[17]

Tracing the political positions of the AFL's national leaders presents little challenge because they occupied visible positions and they often expressed political opinions in writing. But what about the local leaders and rank-and-file workers? We can gain an unusual look into the thinking and reasoning behind workers' political behavior during 1908 because the AFL staff scrupulously saved and maintained its files from these political campaigns. The AFL received hundreds of letters from trade unionists around the country during 1908. Usually, workers asked for assistance or advice, but often they simply offered opinions or analyses. Most of the writers showed a surprising assertiveness as they communicated with their top labor leaders. Indeed, Gompers even received a few abusive letters. One worker addressed himself to "Samy Wind-Bag Gompers." Another wrote to "Samuel Gompers the Insect" and sent an envelope filled with dead flies.[18]

The AFL leaders received many letters from trade unionists – either rank-and-file workers or local leaders – who supported Taft. One worker returned a

[15] Gompers to James Duncan, October 31, 1908; Duncan to Gompers, October 31, 1908; Mitchell to Gompers, October 31, 1908; Daniel Keefe to the Buffalo *Republic*, October 5, 1908; Buffalo *Republic* to Daniel Keefe, October 10, 1908: all *AFL Records*, reels 68 and 69.

[16] For an indication of the tense relations among AFL leaders, see Daniel Keefe to H. A. Stamburgh, October 19, 1908; H. A. Stamburgh to James Duncan, October 21, 1908; Keefe to Gompers, October 17, 1908; Gompers to Keefe, October 22, 1908: all *AFL Records*, reel 69; and see Frank Morrison to Keefe, October 14 and 19, 1908, Morrison Letterbooks.

[17] Keefe to the Buffalo *Republic*, October 5, 1908, *AFL Records*, reel 68; Keefe to Gompers, October 17, 1908, *AFL Records*, reel 69; Keefe to H. A. Stamburgh, October 19, 1908, *AFL Records*, reel 69; Sim A. Bramlett to Gompers, October 18, 1908, *AFL Records*, reel 69; Gompers, *Seventy Years of Life and Labor: An Autobiography* (New York: E. P. Dutton, 1925), 2:266; Foner, *History of the Labor Movement*, 3:360.

[18] No signature to "Samy WindBag Gompers," July 24, 1908; no signature to "Samuel Gompers the Insect," September 3, 1908: both *AFL Records*, reels 66 and 67.

political circular sent out by the AFL, with the following scrawled across it: "When were you told to tell me how to vote? I'll vote to suit meself. Hurrah for TAFT!" Some workers expressed their affection for Teddy Roosevelt – "the best friend that the working man has ever had in this country" – as their reason for supporting Taft. But more often workers pointed to their concerns about economic growth – or, as the discourse of the age put it, their hopes for prosperity. One worker returned an AFL circular with the following message scrawled across it: "We vote as we please. Prosperity First!" Another argued, much as Taft or Roosevelt might, that a Bryan victory would result in factory closings, and that workers would be hurt far worse by unemployment than by any injunction.[19]

Gompers's emphasis on winning anti-injunction legislation seemed misplaced to these workers. A trade unionist from Linton, Indiana, wrote to say that except for one socialist, everyone in his local would vote for Taft: "we are all law abiding citizens and favor the present injunction law without it we think there would be nothing but Riots in case of labor disputes instead of Peace. So you will do me a great favor by not sending such stuff." Another workingman declared that only those who seek to commit wrongful acts ever worried about injunctions.[20]

Socialists and other radicals also excoriated the Federation leaders for their alliance with the Democrats. When Gompers first signaled his determination to engage more actively in politics, early in 1908, Socialists expressed anger that he failed to consider allying with their party.[21] As Gompers grew more committed to running a successful campaign, he began to rely increasingly on anti-socialism, that tool he had used so many times to unite trade unionists around his leadership. This time, though, his attacks on the Socialists grew more sinister than ever.

To begin with, Gompers expressed his outrage that Socialists like Eugene Debs would criticize the AFL campaign program: "So Debs has joined the mob of howling dervishes who are kicking up a great dust and trying to discourage the men in the labor movement from using their political power ... to protect the rights of the masses who toil." According to Gompers, Debs had formed the American Labor Union to help capitalists destroy the AFL and other labor organizations. Recalling the dramatic but unsuccessful Pullman boycott of 1894, Gompers charged that as its leader, Debs caused the "blacklisting and victimization" of

---

[19] AFL circular returned from Grafton, West Virginia, October 16, 1908; H. C. Callaway to Dear Sir, September 26, 1908; H. E. Seelye to Gompers, July 17, 1908; all *AFL Records*, reels 66–68.

[20] James F. Stephens to M. Grant Hamilton, September 22, 1908, *AFL Records*, reel 67; J. Graham to Gompers, August 4, 1908, *AFL Records*, reel 66.

[21] William Bush, Springfield, Missouri, to Gompers, August 20, 1908, *AFL Records*, reel 66; W. F. Dieckhaus et al., North Star Lodge No. 197, IAM, Brainerd, Minnesota, August 10, 1908, *AFL Records*, reel 66; Edward Hourigan, District Lodge No. 15, IAM, New York City, to Gompers, September 9, 1908, *AFL Records*, reel 67.

thousands of railroad workers. For this, he dubbed Debs the "Apostle of Failure." Gompers climaxed his crescendo of accusations by charging that Debs had allied with open-shop employers like C. W. Post and James Van Cleave, and that they, along with the Republicans, were the true financiers of the Socialist "Red Special," the train that carried Debs across the country.[22]

Gompers's allegations enraged leftists of varying persuasions, but especially those Socialists who belonged to AFL unions. In a reaction typical of the labor movement's left wing, the Seattle *Union Record* characterized Gompers's attack as "the whine of a pettish, disgruntled old man."[23] Socialist workers from around the country wrote Gompers personally after he denounced Debs. An angry trade unionist who signed himself "A.S.Ocialist" sent a postcard bearing Debs's picture to "D.E.Mocrat," with the comment: "This photo is a representation of a man who has laid in prison as a result of an infamous injunction issued under a Democratic Government and who worked for Bryan in 1896. He learned better and done better." An Illinois worker warned Gompers that "you are losing the respect of many card men by your attack on Mr. Debs, and this is a kindly tip to desist. . . . Two union molders, not Socialists – said last night that Gompers was making a monkey of himself as a politician."[24]

Besides sticking up for Debs, many Socialist workers expressed their amazement that AFL leaders would support a corrupt old party like the Democrats. The worst working conditions persisted in the South, many noted, a region of low wages, child labor, strikebreaking, convict labor, and, not coincidentally, Democratic rule. Most often, Socialists pointed to the miners' strike that erupted in 1908 near Birmingham, Alabama, when officials announced a 17.5 percent wage cut. Local and state politicians lined up behind the mining companies and played an instrumental role in breaking the strike. Duncan McDonald, a member of the UMW's executive board, declared after visiting Alabama:

I don't want anyone to come to me to talk Bryan and Democracy, as this solid Democratic South is more corporation-cursed and more corrupt even than the trust-owned Republican party. And if Gompers . . . were to tour this district with us I think he would hang his head in shame, for what he has said in defense of the Democratic party.

Similarly, a worker wrote from Independence, Missouri, to say: "I have not forgotten Cleveland's administration, nor the Railroad Strike of 1894. We need not go back as far as that, but turn our eyes to Alabama now and see if Democratic bullets do not kill the same as Republican bullets." As Eugene Debs noted,

---

[22] Samuel Gompers, "Debs, the Apostle of Failure," *AF*, 15 (9), September 1908, 736–40; Max Hayes, "World of Labor," *International Socialist Review*, 9 (4), October 1908, 301–5.

[23] The *Seattle Union Record* is quoted in the Cleveland *Citizen*, September 26, 1908.

[24] A.S.Ocialist to D.E.Mocrat, September 19, 1908; Edward Waring to Gompers, September 6, 1908; Edward Hourigan to Gompers, September 9, 1908; E. B. Latham to Gompers, August 31, 1908; Henry Kaste to Gompers, August 31, 1908; W. Blenks to Gompers, September 1, 1908: all *AFL Records*, reel 67.

"Gompers this year is for the Democratic party, but he does not care to go to Alabama and make speeches."[25]

Another line of criticism expressed by leftist workers closely followed arguments Gompers himself had used for decades, though with a Socialist twist. Partisan politics could only disrupt the labor movement, *unless* based on class interests. George Ashford of Savannah, Illinois, wrote to Frank Morrison: "The present industrial panic coupled with Gompers's politicial [*sic*] action has had a tendency to tear everything to pieces... about one more break endorsing our oppressors, the Capitalist class, will see the end of the AFL or the rule of Gompers." The Wisconsin Federation of Labor wrote Gompers to complain that his policy could result only in "disruption and dissension" within labor organizations. And one worker, who signed himself "A Man with a Card and a Thinking Machine," expressed a common sentiment: "The working class aren't going to be led to slaughter always. One set of capitalist skinners looks as bad to them as another. Every union man I know is going to vote for Debs, the only candidate that has a real union card. Whither is the AFL drifting anyway?"[26]

For all their differences, the workers who wrote the AFL united to a remarkable extent over one issue: Labor's leaders, they argued, had never consulted rank-and-file workers when deciding their political strategy. Now those leaders sought to dictate how American workingmen should vote. A Chicago worker whose union backed Taft wrote to Gompers: "You don't own the members of the AFL ... we do our own thinking, and neither want your advice, nor influence." One worker wrote to say that Gompers's promise to deliver the labor vote to the Democrats had made many workers decide to vote for Taft, "not *being willing* to be regarded, as *merchandise* – to be *sold* and *delivered*, at the *option* of a despotic ruler. A great many – yes *thousands* – think it about time to have a new President – one not so *dictatorial*. . . ." A Michigan trade unionist similarly complained to Gompers: "I have no chain to my nose. . . . When you promised to hand me over to the Democratik Convention you sir counted without your slave."[27]

Many who complained of Gompers's issuing commands argued that neither of the major parties deserved labor's support. Theo Lehmann of Burlington, Iowa, described himself as a "long life Union carpenter," and said: "I have to pay for you sent those Papers out but you [nor] anybody else can tell me to vote. I vote

[25] McDonald is quoted in Max Hayes, "World of Labor," *International Socialist Review*, 9 (3), September 1908, 232–5; and see Hayes's column in 9 (4), October 1908, for a lengthy Socialist critique of the Democratic South; C. L. Munro to Grant Hamilton, September 27, 1908, *AFL Records*, reel 67; and "Debs Calls Gompers Liar," newsclipping from Syracuse, New York, October 3, 1908, *AFL Records*, reel 68. See also Daniel Letwin, "Interracial Unionism, Gender, and 'Social Equality' in the Alabama Coalfields, 1878–1908," *Journal of Southern History*, 61 (3), August 1995, 519–54.

[26] George W. Ashford to Frank Morrison, August 21, 1908, *AFL Records*, reel 66; Fred Brockhauser to the AFL Executive Council, August 7, 1908, *AFL Records*, reel 67; "A Man with a Card and a Thinking Machine," October 12, 1908, *AFL Records*, reel 68.

[27] Thomas P. Maloney to Gompers, August 3, 1908; George H. Simmons, Auburn, Michigan, to Gompers, July 26, 1908: both *AFL Records*, reel 66.

the Social ticket." The secretary of the Pattern Makers' Association of Boston wrote Frank Morrison to say that "when the AFL nominates a candidate this Association will support him and further to remind the Executive Council that President Gompers is in our pay, and ought not take part in the election of either Republican or Democratic [candidates]."[28]

These sentiments, so pervasive in workers' letters and in the labor press, suggest that the Republican charge of "delivering the labor vote" resonated deeply with rank-and-file workers. After all, the Federation's 1908 campaign was a highly centralized affair, one initiated by top leaders with participation neither invited nor accepted from local and state activists. We saw in earlier chapters that the AFL's structure maximized the powers granted the affiliated international unions, while strictly limiting the rights and powers of the state federations and the central labor unions. As a result, no institutions existed in the United States that could make possible a political movement independent of the trade unions, like the *bourse du travail* or the *camera del lavoro* provided in France and Italy. As AFL leaders pushed more deeply into political activism in 1908, they generated tensions within the labor movement as local workers questioned not only the direction of labor politics, but also the manner and method by which the AFL leaders chose that direction.

When the AFL convened its affiliated unions to discuss political action in March 1908, the discussion remained private and the public received word only that everyone had united behind Gompers's "reward and punish" strategy. In fact, at least a few international presidents challenged AFL strategy as limited and narrow. Matthew Woll, president of the Photo Engravers, wrote in a letter read to the conference that "The AFL has heretofore directed mainly its influence, power and forces in the political arena in a negative form." He argued that the Federation should begin a positive campaign to influence the executive branch by working to elect John Mitchell governor of Illinois.[29] The deliberations remained private, so we can only guess at the sort of debate Woll's suggestions might have generated.

Disagreement also emerged in the weeks after the AFL's March conference, when Congress once again proved itself unwilling to respond to labor's demands. In May, William Mahon, president of the Street and Electric Railway Employees, argued to Gompers that representatives at the March conference had agreed if labor's demands were not addressed by Congress, another conference would be called to develop in more detail labor's political strategy. Now Mahon could see from Gompers's latest circular that "you have decided to continue the old policy that has been pursued, and going at it blindly as we have in the past without

---

[28] Theo Lehmann to Whom it May Concern, August 15, 1908; L. W. Powers to Frank Morrison, August 22, 1908: both *AFL Records*, reel 66.

[29] The deliberations of the conference were not made public, so there may have been more leaders who made such suggestions. Matthew Woll, president of the Photo Engravers, wrote down his opinions to be read at the conference because he could not attend. Matthew Woll to the representatives at the Labor Conference, March 18, 1908, *AFL Records*, reel 65.

any definite results, in my opinion." Mahon declared that without a more elaborate strategy, labor would be incapable of conducting a successful campaign.[30]

In Gompers's view, the situation looked very different. He responded to Mahon that the strategy thus far had resulted in significant accomplishments, and he denied that representatives in March had called for another conference. Mahon continued to press his point: "It was specifically understood, . . . that there should be another conference held to outline a specific program. . . . This course should be pursued. I do not know that the Executive Committee now have a right to over-rule the actions of that convention. . . ." Privately, Gompers admitted to an ally that the representatives in March had called for another conference, and in the next weeks, several other international leaders pressed the AFL leadership to carry out those wishes.[31]

In June, Gompers discussed the matter with his Executive Council, but its members voted against an additional conference. Council member Denis Hayes, a Republican and president of the Glass Bottle Blowers, suggested their reasoning in a letter to Gompers: A conference, he believed, might

cause people to believe that [the AFL's political policy] did not receive the whole-hearted approval of the entire labor movement. I did not think it wise to risk the raising of one discordant voice or protest against it which might have happened had such meeting been called. . . .[32]

For the moment, the Council members shelved the matter, yet the pressure continued to build.

While national-level leaders debated how best to proceed, activists at the state and local levels grew restless in their desire to influence the future of labor politics. In Oklahoma, where labor played an unusually prominent political role, helping to write the state's first constitution and elect its first administration, activists wanted some way to unite the nation's state federations of labor around a detailed political strategy.[33] In late March 1908, one of the leaders of that movement, J. Harvey Lynch, wrote every state federation of labor in the country, urging that they hold a convention of state federations to formulate a platform of demands for labor and to secure written pledges of support from every political candidate. Out of this, Lynch hoped there would emerge not a labor party, but a national committee capable of representing labor's political interests. As its founding document, he hoped this body would write a new Declaration of Independence, updating that of 1776 to better reflect the needs of Americans

[30] Mahon to Gompers, May 12, 1908, *AFL Records*, reel 65.
[31] John Frey of the Iron Molders and George Berry of the Printing Pressmen also pushed Gompers to call another conference, and Frey reported that several other executive officers supported the idea. Mahon to Gompers, May 12 and 27, 1908; Gompers to Mahon, May 16 and June 9, 1908; John Frey to Gompers, July 16, 1908; George L. Berry to Gompers, July 30, 1908: all *AFL Records*, reels 65 and 66.
[32] Denis Hayes to Samuel Gompers, August 17, 1908, *AFL Records*, reel 66.
[33] Keith Bryant, "Labor in Politics: The Oklahoma State Federation of Labor during the Age of Reform," *Labor History*, 10 (3), Summer 1970, 259–84.

in the early twentieth century. Lynch received strong backing for this plan: Within a few weeks, twenty-seven state federations out of the thirty-eight then in existence had approved it and declared their intention to participate.[34]

Widespread dissatisfaction existed among state and local activists over the limited nature of AFL politics and the control exercised by the international affiliates. The Ohio Federation's secretary declared: "I don't feel that the conference of International Unions went near as far as I would like to have seen them go. . . ." Another argued that the state bodies had tried to win the attention of the parent body and the internationals at the conventions, but without success. The international leaders benefitted from state-level activists' efforts, but they are "so engrossed with a desire to gain control of members of other affiliated organizations, that they loose [*sic*] sight of the necessity of giving due consideration to the true needs of the different state bodies." Even some officials who reassured Gompers that they did not seek to challenge the rule of the internationals nonetheless pointed out that a larger political role for state federations would be appropriate, because their leaders were best equipped to influence activists at the state level.[35]

Gompers interpreted Lynch's movement as a repudiation of his and his allies' leadership. Treating it as the political equivalent of dual unionism, Gompers immediately wrote all state federations that such a conference would create confusion among workers and assist their opponents. To the AFL Executive Council, he made the rather ludicrous charge that Lynch's real reason for a convention was to nominate Governor Haskell of Oklahoma for the U.S. presidency. Naturally, he argued, such a project would divide labor's efforts.[36] Seventeen state federations quickly responded to console the AFL president that they opposed Lynch's idea. Not a single state official could summon the courage to inform Gompers that they approved of it. Only one of Lynch's peers, the secretary of the Oklahoma federation, wrote to console Gompers that the movement "is not hostile to the American Federation, but on the contrary very friendly." Yet Gompers had apparently convinced other state officials to treat Lynch's proposal as falling outside of their jurisdiction. As the Texas federation's secretary wrote to Lynch, his body would not participate because "such matters are clearly within the province of the American Federation and such a meeting would . . . be a usurpation of the prerogative of our parent body."[37]

[34] Lynch to W. E. Bryan, April 1, 1908; Gompers to Lynch, April 14, 1908; Gompers to the AFL Executive Council, April 15, 1908: all *AFL Records*, reel 65.

[35] Harry D. Thomas, secretary-treasurer, Ohio Federation of Labor, to Gompers, *AFL Records*, reel 65; D. W. Finn, secretary, New Hampshire Federation of Labor, to Gompers, April 17, 1908, *AFL Records*, reel 65; W. E. McEwen, secretary-treasurer, Minnesota Federation of Labor, to Gompers, April 22, 1908, *AFL Records*, reel 65.

[36] See the resolution passed by Carpenters' Unions Nos. 309 and 493, New York, October 4, 1908; and Gompers to the AFL Executive Council, April 15, 1908: both *AFL Records*, reels 65 and 68.

[37] J. Luther Langston to Gompers, April 21, 1908; F. N. Graves to Gompers, April 23, 1908; see also Sim Bramlette to Gompers, April 27, 1908: all *AFL Records*, reel 65.

The gears of Gompers' machine were moving efficiently by now, but Lynch did not seem to notice them. He responded to Gompers's first negative letter by saying merely that he would soon be visiting Washington, D.C., and would explain everything, and then Gompers would understand. Later as he watched his movement die, Lynch wrote passionately to the state Federations in hopes of resuscitating it:

As this is a move among the "grass roots," or the rank and file I can readily see why the Politicians of all parties, and the representatives of corporate wealth would object to it, but just why our national president should object to it I can not understand, since it would vitalize the actual members at the ballot boxes on election day and make the work of our national officers effective.

He noted that the literature sent out from Federation headquarters made little impact, because nothing was being done at the local level to coordinate and extend labor's political movement.[38] Yet after Gompers's strenuous efforts to kill the movement, the other state federations remained deaf to Lynch's appeal.

A third and final effort to convene around questions of political strategy emerged in July. This one succeeded because it seemed safely dominated by the international trade unions. L. W. Quick, secretary-treasurer of the Railroad Telegraphers, sent out a circular to editors of the national and international unions' official journals, suggesting a political conference. He received 38 responses, all but three of them favoring the conference. Nonetheless, first Vice-President James Duncan lobbied against the proposal because it would "create the impression that there was lack of confidence in the proper parties. . . ." The AFL's Labor Representation Committee met and decided to approve the conference, as Gompers put it, "in view of existing conditions as well as the understanding reached at the Protest Conference last March. . . ." The Executive Council concurred with this advice.

Gompers remained nervous about the conference and wired Quick, "Of course if held greatest care must be exercised. There is always danger of matters going wrong." One way to prevent matters from "going wrong" lay in strictly limiting participation. Only the editors of official journals and the presidents of international unions could attend; AFL leaders explicitly *excluded* the editors of the "unofficial" labor press, those newspapers put out by central labor unions, state federations, or independent organs. Even under these exclusionary conditions, Gompers asked Quick to visit Washington and confer personally with him on how to run the conference so it would constitute a smooth endorsement of AFL policy. Gompers also arranged to have allies like Grant Hamilton and John Lennon attend. As a result the conference, according to Lennon's description, was "A–No. 1, [and] showed a solidarity of intent and determination to support the Federation policy." Representatives from forty official organs of international unions attended

---

[38] Lynch to Gompers, April 18, 1908; Lynch to the executive board, Kansas State Federation of Labor, April 24, 1908; J. Luther Langston to Gompers, April 21, 1908: all *AFL Records*, reel 65.

the Chicago conference and passed a resolution affirming their "confidence in the integrity of Samuel Gompers" and declaring support for "the Gompers-Bryan political program." Only one representative, the Socialist secretary of the Brotherhood of Painters, Decorators, and Paperhangers, voted against this resolution.[39]

By the end of the 1908 campaign, AFL leaders and members divided sharply over the proper substance and methods for a genuine labor politics. Although Gompers and his allies pushed the Federation into an alliance with the Democratic Party, workers who favored Republican or Socialist candidates questioned their approach. But tensions rose even higher among AFL workers over the way those decisions were made. Gompers clearly desired to limit popular political activity by rank-and-file workers. He feared that he would lose control over labor's future if a robust political movement – whether Laborite or Socialist in character – emerged. The political circumstances further constrained Gompers. He had chosen to pursue a pressure-group approach to labor politics. Waging a single-issue campaign in collaboration with the Democrats led to Republican charges about delivering the labor vote. But only by establishing discipline on political matters and, in effect, delivering labor's vote to the Democrats, could the AFL leaders prove themselves a worthwhile ally.

Rank-and-file workers and local activists, however, saw things differently. After hearing for decades that labor must stay out of party politics, they watched their leaders enter into a partisan alliance. No one asked them to help choose labor's political strategy. Whereas trade union leaders believed they alone possessed the right and responsibility to make important political decisions, rank-and-file workers reacted differently, arguing that no one should dictate their votes. Even the appearance of such an effort seemed an affront, a violation of their rights as citizens. A Republican campaign worker described the mood among Illinois workers, declaring that he found the rank and file reacting in a "sullen and stubborn" way to Gompers's policies. "Many of them express themselves not only as against Gompers's policies but they will vote in retaliation of Mr. Gompers's presumption to contract their suffrage."[40]

The Local Face of Labor Politics

Any attempt to build discipline and political unity at the national level confronted complex circumstances at the state and local levels. Partisanship still exerted a tremendous influence on the ways workingmen experienced their political relationships, and workers' ethnic and religious dispositions and the regions in which they lived all shaped their political preferences. The AFL political

---

[39] James Duncan to L. W. Quick, July 25, 1908; Gompers to Lennon, July 31, 1908; Quick to Gompers, August 10, 1908; Gompers to Quick, August 14, 1908; Gompers to "Whom It May Concern," August 27, 1908; Lennon to Gompers, September 2, 1908: all *AFL Records*, reels 66 and 67. See also "Support Promised Bryan by Forty Labor Editors," in the *Chicago Tribune*, September 2, 1908.

[40] W. W. C., "Memorandum Report," October 1, 1908, Joseph Cannon Papers, Illinois State Historical Society.

strategy reached out almost exclusively to skilled trade union men, and whereas many found the Democrats' case persuasive, others, and especially nonskilled workers outside of the unions, saw Republicans as more appealing. In the neighboring states of Illinois and Indiana, in the heart of industrial America and at a crossroads of partisan allegiances, two very different contests set these dynamics in motion.

Once again in 1908, AFL leaders mobilized to defeat Speaker of the House Joseph Cannon's bid for reelection. No goal loomed larger in Samuel Gompers's political universe than this one; even his national-level alliance with the Democratic Party was motivated in significant part by a desire to defeat Cannon. "Czar" Cannon's autocratic control of Congress, and his relentless squashing of progressive legislation, had originally been brought to the attention of Americans through the AFL's first campaign against him in 1906. Two years later, opposition to the speaker had grown and a small grassroots movement against him, one that would finally end his reign in 1910, had become visible. Candidates for congressional office in several midwestern states pledged not to support Cannon for speaker, and now when Cannon spoke outside his own district, he sometimes ducked lemons thrown by female protestors. Presidential candidate Taft disclosed to a friend that "Confidentially, the great weight I carry in this campaign is Cannonism." Theodore Roosevelt similarly noted that Cannon had become a detriment to the Republicans: "they have had to cancel his engagements in the very doubtful districts, the candidates being afraid to have him come into their districts."[41]

Yet for all his troubles, Joseph Cannon remained one of the country's most powerful politicians, standing for reelection in a district and a state dominated by his own party. Two years before, and despite organized labor's united opposition, Cannon withstood the challenge of Socialist John Walker like an elephant triumphing over an ant. This time, the AFL leaders hoped to put up a stronger challenge by backing a Democratic candidate. From the beginning, they played the central role in shaping the campaign against Cannon. In June, a lawyer named Henry Bell, who sought the Democratic nomination against Cannon, made a bid for the AFL's support. Gompers and he began a regular correspondence, and during the next weeks, Bell agreed to support the Federation's major demands. Gompers decided Bell was a legitimate candidate and his position on the issues were "all that we could ask of him." In July, Gompers traveled to Chicago to meet with John Lennon, Edward Nockels, M. Grant Hamilton, and John Walker, and together they plotted the AFL's strategy against Cannon.[42]

[41] Jonathan F. White to Cannon, September 21, 1908, Cannon Papers; Newark *Evening News*, October 24, 1908, Cannon Papers; Richard Wayne Parker to Cannon, October 20, 1908, Cannon Papers; E. L. Phillip to Joseph Cannon, October 23, 1908, Cannon Papers; William Rea Gwinn, *Uncle Joe Cannon: Archfoe of Insurgency: A History of the Rise and Fall of Cannonism* (New York: Bookman Associates, 1957), 157; Blair Bolles, *Tyrant from Illinois: Uncle Joe Cannon's Experiment with Personal Power* (New York: W. W. Norton, 1951), 147.

[42] H. C. Bell, Marshall, Illinois, to Samuel Gompers, June 20, 1908; Gompers to H. C. Bell, June 27, 1908: Gompers to John Lennon, June 27, 1908; H. C. Bell to Gompers, June 29, 1908; Lennon to Gompers, June 29, 1908; Gompers to Lennon, July 1, 1908: all *AFL Records*, reel 65.

From that point on until election day, the AFL established a powerful presence in the 18th Congressional district of Illinois. During the remaining summer months, Hamilton and Nockels struggled to lay the basis for an effective campaign by mobilizing local union activists and attempting (unsuccessfully) to establish a labor newspaper in Danville.[43] On Labor Day, Samuel Gompers kicked off the campaign with a speech in Danville, and thereafter the AFL concentrated five additional organizers on the district. The United Mine Workers, under John Walker's leadership, contributed another five men.[44]

The AFL's campaign against Cannon focused on labor's legal demands. In his Labor Day speech, Samuel Gompers rebutted the charge that he sought to deliver labor's votes to the Democrats and he denounced Speaker Cannon's autocratic methods in the House of Representatives. Yet his speech focused mainly on the need for an amendment to the Sherman Anti-Trust Act and an anti-injunction bill. At the AFL's request, Democratic candidate Bell also focused his campaign on labor's legal demands. As in other parts of the country, organizers reported that the emphasis on legal issues made it difficult for some voters to grasp the AFL campaign. Traveling throughout the state, for example, Hamilton discovered that outside of big cities, workers often did not "understand" the injunction question.[45]

There were other problems with the AFL program as well. Democratic organization in the district remained weak, with party activists discouraged by years of Republican domination. Henry Bell, the Democratic candidate, ran a lackluster campaign. Cannon's prestigious position as speaker led some to believe that they should not oppose his reelection, and he ably exploited all the advantages of incumbency as well as his ties to the Old Soldiers' Home. And for all of labor's strength in Danville, unions remained fragile or nonexistent in many of the smaller towns. Farmers far outnumbered working people in the district and, enjoying a period of prosperity, most of them happily supported Cannon.[46]

---

[43] Hamilton to Morrison, August 1, 3, and 15, 1908, *AFL Records*, reel 66.

[44] The Printing Pressmen also sent one organizer to Cannon's district. See Morrison to Jacob Tazelaar, September 9 and 23, 1908, Morrison Letterbooks; Morrison to J. D. Pierce, September 15, 1908, Morrison Letterbooks; Gompers to Hamilton, September 24 and October 8, 1908, *AFL Records*, reels 67 and 68; John Walker to Gompers, September 28, 1980, *AFL Records*, reel 68; Gompers to J. J. Sullivan, September 26, 1908, *AFL Records*, reel 67; Hamilton to Gompers, October 10, 1908, *AFL Records*, reel 68; John F. Geckler to George L. Berry, October 23, 1908, *AFL Records*, reel 69.

[45] "Speech of Mr. Samuel Gompers. At Lincoln Park, Danville, Labor Day, September 7, 1908," Cannon Papers; Hamilton to Morrison, August 8, 1908, *AFL Records*, reel 66; H. C. Bell to Gompers, August 5, 1908, *AFL Records*, reel 66. Bell's literature on the labor injunction was personally approved, word for word, both by Gompers and by Lennon.

[46] Pierce to Gompers, September 26, 1908, *AFL Records*, reel 67; Morrison to J. D. Pierce, September 15, 1908, Morrison Letterbooks; Morrison to Hamilton, September 15, 1908, Morrison Letterbooks. For a lengthier analysis of this race, see Julia Greene, "The Strike at the Ballot Box: Politics and Partisanship in the American Federation of Labor, 1881 to 1917," Ph.D. diss., Yale University, 1990, chapter 5.

Probably the greatest problem faced by the AFL in Cannon's district, however, was caused by the complex dynamics of party politics. Although many trade unionists found Cannon's antilabor record disagreeable, they often shared his broader loyalty to the Republican Party. Railroad unions and the mineworkers dominated Cannon's district, and both groups counted many Republicans among their members. Among the miners, for example, both ex-president John Mitchell and his successor Tom Lewis possessed ties to the Republicans. Miners' leaders in the Danville area more often allied with the Republican Party than any other, and the Socialists came in second in the bid for miners' political allegiance.[47]

A strong labor campaign might have overcome these divisions and persuaded Republican-leaning union men to oppose Cannon. However, the Illinois gubernatorial campaign of 1908 intensified trade unionists' political divisions and helped Cannon win his race. Both of the major party gubernatorial candidates carefully presented themselves as "friends of labor," but the Republican contender, incumbent Charles Deneen, could more convincingly appeal for workers' support. By 1908, Deneen had established himself as a reformer standing for progressive and clean government. During 1907 and 1908 Deneen worked to pass a Health, Safety and Comfort Act and an Occupational Disease Act. Under his administration, legislation was also passed covering convict labor, mine safety, and protection of workers. Democratic nominee Adlai E. Stevenson also possessed extensive political experience, having served as vice-president during the second Cleveland Administration and later as a congressman. Democratic campaigners sought to focus voters' attention on Stevenson's fine character and patriotism. Yet Republicans more effectively emphasized Stevenson's role as a coal operator and charged that he exploited his workers and represented the interests of big business.[48]

Having invested so much politically in the fortunes of the Democratic Party, the national AFL leaders felt tremendous pressure to support Democrat Stevenson. AFL Treasurer John Lennon, who resided in Bloomington, emerged as Stevenson's biggest labor booster. A fierce partisan of the Democrats, Lennon wanted nothing more than to see William Bryan become President: "I am still

---

[47] Cannon perceived the vote of railroad workers and miners as particularly crucial for his reelection. See Cannon to O. J. Ricketts, August 30, 1908, Cannon Papers; "Railroad Men to Work for Deneen," Danville *Commercial-News*, August 29, 1908, p. 1; "Memo," 1908, Cannon Papers; list of mining leaders' political affiliations, Cannon scrapbooks, October 1908, Cannon Papers; Clifford Reed to Gompers, September 18, 1908, *AFL Records*, reel 67; "Row Likely in Illinois Labor," Chicago *Daily Socialist*, October 21, 1908, p. 2; "Illinois Labor for Socialism," Chicago *Daily Socialist*, October 24, 1908, p. 2; Eugene Staley, *History of the Illinois State Federation of Labor* (Chicago: University of Chicago Press, 1930), 193–4; Bolles, *Tyrant from Illinois*, 47–8.

[48] Donald F. Tingley, *The Structuring of a State: The History of Illinois, 1899–1928* (Urbana: University of Illinois Press, 1980), 167–76. The Health, Safety and Comfort Act and the Occupational Disease Act were not passed until after Deneen's reelection: Staley, *History of the Illinois State Federation of Labor*, 264–5 and 277.

wearing the big medallion of Mr. Bryan that I wore at the Council Meeting in
Denver . . . and am going to be just as positive and unqualified in my support
of Bryan as I would be in support of labor men were they on the ticket." The
best argument offered for supporting Stevenson was simply that victory for him
would aid the AFL campaign to defeat Cannon and Taft.[49]

Gompers and the AFL's Labor Representation Committee seemed to agree
with Lennon on the pragmatics of supporting Stevenson to aid the Democratic
cause, but they refused to go as far in their support as he desired. Lennon
attempted to engineer an endorsement for Stevenson by the Illinois labor movement, and toward that end, he pleaded with Gompers to write the leaders of the
Chicago Federation of Labor and commend Stevenson as a worthy candidate.
Gompers replied that although he, too, considered Stevenson the best man,
he did not want to interfere. The Chicago Federation of Labor had recently
decided not to endorse anyone and Gompers did not wish to "stir up a hornet's
nest." When Lennon asked James O'Connell and Frank Morrison of the Labor
Representation Committee to take a stand, both confessed their agreement with
Gompers's position.[50]

The national leaders had good reason to feel wary of Lennon's strategy. Much
of the Illinois labor movement had already rejected Stevenson's candidacy in
favor of the Republican Deneen. In June, the state's central labor unions met
to discuss the coming elections. The delegates united enthusiastically behind
miners' leader John Mitchell as a possible candidate for governor, but soon after
the conference, Mitchell declined to run. Edwin Wright, the president of the
Illinois State Federation of Labor, immediately issued a letter calling on trade
unionists to support Republican incumbent Charles Deneen. Wright, one of the
trade unionists instructed by Gompers to build a campaign against Cannon, was
"a personal and political friend of Governor Deneen," and this friendship gradually led him to other Republican commitments as well. Increasingly, Wright
became unenthusiastic about fighting Cannon, and he urged Gompers not to
focus labor's energies on that one fight. Meanwhile, the AFL's representative
at Democratic headquarters, M. Grant Hamilton, pushed Gompers to intensify
the fight against Cannon. According to Hamilton, Wright had made an alliance
with Deneen, who in turn had allied with Cannon. In fact, Wright apparently
supported the entire Republican ticket. He confided privately to a local union
leader that he remained suspicious of the Democrats in his state, and could not
advise workers to have any contact with them.[51]

---

[49] John Lennon to Gompers, July 24 and August 16, 1908, *AFL Records*, reel 66; Morrison
to J. D. Pierce, September 16, 1908, Morrison Letterbooks.
[50] Edward Nockels to Gompers, July 27, 1908; John Lennon to Gompers, July 24, 1908;
Gompers to John Lennon, July 29, 1908, Lennon to Gompers, July 29, 1908; Gompers
to Lennon, July 31, 1908; Lennon to Gompers, August 3, 1908; Gompers to Lennon,
September 4, 1908: all *AFL Records*, reels 66 and 67.
[51] Edwin R. Wright to City Central Bodies of Illinois, May 22, 1908, *AFL Records*, reel 65;
Chicago Federation of Labor Minutes, Chicago Historical Society, July 5, 1908; Edwin R.

In the context of the AFL's alliance with the Democrats, Wright's Republican sympathies represented troubling dissent. Reports flew that Wright would lose his position as president of the Illinois Federation, and John Fitzpatrick of the Chicago Federation of Labor suggested that charges might be brought against him.[52] But as it turned out, Wright was not the AFL's biggest problem. The Illinois miners also supported Deneen. According to the United Mine Workers Journal, Stevenson had opposed unionization in his mines and threatened workers with arrest simply for discussing unionism. Socialist John Walker, leader of the Illinois miners, endorsed Deneen. As he saw it, the miners owed Deneen their support, "as he has done everything that he could . . . in their interest and . . . for every other measure that was introduced by other organizations during the session of the Legislature here. . . ." The UMW had many measures planned before the next session of the legislature, and as a coal operator, Stevenson would certainly oppose their demands. If a strike occurred, Walker believed Stevenson would side solidly with the operators.[53]

In October, these tensions exploded into the open, as Deneen's campaign relentlessly appealed to labor and portrayed Stevenson as its enemy. Finally, officials of the AFL and the Chicago Federation felt compelled to counter the Republican appeals to labor. Edward Nockles for the Chicago Federation of Labor and M. Grant Hamilton and John Lennon of the AFL issued a letter, widely reprinted in the state's newspapers, stating they had investigated the charges made against Stevenson as unfriendly to labor, and that they now denounced the charges as "false and malicious." In response, John Walker issued his strongest endorsement of Deneen, and wrote Gompers to condemn their action and in particular their failure to consult the miners.[54]

Wright to all officers of the Illinois Federation of Labor, June 25, 1908, AFL Records, reel 65; Edwin Wright to Frank Morrison, July 18, 1908, AFL Records, reel 66; M. Grant Hamilton to Frank Morrison, July 20, 1908, AFL Records, reel 66; Morrison to Edwin Wright, October 2, 1908, Morrison Letterbooks; J. W. Clifton, secretary, Glass Bottle Blowers' Association, Streator, Illinois, to Gompers, October 16, 1908, AFL Records, reel 68.

[52] Privately, Frank Morrison assured Wright that his Republican loyalties would result in no recriminations from the AFL leadership. Edwin R. Wright to Frank Morrison, July 31, 1908, AFL Records, reel 66; Morrison to Edwin Wright, September 24 and October 2, 1908, Morrison Letterbooks; "Political Row on in Unions," Chicago Daily Socialist, July 9, 1908, p. 2; "Political Game of Labor Leads to Disruption," Chicago Daily Socialist, July 16, 1908, p. 1; "Labor Storm is Breaking Over Gompers' Head," Chicago Daily Socialist, July 20, 1908, p. 1; "Yates Adds to Labor Muddle," Chicago Daily Socialist, July 22, 1908, p. 1.

[53] Eugene Staley, History of the Illinois State Federation of Labor, 191; Tingley, The Structuring of a State, 173; John Walker to Gompers, October 31, 1908, AFL Records, reel 69.

[54] Edward Nockles, M. Grant Hamilton, and John Lennon to no one, October 28, 1908, AFL Records, reel 69; John Walker to Gompers, October 31, 1908, AFL Records, reel 69. Lennon and Hamilton's closeness to the Democratic Party suggests that its leaders may have pressured (or at least influenced) them to write the controversial letter about Stevenson's fairness to labor. The Chicago Daily Socialist (October 30, 1908, p. 1) reported that the Democratic State Central Committee put out a letter praising Stevenson's labor record, and the signers included Lennon, Nockels, Fitzpatrick, and M. Grant Hamilton.

Startled by Walker's anger, Ed Nockels of the Chicago Federation of Labor wrote to him soon thereafter. Nockels confessed he had not until then grasped the intensity of the UMW's opposition to Stevenson, and he regretted his and others failure to seek the miners' counsel before issuing the pro-Stevenson letter. Yet he also belittled Deneen's assistance to the miners: "this has been the case the world over among politicians who always point out some organization that they have befriended. . . ." For his part, Walker learned from the conflict that, more than ever, labor needed its own party. "It would clarify the situation . . . if we were to start a labor party of our own and I guess we will have to do that yet, as it appears that we are not going to be able to get you fellows into the Socialist party." Referring perhaps to the role Edwin Wright had played, Walked noted that "Labor Politicians" sometimes work for their own interests alone, and exploit their organizations for themselves: "That is the real danger in Labor Unions tackling the political question. It is not politics that is dangerous, it is the politician."[55]

This split over the governor's race suggests the difficulties involved in attempting to tie organized labor to one party across the United States. A great many workers remained loyal to the Socialists or the Republicans, and would not heed Gompers's advice to vote Democratic. Furthermore, workers might support Bryan for national office, but circumstances at the local or state levels could make the Democratic candidates unattractive. In Illinois, the support so many trades unionists gave to Governor Deneen clearly hurt the AFL's crusade against Joe Cannon. As the campaign evolved, Cannon worried less about labor's opposition and focused more on combatting his prohibitionist critics. A labor organizer sent into Cannon's district by the Republican Party observed, "Efforts to bolster Governor Deneen's candidacy by the labor vote is largely destroying labor's efforts to defeat Cannon." In the end, Cannon won with more than 7,000 votes to spare out of the total 53,000 cast by voters.[56]

In the neighboring state of Indiana, AFL strategy met with a different fate. James Watson, a congressman closely allied with Joseph Cannon and with the open-shop employers in NAM, ran for the governorship in one of the year's most closely watched state battles. AFL leaders strenuously opposed Watson's candidacy from the beginning. If Speaker Joseph Cannon represented to Gompers

---

[55] Nockels to Walker, November 2, 1908, *AFL Records*, reel 69; Walker to Nockels, November 5, 1908, *AFL Records*, reel 69. Walker's comment to Nockels seems prophetic of his later actions. In 1916, the Socialist Party expelled Walker for endorsing President Woodrow Wilson and Illinois Governor Edward Dunne over Socialist candidates. In 1918 and 1919, Walker worked with leaders of the Chicago Federation of Labor to build a statewide labor party that, after acquiring support from farmers' organizations, adopted as its name the Farmer-Labor Party. See John H. Keiser, "John H. Walker: Labor Leader from Illinois," in Donald Tingley, ed., *Essays in Illinois History: In Honor of Glenn Huron Seymour* (Carbondale and Edwardsville: Southern Illinois Press, 1968), 75–100; and Douglas Carlson et al., "Biographical Sketch," in *Guide to the Papers in the John Hunter Walker Collection, 1911–1933*, Illinois Historical Survey, University of Illinois.

[56] W. W. C., "Memorandum Report," Peoria, Illinois, October 1, 1908, Cannon Papers; Gwinn, *Uncle Joe Cannon*, 275–7.

the "Mephistopheles of American politics," James Watson served as "the Faust who helps to despoil the American people's rights." Elected to Congress in 1894, Watson became majority whip – and hence Cannon's right hand – in 1901. He served in that capacity until 1908, when he stepped down to run for governor.[57]

The state of Indiana loomed large in American politics. The competitiveness that characterized political races there, with the winning party (usually Republican) rarely receiving more than 51 percent of the vote, gave the state influence in deciding the outcome of national races.[58] Indiana also boasted one of the country's most formidable open-shop movements. Indianapolis was home not only to NAM activist David Parry, but also to the Employers' Association of Indianapolis (EAI), an influential open-shop organization. Created in 1904, by 1908 the EAI claimed major victories over the machinists and the building trades workers, establishing the open shop in each case. What had once been headquarters to the trade union movement was on its way to becoming, in the words of a union activist, "The graveyard of union aspirations; the scabbiest hellhole in the United States."[59]

NAM employers hoped to win the governorship for Watson not only to reward a friend, but also to satisfy loftier political ambitions. They desired respect from Republican leaders, and they hoped for the ascendancy within the party of conservatives like Cannon and Watson. The campaign thus represented the NAM's most ambitious bid for legitimacy and power within the Republican Party. As NAM Secretary Schwedtman wrote to Martin Mulhall, the association's top political worker:

your campaign in Indiana should mark a new departure from old campaign methods. Once the politicians understand that they will have to reckon with us, and . . . that they need not be afraid of having their connection with us known, they will be most careful to consult us in all important State and National movements.[60]

---

[57] Gompers is quoted in "Democrats Sway State Federation," *Indianapolis Star*, October 1, 1908, p. 1; James E. Watson, *As I Knew Them: Memoirs of James E. Watson* (Indianapolis: Bobbs-Merrill, 1936), 13, 27, and 56.

[58] John H. Madison, *The Indiana Way: A State History* (Bloomington: Indiana University Press, 1986), 208–10; Charles S. Hyneman, C. Richard Hofstetter, and Patrick F. O'Connor, *Voting in Indiana: A Century of Persistence and Change* (Bloomington: Indiana University Press, 1979), 83–111; and Philip R. VanderMeer, *The Hoosier Politician: Officeholding and Political Culture in Indiana 1896–1920* (Urbana, IN, 1985).

[59] Clarence Bonnett, *Employers' Associations in the United States: A Study of Typical Associations* (New York: Macmillan, 1922), 499–532; Orlando B. Iles and Andrew J. Allen, *Labor Conditions and the Open Shop in Indianapolis*, pamphlet published by the Associated Employers of Indianapolis, Inc., 1920, Indiana State Library, Indianapolis.

[60] Schwedtman to C. W. Post, November 2, 1908, U.S. Senate, *Maintenance of a Lobby to Influence Legislation: Hearings Before a Subcommittee of the Committee on the Judiciary*, 63rd Congress, 1st Session, 1913 (hereafter cited as *Maintenance*), Vol. 2, pt. 2, p. 2323; Schwedtman to Mulhall, October 14, 1908, *Maintenance*, Vol. 2, pt. 2, p. 2206; Van Cleave to Parry, August 27, 1908, *Maintenance*, Vol. 2, pt. 2, p. 1939. On the NAM's relative lack of enthusiasm about Taft's campaign, see Schwedtman to Mulhall, November 3, 1908: "as a matter of fact, we are more interested in Watson's election than we are in Taft's." *Maintenance*, Vol. 2, pt 2, p. 2325.

Union activists, meanwhile, rallied to the candidacy of Democrat Tom Marshall. The Indiana State Federation of Labor attempted unsuccessfully in the spring of 1908 to oppose Watson's bid for the Republican nomination. That September, delegates to the annual convention passed a resolution strongly endorsing the AFL campaign program.[61] Gompers himself conducted a four-day train tour of Indiana, accompanied by state and national labor leaders, to make dozens of speeches throughout the state. His visits provided the opportunity for political agitation by local activists, who blanketed towns with leaflets and fliers publicizing the Gompers meeting. Thousands of workingmen greeted Gompers and his comrades.[62]

Indiana trade unionists and the Democrats, like their counterparts throughout the country, stressed the need for anti-injunction legislation in this campaign, whereas the Republicans focused on economic prosperity. As Watson put it, the Republican Party seeks to "keep wages high, to keep factories open, and to keep hopes in the hearts of the workmen." Democrats and labor activists pointed to the acute recession just ending as a challenge to Republican claims about prosperity. In the context of closed factories and unemployed workers, Gompers declared to Indiana factory workers, "Dangling a dinner pail in the faces of honest workingmen is a shame. . . ." Yet Bryan and Gompers provided no positive program other than injunction reform.[63]

In a campaign so dominated by appeals to labor, Watson's effort among workingmen became particularly important. The Republican candidate spoke more often to labor crowds than any other. During the last weeks before election day, Watson added regular noon day factory meetings to his schedule, speaking at iron works and machine shops. Indianapolis's Republican newspaper targeted workers more than any other social group, with daily editorials, articles, and letters to the editor addressing labor issues or attacking the unions' political role.[64]

But the key to the Republican labor campaign lay with Martin Mulhall and the NAM's organizing among manufacturers and workers. Focusing his effort in the city of Indianapolis, and working closely with Republican leaders, Mulhall

---

[61] "Democrats Sway State Federation," *Indianapolis Star*, October 1, 1908, p. 1; editorial in *The Union*, October 10, 1908; "Union Makes Protest," *Indianapolis Star*, September 15, 1908, p. 3.

[62] Gompers spent more time touring through Indiana in 1908 than in any other state. Edgar Perkins to Gompers, October 10, 1908, *AFL Records*, reel 68; O. P. Smith to Gompers, November 4, 1908, *AFL Records*, reel 69; Samuel Gompers to Edgar A. Perkins, October 6, 1908, *AFL Records*, reel 68; "Gompers in Indiana," *The Union*, October 24, 1908, p. 1; "Gompers in Indiana," *Indianapolis Star*, October 17, 1908, p. 5.

[63] "Gompers in Indiana," *Indianapolis Star*, October 17, 1908, p. 5; "Watson Lauds Taft," *Indianapolis Star*, October 21, 1908, p. 14; "Full Dinner Pail Empty Says Bryan," *Indianapolis Star*, October 23, 1908, p. 2.

[64] For a sample of Watson's work among labor, see "Hold Noon Meetings," *Indianapolis Star*, October 13, 1908, p. 3; "Workingmen Hear Watson," *Indianapolis Star*, October 15, 1908, p. 4. To follow the *Indianapolis Star's* appeals to workingmen, see "Business in the Elections," October 8, 1908, p. 6; and "Gompers and the Labor Vote," October 18, 1908, p. 6. The Democrats, of course, also conducted innumerable noonday factory meetings: see the *Indianapolis Star*, October 3, 1908, p. 3.

created an organization of conservative factory operatives who attempted to mobilize other workers behind Watson's candidacy. Most men who joined this group, the Workingmen's Protective Association (WPA), came from the factories owned by prominent members of the Employers' Association of Indianapolis. At the first meeting of employees on September 11, Mulhall happily observed the new members: "The men who were selected by the employers, were . . . high-grade, intelligent, well-appearing mechanics. . . ." By October, Mulhall reported that more than 100 workers were attending the meetings, and he had them performing a number of services for the manufacturers. They strove to convince co-workers to support the Republican ticket both at the state and national level. The group's members also conducted polls of workplaces to determine how many workers would vote Republican, taking down the names and addresses of those brave enough to confess plans to vote the Democratic, Socialist, Prohibition, or Independent tickets. A clerk then delivered packets of political leaflets to such workers, hopefully to change their minds and bring them around to the Republican Party.[65]

The WPA presented itself as a legitimate workers' endeavor. A letter to manufacturers referred to the WPA as an organization "in which the employer has no say for this is a workingmen's organization."[66] In political literature urging support for Watson, the WPA described itself as representing 8,000 wage earners: "At heart we have only the best interests of the working people, of which we are a part." It urged workers not to be "intimidated or coerced or sold out to the Democratic party" by anyone who preaches "class hatred – the classes against the masses." At the same time, NAM instructed members not to mention the group or its activities to any person, "since the most effective results can be accomplished . . . by quiet activity."[67]

The WPA's next step lay in reaching out to the vast mass of industrial workers by creating Republican factory clubs. At Nordyke and Marmon, a manufacturing plant employing some 500 people, WPA workers formed both a Taft-Sherman-Watson club, with 350 members, and a drum corps of 30 men, "well equipped and uniformed." All across town Republican clubs, including fife, drum, and bugle corps, sprang up, particularly in factories owned or managed by open shop employers.[68]

With the manufacturers' committee active, the WPA hustling votes, and Republican clubs established in many factories, NAM had laid a strong foundation

[65] Mulhall to Schwedtman, September 22, 1908, p. 2093; C. C. Hanch to Dear Sir, September 26, 1908, p. 2127; C. C. Hanch to Dear Sir, September 26, 1908, pp. 2046–7. All from *Maintenance*, Vol. 2, pt. 2.

[66] C. C. Hanch to Dear Sir, September 26, 1908, *Maintenance*, Vol. 2, pt. 2, pp. 2126 and 2046–8.

[67] Workingmen's Protective Association to Dear Sir, October 21, 1908, p. 2246; A. J. Allen to Dear Sir, 1908, p. 2129: both *Maintenance*, Vol. 2, pt. 2.

[68] Mulhall to Schwedtman, September 15 and October 7, 1908, *Maintenance*, Vol. 2, pt. 2, pp. 2041 and 2152.

for its political campaign. As a climax, Mulhall orchestrated a series of grand industrial parades. Almost each week during the last stages of the campaign, workers gathered to march the streets on behalf of Republican candidates. When presidential nominee William H. Taft visited, or when James Watson came to town, Mulhall punctuated the event dramatically with a procession of some four thousand workers from the factories of Indianapolis.[69]

The parades seem to have been buoyant occasions, in keeping with the tradition of American political spectacle. They occurred at night, with men and women waving torches as they marched down the streets. Although the processions celebrated industry and the workers whose skill and artistry made it possible, however, they also represented quite clearly the employers' vision. Workers were organized not according to craft, but according to the firm where they worked. They marched under banners and rode in wagons identifying them as the workers of the Van Camp Packing Company, the American Car and Foundry Company, the Foster Lumber Company, and some two dozen others.[70]

Workers relied on banners not only to identify their employers, but also to display their political sentiments. One common banner declared, "With Taft Prosperity Begins." Another pronounced more simply, "Watson Looks Good to Us." A delegation from a saw-manufacturing plant created its own "saw Corps," parading through town while beating on circular saws, and carried a banner that praised the Republican tariff policy: "American Saws Are Good Enough for Us!"[71]

NAM activists saw these industrial parades as their crowning achievement. David Parry wrote happily to James Van Cleave: "Colonel Mulhall is certainly a trump and past master in political art. Of course our Democratic friends have been howling like a pack of hurt hounds, . . . but they have gotten on to the conditions too late to stop our purpose." Mulhall reported to NAM headquarters that the parades had achieved their purpose, because Republican leaders finally treated him with respect. Now NAM activists only had to wait confidently for election day when, they knew, Watson would win the governor's election.[72]

Unfortunately for Mulhall and the NAM, Democrat Tom Marshall soundly defeated Watson for the governorship. In an otherwise narrow election, Marshall won by nearly 15,000 votes out of a total of some 700,000. For the first time since 1893, Democrats took control in Indiana. Democrats also won eleven out of thirteen seats in Congress, a majority in the lower house of the state legislature, and the offices of lieutenant-governor and Superintendent of Public

[69] Mulhall to Schwedtman, September 23, October 7 and 17, 1908, *Maintenance*, Vol. 2, pt. 2, pp. 2099, 2152, and 2230; "Thousands Parade and Cheer Senator," *Indianapolis Star*, November 1, 1908, p. 11.

[70] "Thousands Parade and Cheer Senator," *Indianapolis Star*, November 1, 1908, p. 11; "Taft Reviews Big Parade," *Indianapolis Star*, October 24, 1908, p. 3.

[71] "City Gives Watson Assuring Ovation," *Indianapolis Star*, October 17, 1908, p. 1. "Taft Cheered by Throng," *Indianapolis Star*, October 24, 1908, p. 1; Mulhall to Schwedtman, October 24, 1908, *Maintenance*, Vol. 2, pt. 2, p. 2264.

[72] Mulhall to Schwedtman, October 17 and 24, 1908, pp. 2227 and 2264; David Parry to Schwedtman, October 17, 1908, p. 2230; all *Maintenance*, Vol. 2, pt. 2.

Instruction. Yet the Republicans won the presidency in Indiana and swept every other state office, from treasurer and attorney general down to the Bureau of Statistics.[73] Voters had specifically repudiated the Republican gubernatorial ticket, the Democrats had their best results in fifteen years, and labor won its biggest victory of the year. How did this happen?

Three factors came together in 1908 to defeat Watson: traditional partisan loyalties, the liquor question, and the labor vote. During the Progressive era, the state of Indiana still exhibited many characteristics associated with the political culture of the Gilded Age. Partisan loyalty continued to be worn like a proud badge in Indiana, the newspapers still marched to a partisan beat, and as recently as 1897 the state had passed a law requiring that voters state their party affiliation when asked by poll takers.[74] Historically, the parties divided the state between them, with Democrats dominating in the southern counties and in some cities, especially where brewing interests were strong, and the Republicans enjoying hegemony in the northern counties and in most manufacturing areas. Southern Indiana was a region of poorer farms, often inhabited by German-Americans, where discontent was common, whereas northern Indiana was wealthier, more populous, and more Yankee.[75]

The Democrats in Indiana benefitted in 1908 as the question of prohibition tore the Republican Party apart. By 1908, the progressive faction of the Indiana Republican Party was quite strong, having elected the reformist Governor Hanley in 1904. An old-fashioned Republican, J. Frank Hanley's reform spirit focused especially on things he considered immoral: gambling, tobacco, and, above all, prohibition of alcohol. In the spring of 1908, Governor Hanley, who was not running for reelection, convinced the Republican state convention to adopt a plank endorsing local county option. This proposal pitted rural against urban voters, allowing the mostly rural supporters of temperance to outlaw liquor for an entire county, despite the opposition of urban voters. In September, Hanley called a special session of the General Assembly to pass the county option law – and succeeded by a narrow margin.[76]

---

[73] For voting returns, see the *Report of the Secretary of State of Indiana, 1908* (Indianapolis: Indiana State Library).

[74] VanderMeer, *The Hoosier Politician*, 24–8.

[75] See Clifton Phillips, *Indiana in Transition: The Emergence of an Industrial Commonwealth, 1880–1920*, Vol. 4 of *The History of Indiana* (Indianapolis: Indiana Historical Society, 1968), 4.

[76] Labor's opposition to Watson was hardened by the Republican Party position on liquor: both the State Federation and the Indianapolis Central Labor Union strongly condemned the local county option bill, arguing that it would cost workers' jobs and violate individuals' rights to drink as they please. "Politics Menaces Life of Federation," *Indianapolis Star*, October 2, 1908, p. 1. On the Republicans and liquor, see Phillips, *Indiana in Transition*, 97–101; Mulhall to Schwedtman, August 15, 1908, *Maintenance*, Vol. 2, pt. 2, p. 1887; [Mulhall] to Ferdinand [Schwedtman], August 17, 1908, *Maintenance*, Vol. 2, pt. 2, pp. 1889–90; [Mulhall] to J. P. Bird, August 14, 1908, *Maintenance*, Vol. 2, pt. 2, p. 1883; Mulhall testimony, *Maintenance*, Vol. 3, p. 2828.

Hanley's crusade against liquor had peaked even as the Republican convention chose its next gubernatorial candidate from the party's conservative wing. By pushing hard for county option amidst a gubernatorial election, Hanley showed where his priorities lay: He wanted to get rid of alcohol even if it allowed Democrats into the state house. James Watson disliked and evaded the prohibition issue, and this Republican split over moral reform greatly weakened its 1908 campaign. Progressive Republicans refused to rally enthusiastically around Watson: To a friend, Albert Beveridge called Watson a liar, a man who represented "a regime which had cut the throat" of progressive Republicans. Hanley told Watson he was "morally unfit" to be governor, and departed at the height of the campaign to lecture outside the state on the evils of alcohol.[77]

Meanwhile, the NAM campaign helped push workers into the Democratic camp and linked labor and liquor together with traditional loyalties into a bundle that defeated the Republican ticket. Analysts agreed after the election that the labor vote had been critical. As the Republican newspaper put it, workers "were determined to strike a blow, they wanted to show their strength, and they have done so." Certainly, the NAM's work united organized labor against the Republican ticket. NAM leaders gambled that by creating a more public campaign, they would gain acceptance as a legitimate political power and through this win Republican leaders' fear and respect. The NAM strategy instead invited an exposé of manufacturers' political coercion that angered many working men and alienated Republican Party leaders.

After the WPA began distributing political literature at Indianapolis factories, word of it leaked out to Democratic and union leaders and both groups relentlessly investigated the matter. The Democratic newspaper speculated about the "Mysterious Letters" sent to coerce and intimidate workers in the large factories. Within days, they traced the letters to Mulhall, operating out of an office adjoining that of the Indianapolis Employers' Association. Mulhall thickened the muddy waters by declaring he was working for the Republican National Committee.

The situation grew more explosive in the following days as every group involved in Mulhall's schemes (the Republican National Committee, the Indianapolis Employers' Association, and the NAM) denied any association with him. But labor leaders and journalists soon pieced together the evidence and demonstrated that Mulhall was indeed connected to all three organizations. The scandal proved to many workers that a link existed between Watson and open-shop employers. Labor newspapers grew vehement in their condemnations of Watson, and activists distributed tens of thousands of circulars across the state warning workers about Mulhall's activities "in conjunction with labor-crushing employers." As

---

[77] Lawrence M. Bowman, "Stepping Stone to the Presidency: A Study of Thomas Riley Marshall's 1908 Indiana Gubernatorial Campaign," Ph.D. diss., University of Kansas, 1967, 19–20 and 166. William Foulke was another prominent Indiana Republican who opposed Watson, indeed much more fiercely than did Hanley or Beveridge.

the circular noted, "No wage worker with a trace of American patriotism in him will countenance this effort . . . to rob him of his franchise."[78]

Indiana's voting returns suggest how partisan loyalty combined with the issues of liquor and labor to defeat the Republican gubernatorial ticket in 1908. County returns demonstrate remarkable consistency in partisan associations: The south remained overwhelmingly Democratic, and the Republican Party continued to dominate in northern counties. Marshall's home territory in the Northeast helped him win some Republican areas, but otherwise, when southern or northern counties stepped outside this larger pattern, they had usually done so in previous elections as well.[79] Voting in areas with many working-class residents followed a regional and trade unionist axis. Northern cities tended to vote Republican, especially when organized labor possessed little foothold (as in Gary and East Chicago), and southern towns tended to vote Democratic, particularly those in labor strongholds such as Terre Haute. Vanderburgh county in southern Indiana, with Evansville as its major city, provides a useful example. Historically, it voted Republican, unusual for a county in the southern tip of the state. Deep in the heart of mining country, Evansville in 1908 continued to vote straight Republican, with a plurality of approximately one thousand votes in each case, *except* when it came to the governorship: For that office, Vanderburgh went Democratic by some three hundred votes. Indeed, in the mining counties of southwestern Indiana, which typically voted Republican, most in 1908 supported the Democrat Marshall for governor.[80]

The key to gauging the impact of the NAM campaign, however, lies with Marion County, itself dominated by the city of Indianapolis. The state's most populous city, Indianapolis served as Mulhall's headquarters. Both the NAM and the AFL focused their campaigns there. Historically Republican, in 1908, Marion County voted Democratic across the board except for one office – the presidency. In that case, county residents supported Republican candidate William Taft. Marion County's sizeable working class was predominantly German-American, with only a small new immigrant and African-American population. German-Americans represented one of the major ethnic groups that had begun fleeing the Democratic Party during and after 1896. Yet they stood at the heart of Indianapolis's labor movement and were most likely unsympathetic to Watson's alliance with open-shop employers, just as they disliked his party's position on prohibition. Together, the labor factor and liquor pushed German-Americans

---

[78] "Against Mulhall's Campaign," *Indianapolis News*, October 15, 1908, p. 3; "Political Circulars to Employes Are Traced," *Indianapolis News*, October 7, 1908, p. 3; "Colonel Mulhall and the Manufacturers' Association – A Fable," *The Union*, October 10, 1908.

[79] *Report of the Secretary of State of Indiana*, 1900, 1904, and 1908.

[80] Mining counties that supported Marshall included Vigo, Clay, Owen, Greene, Sullivan, Knox, Dubois, Martin, Vanderburgh, and Posey; those that supported Watson were Vermillion, Parke, Davies, Pike, Gibson, Warrick, and Spencer: *Report of the Secretary of State of Indiana*, 1908.

back to the Democratic Party for the gubernatorial vote, though they continued
to vote Republican in the national contest.[81]

Indiana's gubernatorial race reminds us that conflicts between labor and capital never operated in a vacuum. The political parties shaped the context in which
groups like the NAM and the AFL mobilized, even at a time when they were
growing less popular. Voters in Indianapolis, particularly when apprised of the
NAM's machinations, rejected the employers' candidate as too closely identified
with a particular group interest. In Illinois, AFL leaders succeeded little better
at attracting voters to support their candidates. Understanding the political fortunes of workers and employers thus requires close attention to the resilient role
played by the structures and culture of the party system.

Workers Deliver Their Votes

On the eve of the election, AFL organizers continued to send in optimistic
reports. A trade unionist in Kansas City described Bryan's appearance in his city
just before the election: "They came from North South East and West to hear
Bryan this morning until the Huron Place could not contain the multitude. . . .
On for victory against tyranny." Yet despite such optimism, Bryan lost by a
sizeable margin: he received only 162 electoral votes to Taft's 321. Outside of the
"Solid South", Bryan won only Kentucky, Oklahoma, Nebraska, Colorado, and
Nevada – each of them hardly critical for determining a presidential contest.[82]

The returns did bring some cheering news to the Democrats. The Republicans'
lead in popular votes was cut by half in 1908 as compared to 1904, and the
Democrats were growing stronger, particularly in the West. Most importantly,
Democratic governors won in Indiana, Ohio, Minnesota, North Dakota, and
Montana, all states that had been in Taft's column in the electoral vote. These
Democratic victories show the impact Roosevelt's endorsement of Taft had in
some places: Voters might support Taft with Roosevelt behind him, but they
would not support conservative Republicans as governors.[83]

Democrats could not ignore the fact, however, that the northeastern states
had gone solidly to Taft. The popular vote for Taft was particularly high in that

[81] For a lengthier analysis of voting behavior in Indiana during 1908, see Julie Greene,
"Dinner-Pail Politics: Employers, Workers, and Partisan Culture in Progressive America,"
in Eric Arnesen, Julie Greene, and Bruce Laurie, eds., *Labor Histories: Class, Politics, and
the Working-Class Experience* (forthcoming, University of Illinois Press).

[82] William Gilthorpe, Kansas City, to Gompers, November 2, 1908, *AFL Records*, reel 69;
Paolo E. Coletta, "Election of 1908," in Arthur M. Schlesinger, Jr., ed., *History of American
Presidential Elections, 1789–1968* (New York: McGraw-Hill, 1971), 2087–8. For more of
the AFL's optimism, see Lennon to Gompers, October 29, 1908, *AFL Records*, reel 69;
Morrison to E. M. Howard, October 28, 1908, Morrison Letterbooks; Morrison to Hugh
Frayne, October 27, 1908, Morrison Letterbooks.

[83] Marc Karson, *American Labor Unions and Politics, 1900–1918* (Carbondale: Southern
Illinois University Press, 1958), 64; George Mowry, *Theodore Roosevelt and the Progressive
Movement* (Madison: University of Wisconsin Press, 1946), 31–2.

region. This boded ill for the AFL campaign program because in the northeast, trade union membership was high and the AFL had centered its campaign there. It is difficult to be precise about workers' voting behavior in 1908 because we lack a detailed study of the subject. Examining voting returns for twenty-two counties where the AFL focused its campaign – all of them possessing a high proportion of wage earners and an active labor movement – can provide a guide to unionists' political behavior.

These counties ranged from Maine to California, but they centered in northern industrial states like New York, Pennsylvania, Ohio, Illinois, and Indiana. They included the cities where AFL members fought their biggest battles: Pittsburgh, Chicago, Detroit, Indianapolis, Youngstown, as well as smaller cities like Danville, Illinois. In all but four of these counties, Bryan lost to Taft, and usually by a wide margin. In the county dominated by Cleveland, Ohio, for example, Bryan won only thirty-three percent of the vote to Taft's sixty-one percent; in Chicago, Bryan won thirty-seven percent to Taft's fifty-five percent. In these twenty-two counties, Bryan's victories came only in New York City and in western counties in Colorado, Missouri, and Nebraska. To the credit of Bryan and the AFL, in most of these counties, the Democrats won significantly more votes than had Alton Parker in 1904. Yet the gains were not nearly enough to bring victory to the Democrats. These results suggest that in labor's stronghold – especially in northeastern and midwestern states like New York, Ohio, and Indiana – the AFL program did not succeed in rallying trade unionists to the Democratic banner.[84]

A number of factors intervened to make some workers vote for Taft or Debs rather than Bryan, and many of these fell outside of the labor movement's control. In this category, we might include the Republican Party's tremendous financial advantage over the Democrats and the powerful pull of traditional partisan loyalties. However, our exploration of workers' political opinions and behavior suggests three additional factors that limited the AFL program in 1908.

[84] Voting data came from the Inter-University Consortium for Political and Social Research, Ann Arbor, Michigan, Data File 8611, principal investigators Jerome Clubb, William Flanigan, and Nancy Zingale. My thanks to Susan Brumbaugh for her technical assistance. The counties examined were Los Angeles and San Francisco Counties; Pueblo County, Colorado; Fairfield and New Haven Counties, Connecticut; Cook County (dominated by Chicago) and Vermilion County (Danville), Illinois; Marion County (Indianapolis), Indiana; Knox County (Rockland), Maine; Essex County (Lawrence), Massachusetts; Wayne County (Detroit), Michigan; Jackson County (Kansas City), Missouri; Douglas County (Omaha), Nebraska; Atlantic County (Atlantic City), New Jersey; New York County and Kings County (Brooklyn), New York; Cuyahoga County (Cleveland), Lucas County (Toledo), and Mahoning County (Youngstown), Ohio; and Allegheny County (Pittsburgh), Lackawanna County (Scranton), and Lycoming County (Williamsport), Pennsylvania. Out of these, only in New York County, Jackson County, Missouri, Douglas County, Nebraska, and Pueblo County, Colorado, did Bryan defeat Taft. S. D. Lovell examined counties with a high proportion of wage earners, all of them in northeastern states, and found voting patterns similar to what I found. See his *The Presidential Election of 1916* (Carbondale: Southern Illinois Press, 1980), 168–9; also Karson, *American Labor Unions*, 64.

First, tensions between the AFL's national-level agenda and the particularities of politics at the state and local levels profoundly shaped labor's role in the 1908 campaign. In its campaign for Bryan, the AFL attempted to build unity on a national level. As we saw in the case of Illinois, though, local- and state-level complexities could make such unity impossible to achieve. In that state, workers' loyalty to a Republican candidate for governor, felt especially by miners and railroad workers, fatally disrupted the AFL's attempt to defeat both Joseph Cannon and William Howard Taft.

Secondly, the Republican Party and its allies in the National Association of Manufacturers also mobilized effectively among working-class voters, and together these groups possessed powerful weapons: These included the affection many workers felt for Theodore Roosevelt, the Republican Party's support among the majority of newspapers (particularly in the Northeast), and the open-shop employers' ability, at least some of the time, to manipulate their employees' political behavior. Most influential of all, though, the Republicans and open-shop employers created a discourse based on "prosperity politics" that appealed to more workers than did the Democrats' emphasis on legal rights.

In 1908, the Democratic Party was still looked on overwhelmingly as the party of depression. Economic depressions are one of the most powerful persuaders in the world of politics. Few events cause voters to lose sympathy and trust in a political party, and for a longer period of time, more than economic crises. The Republicans' steady reliance on issues of prosperity heightened the association of the Democratic Party with depression. Constantly, the Republicans reminded Americans that whereas the Democrats would return the country to desperate poverty, the Republicans represented a safe and prosperous alternative, a "full dinner pail" for everyone. The success of this tactic is particularly startling because in the autumn of 1908, the United States was still recovering from its recent depression.

In comparison, the Democrats and the AFL appealed to workers with themes of legal and constitutional rights. Although many of Bryan's issues would have been of interest to workers (e.g., his calls for expanding democracy, or for fighting corporate greed), when addressing working-class audiences, the Democrats, like the AFL, focused almost entirely on the need for an anti-injunction law and an amendment to the Sherman Anti-Trust Act. Yet these were trade union demands, difficult issues for building a mass movement.

Grant Hamilton, who worked politically throughout the Mid-West for several weeks before settling in to run the Democratic National Committee's Labor Bureau, stressed repeatedly to Gompers and Morrison that the legal issues emphasized by the AFL were not catching on with workers: "I find that while we have been hammering injunction and anti-trust bills much ignorance exists relative to these questions, which can only be removed by an intelligent handling of the subject upon the floor of their meeting halls." Months later, watching as correspondence arrived in response to the Minute Men campaign,

Hamilton still warned that "a full understanding of the AFL policy is not as yet complete."[85]

After the election, Frank Morrison reflected on the impact of the AFL campaign: "We certainly made the political party 'sit up and take notice'; in fact, the last of the campaign seemed to center around the injunction and the Sherman Anti-Trust law." Labor's legal rights did become an important issue as the campaign went on and as the Republicans, feeling stronger, tackled labor and the Democrats in their own territory. But despite Morrison's satisfied tone, this did not represent a victory for organized labor. Although Roosevelt's intervention on the injunction issue undoubtedly swayed some workers, his argument, that only those workers who did something wrong needed to fear the labor injunction, was persuasive. And the Republican challenge to the AFL-Democratic emphasis on legal rights was especially damaging because the latter's campaign program relied on few other issues for appealing to workers.

John Lennon recounted to Gompers a revealing conversation about these matters in Chicago a few days before the election:

I met the newspaper boys that are our friends and they are in touch with the situation if anyone. They told me then that the organized workers of Chicago were not for Bryan, except the officers. That they are afraid of the bread-and-butter question and that appeared bigger to them than the possibility of being deprived of their rights and liberties. I know by the way the boys talked that they meant it. And, while I still hoped the situation would turn out differently, I find this morning that their statement was correct and where organized labor is strong, we haven't made any showing.

Undoubtedly most workers would not make such a black-and-white choice as prosperity over constitutional rights. In most cases, the decision would be more complex, balancing fears of unemployment and hopes of a "full dinner pail" against fears of legal harassment. But ultimately the Republican Party's broad economic appeal persuaded more trade unionists than did the relatively narrow "trade union rights" appeal used by the Democrats and the AFL.[86]

A third element in understanding the limitations of the AFL campaign program involved the Federation's strategy of political mobilization. In 1906, the AFL had sought the greatest possible degree of mass mobilization and toward this end its officers allowed local autonomy whenever feasible. But in 1908, AFL policy grew more centralized and bureaucratized, and popular politics virtually ceased to exist. The centralization, and the decline in excitement and spontaneity that it caused, made the AFL's campaign program less effective in 1908. Pressures from outside of the AFL and dissent within led leaders to centralize their political program and to retreat on the popular aspects of the strategy. This in turn helped dampen local workers' enthusiasm for the strategy,

---

[85] Hamilton to Morrison, July 25, 1908; Hamilton to Gompers, September 22, 1908; see also Hamilton to Morrison, August 8, 1908: all *AFL Records*, reels 66 and 67.

[86] John Lennon to Gompers, November 4, 1908, *AFL Records*, reel 69.

which strengthened the AFL leaders' need to control and enforce their program. In this complex way, the AFL national leaders' strategic choices, and the AFL members' responses to them, played a significant role in the failure of their campaign program. This dynamic highlights the significance of mobilization strategies for understanding the political behavior of social groups. It is important not to abstract workers' voting habits from what happened before election day, but to assess both who controlled the mobilization efforts and how they were undertaken. A more democratic AFL, one more responsive to local initiative, would have generated undoubtedly a greater degree of political participation by its members.

On election day in 1908, American trade unionists delivered their vote not only on the U.S. presidency, but also on the political strategy chosen by their national union officials. Repudiating Gompers's choice for the land's highest office, organized workers also renounced his political strategy. Mass mobilization would not dominate AFL political policy again during Samuel Gompers's lifetime. Instead, the tensions and conflicts it generated led national union officials to rely henceforth on more discreet and still more elite political strategies. The AFL program had always possessed a two-sided potential: On the one hand, there appeared the promise of popular politics, with energized rank-and-file members building a political movement. On the other hand, the program threatened merely to advance the interests of national leaders, providing them with a way to shape and control American labor politics. The latter became dominant in 1908, and the potential of popular activity was squandered. During the heat of the campaign, Gompers had once observed: "The fact that the workers intend to deliver their own votes causes consternation."[87] Gompers had been more correct than he realized, and ultimately he shared in the consternation. As the 1908 campaign showed, only the workers themselves could deliver the labor vote.

[87] Samuel Gompers, "Candidate Taft, Take Notice!" *AF*, 15 (11), 960.

Fig. 1. A common scene in early twentieth-century America: the political parade. (Courtesy of the Library of Congress.)

Fig. 2. William Jennings Bryan at the start of his 1908 campaign at the Nebraska State Capitol, seated here with Democratic Party Chairman Norman Mack, center, and vice-presidential nominee John Kern of Indiana, right. (Courtesy of the Nebraska State Historical Society.)

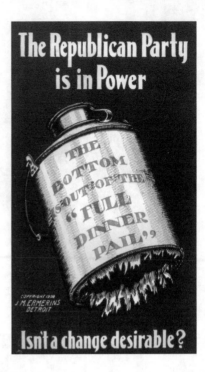

The Republican Party is in Power

THE BOTTOM IS OUT OF THE "FULL DINNER PAIL"

COPYRIGHT 1908
J.M.ERMERINS
DETROIT

Isn't a change desirable?

Fig. 3. In 1908, much of the Democratic Party's campaign material, like this postcard, appealed to workers by challenging the Republicans' claim that they would bring prosperity and a "full dinner pail." (Courtesy of the Nebraska State Historical Society.)

Fig. 4. Railroad workers in Havelock, Wisconsin, listening to Republican presidential nominee William Howard Taft in 1908. (Courtesy of the Library of Congress.)

Fig. 5. William Jennings Bryan speaking in his characteristic animated style during the 1908 campaign. (Courtesy of the Library of Congress.)

Fig. 6. Frank Walsh of the Commission on Industrial Relations in a classic pose, taken in 1915. (Courtesy of the Library of Congress.)

Fig. 7. Samuel Gompers, president of the American Federation of Labor, proudly casts a ballot as others watch. (Courtesy of the Library of Congress.)

PART THREE

The Retreat from Popular Politics

Organized labor has learned the lesson that, for a time at least, **silent yet constant and persistent effort** would bring its best achievement. . . .

Samuel Gompers, *American Federationist*,
October 1910, 898

If Wilson would only go the whole limit on the people's side, I believe we would win a tremendous popular victory.

Frank Walsh, in a letter to Basil Manley,
June 26, 1916, Frank Walsh Papers

CHAPTER SEVEN

Quiet Campaigns

The AFL's humiliating political defeat in 1908 emboldened many of Samuel Gompers's enemies and produced some of his darkest hours. The political strategy he and his allies had developed over several years – nonpartisan in theory though pro-Democratic in fact – appeared to have no future. The popularity of both labor partyism and socialism grew after 1908, whereas in the economic sphere a renewed militancy among unskilled workers challenged the AFL's exclusivist orientation. These pressures seemed likely to push organized labor toward a broader and more ambitious political strategy, but instead AFL leaders adopted the opposite course. Hardly in the mood for political gambling, Samuel Gompers retreated from the high-stakes mobilization strategies he had developed since 1906, and sought refuge instead in the realm of lobbying and negotiations with top Democratic leaders. Although the debacle of 1908 could not sever the ties between labor and the Democratic Party, it did force a complete reevaluation of strategy and tactics. Never again would the AFL leaders risk everything on their presumed ability to deliver workers' votes.

Rebellion Within and Without

As the dust settled after Bryan's defeat in late 1908, commentators noted regularly that the AFL's pure and simple leaders had been humiliated by rank-and-file workers who refused to follow their leaders' political advice. "Injunction Judge" Taft now entered the White House and prominent labor enemies like Joseph Cannon and John Dalzell returned to Congress. Those who had supported the AFL policy and hoped it would bring labor some degree of political success felt disheartened and discouraged. Having thrown themselves into political mobilizing, trade unionists found their organizing work suffered as a result. AFL membership hardly budged during 1908, and unionists commonly attributed this both to the lingering impact of 1907's economic panic and to the political distractions caused by the 1908 campaign.[1] Workers loyal to the Republicans still

---

[1] See the Cleveland *Citizen*, November 28, 1908.

felt stung by Bryan supporters' accusation that they had betrayed the labor movement. And Socialist members of the AFL, vilified by Gompers and his allies during the campaign, felt more alienated from their pure and simple leaders than ever before. For solace, they looked to Bryan's poor showing on election day and rejoiced that now, surely, the Democratic Party had met its final death. In the future, workers would undoubtedly shift their allegiances to the Socialist Party or, failing that, at least to an independent labor party.[2]

Whereas Gompers's heartiest supporters attempted to resume a pleasant countenance (the Washington *Trade Unionist*, a stalwart pro-Gompers paper, noted: "Government by injunction has been approved by the people; so cheer up, and make the best of it"), other trade unionists appeared ready for more dramatic change. In the years following the 1908 election, labor parties and socialism both enjoyed unprecedented popularity. In Chicago, for example, the city's Federation of Labor voted unanimously in 1910 to request that the AFL create a labor party uniting workers with farmers and other groups seeking reform: "to the end that the democracy of the nation, now scattered among all existing political parties, ... be welded into one great industrial political movement, having for its purpose industrial liberty...." When the AFL leaders failed to respond to this proposal, Chicago activists began mobilizing on their own to establish a statewide labor party. Ultimately, however, the plan fizzled when Chicago's powerful craft unions refused to support it.[3]

Unionists advocating a new approach to politics enjoyed more success in New York City and Philadelphia, as labor parties emerged in both places. In Philadelphia, a general strike in support of streetcar workers led local unions affiliated with the AFL to create a labor party in March 1910, and its leaders made plans to extend the party throughout the state. The Union Labor Party's far-reaching platform included women's suffrage and injunction law reform, as well as municipal ownership of public utilities, government ownership of railroads, and the abolition of trusts.[4]

But western workers provided the best example of what united action could achieve when they created, in Arizona, a labor party focused on influencing the state's Constitutional Convention. In July 1910, members of the Typographers, the Western Federation of Miners, the Carpenters and Joiners, and the Blacksmiths' unions rallied around a platform supporting the initiative, referendum, and recall; female suffrage; the eight-hour workday; a secret ballot, direct primary, and popular election of U.S. Senators; and an anti-injunction law. The labor party pledged to its platform many candidates running for the position of

---

[2] See, for example, Victor Berger, "Exit – The Democratic Party!" *Social Democratic Herald*, November 7, 1908; and the Cleveland *Citizen*, December 5, 1908.

[3] Chicago Federation of Labor Minutes, April 17, July 3 and 17, and August 7, 1910, Chicago Historical Society; and see Julia Greene, "The Strike at the Ballot Box." Ph.D. diss., Yale University, 1990.

[4] Philip Foner, *History of the Labor Movement in the United States*, Vol. 5, *The AFL in the Progressive Era* (New York: International, 1980), 93–5.

Constitutional delegate – all of them Democrats – and successfully worked for
their election. The resulting constitution included provisions for the eight-hour
day, abolition of convict labor, and the initiative, referendum, and recall. The
latter caused controversy when it came time for Congress to admit Arizona as
a state, because it allowed even for recall of judges. Labor activists around the
country petitioned Congress to admit Arizona and finally succeeded in August
1911, only to have President Taft veto the bill because its constitution allowed
for recall of all elected officials. Ultimately, Arizona withdrew the controversial
provision, achieved statehood, and then reinserted the recall of judges into its
constitution.[5]

Of course, as enthusiasm for progressive reform spread during these years,
workers by 1910 were playing important roles in reform coalitions throughout
the nation. J. Joseph Huthmacher and John Buenker established decades ago that
new immigrant workers participated in progressive era reforms by supporting
them with their votes. Shelton Stromquist has demonstrated, moreover, that
working-class voters not only helped elect reform administrations but beyond
that, "a working class political agenda and mobilization of working class voters
behind that agenda acted as a powerful, if sometimes invisible, undercurrent
within variously constituted reform constituencies." In cities like Detroit, Cleveland, and Chicago, and on the state level in California, Illinois, and Massachusetts,
among other places, this working-class agenda focused on issues like municipal
ownership and tax reform, and as Stromquist argues, "gave form and substance
to urban progressivism."[6] The mode of operation varied considerably, from independent or Socialist Party efforts in San Francisco and Milwaukee, to alliances
with Democrats or (less often) Republicans, to nonpartisan pressure tactics.
Workers' involvement in municipal- and state-level political mobilizations had
increased throughout the early twentieth century, undoubtedly helping to push
the AFL to embark on political activity back in 1906. At the same time, the
AFL's highly visible campaigns, especially in 1908, likely encouraged even more
workers to become politically active.

Rumors abounded in these years that the AFL would soon launch an independent labor party, although in hindsight it appears clear that Samuel Gompers
and his allies had no intention of taking such a step. Sentiment in favor of independent action seemed strong among trade unionists. Reporting on the AFL's
1908 convention, the Cleveland *Citizen* noted that many delegates traditionally
linked to the Democratic Party or Republican Party now hoped to see a labor
party created, and they wondered why the Socialists would not create one.[7] Many

[5] Ibid., 50–3.
[6] J. Joseph Huthmacher, "Urban Liberalism and the Age of Reform," *Mississippi Valley
Historical Review*, 44, September 1962, 231–41; John Buenker, *Urban Liberalism and
Progressive Reform* (New York: Charles Scribner's Sons, 1973); Shelton Stromquist, "The
Crucible of Class: Cleveland Politics and the Origins of Municipal Reform in the Progressive
Era," *Journal of Urban History*, 23 (2), January 1997, 192–220.
[7] Cleveland *Citizen*, Nov. 28, 1908.

Socialists, and the editors of the *Citizen* were among them, feared a nationwide labor party as much as did Gompers and his conservative peers. In these years, with political passions running high, the issue came close to tearing apart the Socialist Party.

Since 1906, the Socialist Party had grown increasingly divided between right-wing and left-wing factions. The left wing emphasized industrial action, especially through the Industrial Workers of the World, and saw political work as useful primarily for educational reasons. The right and center coalition focused on broad social and political reforms, seeking to achieve socialism gradually through "constructive" reforms. This right wing thus put more faith in politics as an agent of change, and was less critical of the AFL than the left wing. The right wing also dominated the positions of leadership in the party. Most of the National Executive Committee by 1910 belonged to the right wing of the party.[8]

Socialists of every faction had watched the AFL's political campaigns with great interest and sometimes with anxiety, waiting and hoping that it would lead workers to embrace political action and, ultimately, the socialist approach. The 1908 election proved a disappointment for Socialists, the vote for their presidential candidate Eugene Debs barely climbing above that of 1904. Some attributed this to the AFL's political campaign and more precisely to Gompers's attacks on Debs. Others, like left-winger Charles Kerr (the editor of the *International Socialist Review*), took solace in the fact that the worst defeats had been suffered in places where right-wing Socialists dominated. But for most Socialists, labor's recent political struggles generated careful reflection over the best strategy to adopt in the future.[9]

Right-wing Socialists grew the most introspective, wondering amongst themselves if the time had come to embrace an independent labor party. Immediately after the 1908 election, Los Angeles lawyer Job Harriman wrote Morris Hillquit to propose that the Socialists jointly call a conference with the AFL for the purpose of creating a labor party. "For the first time in the history of the labor movement here I find the labor leaders are ready to consider the question of independent politics, and an amalgamation with the Socialist party." He suggested that they attempt at this convention to pass a fairly conservative platform, including the eight-hour day, a closed shop, an anti-injunction law, a child labor law, and public ownership of monopolized industries. Assessing the status

---

[8] The most useful source for information about factions in the nationwide Socialist Party is Ira Kipnis, *The American Socialist Movement, 1897–1912* (New York: Columbia University Press, 1952). See also David Shannon, *The Socialist Party of America: A History* (New York: Macmillan, 1955).

[9] Debs received 402,895 votes in 1904 and 420,890 in 1908. See Arthur M. Schlesinger, Jr., ed., *History of American Presidential Elections, 1789–1968* (New York: Chelsea House, 1971), 3:2046 and 3:2131. For Socialist reactions to the election, consult *The Bakers' Journal*, November 7, 1908; Charles Kerr in the *International Socialist Review*, January 1909, 7 (6), 532.

of the AFL, Harriman noted: "Gompers' policy has failed, but Gompers has not failed. We must not believe it. He is very much alive." The way to crush him, Harriman argued, was to appear lenient and willing to support a modest platform in the larger interest of working-class political unity.[10]

During the next year, Harriman's proposal grew more popular among Socialist leaders. In November 1909, Algie Simons, right-wing editor of the Chicago *Daily Socialist*, attended the AFL's annual convention. What he saw there startled Simons. Talking with delegates, he discovered among many unionists what he called, in a letter to his friend William English Walling, an "intense hatred against the Socialist Party combined **with a perfect willingness to accept the philosophy of Socialism**." A large majority of delegates, he believed, favored the creation of a labor party, but would never join the Socialist Party. Simons argued that the British Labour Party was much more effective than the American Socialist movement, that the latter must be thoroughly reorganized to become a true working-class party, and last that the "demagogical politicians" (i.e., presumably, the left wing) must be driven out of the Socialist Party.[11]

Walling reacted to this letter with great hostility. He immediately wrote scores of prominent Socialists to alert them that the right-wing leaders (namely, Simons, Robert Hunter, John Spargo, Victor Berger, and Morris Hillquit) planned to solidify their control over the party machinery and turn it into a labor party allied with the AFL. Soon thereafter, Walling sent Simons's letter to Charles Kerr, who published it in his influential *International Socialist Review* and asked each person nominated for a position on the National Executive Committee in the coming elections to state whether they favored merging the Socialist Party into a labor party. Phrasing the question that way led most nominees to vote "no," but privately, the right-wing leaders did appear quite interested in working with a labor party.[12] As Hillquit wrote to J. G. Phelps Stokes, "if a bonafide workingmen's party should be organized in this country . . . on a true workingmen's platform, and upon the principle of independent and uncompromising working class politics, our party could not consistently oppose such an organization. . . ." Certainly Berger, Hunter, Simons, and Spargo would join him in favoring cooperation with such a party, he argued, as would the majority of Socialist Party members.[13]

The coup engineered by Walling and Kerr helped kill any Socialist-sponsored efforts to build a labor party. By spring 1910, national chairman J. Mahlon Barnes could describe Socialist policy accordingly: "this is our year to side-track the Gompers program . . . on independent political action and to forestall an

---

[10] Harriman to Hillquit, November 10, 1908, Morris Hillquit Papers, Wisconsin State Historical Society, Madison.

[11] Algie M. Simons to William English Walling, November 19, 1909, reprinted in *International Socialist Review*, 10 (7), January 1910, 594–7.

[12] "A Labor Party," *International Socialist Review*, 10 (7), January 1910, 594–609 and 654–62.

[13] Hillquit to Stokes, December 3, 1909; Stokes to Hillquit, December 2, 1909; and Berger to Hillquit, December 6, 1909: all Hillquit Papers.

independent labor party." Soon after this battle, Socialist Party leaders sent an organizer to Arizona to discourage the creation of a labor party there.[14] As we will see, the failure of these efforts to broaden the Socialists' appeal ironically may have helped the Democrats steal their thunder in 1916.

But for the time being, circumstances appeared to prove the wisdom of the left-wing Socialists. In the next years, the party grew stronger and more popular. From a membership of only 20,000 in 1904, the Socialist Party peaked at 150,000 members in May 1912. Electorally, the party's successes began to add up: In 1910, it elected its first congressman, Victor Berger of Milwaukee. By the end of 1911, more than 1,100 Socialists had been elected to public office nationwide, including fifty-six mayors. The towns voting Socialists into power ranged widely across the United States, but midwestern towns with populations under 50,000 people seemed to produce the strongest Socialist victories. At the national level, the party recovered from its poor 1908 showing to record, in 1912, its best vote ever in a presidential race. It more than doubled its 1908 showing to poll over 900,000 votes, or 6 percent of all those cast, for candidate Eugene Debs.[15]

The growing popularity of socialism naturally threatened Samuel Gompers's conservative vision of labor politics. During these years, moreover, the Socialist movement began to challenge pure and simple leaders in their own territories. During 1911 and 1912, Socialist-led rebellions in several international unions removed conservative leaders, including James Moffitt of the hatters, William Huber of the carpenters, Hugh Frayne of the sheet-metal tradesmen, John Lennon of the tailors, and James O'Connell of the machinists. Each of these men belonged to the conservative bloc, led by Samuel Gompers, that ruled over the AFL, and most had been prominent supporters of Gompers's political strategy. O'Connell and Lennon in particular were among the most partisan Democrats in the AFL and each had played a vital role in designing and implementing the Federation's alliance with the Democratic Party.[16] Within the AFL itself, the height of Socialist influence came in 1912 when approximately 100 delegates to the AFL convention, or 25 percent, were affiliated with the Socialist Party.

---

[14] Barnes to Hillquit, May 3, 1910, Hillquit Papers; for continued labor party agitation among other Socialists, see correspondence between Adolph Germer and Robert Hunter, March 18 and 28, 1910, Adolph Germer Papers, Wisconsin State Historical Society, Madison. Hunter proposed that Socialists in the UMW, WFM, Tailors, IAM, Bakers, and Brewers call a conference to launch a labor party. Socialist opposition to labor parties dated back to 1901, but seems to have grown more aggressive after this fight. See Foner, *History of the Labor Movement*, 3:277–9 and 5:90.

[15] Richard Judd, *Socialist Cities: Municipal Politics and the Grassroots of American Socialism* (Albany: SUNY Press, 1989), 19–25; Kipnis, *The American Socialist Movement,* 339–68; and Schlesinger, *History of American Presidential Elections*, 3:2242.

[16] David Montgomery, *The Fall of the House of Labor: the Workplace, the State, and American Labor Activism* (New York: Cambridge University Press, 1987), 289–90; Warren Van Tine, *The Making of the Labor Bureaucrat: Union Leadership in the United States, 1870–1920* (Amherst: University of Massachusetts Press, 1973), 158.

Socialists nominated their own Max Hayes for the AFL presidency against Samuel Gompers, and nearly one-third of the delegates voted for him. Every delegate representing five unions voted for Hayes: the bakery workers, cloth hat and cap makers, machinists, shingle weavers, and the Western Federation of Miners. Hayes also received half or more of the votes from delegations representing the United Mine Workers, the Brewery Workers, the Journeymen Tailors, the Painters and Decorators, and the Quarry Workers. The Socialist candidate for AFL vice-president received even more votes than Hayes. William Johnston, the Socialist militant elected leader of the International Association of Machinists, ran for third vice-president against the incumbent (Machinists' ex-president) James O'Connell. O'Connell beat Johnston by 10,800 votes to 6,200.[17]

As Socialists challenged the AFL leaders on their own turf, another dramatic set of events suggested the narrowness of the Federation's craft organization. Beginning in 1909, unskilled workers in several industries demonstrated their potential for solidarity and militancy. In the steel industry at McKees Rocks, Pennsylvania, unskilled workers aided by the IWW struck and won, succeeding where the aristocratic craft workers had failed. Their story repeated itself in the following months in a number of other steel towns. In New York, unskilled female shirtwaist workers united in the "uprising of the 20,000" and won their strike after three months. More strikes by female garment workers followed, in New York and Chicago, leading in 1914 to a rebellion against the conservative leadership of the United Garment Workers and the establishment of a new industrial union, led by the young Sidney Hillman. These and other strikes disproved some key assumptions on which the AFL had been built: Immigrants, women, and the unskilled could not be organized, and craft organization was superior to industrial unionism. In the process, this new movement of unskilled workers exposed the narrow exclusivism of the venerable AFL and its resulting limitations as a working-class institution.[18]

A last critical problem for the AFL leaders, and for all of union labor, resulted from labor's continuing war against open-shop employers. This time the battle centered in Los Angeles. One of the open-shop movement's main strongholds, Los Angeles included prominent anti-union leaders such as Harrison Gray Otis, the publisher of the Los Angeles *Times*. By 1910, the growing conflict between workers and employers focused on Los Angeles's best-organized industry, the metal trades. On June 1, 1910, metalworkers went on strike, and within two weeks, 1,500 workers had left their jobs. Injunctions and antipicketing ordinances failed to break the strike and the labor movement grew stronger. Over the next months, tensions in Los Angeles escalated, and in the early morning

---

[17] Kipnis, *The American Socialist Movement*, 339–68.

[18] See David Montgomery, "The 'New Unionism' and the Transformation of Workers' Consciousness in America, 1909–1922," *Journal of Social History*, 7, Summer 1974, 509–35; James Green, *The World of the Worker: Labor in Twentieth Century America* (New York: Hill and Wang, 1980); and Susan Glenn, *Daughters of the Shtetl: Life and Labor in the Immigrant Generation* (Ithaca, NY: Cornell University Press, 1990).

of October 1, 1910, a bomb exploded in the open-shop offices of the *Times,* destroying the building and killing twenty-one people.[19]

Some six months later, police arrested John McNamara, secretary-treasurer of the International Bridge and Structural Iron Workers, and his brother James for the *Times* bombing. AFL leaders joined most other labor activists in declaring immediately that the McNamaras had been framed, and Gompers personally convinced a reluctant Clarence Darrow to take the case. When Darrow warned that defense of the McNamara brothers would cost $350,000, Gompers promised to raise the money. The AFL then launched an aggressive campaign in support of the McNamaras. Workers created defense leagues throughout the country, AFL leaders commissioned a film honoring John McNamara, and Labor Day, 1911, was proclaimed "McNamara Day" and honored by thousands of demonstrating workers across the country.[20] The AFL's prestige and honor rested on the validity of its argument that the McNamara brothers were innocent victims of a frame-up.

Soon after the brothers' trial began in the fall of 1911, however, the defense team's strategy fell apart. In November, Darrow was charged with attempting to bribe a jury member. Then on December 1, 1911, James McNamara pleaded guilty to the charge of murder and confessed that he had planted a suitcase of dynamite near the *Times* office building. His brother pleaded guilty as an accessory to the bombing of an ironworks soon thereafter. Rarely has American labor faced a darker moment than the day when the McNamara brothers changed their pleas. On learning the news, Samuel Gompers reportedly broke into tears, feeling, he later said, "horror struck and amazed." Like millions of American workers, Gompers had believed deeply in the brothers' innocence.[21]

The McNamaras' confession generated an antilabor fever throughout the country. Employers charged that the brothers represented merely the beginnings of a vast bombing conspiracy. Every member of the working class, and especially union activists, became suspect. Detective William Burns, who led the *Times* investigation, charged that the blame for the bombing should be placed

---

[19] Foner, *History of the Labor Movement,* 5:7–12; Luke Grant, *The National Erectors' Association and the International Association of Bridge and Structural Ironworkers* (New York: Arno Press, 1971); Louis Adamic, *Dynamite: The Story of Class Violence in America* (New York: Macmillan, 1934); Graham Adams, Jr., *Age of Industrial Violence, 1910–1915: The Activities and Findings of the U.S. Commission on Industrial Relations* (New York: Columbia University Press, 1966); and Grace Hilman Stimson, *Rise of the Labor Movement in Los Angeles* (Berkeley: University of California Press, 1955). Also useful is the account by the fiercely antilabor detective who investigated the case: William J. Burns, *The Masked War: The Story of a Peril that Threatened the U.S.* (New York: George H. Doran, 1913).

[20] Report of James McHugh, Andrew Furuseth, and John Colpoys, McNamara Defense Fund Auditing Committee, April 27, 1912, *American Federation of Labor Records: The Samuel Gompers Era* (Microfilming Corporation of America, 1979) (hereafter cited as *AFL Records*), reel 75; Foner, *History of the Labor Movement,* 5:17–23.

[21] Adamic, *Dynamite,* 231–40; "Live Labor Topics of the Day. Gompers Speaks for Labor," *American Federationist* (hereafter cited as *AF*), 19 (3), March 1912, 201–6.

at the door of Samuel Gompers, and newspapers eagerly picked up and publicized his accusations. The New York *Evening Journal,* for example, focused its front page for December 7 on a vast headline proclaiming: "GOMPERS MAN HIGHER UP – STATEMENT OF DETECTIVE BURNS." In repeated editorials and articles, Gompers defended the labor movement, the AFL, and himself, arguing that the American trade union movement was "lawful and progressive," and that it had nothing to hide. He offered to open AFL files and account books to interested persons and concluded: "What has happened has been a deplorable incident, a misfortune, an exceptional course of action, but . . . [it] does not touch the essentials of trade unionism."[22]

For decades, conservative labor leaders had struggled to demonstrate the respectability of their union movement, while painting the Socialists and Wobblies as violent ruffians. In the rhetoric of open-shop employers, however, no difference existed between a Wobbly, a Socialist, or an AFL worker: All were thugs disposed toward riotous actions. The McNamaras' confession appeared to demonstrate the validity of this charge and thereby represented a spectacular public relations victory for anti-union employers everywhere. Reeling from this blow to the labor movement's public image, Gompers simultaneously faced challenges to his authority from Socialists and from unskilled workers mobilizing victoriously around the country without assistance from his craft-oriented federation. Facing such problems, Gompers and his allies were not likely to undertake major political gambles. On the other hand, if the opportunity arose, they could surely use some friends in powerful places.

Labor's Elite Politics

This larger context and the devastating setbacks incurred in the 1908 political campaign explain why AFL politics shifted gears so dramatically during the years from 1909 to 1913. Popular mobilization of AFL members, and the highly visible political posturing by Gompers that accompanied it, never dominated AFL politics again the way they had between 1906 and 1908.

This is not to say that AFL leaders retreated from politics, but rather that their mode of operation changed radically. Instead of grassroots mobilization campaigns, the AFL now focused its efforts on the elite world of lobbying and high-level contacts with Democratic Party leaders. In 1909 and 1910, the AFL leadership continued watching Congress, looking for progress that never came on measures like injunction reform. Speaker Cannon's control over the House of Representatives kept the AFL's bills bottled up in committee, and President Taft did not encourage Cannon to abandon his standpat strategies. During 1909,

---

[22] Gompers, "Labor's Position Lawful and Progressive," *AF,* 19 (1), January 1912, 29–32; Gompers, "'The Man Higher Up' Outcry," *AF,* 19 (2), February 1912, 132–5; "Live Labor Topics of the Day. Gompers Speaks for Labor," *AF,* 19 (3), March 1912, 201–6; "Burns' Frenzy Running to Seed," *AF,* 19 (3), March 1912, 206–7.

Gompers encouraged Democratic congressmen to unite with insurgent Republicans in an effort to rein in the autocratic House speaker, giving the group meeting space at Federation headquarters and acting, in his own words, as an unofficial advisor. This effort bore fruit in March 1910 when a majority of congressmen voted to change House rules and strip Speaker Cannon of much of his power.[23]

The AFL's most strenuous effort to solve its legal crisis during these years emerged from a meeting between the "Labor Group" in Congress – those congressmen elected as a result of the AFL's political work in 1906 and 1908 – and Gompers and Morrison. It generated a new attempt by Congressman William Hughes of New Jersey to exempt labor from the provisions of the Sherman Anti-Trust Act. He introduced a rider to the Civil Supply Bill, which provided funds for antitrust prosecutions under the Sherman Act. The Hughes amendment prohibited the use of such funds for prosecuting labor organizations. Though both the House and the Senate defeated this amendment, representatives' votes on it became the acid test by which the AFL officially decided who deserved labor's support in the 1910 elections.[24]

That June, the AFL Executive Council laid out a four-pronged strategy for the 1910 campaigns: First, Federation leaders would communicate with the political parties in each congressional district to urge the nomination of unionists for Congress; second, it would instruct the insurgents in Congress that opposition to Cannon by itself would not guarantee labor's support; third, AFL leaders would determine how congressmen voted on the Hughes amendment to exempt labor from the Sherman Act; and, lastly, each AFL affiliate would be voluntarily assessed in order to raise funds.[25] Through its assessment, the AFL raised $3,148.78 (less than half the amount raised in either 1906 or 1908), with which it printed and distributed campaign literature and put organizers in the field. As in earlier campaigns, the AFL targeted powerful enemies of labor, pouring much of its resources into those contests, and worked to encourage trade unionist candidates. As with other campaigns, the AFL national headquarters determined which districts would receive literature and organizers, and which candidates would receive Gompers's support. Last, the AFL compiled information on the records of incumbent congressmen, supplying it to interested local- or state-level activists.[26]

---

[23] For the fullest discussion of the Democratic-Insurgent coup against Speaker Cannon, see Kenneth W. Hechler, *Insurgency: Personalities and Politics of the Taft Era* (New York: Russell and Russell, 1964), 49–78; for Gompers's role, see Samuel Gompers, *Seventy Years of Life and Labor: An Autobiography* (New York: E. P. Dutton, 1925), 2:250–2.

[24] Foner, *History of the Labor Movement*, 5:92–3.

[25] Extracts from the Executive Council Minutes, June 1910, *AFL Records*, reel 71.

[26] Morrison to Cal Wyatt, September 30, 1910, Morrison Letterbooks; Morrison to Sim Bramlette, October 18, 1910, Morrison Letterbooks; Gompers to William Hughes, October 28, 1910, *AFL Records*, reel 72; Morrison to John Moffitt, October 13, 1910, Morrison Letterbooks; Morrison to Martin Lawler, October 22, 1910, Morrison Letterbooks; Gompers to U. H. Long, August 5, 1910, *AFL Records*, reel 72; Foner, *History of the Labor Movement*, 5:97.

Gompers and AFL Secretary Frank Morrison deliberately designed this campaign as a quieter and less visible alternative to their boisterous strategy of years before. Their approach suggests the lessons they had learned during 1908. As Gompers put it, in previous campaigns, "labor entered into the open arena of political battle and drew all the concentrated opposition fire upon its ranks." Although this approach resulted in some victories, it was not sufficiently successful. Therefore, "Organized labor has learned the lesson that, for a time at least, **silent yet constant and persistent effort** would bring its best achievement. ..." Similarly, Morrison wrote to an organizer in mid-October that "The quiet campaign all along the line that we have been carrying on is bearing good fruit; it is 100 percent more satisfactory than any other campaign that we have had to deal with."[27]

In every sphere of its campaign, the AFL played a more subdued role than in 1906 and 1908. Workers sent in few requests for their congressmen's records and generally gave little indication that they were mobilizing behind the campaign. Similarly, the AFL utilized few organizers for its 1910 campaign. Rather than the scores of organizers assigned to political duty in previous contests (42 in 1906 and more than 100 in 1908), the AFL shifted only 15 organizers onto political campaigns in 1910. Even these few organizers did not work for very long, typically contributing only between one and three weeks to political duties.[28]

Most of the AFL's limited funds went into printing and distribution of literature. As earlier, the AFL leaders focused their campaign strategy on the voting records of congressmen. The AFL spent nearly $2,000 to print and distribute 250,000 copies of a leaflet providing the record of congressmen's votes on the Hughes amendment. At local workers' request, the AFL sent this leaflet out in quantities of 500, 1,000, or more. The national leadership believed congressmen's votes on this issue perfectly represented who was or was not a friend to labor. As Morrison put it, "Those men who voted against the Hughes amendment were antagonistic on all other labor measures; so it is as true a line-up as we could have secured as to the attitude of the members of the House of Representatives." Apparently, this leaflet was the only one put out by the AFL during the 1910 campaign.[29]

The AFL focused its strategy on approximately half a dozen races. Above all, it worked to defeat top lieutenants of Speaker Cannon's: John Dalzell of Pittsburgh, whom the AFL had fought heatedly in 1906; and John Gardner of

---

[27] Gompers, "Labor's Political Opportunity," *AF*, 17 (10), October 1910, 898; Morrison to M. Grant Hamilton, October 10, 1910, Morrison Letterbooks.

[28] See Greene, "The Strike at the Ballot Box," 544–5.

[29] Morrison to M. Grant Hamilton, October 10, 1910, Morrison Letterbooks; Morrison to Thomas Flynn, October 10, 1910, Morrison Letterbooks. The leaflet was entitled: "Record Vote of Congressmen For and Against Labor. Roll Call of Congressmen in the House of Representatives by States on the Hughes Amendment." See the *AFL Records*, reel 72, October 19, 1910.

New Jersey, another standpatter who had years earlier been an important ally of the AFL. It also assigned several organizers to help leading trade unionists running for congressional seats. Miner William B. Wilson of Pennsylvania received assistance from several organizers, as did James Maher of Brooklyn, a member of the Hatters' union. Both won election to Congress. Last, the AFL worked to elect D. J. McGillicuddy of Lewiston, Maine, to Congress. In 1906, McGillicuddy had failed to defeat labor enemy Charles Littlefield in a much publicized campaign. In 1908, Littlefield had chosen not to run for reelection and had been succeeded by another Republican. Now in 1910, the AFL leaders tried for a third time to elect McGillicuddy, and finally succeeded. Organizer Harry Eichelberger exulted: "Your work here four years ago and the work two years since has borne fruit."[30]

This comment captured the mood among AFL activists throughout the country. Morrison wrote cheerfully in mid-October: "Everything looks good for the AFL this year. I am sure a sufficient number of friendly Representatives will be elected to Congress this fall to ensure the passage of legislation that we have been working for for quite a number of years."[31] And indeed, the AFL's more discreet political strategy seemed to pay off. The number of trade unionists in Congress continued its slow but steady climb, increasing from 8 to 13 as a result of the 1910 elections. The Labor Group in Congress now included nine Democrats, three Republicans, and one Socialist, who represented the following unions: United Mine Workers (2 congressmen), Commercial Telegraphers (2), Typographers (2), Locomotive Firemen, Blacksmiths, Bridge and Structural Ironworkers, Railroad Telegraphers, Musicians, Metal Miners, and Hatters.[32]

In addition, the Democrats regained firm control of the House of Representatives, with a majority of 73, for the first time in sixteen years. The Republicans

---

[30] Eichelberger to Gompers, September 12, 1910, *AFL Records*, reel 72.

[31] Morrison to John Badry, October 14, 1910; see also Morrison to Andrew Furuseth, October 17, 1910: both Morrison Letterbooks.

[32] "President Gompers' Report," *AF*, 19 (1), January 1912, 33. Two other congressmen (Isaac Sherwood of Toledo, Ohio, and William Hughes of Paterson, New Jersey) had won inclusion in the "Labor Group" through their stalwart support for labor reform, thus bringing the total number of labor congressmen to fifteen. The "card men" elected to Congress in the 1910 election included the following: Robert Lee, a Democrat and blacksmith from Pottsville, Pennsylvania; William B. Wilson, a Democrat and miner from Blossburg, Pennsylvania; E. E. Roberts, a Republican metal miner from Carson City, NV; Carl C. Anderson, a musician and Democrat from Fostoria, Ohio; Charles B. Smith, a Democrat and railroad telegrapher from Buffalo, New York; David Lewis, a Democrat from Cumberland, MD and a mineworker; Frank Buchanan, Democrat from Chicago, worked as a bridge and structural ironworker; James McDermott of Chicago, commercial telegrapher and Democrat; James Maher, Democrat and hatter from Brooklyn, New York; William J. Cary, a commercial telegrapher and Republican from Milwaukee; John Martin, a Democrat from Pueblo, Colorado, and a locomotive fireman; John Farr, a Republican typographer from Scranton, Pennsylvania; and Victor Berger, a Socialist typographer from Milwaukee. Information on these men comes from "President Gompers' Report," cited earlier, and from the *Congressional Directory*, 62nd through 65th Congresses (Washington, DC: Joint Committee on Printing).

maintained their hold on the U.S. Senate, but Democrats significantly increased their standing in that body, and when combined with Republican insurgents, they could now dominate it. Progressive Democrats also won gubernatorial races in New York, Connecticut, Maine, Massachusetts, and New Jersey, among other states.[33] Although the AFL leaders seemed uncertain after the debacle of 1908 about what the future held for their relationship with the Democratic Party, Gompers clearly sensed that this Democratic victory posed an opportunity that, if not seized, could spell disaster for his vision of American labor politics. Thus, he released a statement to the media on March 4, 1911, as the new Democratic Congress prepared to open. Gompers warned that because the Democrats had won a majority of seats in Congress, organized labor had now better see action on its demands: "Unless the Democratic party shall take hold of the interests of the masses, . . . it is not going to be the party of the future. . . . I feel that the time has come when we shall have a constructive, progressive, radical labor party, unless the Democratic party shall perform its duties." In a memo to the AFL Executive Council explaining the reasons for this letter, Gompers argued that if the Democrats failed to act on labor's demands, the AFL would be incapable of preventing the creation of an independent labor party: "By pointing this out to the Democrats before the new session of Congress begins, we can make them understand that they can prevent this new party from rising by proving that there is no need for it." This was not the first time Gompers had exploited Socialist and labor party sentiment within the Federation to achieve his own political ends.[34]

As it turned out, Gompers had nothing to fear from the new Congress. As the session opened, Democratic congressmen quickly elected Missourian Champ Clark, a progressive and strong Bryan supporter, as Speaker of the House. They elected William B. Wilson, an ex-official of the United Mine Workers and a leading member of the Labor Group in Congress, as chairman of the Labor Committee, and three trade unionists soon joined Wilson there as well: David Lewis (UMW), Frank Buchanan (Structural Iron Workers), and James Maher (Hatters). Indeed, the president of the National Association of Manufacturers attacked the Democrats for "so constituting the . . . [Labor Committee] as to place it under the domination of present or ex-labor union officials who sit in Congress."[35]

Suddenly, a very different sort of congressional politics became possible. Though thirteen labor congressmen by themselves remained a small minority in the House of Representatives, nonetheless they combined to create an audible chorus of voices. Through their efforts, a broader and more ambitious series of labor reforms made their way to the House floor. Proposals made by members

---

[33] George Mowry, *The Era of Theodore Roosevelt 1900–1912* (New York: Harper & Row, 1958), 272–3; David Sarasohn, *The Party of Reform: Democrats in the Progressive Era* (Jackson: University Press of Mississippi, 1989), 87–92.

[34] Foner, *History of the Labor Movement*, 5:98–9.

[35] "President Gompers' Report," to the 1911 convention of the AFL, reprinted in the *AF*, 19 (1), January 1912, 33; Sarasohn, *The Party of Reform*, 96.

of the Labor Group included bills proposing to raise wages for the women who cleaned the House office building; conduct government investigations into the causes of unemployment, the Harriman railroad strike, and the Lawrence textile strike; regulate the hours of work in continuous working factories throughout the United States; return control over their destiny to the people of the Philippines; and create an old-age pension for wage earners, or in other words, for those men and women who work "on the battle field of industry."[36]

None of these proposals made it out of their committees. But when the labor congressmen united with likeminded politicians, usually Democrats, they could have a more potent effect. Through the efforts of the Labor Group, numerous bills favored by organized workers won passage in the house, and occasionally in the Senate as well. Both Houses of Congress passed an eight-hour bill for government employees and President Taft signed it into law, just as he did a bill placing a high tax on white phosphorus matches (to discourage use of the same, so as to protect the industry's workers). Furthermore, several measures that the Labor Group introduced or lobbied for passed the House and awaited passage in the Senate. These included bills that would limit injunctions, provide for a jury trial in cases where contempt charges resulted from injunctions, create a Department of Labor with a cabinet-level secretary possessing power to mediate in trade disputes, create a Commission on Industrial Relations to ascertain methods for dealing with labor conflicts, investigate Taylorism to protect workingmen from too great a speedup of the work process, and regulate convict labor. Several of these bills were ultimately signed into law. Most notably, the creation of the Department of Labor and the Commission on Industrial Relations would each emerge as watershed events in the political history of the working class, helping to restructure American politics and create a more fruitful environment for labor and progressive reform.[37]

Despite these successes, Gompers indulged in propaganda when he argued, in the *American Federationist,* that the labor congressmen transcended their party affiliations to unite around political issues. Even in Congress, labor politicians struggled against partisan divisions. The Democratic labor congressmen dominated in the group, and on the floor of the House of Representatives, members manifested their disagreements as often as they did the unity Gompers so preferred. Victor Berger, the lone Socialist, attacked the Democratic Party's record as musician Carl Anderson defended it. Democratic miner William Wilson made

---

[36] *Congressional Record* (referred to hereafter as *CR*), Vol. 48, pt. 1, 62nd Congress, 2nd Session, December 4, 1911 to January 17, 1912, p. 464; *CR*, Vol. 48, pt. 2, January 18 to February 14, 1912, p. 1602; *CR*, Vol. 48, pt. 3, 62nd Congress, 2nd Session, February 15 to March 9, 1912, p. 2488; *CR*, Vol. 49, pt. 4, 62nd Congress, 3rd Session, February 13–26, 1913, p. 3624; *CR*, Vol. 47, pt. 2, 62nd Congress, 11st Session, May 6 to June 14, 1911, p. 1478; and *CR*, Vol. 48, pt. 9, 62nd Congress, 2nd Session, June 21 to July 22, 1912, p. 9246.

[37] Samuel Gompers, "Organized Labor and Federal Legislation," *AF*, 19 (8), August 1912, 628–30; "President Gompers' Report," reprinted in the *AF*, 19 (1), January 1912, 33; *CR*, Vol. 48, pt. 3, 62nd Congress, 2nd Session, February 15 to March 9, 1912, p. 2489; and comments by W. B. Wilson in *CR*, Vol. 48, pt. 11, 62nd Congress, 2nd Session, August 9–26, 1912, pp. 10679–82.

an emotional pitch for his party, and Republican typographer John Farr took shots at the Democrats' judgment. Besides demonstrating the hold of partisan loyalties, the labor congressmen could and did divide over specific issues. Immigration restriction, for example, generated tense debates. Although some in the Labor Group loyally repeated the AFL position in favor of restriction, many others refused and insisted on liberal immigration policies.[38]

The Labor Group had far to travel before it could become a united and powerful bloc within the House of Representatives. Organized labor's biggest gains continued to come not from the efforts of labor congressmen alone, but from their alliance with Democrats. At a time when AFL leaders felt unsure of their alliance with the Democrats after the debacle of 1908 and the decline in William Jennings Bryan's power, the party's receptiveness to labor reform in the new session of Congress suggested that it would prove more than a temporary convenience.

The Changing Terrain of American Politics

In fact, by the summer of 1912, a strong foundation had been established for a political partnership uniting organized labor and the Democrats. The two groups continued to share certain predispositions that boded well for a political alliance: Both were suspicious of concentrations of power; both grimaced under conservative Republican domination of the White House and Congress; both saw themselves as outsiders fighting entrenched financial and political interests; and, last, both shared the extreme racism of the age and defined "the masses" in a way that excluded African-Americans. At the state and municipal levels, these shared beliefs allowed trade unionists and Democrats to establish productive working relationships in many regions of the country and these, regardless of the desires of individual leaders, continued to make possible a national-level alliance. Between 1908 and 1912, the Democratic Party won control of major two-party states such as Ohio, Indiana, New York, New Jersey, Massachusetts, and Illinois. In each case, organized labor worked with the Democracy to pass significant progressive legislation, and particularly, labor reforms. In Ohio, for example, labor activists pushed Governor Judson Harmon and his successor James Cox to sponsor and support a broad range of labor reforms. Their achievements included a compulsory workmen's compensation act, a ban on child labor, a nine-hour workday for women, the initiative and referendum, and mine and railroad safety regulations. Perhaps a more famous case of labor-Democratic cooperation at the state level emerged in New York, where the labor and women's movements

---

[38] For Berger debating Anderson, see the *Congressional Record*, Vol. 48, pt. 9, 62nd Congress, 2nd Session, June 21 to July 22, 1912, p. 9246; for Wilson and Farr's partisan appeals, see *CR*, Vol. 48, pt. 11, pp. 10679–82, and Vol. 47, pt. 1, pp. 505–6; for conflicting opinions on immigration, where John Farr opposed William Hughes and William Wilson, see *CR*, Vol. 48, pt. 2, January 18 to February 14, 1912, pp. 1449–50; similarly, for opposition to immigration restriction expressed by Victor Berger and John Martin, see *CR*, Vol. 49, pt. 4, February 13–26, 1913, pp. 3422–3.

mobilized after the Triangle Fire of 1911 to demand reforms. The state legislature bowed to the pressure and created a Factory Investigation Commission with
members including Mary Drier of the Women's Trade Union League, and Samuel
Gompers, while two young legislators representing Tammany Hall, Robert
Wagner and Alfred Smith, served respectively as chairman and vice-chairman.
During the next four years, the commission investigated working conditions
and proposed reforms to address the most egregious problems. Ultimately the
commission pushed a spectacular set of labor reforms through the legislature.
By the end of the progressive era New York State possessed the most advanced
and progressive labor legislation in the nation.[39]

The Democratic Party itself underwent a transformation during these same
years, one that complicated the project of building a permanent alliance with
organized labor. After more than a decade, it finally seemed William Jennings
Bryan would no longer stand at the party's helm when the next presidential election took place. Democrats around the country nervously agitated for this or
that candidate to replace him. With the party gaining in power at the state level,
a number of possible candidates emerged. By early 1912, the strongest ones
appeared to be Oscar Underwood, a southerner and representative of the party's
conservative wing; Champ Clark of Missouri, Speaker of the House, a firm
Progressive and the apparent inheritor of Bryan's mantle; and Woodrow Wilson,
the ex-President of Princeton elected in 1910 to the New Jersey governorship.
Wilson had the prestige and grooming to place him as a likely presidential nominee, but he was also the least tested of the candidates and his political sympathies remained somewhat mysterious.

The AFL leaders watched closely during 1912 as the Democrats chose their
new leader. Fervently, they desired that Champ Clark should win the nomination. Champ occupied a position in the political spectrum similar to Bryan's,
and enjoyed a closer personal relationship with Nebraska's "Peerless Leader."
As a result Clark won much of Bryan's following, especially in the West and
Midwest. Clark had served in Congress since the 1890s and had consistently
supported progressive causes within that body. As Speaker of the House since 1910,
Clark had fought successfully to pass a series of reforms impressive enough
that, according to labor Congressman W. B. Wilson, the House had fulfilled
each of its promises made to labor during the 1908 campaign.[40]

[39] Sarasohn, *Party of Reform*, 111–18; Hoyt L. Warner, *Progressivism in Ohio, 1897–1917*
(Columbus: Ohio State University Press, 1964), 368–83 and 401–12; Irwin Yellowitz, *Labor
and the Progressive Movement in New York State, 1897–1917* (Ithaca, NY: Cornell University Press, 1965), 94 and 133–6; Robert Wesser, *A Response to Progressivism: The Democratic Party and New York Politics, 1902–1918* (New York: New York University Press,
1986), 70–4 and 225–6.

[40] Not only the AFL, but also William Randolph Hearst (and his influential newspapers) supported Clark strongly. Arthur S. Link, *Woodrow Wilson and the Progressive Era, 1910–1917*
(New York: Harper & Row, 1954), 10–14; Gompers, "Labor on Guard and Insistent –
No. 2," *AF*, 19 (8), August 1912, 623–8; for W. B. Wilson's comment, see *CR*, Vol. 48,
pt. 11, 62nd Congress, 2nd Session, August 9–26, 1912, pp. 10679–82.

Governor Wilson presented Clark's stiffest competition, but trade unionists had reasons to distrust him politically. Wilson's political roots lay firmly with the conservative wing of the Democratic Party. He deserted Bryan in 1896 and supported the Gold Democratic ticket, and again in 1908, he opposed Bryan for the Democratic nomination. In that latter year, Wilson, then president of Princeton, was first mentioned as a possible presidential nominee, but conservative editors like George Harvey of *Harper's Weekly* provided his only support. In 1910, conservative New Jersey boss James Smith picked Wilson as his nominee for governor, and the Princetonian handily won the election. Wilson's political orientation had begun to shift from conservative to progressive sometime between 1908 and 1910. Immediately after the election Wilson dramatically pronounced his break with conservative boss politics by defeating Smith's bid for a senatorial nomination. He then pushed through the legislature a set of reforms that included a workmen's compensation act, a law allowing municipalities to adopt the initiative, referendum, recall, and commission form of government, and a corrupt-practices act, thus turning New Jersey into a model progressive state. At the same time, Wilson moved gradually closer to Bryan's stance on a number of issues, announcing, for example, his support for Bryan's pet issue, the initiative and referendum, in May of 1911. Although some began to worry that Wilson was becoming too much a "Bryan candidate," the New Jersey politician easily dissociated himself from agrarian radicalism. Wilson's intellectualism, urban background, and upper-class bearing all created a certain respectability that Bryan would never attain, allowing him, even as he moved to the left, to maintain his support among Cleveland Democrats and moderate editors who had felt profoundly alienated from Bryan.[41]

Thus by early 1912, Wilson had transformed himself into a leading progressive candidate, but one who could nonetheless attract conservative support. As Wilson's reputation as a progressive spread, however, many workers remained unimpressed. As recently as June 1910, Wilson, then president of Princeton University, had made a sharply antilabor address at his university's baccalaureate, calling trade unions "economically disastrous." The New Jersey labor movement vehemently opposed Wilson's candidacy for governor that year, state Federation of Labor leaders calling him the "tool . . . [of] Wall Street's interests. . . ." And although Wilson's record as governor between 1910 and 1912 finally won him the support of New Jersey labor, the movement's national leaders could not shake their suspicions about his sincerity – particularly on labor issues.[42]

---

[41] Arthur Link, *Wilson: The Road to the White House* (Princeton: Princeton University Press, 1947), 96–155 and 237–73; Sarasohn, *Party of Reform*, 119–23; Blum, *Woodrow Wilson and the Politics of Morality* (Boston: Little, Brown, 1956), 48–50.

[42] For Wilson's baccalaureate address see Arthur Link, ed., *The Papers of Woodrow Wilson* (Princeton: Princeton University Press, 1966), 19:242–3; for Wilson's attempt to appeal to the labor vote during the 1910 campaign, see "News Report of a Campaign Address in Bayonne," in ibid., 485–92; see also Link, *Wilson: The Road to the White House*, 159 and 387; and David Sarasohn, "The Democratic Surge, 1905–1912: Forging a Progressive

With the choice between Clark and Wilson in their minds one between a friend and foe of labor, the AFL leaders attempted for the first time in 1912 to influence the Democrats' choice of a presidential candidate, sending at least one organizer out to the Midwest to work on Clark's behalf.[43] Two months later, Clark arrived at the Democratic convention with more delegates committed to him than any other candidate, and initially it appeared that he would win the nomination. Late in the balloting, however, a trend developed in favor of Wilson. Bryan played a central role in this process by declaring, shortly after New York had gone to Clark, that he could ally with no candidate supported by Tammany Hall. Hearst's support for Clark also became increasingly visible and the Wilson camp effectively focused its criticism of Clark's candidacy on his relationship with the newspaper magnate.[44]

A Clark supporter to the very end, Gompers felt "disheartened" by Wilson's nomination. AFL leaders like John Lennon who strongly supported the temperance cause found Wilson palatable but disliked his vice-president, Thomas Marshall, Indiana's popular governor who opposed prohibition of alcohol. However, by 1912, the AFL's alliance with the Democratic Party had sufficiently deep roots, and it served simultaneously to bolster Gompers's dominance over labor's political culture that it could not be shaken by a presidential candidate who won only lukewarm support from the labor movement. Whatever the AFL's suspicions of Wilson, his party had proved itself a loyal friend to the Federation once it won control over the House of Representatives in 1910. Now, in 1912, convention delegates endorsed the same labor planks that AFL leaders had influenced and then praised profusely in 1908. Furthermore, the AFL leaders still looked to Bryan for political leadership. The instrumental role Bryan played in winning the nomination for Wilson undoubtedly helped warm Gompers and his allies to the New Jersey governor's candidacy.[45]

Democratic leaders similarly saw their burgeoning alliance with labor as too valuable to surrender. The formula first devised by Bryan continued to dominate party leaders' strategizing: In order to win the White House, the party must unite labor with other outsiders (southerners, westerners, and farmers above all). Josephus Daniels continued to serve as a top advisor when party leadership shifted from Bryan to Wilson (he worked as publicity director for the latter),

Majority," Ph.D, diss., University of California at Los Angeles, 1976, 237–41. Sarasohn refers to Wilson's antilabor speech as "an incredible move for anyone then cultivating national ambitions. . . ."

[43] Daniel Harris, Kansas City, to Gompers, February 27, March 26, and April 10, 1912, *AFL Records*, reel 74; W. D. Jamieson to Gompers, February 29, 1912, *AFL Records*, reel 74.

[44] The complex processes that won the nomination for Wilson may be traced by looking at Sarasohn, *Party of Reform*, 135–43; Link, *Woodrow Wilson and the Progressive Era*, 7–13; idem, *Wilson: The Road to the White House* (Princeton: Princeton University Press, 1947); and William Jennings Bryan, *A Tale of Two Conventions* (New York: Funk and Wagnalls, 1912).

[45] Gompers, *Seventy Years*, 2:282; on Lennon's disapproval of Thomas Marshall's candidacy, see Greene, "The Strike at the Ballot Box," 567–70.

and he expressed this common view in a letter to William McAdoo during the 1912 campaign, "If we get our share of [the labor vote] . . . there is nothing in the world that can defeat us. It is the crux of the situation."[46]

At the same time, the AFL leaders and Wilson shared a common approach to the dominant political question of the day: the nature and role of the state. The progressive movement had sufficiently matured by 1912 to define the leading issues in American political culture and this meant, first and foremost, a rejection of laissez-faire economics. While Taft and the Republicans would continue to stress the virtues of a self-regulating economy aided by the courts, the political momentum clearly belonged in 1912 to Woodrow Wilson and to Teddy Roosevelt's Progressive platform. Both candidates accepted the need for an expanded federal government, but they disagreed fundamentally over the shape that expansion should take. Roosevelt's political vision most resembled a statist solution. He proposed extensive powers for the government, for example, in the licensing and oversight of corporate activities. A Rooseveltian state would also pursue social justice by regulating a minimum wage and maximum hours for women and children.

Like Roosevelt, Wilson embraced the need for extensive reform, but his enthusiasm for relying on the federal government was tempered by traditional Democratic distaste for an interventionist state. Under the tutelage of Louis Brandeis, a Massachusetts lawyer and reformer with close ties to organized labor, Wilson developed an approach he called "The New Freedom." He argued that Roosevelt's vision of a regulatory administrator state would fail because the economic power of trusts would soon be translated into political power; ultimately, they would control the regulators as well. Wilson countered with a strategy he believed would restore free enterprise by "regulating competition," a concept that sounded appealing in its emphasis on liberty but remained forever vague in its details.[47]

Wilson's approach to the labor question spoke more directly to the AFL leaders' concerns. Although Roosevelt's program offered to do many things for workers, in Wilson's eyes it constituted paternalism. Roosevelt's Progressive platform, Wilson argued, "legalizes monopolies and systematically subordinates workingmen to them and to plans made by the Government. . . ." Indeed, the very monopolies Roosevelt sought to legalize were the same ones that "have been more inimical to organized labor than any other class of employers in the United States. . . . They have made it most difficult that you should take care of yourselves. . . ." Furthermore, "No federal legislation can change that thing. The

---

[46] Josephus Daniels to William McAdoo, October 14, 1912, William McAdoo Papers, Library of Congress, Manuscripts Division.

[47] Link, *Wilson: The Road to the White House*, 488–91; Martin Sklar, *The Corporate Reconstruction of American Capitalism, 1890–1916* (New York: Cambridge University Press, 1988); for Brandeis's views, see "Labor and the Trusts," *Collier's*, September 14, 1912; and Brandeis, "Labor and the New Party Trust Program," *La Follette's Weekly Magazine*, 4, October 12, 1912, 6–8 and 19–22.

minute you are taken care of by the government, you are wards, not independent men." In a Labor Day address in Buffalo, Wilson sounded very much like
Gompers, declaring that workers must depend on themselves and their organizations rather than the government: "I have yet to learn of any instance where
you got anything without going and taking it."[48]

Wilson's approach to winning the trade union vote was thus quite different
from Roosevelt's. In his speeches, he spent more time attacking the Progressive
Party's plan to expand the government's powers than on any other issue. He
dutifully defended labor's right to organize, and he discussed the Democratic
position on the tariff with regard to working people, arguing that lowering it
would lead to greater prosperity and hence aid workers more than Republican
protectionism ever had. But his primary appeal among workingmen consisted
of antistatism. Gompers might still feel suspicious of the degree to which Wilson
accepted labor's agenda as his own, but in their attitudes toward the state, the
presidential nominee and labor's leading statesman found much on which they
could agree.[49]

When it came to building campaign strategy, Wilson and his lieutenants
approached things very differently than had Bryan. As in 1908, the Democrats
appealed to labor strenuously and repeatedly, making the "labor question" one
of their top three or four issues. But the close working relationship that existed
between the Democracts and the AFL leaders that year, when they made strategic decisions together and even pooled their financial resources, did not
reappear in 1912. Samuel Gompers and the AFL leaders maintained a studied
distance from the Democrats' campaign, supporting them in editorials, but playing absolutely no role in directing and supervising the campaign. Both Gompers
and Lennon appeared open to picking up where their strategy left off in 1908,
but after a lengthy conference in Trenton between Gompers and Wilson in
July 1912, the connections broke off almost entirely.[50]

Although little written record has survived to document why the relationship
changed so dramatically, both the Democrats and the AFL leaders had reasons
to prefer a less public alliance. The 1908 campaign taught the Democrats that
a highly visible partnership with organized labor proved more a liability than
an asset. Seeking to recruit labor's support, William Jennings Bryan thought his
priority must be to win over AFL leaders. With that accomplished, he followed
their lead on most matters regarding the working class. That strategy blew up

---

[48] Woodrow Wilson, "Labor Day Address in Buffalo," in Link, *Papers of Woodrow Wilson*,
69–79; idem, *Wilson: The Road to the White House*, 490–2.

[49] For Wilson's appeals to workers, see his "Address at a Workingmen's Dinner in New York,"
September 4, 1912, in Link, *Papers of Woodrow Wilson*, 25:98–106; "Address to Work-
ingmen in Fall River, Massachusetts," September 26, 1912, ibid., 257–69; and "Speech to
Workingmen in Peru, Indiana," ibid., 332–8.

[50] Lennon to Gompers, July 2 and 3, 1912, *AFL Records*, reel 75; Gompers to Lennon,
July 9, 1912, *AFL Records*, reel 75. For a lengthier consideration of the reasons behind
these changes, see Greene, "The Strike at the Ballot Box," 567–72.

in the Democrats' collective face, however, and with the 1912 campaign following so shortly on the heels of the McNamara scandal, Woodrow Wilson surely needed little prodding to realize that Samuel Gompers could greatly damage his and his party's image. Gompers had learned a similar lesson from 1908. Years later, he explained his inactivity in 1912, pointing out that "Experience in the previous presidential campaign after the attacks were made against my associates, and particularly against me, indicated that I could best help in the campaign by counsel and assistance rather than conspicuous service that would focus attacks upon me."[51]

Thus, AFL politics looked very different in 1912 as its campaign program of earlier years, based on popular mobilization, almost entirely collapsed. Samuel Gompers examined each party's record in editorials and concluded that the Democrats possessed the best record on labor matters. AFL leaders supplied congressmen's records to trade unionists who requested them, but few did so. The AFL continued to emphasize the importance of electing trade unionists to Congress, but did little to further such a goal other than writing favorable letters for candidates known personally by Gompers or Morrison. The only other action taken by AFL national leaders consisted of publishing and distributing approximately 100,000 copies of a *Weekly Newsletter* that presented the AFL position on political matters, primarily listing the party platforms and avoiding any strong support for any party or candidate. Gompers did not exhort trade unionists to undertake a concrete program of activity, as he had in earlier years. The AFL assigned no volunteer or salaried organizers to political work and its leaders made no appeals to affiliated unions for money to fund a political program. Not since 1900 had the American Federation of Labor done so little for a national election.[52]

The Democratic National Committeemen nonetheless worked diligently to create a labor campaign in 1912, similar to their pioneering program of 1908, but they did not work through the AFL leaders in doing so. Instead, they called on lesser AFL lieutenants who had helped them in 1908. Herman Robinson, who led the Democratic labor strategy at its New York headquarters in 1908, continued to lead it now. Robinson's duties included building a labor campaign in seven Middle Atlantic and New England states. He planned to assign organizers to conduct political organizing in each state, and as in 1908, he hoped

---

[51] Gompers, *Seventy Years*, 2:282–3.

[52] The AFL's limited role is documented in Gompers to Joseph Murphy, June 29, 1912, *AFL Records*, reel 75; Gompers to Charles Case, August 30, 1912, *AFL Records*, reel 75; Gompers to Timothy Healey, September 30, 1912, *AFL Records*, reel 75; Gompers to Samuel Prince, October 6, 1912, *AFL Records*, reel 75; Gompers to William Rial, October 8, 1912, *AFL Records*, reel 75; Morrison to Gompers, September 27, 1912, *AFL Records*, reel 75; Morrison to James Morrison, October 16, 1912, Morrison Letterbooks. The AFL did pay the railroad fare, but nothing else, to send one organizer into candidate William B. Wilson's district to help him campaign. See Morrison to W. B. Wilson, October 29, 1912, Morrison Letterbooks. On the AFL's decision to raise no funds for the 1912 campaign, see Gompers to P. E. Duffy, September 5, 1912, *AFL Records*, reel 75.

AFL organizers could be engaged to do the job, but this time at the Democratic Party's expense. Robinson expected to assign one organizer and between one and four assistants to each major city for distributing literature. If Robinson's plans for developing labor's role were at all typical, this indicates a significant labor campaign, although one much more modest than that of 1908.[53]

Political organizers worked to mobilize the vote for Wilson primarily by giving speeches and distributing literature. One Democratic worker wrote to Gompers in late October and described his work. He often held night meetings, he said, and closed the meetings by showing his "lantern slides." Among the slides were pictures of Samuel Gompers and Woodrow Wilson: "in industrial centers you share the applause and the honors especially when I announce that you are not supporting Debs or Taft or Teddy – but upon deep investigation – have decided to support Wilson." In addition to using political organizers, the Democratic Party also appealed to workers by creating at least two special pamphlets that focused on what the Democratic-controlled House of Representatives had accomplished for labor.[54]

Gompers rarely communicated with the Democratic campaign in 1912. He advised Herman Robinson on campaign tactics a few times, but treated coolly any other Democratic requests for help. In early September, Martin Wade, who led the Democratic Party's labor campaign, wrote Gompers to ask that he cooperate with their work as in 1908 and that he assign Grant Hamilton to the Chicago headquarters. Gompers did not answer Wade's letter. A week later, Robinson informed Gompers which labor representative would be working at the Democrats' Chicago headquarters, which indicates that Gompers played no role in choosing the person for that position. Similarly, Robinson's request for suggestions of organizers who could do political work for the Democrats ended with him stressing that any help Gompers could give would be kept confidential. And when T. C. Spelling, a lawyer who had long worked with the AFL on legislative matters, requested that Gompers or some other leader of the AFL join him on a tour for the Democratic Party, Gompers's response again remained aloof: "I have no right to recommend to you anyone to accompany you. . . ." He recommended that Spelling contact Herman Robinson for suggestions.[55]

In early November 1912, voters elected Woodrow Wilson to the presidency by a comfortable margin and gave the Democratic Party control over both houses of the U.S. Congress for the first time in decades. In addition, seventeen of the

---

[53] Herman Robinson to Samuel Gompers, September 10, 1912, *AFL Records*, reel 75.

[54] F. S. Marnett to Gompers, October 23, 1912, *AFL Records*, reel 75; Foner, *History of the Labor Movement*, 5:117; on the Democrats' use of working-class organizers, see also Sarasohn, *Party of Reform*, 144.

[55] It is possible that Gompers responded to Wade by phone, although the letter is marked "no answer," indicating that no response was made. M. J. Wade to Gompers, September 4, 1912; Robinson to Gompers, September 10, 1912; Gompers to Robinson, September 11, 1912; T. C. Spelling to Gompers, September 13, 1912; Gompers to Spelling, September 16, 1912: all *AFL Records*, reel 75.

elected congressmen possessed union cards. At a press conference held by the AFL immediately after the election, Gompers claimed his Federation had played a significant role in the Democratic victory: "We did not go into the open this time but we made our fight just the same."[56]

Wilson won with a landslide in the Electoral College, though his victory as measured by popular votes was less impressive. With Wilson receiving just slightly fewer votes than Bryan had in 1908, the votes for Taft and Roosevelt together outnumbered the Democratic tally. This fact has led historians to attribute Wilson's victory to the fluke of Republican division, yet David Sarasohn has recently demonstrated the flaws with that particular logic. It assumes that if only one of Wilson's opponents had run for the office, say perhaps Taft, he would have won support from all those who voted for Roosevelt. In fact, however, many Rooseveltian progressives would have preferred Wilson if faced with a choice between him and Taft, just as many Taft supporters would have chosen Wilson over Roosevelt.[57]

Voting returns from the twenty-two counties where organized labor engaged in active campaign work during these decades allow a way to explore trade unionists' political reactions in 1912. These counties included many of the country's large industrial cities, such as Pittsburgh, Chicago, New York, Kansas City, and San Francisco; they also included smaller industrial cities such as Lawrence, Massachusetts, and mining regions in Pennsylvania and Illinois. Voters in these counties reacted in very diverse ways to the 1912 campaign. In more than half of the counties, including almost all of those in Pennsylvania, Ohio, Indiana, Illinois, and Michigan, voters gave Woodrow Wilson fewer votes than they gave Bryan in 1908. Counties in New England and the Middle Atlantic region, on the other hand, gave Wilson more votes than they had given Bryan, reflecting the latter's inability to penetrate eastern regions in 1908. Yet San Francisco and Los Angeles also preferred Wilson, thus demonstrating the Democratic candidate's ability to appeal to voters outside of the East. These mixed results suggest that the collapse of the AFL program and the Democrats' rather lackluster campaign resulted in less support from unionists for the party's standard-bearer. Yet although faring worse than Bryan had in many cases, Wilson still won fifteen of the twenty-two counties despite competition from the Republican, Progressive, and Socialist parties. This reflects the continuing viability of the alliance between trade unionists at the grassroots level and the Democratic Party.[58]

[56] Foner, *History of the Labor Movement*, 5:118.   [57] Sarasohn, *Party of Reform*, 148–54.

[58] Voting data come from the Inter-University Consortium for Political and Social Research (ICPSR), Ann Arbor, Michigan, Data File 8611, principal investigators Jerome Clubb, William FLanigan, and Nancy Zingale. The counties examined were Los Angeles and San Francisco Counties; Pueblo County, Colorado; Fairfield and New Haven Counties, Connecticut; Cook County (dominated by Chicago) and Vermilion County (Danville), Illinois; Marion County (Indianapolis), Indiana; Knox County (Rockland), Maine; Essex County (Lawrence), Massachusetts; Wayne County (Detroit), Michigan; Jackson County (Kansas City), Missouri; Douglas County (Omaha), Nebraska; Atlantic County (Atlantic City), New Jersey; New York County and Kings County (Brooklyn), New York; Cuyahoga County

The Socialist Party also won more votes in these twenty-two industrial coun-
ties, another probable consequence of the AFL's retreat from political mo-
bilization. The Socialist vote decreased only in Knox County, Maine, where
Woodrow Wilson won an overwhelming victory, and in the mining region around
Scranton, where Theodore Roosevelt, still very popular among miners, battled
Wilson for the vote. In every other county where the AFL had historically
centered its campaign, Socialists saw a dramatic increase in their vote totals. In
Chicago, their vote rose by 7.5 percent, in Youngstown by 9 percent, and in
Pittsburgh by nearly 10 percent. Nationwide, 900,672 voters chose Eugene Debs,
and more than half of those voted Socialist for the first time. After 1908, one
could sense rank-and-file trade unionists' discontent when their movement
refused to move forward toward Socialist or Labor Party activity. By 1912, this
sentiment pushed more workers than ever before to support Eugene Debs for
the presidency. In the years to come, Woodrow Wilson and the Democratic Party
would endeavor to win over not only the Progressives who supported Roosevelt
in 1912, but also those workingmen who supported Debs.[59]

As the humiliation of 1908 faded into distant memory, the pure and simple leaders
of the AFL by 1912 could look more contentedly on the arena of American
politics. Although voting statistics indicate that American workingmen still were
not supporting the Democrats overwhelmingly, in 1910 Democratic congressmen, whose numbers included a growing number of trade unionists, finally won
control over the House of Representatives. Then, in 1912, Democrat Woodrow
Wilson won the presidency with formal support from the AFL. Still uncertain
how fruitful for labor this new Democratic president might prove, Samuel
Gompers nonetheless must have felt his heart leap at the vision of his Republican
enemies finally scurrying out of power. A campaign leaflet circulated during
1912 aptly caught the buoyant mood of the Democrats and their supporters.
Ostensibly a bill announcing a public auction, it proclaimed: "Republican Junk
for Sale – Notice of Public Auction – March 5, 1913." Uncle Joe Cannon would
serve as auctioneer, helping his fellow Republicans get rid of their unneeded
baggage as they returned to public life. Auctioned items included one elephant,

---

(Cleveland), Lucas County (Toledo), and Mahoning County (Youngstown), Ohio; and
Allegheny County (Pittsburgh), Lackawanna County (Scranton), and Lycoming County
(Williamsport), Pennsylvania. S. D. Lovell examined voting returns in counties with the
highest proportion of wage earners, and found a more dramatic shift: Wilson's popular
vote grew over Bryan's in every case, and sometimes by a large margin. In New Britain,
Connecticut, for example, 38 percent of the population supported Wilson, whereas only 32
percent had voted for William Jennings Bryan. All of these counties, however, are situated
in the northeastern region, and mostly in New England. Thus, the results would seem to
reflect a regional bias more than a class preference. See S. D. Lovell, *The Presidential
Election of 1916* (Carbondale: Southern Illinois University Press, 1980), 168–9.
[59] County-level voting returns are from the data files of ICPSR – see note 58. See also George
E. Mowry, "The Election of 1912," in Schlesinger, *History of American Presidential
Elections*, 3:2135–66, esp. 3:2163.

one set of injunctions and antitrust laws, one financial system, one failed method of tariff revision, and "a large quantity of GOP bric-a-brack, consisting of old dinner pails, prosperity gags, Taft smiles . . . [and] panic threats. . . ."[60] With the Republicans gone, a new question emerged: How would a Democratic president shape the terrain of American labor politics?

[60] This leaflet is filed with J. M. Camden's letter to William McAdoo, November 4, 1912, William McAdoo Papers, General Correspondence, Box 94, Library of Congress, Manuscripts Division.

CHAPTER EIGHT

The Making of Labor's Democracy

After 1912, a growing consensus that the government must do more to correct the evils of industrial capitalism took hold through much of the United States, helping to recast political relationships and strategies along the way. Woodrow Wilson had won the presidency in 1912 by articulating a vision of only very modest state action. Poised between Theodore Roosevelt, who advocated a more interventionist state, and William Taft, who celebrated the virtues of laissez-faire relationships and viewed the government's role negatively, Wilson took the middle road. More government was needed, he seemed to say, but not much more. When campaigning among workers that year, Wilson sounded remarkably like Samuel Gompers, warning that a powerful government could turn virtuous workingmen into dependent wards of the state.[1]

Once elected, Wilson found his vision difficult to implement because numerous pressures encouraged him to use his power in more positive ways. Both the Progressive and Socialist movements enjoyed great vitality during these years, and activists from both movements clamored for expanded governmental responsibilities, demanding everything from free schoolbooks for children, to pensions for mothers, to laws regulating child or female labor. Wilson's own actions, and especially his role in forming the Commission on Industrial Relations in 1913, helped focus public attention on the government. Organized labor continued fighting to win anti-injunction legislation and exemption from the Sherman Anti-Trust Act. Whereas at the beginning of his presidency Wilson rejected labor's demands as the pleading of a special interest group, by 1916 his desire to win reelection began to force a different perspective. In August of that year, when 350,000 workers on fifty-two different railroads demanded an eight-hour day to prevent a nationwide strike, Wilson used the machinery of government to settle the dispute. The Adamson Act, passed in September by Congress, granted railroad workers the eight-hour day.

These changes in American political culture affected those old allies, the AFL and the Democratic Party, in very different ways, but they forced both groups

---

[1] On the views of Wilson, Roosevelt, and Taft, see Martin Sklar, *The Corporate Reconstruction of Capitalist America, 1890–1916* (New York: Cambridge University Press, 1988).

to develop new styles and strategies if they were to remain effective. The AFL found it much more difficult under these circumstances to exercise influence over the course of American labor politics. A Gompersian political vision could imagine only a negative state, and it represented a small and exclusivist group of trade unionists. The Democrats, meanwhile, felt ready for new allies and they suspected a broader coalition would be needed if the president were to win his reelection campaign. Early in 1916, one activist allied with the Democratic Party, lawyer Frank Walsh, dreamed aloud of an election campaign pitched as "a battle between big business and the people; also 'the empire against democracy.' If Wilson would only go the whole limit on the people's side, I believe we would win a tremendous popular victory."[2] What new actors and new institutional arrangements would make such a campaign possible?

AFL Politics and the New Democratic Order

Samuel Gompers and his pure and simple allies in the AFL had aggressively pursued their narrow and antistatist agenda for more than a decade, employing a partisan alliance as the major tool for achieving their goals. In 1912, a Democratic candidate to whom they gave only lackluster support won the presidency. Wilson's victory created a more promising environment for labor reform, and the AFL leaders worked hard in the following years to take advantage of the new circumstances. Though Gompers trumpeted their achievements as a vindication of his political vision and strategy, in fact, the AFL's success under Wilson's first administration remained mixed at best.

Despite the distance he had maintained from the AFL during the 1912 campaign, Wilson made friendly overtures toward Federation leaders immediately afterwards. A few weeks after election day, Gompers traveled to Trenton and met with the president-elect. To the labor chief's pleased surprise, Wilson spent more than ninety minutes conferring with him about labor's legislative needs. Gompers outlined the AFL's priorities: an anti-injunction bill, a bill guaranteeing jury trials for indirect contempt charges, and a bill creating a Department of Labor. Gompers further urged that someone friendly to organized labor, preferably William B. Wilson, head the new department. Once an official of the United Mine Workers, Wilson had first won election to Congress in 1906. In 1910, when the Democrats gained control over the House of Representatives, he became chairperson of the Committee on Labor. In the recent election, however, William Wilson had lost his bid for reelection.[3]

---

[2] Frank Walsh to Basil Manley, June 26, 1916, Frank Walsh Papers, New York Public Library.

[3] Gompers to Woodrow Wilson, December 16, 1912, Woodrow Wilson Papers, Series 2, Library of Congress; Governor Wilson's Secretary to Gompers, December 17, 1912, Wilson Papers, Series 2; Gompers to the AFL Executive Council, December 21, 1912, *American Federation of Labor Records: The Samuel Gompers Era* (Microfilming Corporation of America, 1979) (hereafter cited as *AFL Records*), reel 75; internal AFL memo, December 13, 1912, *AFL Records*, reel 75.

This visit began a long relationship between Samuel Gompers and Woodrow Wilson. Gompers visited and corresponded often with the president during the next eight years, writing him an average of twice per month. In many cases, Gompers made his requests for legislation directly to the president; conversely, Wilson often asked Gompers for advice about appointments or legislation. Furthermore, Gompers played a role in developing most labor bills passed during the Wilson years. The friendship Wilson felt for the AFL was symbolized in his agreeing to attend, as guest of honor, the dedication of its new headquarters building on July 4, 1916. This relationship between the AFL and Wilson's White House gave Gompers and his allies an unprecedented admission into the exhilarating realms of national policy making. It was also deeply gratifying to Samuel Gompers, providing him with the status of elder statesman that he had long sought.[4]

In addition to his new friendship with Woodrow Wilson, Gompers could count a number of old allies in the president's cabinet. William Jennings Bryan, Gompers's partner in creating the alliance between the AFL and the Democratic Party, now served in Wilson's administration as the Secretary of State. Josephus Daniels, a longtime friend of organized labor, occupied the office of Secretary of the Navy. Miner William B. Wilson, a stalwart confederate of Gompers's since the 1890s, became the first Secretary of Labor in 1913. Thus, Gompers could count as friends three cabinet secretaries plus the President of the United States, and organized labor had suddenly achieved unprecedented access to very real sources of power within the federal government. More concretely, these men ensured that the AFL's long partnership with the Democratic Party would not go unrewarded.[5]

From the AFL leaders' perspective, the most significant of these appointments, by far, was that of ex-miner William Wilson. As a congressman and as

---

[4] This relationship has been examined in depth in John S. Smith, "Organized Labor and Government in the Wilson Era, 1913–1921: Some Conclusions," *Labor History*, 3 (3), Fall 1962, 265–86; Melvyn Dubofsky, "Abortive Reform: The Wilson Administration and Organized Labor,1913–1920," in James E. Cronin and Carmen Sirianni, eds., *Work, Community, and Power: The Experience of Labor in Europe and America, 1900–1925* (Philadelphia: Temple University Press, 1983); Dallas Lee Jones, "The Wilson Administration and Organized Labor, 1912–1919," Ph.D. diss., Cornell University, 1954; Philip Foner, *History of the Labor Movement in the United States*, vol. 5, *The AFL in the Progressive Era*, and vol. 6, *On the Eve of America's Entrance into World War I* (New York: International, 1980 and 1982). For an example of Gompers providing the Wilson Administration with the AFL's opinion of a possible appointment to the Supreme Court, see Gompers to William B. Wilson, July 13, 1916, *AFL Records*, reel 81; and internal memo written by R. Lee Guard, July 14, 1916, *AFL Records*, reel 81.

[5] Besides these members of Wilson's cabinet, a large number of trade unionists and labor sympathizers won appointments within the Democratic administration. Perhaps the most notable was Louis F. Post, Chicago single-tax activist and great friend to the labor movement, who became Assistant Secretary of Labor. For more discussion of personnel in Wilson's first administration, see D. L. Jones, "The Wilson Administration and Organized Labor, 1912–1919," Ph.D. diss., Cornell University, 1954, chapter 3.

Chairman of the Committee on Labor between 1911 and 1913, Wilson had shep-
herded through the bill that created a Department of Labor. Now serving as the
nation's first Secretary of Labor, Wilson became the first representative of the
working class to enter the highest level of government office. During his eight
years as secretary, Wilson served working people and the labor movement in
multifaceted ways. Wilson himself believed that his most important duty lay in
carrying "the viewpoint of labor into the councils of the President." Certainly
he performed that function, helping to educate President Wilson about workers'
needs and problems, but he also carried the president's view out to American
workers. Workingmen's faith in their federal government undoubtedly increased
by virtue of watching a labor representative operate within its highest levels.

Though we lack a comprehensive study of this pathbreaking "workers' dominion" within the federal government, it appears that Wilson's greatest practical
achievement lay in establishing procedures to mediate between labor and business and in involving the government in this process. He appointed numerous
labor activists, especially members of the United Mine Workers, to staff his
department and especially its mediation services. Under Wilson's leadership, the
Department of Labor began mediating labor conflicts as early as 1915, and in
1917, the U.S. Conciliation Service was formed within the Department of Labor.
This established the precedent for regularized government intervention in labor
disputes, but Wilson's mediators worked not only to defuse conflict. They also
promoted trade unionism, urging employers to recognize the AFL and its affiliated unions. Between early 1913 and the summer of 1916, the Department of
Labor mediated in 238 industrial disputes, and helped employers and workers
reach an agreement in 149 of those cases.[6]

With a foundation of support within President Wilson's administration, centered particularly in the Department of Labor, the AFL was well positioned to
exert a new level of political influence. In addition to these friends in the executive branch, the AFL leaders could now work also with a Democratic House
and Senate. Democrats possessed solid majorities in both houses of Congress,
and the number of labor congressmen continued to grow during these years. The
latter gave Samuel Gompers and his AFL peers a wedge of influence within the
House of Representatives. William Hughes served as spokesman for this labor
group, and David Lewis, a former miner from Maryland, took over William B.
Wilson's position as Chairman of the Labor Committee. The labor congressmen

[6] In fifty-two of these cases, efforts were still being made to come to an agreement. On Wilson
and the Department of Labor, see Dubofsky, "Abortive Reform" (the quote is on p. 203);
Jones, "The Wilson Administration," 83–94; John Lombardi, *Labor's Voice in the Cabinet*
(New York: Columbia University Press, 1942). Figures on the number of cases mediated
comes from remarks made by Congressman David Lewis, *Congressional Record*, Vol. 53,
pt. 15, 64th Congress, 1st Session, 1916, pp. 1369–71. My reference to the "workers' dominion" builds on Robyn Muncy's book, *Creating A Female Dominion in American Reform,
1890–1935* (New York: Oxford University Press, 1991). The Department of Labor has
received a great deal less attention than its offspring, the Children's Bureau, which is the
subject of Muncy's study.

proposed a wide variety of bills (e.g., favoring woman suffrage and asking for an investigation into labor conditions on the Panama Canal), but their most important services came in fighting for the AFL's agenda and, most notably, for a bill that would exempt labor from prosecution under the Sherman Anti-Trust Act.[7]

Yet for all that the AFL gained during these years, when it came to the hard work of passing legislation, President Wilson's record remained profoundly disappointing. He lagged behind his party on questions of labor reform, tending to see the union movement as part of a broader trend toward concentration of power. Many of the reforms sought by organized labor and its friends Wilson rejected as favoritism, calling them legislation for a special-interest group. As a result, significant conflicts emerged during these years between AFL leaders and the president.

Time and again Wilson waffled on or actively opposed bills the AFL keenly desired. Soon after his inauguration, labor's legislative energies focused on attaching a rider to the Sundry Civil bill of 1913, which would prohibit the Justice Department from using funds allocated by the Sherman Act for the prosecution of labor or farm organizations. Wilson considered vetoing the bill and although he ultimately signed it, he stated that it merely expressed the opinion of Congress and that he would find the funds necessary for prosecuting unions in violation of the Sherman Anti-Trust Act. The Justice Department, in short, would not be prevented from prosecuting unions for actions considered unlawful. Similarly, on the issue of seamen's rights, the AFL continued its decade-long battle for legislation abolishing involuntary servitude and mandating improvements in sailors' working conditions. Wilson reversed his position on this bill numerous times. It ultimately passed Congress despite his opposition, and Andrew Furuseth, Robert La Follette, and William Jennings Bryan only narrowly succeeded in convincing him not to veto the bill.[8]

The AFL's effort to win reforms in the nation's injunction law exemplifies the problems facing AFL leaders and allies as they adapted to a Democratic executive and Congress. The process, which would result in passage of the Clayton Anti-Trust Act, began in early 1914 when President Wilson undertook a reframing of antitrust legislation. To a joint session of Congress he outlined his intentions in unusual detail, but to the chagrin of the AFL's national leaders, the president said nothing about labor. On the contrary, Wilson stressed his conciliatory intentions toward the business world. AFL leaders decided to try and

---

[7] For an example of bills proposed by labor congressmen, see the *Congressional Record*, Vol. 50, pt. 3, 63rd Congress, 1st Session, June 17 to August 3, 1913, p. 2071; and ibid., Vol. 52, pt. 2, 63rd Congress, 3rd Session, January 7–23, 1915, pp. 1461–2. For more on the labor congressmen, see Jones, "The Wilson Administration," 140–82.

[8] On these legislative matters, consult Foner, *History of the Labor Movement*, 5:122–7; and Link, *Woodrow Wilson and the Progressive Era, 1910–1917* (New York: Harper and Row, 1959), 55–6 and 61–3.

include provisions limiting injunctions and exempting labor from antitrust regulations in this new bill, rather than attempting to pass additional legislation. However, President Wilson and most members of Congress remained unyielding on these questions. Their compromise solution only offered the AFL provisions allowing for jury trial in cases of criminal contempt, modest limits on the issuance of injunctions in labor disputes, and an explicit statement that farm and labor unions should not be considered illegal combinations when they lawfully sought to obtain legitimate objectives.

Several labor congressmen visited the White House to protest this compromise and threatened to unite with Republicans to kill the bill. During this crucial period, however, AFL leaders took no steps to mobilize trade unionists behind their position. Unlike earlier battles, Gompers did not ask AFL members to write letters or hold demonstrations and protest meetings. Nor did Gompers threaten, as he had consistently until 1912, that Republican *or* Democratic failures to meet labor's demands would force workers to take action at the polls.[9] When Wilson finally refused to grant labor anything more, AFL leaders accepted the compromise. The House of Representatives passed this bill, the Clayton Antitrust Act, in June 1914. It is remarkable that the AFL leaders accepted so limited a bill, because their entire political program for the last twenty years had focused on remedying judicial harassment based on the existing injunction and antitrust legislation.

In the next months, the AFL waited for the Senate to vote on the Clayton Act. At this late stage, Gompers did urge trade unionists to write letters and hold meetings to ensure that the bill pass the Senate. At the same time, employers' allies in the Senate attempted to weaken the labor provisions, whereas labor's allies tried to strengthen them. The AFL won addition of a sentence reading "The labor of a human being is not a commodity or article of commerce," which labor leaders later celebrated as a tremendous victory. Employers won more substantive changes: In a number of places, the National Association of Manufacturers successfully added the words "lawful" or "lawfully" that significantly circumscribed the scope of the bill and later provided the basis for judicial interpretations rendering the bill nearly meaningless for workers' rights.[10]

---

[9] Link, *Woodrow Wilson and the Progressive Era*, 68–71; Foner, *History of the Labor Movement*, 5:130–5.

[10] Link, *Woodrow Wilson and the Progressive Era*, 70–4; Foner, *History of the Labor Movement*, 5:135–9. The two key provisions of the Clayton Act regarding labor are Sections 6 and 20. Section 6 reads, in addition to the quoted statement that labor is not a commodity:

Nothing contained in the anti-trust laws shall be construed to forbid the existence and operation of labor or agricultural organizations ... or to forbid or restrain individual members from lawfully carrying out the legitimate objects thereof; nor shall such organizations be construed to be illegal combinations or conspiracies in restraint of trade under the anti-trust laws.

See Lewis Lorwin, *The American Federation of Labor: History, Policies, and Prospects* (Washington, DC: The Brookings Institution, 1933), 121.

Once the Clayton Act became law in October 1914, the AFL leaders quickly moved to broadcast and celebrate the significance of the new legislation. Gompers hailed the act as labor's "Magna Carta," and emphasized its declaration that human labor is not a commodity. That statement, he pronounced to the AFL Executive Council, was "the most important ever made by any legislative body in the history of the world . . ." because it would protect labor from all future court attacks. It also demonstrated the essential soundness of the political policy followed by AFL leaders since 1906.[11]

The Clayton Act did guarantee trade unions' right to exist, and it provided for a jury trial in charges of criminal contempt. These were important gains, and labor had fought for them for years. In the context of recent court decisions, particularly *Hitchman Coal and Coke Co. v. Mitchell*, which held that the UMW could be prosecuted as a conspiracy under the Sherman Anti-Trust Act, the formal guarantee of the right to exist should not be underestimated.[12] However Wilson, his chief aides, the majority of congressmen and senators, and most contemporary observers believed that the Clayton Act would not protect workers from prosecution under antitrust legislation. Despite Gompers's hopes and pronouncements, these observers proved correct. In a series of cases beginning in 1917, the courts interpreted the Clayton Act as having little effect on labor-employer relations. Most significantly, the U.S. Supreme Court held in 1921 in *Deering v. Duplex Printing Company* that the Clayton Act should not prevent federal courts from restraining activities which they considered illegal.[13] Thus, the Wilson Administration had done little to help AFL leaders win their pre-eminent demand since the 1890s, even though the Democratic platforms in 1908 and 1912 had strongly called for limitation of the labor injunction and exemption of labor from the antitrust laws. Gompers would have had good reason for distancing himself from the Democratic Party, but to the contrary, the Clayton Act became his key piece of evidence in his effort to defend and justify the AFL's political policy. Although in fact the AFL's program had stalled and Wilson had proved remarkably unsympathetic to organized labor's requests, the alliance between the AFL and the Democrats appeared, at least at the level of elite politics, to be stronger than ever.

[11] Foner, *History of the Labor Movement*, 5:138.
[12] On this point, see Foner, *History of the Labor Movement*, 5:122–7. For an exploration of the debates surrounding the Clayton Antitrust Act, see Stanley Cutler, "Labor, the Clayton Act, and the Supreme Court," *Labor History*, 19 (3), Winter 1962, 19–38; Dallas L. Jones, "The Enigma of the Clayton Act," *Industrial and Labor Relations Review*, 10 (2), January 1957, 201–21; Martin J. Sklar, *Corporate Reconstruction of American Capitalism*, 330–1; William Forbath, "The Shaping of the American Labor Movement," *Harvard Law Review*, 102 (6), April 1989, 1225–7; Arthur Link, *Wilson: The Road to the White House* (Princeton: Princeton University Press, 1947), 427–44.
[13] Link, *Woodrow Wilson and the Progressive Era*, 73; Taft, *The A.F. of L. in the Time of Gompers* (New York: Harper, 1957), 298–9. For examples of contemporary opinion of the Clayton Act, see "Labor Is Not a Commodity," 9, December 2, 1916, *New Republic*, 112–14; and Edwin W. Witte, "The Clayton Bill and Organized Labor," *The Survey*, 33, July 4, 1914, 360.

Recasting American Labor Politics

In 1915, Sam Gompers observed, "There is a strange spirit abroad in these times. The whole people is hugging the delusion that law is a panacea."[14] By the second decade of the twentieth century, American politics was undergoing a sea change, one that created a dramatically different environment for labor reform. The maturing of diverse reform movements and the popularity of both the Socialist and Progressive parties combined to make the question of government intervention central to American political culture. How and to what extent should the government intervene to correct social and economic ills? Meanwhile President Wilson and his Democratic colleagues in the House and Senate reacted to this new political environment in ways that helped them win influential new friends. Together these changes would make possible an alternative foundation for American labor politics.

Perhaps President Wilson's most important contribution to creating this new coalition came with his nominees to the Commission on Industrial Relations (CIR). The idea for a government investigation into the causes of industrial conflict first emerged in 1910, with the bombing of the *Los Angeles Times* building providing immediate inspiration. Social reformers, labor activists, and members of the Taft Administration worked together to pass the legislation that created the CIR. Ironically, Taft chose for labor's representatives on the commission two leaders with strong loyalties to the Democratic Party, John Lennon and James O'Connell of the AFL (a third leader, Austin Garretson, represented the Order of Railway Conductors). On assuming the presidency, Woodrow Wilson reassessed Taft's appointments and rejected many of his choices. He accepted without change the original labor representatives (even though social reformers complained that they represented only the most narrow and conservative wing of the labor movement), but he shifted the personnel representing business and the public significantly to give the commission a more progressive and prolabor agenda. Wilson rejected the appointment of NAM leader Frederick Schwedtman, while he added such labor sympathizers as Florence Harriman and John Commons. President Wilson also rejected Taft's nominee for the chairmanship (conservative Senator George Sutherland of Utah) and replaced him with midwestern labor lawyer Frank Walsh. Walsh's appointment radically changed the nature of the commission and the role it would play in American politics.[15]

An Irish-American from Kansas City, Walsh grew up in poverty and took his first wage-earning job at the age of ten. After studying law at night school, Walsh made an early name for himself by winning some dramatic cases and by successfully fighting Missouri's political bosses. Throughout his life, Walsh

---

[14] Gompers, "Self-Help Is the Best Help," *American Federationist* (hereafter cited as *AF*), 22 (2), February 1915, 113–15.

[15] Dubofsky, "Abortive Reform," 204–5; James Weinstein, *The Corporate Ideal in the Liberal State, 1900–1918* (Boston: Beacon Press, 1968), 172–213; and Graham Adams, Jr., *Age of Industrial Violence, 1910–1915* (New York: Columbia University Press, 1966).

defended workers and their unions. His more famous clients included Tom
Mooney and William Z. Foster. Walsh's politics placed him in extraordinary
company: a left-leaning activist with sympathies for the single tax, municipal
ownership, women's suffrage, and Irish independence, he also believed devoutly
in Catholicism, Woodrow Wilson, and the Democratic Party. Capable of fiery
agitation on behalf of radical causes, Walsh also possessed close ties with mainstream politicians.[16]

By 1910, Walsh had established himself as an innovative progressive. He
created in Missouri the People's Lobby, which brought together labor and business representatives, along with church people and professionals, to counter the
lobbies maintained by powerful interests like the railroads. He also engaged
actively in a wide variety of social justice and community service causes. In
1912, unable to decide whether to support Roosevelt or Wilson, Walsh met privately with the latter. Wilson convinced Walsh of his commitment to progressive reform and won his support, appointing him to head a Social Service Bureau
for the Democrats.[17]

After the election, as chairman of the Commission on Industrial Relations,
Walsh rocketed to nationwide fame by turning the body into a dramatic labor
tribunal. Interrogating labor enemies like John D. Rockefeller, Jr., and investigating such crises as the Ludlow massacre and the Lawrence textile strike, Walsh
flamboyantly generated publicity and used it to crusade for social justice. Commission members traveled across the country to conduct public hearings, and
consistently Walsh turned their proceedings into a brilliant political theater, one
that championed oppressed workers, their unions, and even radical organizations
like the IWW, while it rebuked the nefarious activities of employers. Some, like
his colleague on the Commission, Florence Harriman, found Walsh biased: "He
is a born agitator with a very engaging personality, and has his place, but not
in the position of a judge. To me he was always the lawyer, not the judge, –
always cross-examining as though capital were in the dock and always helping
labor with the sympathetic spotlight." But to others, Walsh emerged as one
of the most popular heroes in the world of labor. Newspaper accounts of his
speeches during these years provide evidence of workers' great affection for
him: "The father of the workers!" cried out a supporter in New York City. A
labor newspaper in Pittsburgh, Kansas, called Walsh "the most powerful influence for good among all the champions of labor."[18]

---

[16] This portrait of Walsh is drawn from his papers, held at the New York Public Library, and
especially from Ralph Sucher, "Biographical Sketch of Frank P. Walsh," Walsh Papers. For
additional background on Walsh, see Sister Maria Eucharia Meehan, "Frank P. Walsh and the
American Labor Movement," Ph.D. diss., New York University, 1962; and Harold Charles
Bradley, "Frank P. Walsh and Postwar America," Ph.D. diss., St. Louis University, 1966.

[17] Mrs. J. Borden Harriman, *From Pinafores to Politics* (New York: Henry Holt, 1923), 131;
Sucher, "Biographical Sketch of Frank P. Walsh," Walsh Papers.

[18] Harriman, *From Pinafores to Politics*, 136; New York *Call*, July 5, 1916, Walsh Papers;
Pittsburgh, KS, *Workers' Chronicle*, June 30, 1916, Walsh Papers; on the Commission, the
definitive source is Adams, *Age of Industrial Violence*.

Over nearly two years, CIR members and their staff traveled across the country and talked with scores of people. Finally the Commission concluded its proceedings in 1915. Walsh's assistant, Basil Manley, drafted a final report that presented in passionate detail the problems facing American workers and proposed solutions for them. Signed only by Walsh and the three labor commissioners, the final report was regarded as too sympathetic to labor by the public and business representatives, and each of these factions submitted its own report. Indeed, Manley's report presented a stunning analysis of the labor question, one that simultaneously demonstrated the limitations of AFL and Democratic politics. It pinpointed four major causes of labor unrest in the United States: the unjust distribution of wealth and income; unemployment; the denial of equal justice to workers; and the denial of the right to organize and bargain collectively. As remedies, the Commission's report called for a stiff inheritance tax (it would not allow anyone to inherit more than one million dollars); a tax on owners of nonproductive land; restrictions on private detective agencies; and laws and constitutional amendments to guarantee workers' right to organize and to free them from harassment by government agencies and by employers.[19]

This report broke firmly with decades of antistatism as propounded by the national leaders of the AFL, reaching out with one arm to political visions of the Gilded Age labor-populist movement, and with another to state- and local-level political activists since that time. Resolutely Walsh, Manley, and the labor commissioners advocated state intervention on behalf of working Americans: "the entire machinery of the Federal Government should be utilized to the greatest possible degree for the correction of such deplorable conditions as have been found to exist." As examples of the greater role the state could and should play, the report recommended expanded social services, more money to education, and the development of large construction projects run by the government as a solution to unemployment. Yet there remained some important limits to the state as this report envisioned it. The report explicitly rejected the German path, or in other words, the development of a "huge system of bureaucratic paternalism." Rather, the author recommended that the government remove obstacles preventing workers from organizing, "reserving for performance by the Government only those services which can not be effectively conducted by voluntary organizations and those which are of such vital importance to the entire Nation that they should not be left to the hazard of private enterprise." Although this conceptualization bowed in the direction of both Samuel Gompers's and Woodrow Wilson's political philosophies, it nonetheless provided a more expansive view of the state's role and responsibilities.[20]

---

[19] Adams, *Age of Industrial Violence*, 214–23; U.S. Commission on Industrial Relations, *Final Report and Testimony Submitted to Congress by the Commission on Industrial Relations*, Senate Document No. 415, 1st Session (Washington, DC: U.S. Government Printing Office, 1916), 1:17–167.

[20] U.S. Commission on Industrial Relations, *Final Report and Testimony*, 1:18–19.

The Commission's final report thus pointed the way toward a very different political coalition within the world of labor, one no longer dominated by the AFL. Politically, its analysis of the causes of industrial unrest and its recommendations for solutions both placed the Commission report closer to the Socialist than the Democratic Party. Although Samuel Gompers had worked for decades to send Socialists into exile, Frank Walsh and his final report promised to return them to the center of American labor politics. With its concern for issues such as social services that would not be limited to skilled craft unionists, the report's vision potentially reached beyond the privileged and exclusivist boundaries of the AFL's membership. Furthermore, Walsh's report forcefully addressed the needs and problems of groups, such as female workers and tenant farmers, long ignored by the AFL. Speaking to women's employment, for example, it recommended that women receive wages equal to men's and that the government encourage unionism among them.[21]

Yet in certain respects, Walsh's conception of "labor" was not so different from that of Samuel Gompers. The Commission's final report typically spoke not to the entire working class, but to that segment affected by unionism. Repeatedly, it saw the solution to workers' problems as lying in the union movement. It failed to address the problems confronted by workers of African or Hispanic descent. The report recommended that the government use literacy tests to restrict European immigration (though Frank Walsh formally dissented from this provision of the report). A special section on Chinese exclusion assessed ways to enforce the law more efficiently, suggesting, for example, special measures against individuals who smuggled Chinese workers into the country. And whereas the commissioners championed unionism for women, they seemed to prefer that women stay out of the work force altogether. Calling on employers to pay their male workers a family wage, the report declared that "Under no other conditions can a strong, contented, and efficient citizenship be developed." Further, the commissioners called women's labor a "direct menace to the wage and salary standards of men."[22]

For all its limitations, the Commission's final report presented a remarkably radical analysis of industrial unrest, one that examined conditions from the perspective of workers and their problems. John Commons refused to sign the report, declaring that it looked too much to "politics" for solutions when workers should focus on collective bargaining. Florence Harriman rejected the report as "socialistic" and "revolutionary," saying it was "like using the Government to organize one class for swallowing up another." Their minority report took comfort in applying a putatively neutral and objective perspective to the problem of labor relations. Despite their efforts at neutrality, as Melvyn Dubofsky has recently pointed out, they endorsed the idea of open shops and made no distinction between company and independent unionism. And politically they

[21] Ibid., 1:71–3; Schenectady *Citizen*, October 20, 1916, Personal Scrapbooks, Walsh Papers.
[22] U.S. Commission on Industrial Relations, *Final Report and Testimony*, 1:68 and 71–2.

took a very different approach than had Walsh and the labor commissioners. Explaining why they refused to sign Walsh's report, they complained that it called too soon and too often for legislative relief: "Here is probably the greatest cause of industrial unrest, for as soon as people lose confidence in the making of laws by the legislature, in their interpretation by the courts, and in their administration by officials, they take the law into their own hands. This is now being done by both employers and employees." Commons and Harriman, like Walsh, looked to the government for a solution but they preferred a different branch. They envisioned "experts" chairing nonpartisan labor-management boards that would administer and enforce the existing laws. American conditions, they argued, required that industrial relations be removed entirely from politics. This approach would also "strengthen unionism at its weakest point" by making it unnecessary for union activists to engage in disruptive political action.[23]

Thus, the Walsh and Commons reports envisioned strikingly different paths for the future of industrial relations. Whereas Walsh politicized the industrial debate and made a broad coalition of unionists central to American political culture, Commons shifted responsibility to experts and bureaucrats. Interestingly, *both* looked to the state for solutions. Despite their disagreements – or perhaps, because of them – the rival reports shaped the growing discussions about the government's role and helped ensure that debates about labor reform would now center on the state.[24]

Another reason the Commission exercised such a lasting political influence is that Walsh and his assistants refused to let it wither away after their adjournment in October 1915. Seeing the degree to which his investigation had galvanized the country, and perhaps realizing that its final report could stand as the centerpiece of a new political movement, Walsh decided to form the Committee on Industrial Relations in order to continue the Commission's work. UMW President John White sent Walsh an unsolicited $2,000 to aid in his work, and a diverse group of reformers and trade unionists, including Agnes Nestor and Helen Marot of the Women's Trade Union League, union activists John Lennon, James O'Connell, and John Fitzpatrick, Progressive Party leader Amos Pinchot, and journalist Frederic Howe, joined forces with the new Committee.[25] The Committee worked at a double-fisted goal: maintaining the grassroots enthusiasm about the Commission's final report, while simultaneously pushing Congress to

---

[23] John Commons, *Myself* (New York: Macmillan, 1934), 167–8; Florence J. Harriman, *From Pinafores to Politics*, 174–5; Melvyn Dubofsky, *The State and Labor in Modern America* (Chapel Hill: University of North Carolina, 1994), 55; U.S. Commission on Industrial Relations, *Final Report and Testimony*, 1:171–230, esp. 1:171, 1:187, and 1:191.

[24] Montgomery, *The Fall of the House of Labor, The Workplace, the State, and American Labor Activism, 1865–1925* (New York: Cambridge University Press, 1987), 361.

[25] John White to Frank Walsh, November 16, 1915, Frank Walsh Papers, New York Public Library; "A Follow-Up Committee on Industrial Relations," *Survey*, 35. November 13, 1915, 155; Adams, *Age of Industrial Violence*, 220.

translate its recommendations into legislation. Its members organized local support groups around the country, mobilized behind striking workers in Chicago, Youngstown, and Pittsburgh, and commissioned motion pictures. The Committee's role in strikes won it a certain notoriety, as employers denounced its activities and, in Pittsburgh, charged that Walsh "should be assassinated." Meanwhile, Basil Manley agitated for legislation to end income tax evasion by wealthy individuals and corporations.[26] These diverse activities by members of Walsh's Committee would become central to Democratic politics as President Wilson sought reelection in 1916.

While the Commission had been interrogating John D. Rockefeller and listening sympathetically to workers' problems, another investigation undertaken by the Democrats exposed the political machinations of open-shop employers. In 1913, Martin Mulhall, the energetic strikebreaker and political hustler employed for the last decade by the National Association of Manufacturers, quarreled with his employers and lost his job. Angry over his firing and bitter about the sins he had committed for his NAM bosses, Mulhall went public with vivid stories of the NAM's activities since 1902. Lurid front-page headlines in the Chicago *Tribune* and New York *World* announced Mulhall's tales of political corruption and bribery. Besides confessing his work to mobilize workers behind conservative causes (explored earlier in Chapter 6), Mulhall charged that the NAM had for years been bribing senators, congressmen, and congressional pages. Newspapers wailed about the "invisible government" controlling Washington, D.C., a government made up of self-interested and antilabor employers. Both houses of Congress carried out lengthy investigations over the next years, calling the leaders of the NAM and hundreds of other witnesses to testify before them and subpoenaing all their organizational records. The investigations clearly demonstrated that the NAM had established a systematic lobby to influence the government, one that engaged regularly in inappropriate actions. Little of substance resulted from the investigations, as efforts to pass reforms never survived their committee. The House formally condemned the NAM for improper actions, and it began proceedings to censure one representative, James T. McDermott from the packinghouse district of Chicago. Ironically for Samuel Gompers and the AFL, McDermott formed one part of the "labor group" of congressmen. By training a telegrapher, McDermott had been elected originally in 1906 as one of four trade unionists the AFL's new political program sent triumphantly to Congress. Now the House report condemned McDermott, declaring that "there never has been a lobbyist or a tool in Washington who is more subservient to the trusts than Mr. James T. McDermott." McDermott resigned

---

[26] See Joseph McCartin, "'No Haven of Ideas': Frank P. Walsh, The Struggle for Industrial Democracy, and the Unravelling of Progressivism, 1913–1920," unpublished manuscript; on Manley and income tax evasion, see S. T. Hughes for the Newspaper Enterprise Association to President Wilson, May 19, 1916, Woodrow Wilson Papers, Library of Congress.

his position as congressman rather than face the public humiliation of a formal House censure.[27]

Between the NAM investigations and Walsh's Commission on Industrial Relations running concurrently, American employers had never looked so bad. Together, the two helped generate an empathy for workers' problems in American political culture. Increasingly the question became not whether, but *how* the government should intervene to assist working men and women. A diverse group of Americans worked alongside Frank Walsh and his Commission in pushing for social reforms. Settlement house workers, professionals, and the men and women mobilized through groups like the National Child Labor Committee, the General Federation of Women's Clubs, the National Association of Colored Women, the American Association for Labor Legislation, and the National Consumers' League were among those lobbying for legislation at state and national levels.[28]

Conservative AFL leaders like Samuel Gompers saw this new emphasis on the state as at best a waste of time. Amidst all the changes that AFL politics had undergone since the nineteenth century, those in control of the Federation remained quite consistent in their attitudes toward the state. As Gompers pronounced in 1898, "Our movement stands for the wage-earners doing for themselves what they can toward working out their own salvation. But those things

---

[27] U.S. Senate, *Maintenance of a Lobby to Influence Legislation: Hearings Before a Subcommittee of the Committee on the Judiciary*, 63rd Congress, 1st Session, 1913; U.S. House of Representatives, Committee on Judiciary, *Charges Against Members of the House and Lobby Activities of the National Association of Manufacturers and Others; Final Report #113*, 63rd Congress, 2nd Session, 1913; U.S. House of Representatives, Resolutions 341 and 342, *Congressional Record* (December 9, 1913), Vol. 51, pt. 1, 584, p. 659; for McDermott's resignation, see U.S. House of Representatives, *Congressional Record* (July 21, 1914), Vol. 51, pt. 12, pp. 12431–2; Robert Hunter, *Labor in Politics* (Chicago: Socialist Party of America, 1915). For an excellent exploration of the NAM investigation, see Erika A. Fedge, "Devious Lobbyists and Exalted Congressmen: Honor and Respectability in Progressive American Politics – The 1913 Congressional Lobby Investigations," B.A. thesis, University of Colorado, 1996. Notoriety had followed McDermott through much of his congressional career. In 1909, when a coalition of insurgent Republicans and Democrats attempted to reform the House rules in order to rein in the power of House Speaker Joseph Cannon, McDermott was one of a small group of Democratic congressmen who bolted his party, opposed the reform, and hence kept Cannon's power undiminished. Amongst congressmen at the time, it was said that McDermott had been persuaded by the Chicago packing interests to side with Speaker Cannon in this battle. On this, see Kenneth W. Hechler, *Insurgency: Personalities and Politics of the Taft Era* (New York: Columbia University Press, 1940), 57–8.

[28] For more on efforts in favor of government intervention, see Theda Skocpol, *Protecting Soldiers and Mothers: The Political Origins of Social Policy in the United States* (Cambridge: Harvard University Press, 1992); Kathryn Kish Sklar, "The Historical Foundations of Women's Power in the Creation of the American Welfare State, 1830–1930," in Seth Koven and Sonya Michel, eds., *Mothers of a New World: Maternalist Politics and the Origins of Welfare States* (New York: Routledge, 1993); Molly Ladd-Taylor, *Mother-Work: Women, Child Welfare, and the State, 1890–1930* (Urbana: University of Illinois Press, 1994).

that they can not do for themselves the Government should do." According to this formula, labor should seek only limited legislation to establish unions' right to use tools like strikes, picketing, and boycotts; to free trade unions from unfair competition with cheaper labor sources (thus, the AFL worked to restrict immigration and convict and child labor); and to make the government itself into a model employer.[29]

During the first decade of the twentieth century, with progressive reform blocked by standpat conservatives, Gompers had rarely expressed these anti-statist ideals other than when attacking the Socialist Party. But after 1912, when the Bull Moose, Socialist, and Democratic parties all began promoting more positive visions of the government, Gompers more emphatically stressed the evils of state intervention. By 1912 Gompers also had to contend with energetic reformers like Florence Kelley or Edward Devine, whose visions invited more positive government intervention. As a result, Gompers began inveighing regularly against proposals for eight-hour laws, minimum wage laws, municipal ownership, government-sponsored health insurance, and similar measures. When the American Association for Labor Legislation demanded a reform such as health insurance, Gompers attacked its leaders as "barnacles" hanging on to the labor movement. How dare they presume to know what the workers need or want?[30]

But while Gompers raged against "outsiders" who called for state intervention, labor activists at the local and state levels were building successful political programs that pressed the government for expanded or improved services. In city after city, workers participated in coalitions that called for intensified regulation of business and municipal ownership of utilities. Working-class demands on the state had been blocked at the national level for years by the antistatism of their own trade union leaders. Suddenly now President Wilson, the Democrats, and progressive Republicans appeared unusually open to using state power in the interests of working people. As a result, the AFL's antistatist agenda grew less relevant and AFL national leaders themselves became marginalized by the changing political culture. Meanwhile, the AFL's failure to deliver the labor vote in 1908 continued to keep it strategically marginal as well.

In early 1916, Wilson and his advisors evaluated their political position in light of the approaching presidential election. Facing pressure from different sides, they realized that the President's record thus far on progressive legislation was rather desultory. Wilson's only chance to win reelection lay in strengthening his record during the months remaining before election day in order to convince reformers that he backed their agenda. In 1910, Wilson had quickly remade himself from a conservative into a reform Democrat; now he recreated

---

[29] Samuel Gompers, "Eight Hour Constitutional Amendment," *AF*, 5 (6), June 1898, 110–13; Louis Reed, *The Labor Philosophy of Samuel Gompers* (Port Washington, NY: Kennikat Press, 1966); Fred Greenbaum, "The Social Ideas of Samuel Gompers," *Labor History*, 7 (1), Winter 1966, 35–61.

[30] Samuel Gompers, "Municipal Ownership and Organized Labor," *AF*, 23 (2), February 1916; idem, "Labor vs. Its Barnacles," *AF*, 23 (4), April 1916, 268–74.

himself again to become more thoroughly a progressive. This transformation included greater support for organized labor's demands than ever before. During 1916, Wilson thrilled labor activists by nominating Louis Brandeis to the U.S. Supreme Court, by supporting a model workmen's compensation bill (which finally passed Congress in August) and a rural credits bill (after he had opposed it for years), and by personally and successfully pleading with senators to pass the Keating-Owen Child Labor bill. With little involvement by Wilson, the Democrats also pushed through Congress a new revenue act, which doubled the normal income tax, raised the surtax on higher incomes from 6 to 10 percent, placed a tax on munitions manufacturers, and levied a new tax on estates over $50,000. For decades, activists had agitated for a more progressive taxation policy at the federal level, one capable of challenging propertied wealth. When the Revenue Act became law in September 1916, they achieved a great victory.[31]

The Democrats' most impressive contribution to labor legislation, however, derived from Wilson's work to avert a nationwide railroad strike during the late summer of 1916. Throughout the year President Wilson warily watched the railroad brotherhoods' fight for the eight-hour day and for time and a half for overtime. With the Pullman boycott of 1894 a vivid memory, Wilson undoubtedly hoped to avoid a nationwide railroad strike, particularly during an election year. And with Europe at war, Wilson needed to keep supplies moving overseas. On March 30 the Brotherhoods submitted their demands to the general managers of the railroads, and soon thereafter the AFL indicated its desire to help the brotherhoods in their battle. The Brotherhoods of Locomotive Engineers and Firemen listened to Frank Walsh in July proclaim the eight-hour day "Man's Inalienable Right": "You have the might and the right, through your collective bargaining power, to establish economic and industrial justice for yourselves and your families."[32]

The railroad managers that same month rejected their workers' demands and President Wilson attempted to engage both sides of the conflict in mediation. By early August, it became clear that the U.S. Board of Mediation could not solve the crisis, and the Brotherhoods approved plans for a general strike. On August 13 and 14, Wilson invited the Brotherhood chiefs and the railroad managers to the White House for talks. He stressed the catastrophic consequences a strike would inflict on both the nation's economy and his preparedness program. He asked both sides to compromise and when they refused, Wilson proposed his own solution: concession of the eight-hour day, but postponement of the issue of overtime until a special commission could study the costs of such a plan.

---

[31] Link, *Woodrow Wilson and the Progressive Era,* 192–6 and 224–9. Link notes in regard to this period that Wilson "became almost a new political creature, and under his leadership a Democratic Congress enacted the most sweeping and significant progressive legislation in the history of the country up to that time."

[32] Lorwin, *American Federation of Labor,* 132–3; Denver *Labor Bulletin,* July 14, 1916, report of Walsh's address to the brotherhoods, in Walsh Scrapbooks, Walsh Papers.

The Brotherhoods happily accepted Wilson's unprecedented proposal, but the railroad managers continued to reject any compromise. During the next 10 days Wilson worked fruitlessly to win the managers' acceptance. On August 27, the Brotherhoods' representatives left Washington, escalating their plans for a nationwide strike to begin on September 4. Then, on August 29, before a joint session of Congress, Wilson outlined ambitious legislation to avert a strike by granting railroad workers the legal right to the eight-hour day, and to prevent such a nationwide crisis in the future. By endorsing the eight-hour day as a basic right that should not be arbitrated, Wilson had struck a great blow for the advancement of the labor movement. Democratic congressmen immediately drafted a bill imposing the eight-hour day, which President Wilson and the congressional leaders approved. By September 2, both houses of Congress had passed this bill, known as the Adamson Act. Wilson's role in the crisis constituted one of the most stirring prolabor interventions in a labor conflict to date by a U.S. president. This not only averted the railroad strike, it made Wilson a hero to workers and thus transformed the emerging presidential campaign of 1916.[33]

Why did Wilson take such dramatic steps? As with his broader political transformation during the year, a combination of political ambition, a desire for reelection, and the arguments of progressives he trusted seems to have convinced the president to take action that he earlier would have rejected as "class legislation." At the height of the railroad crisis, Wilson sent for Frank Walsh and conferred with him at length. Walsh fervently believed in the eight-hour day as a step toward social justice; just as strongly, he believed that workers' votes were essential for reelecting the president. Undoubtedly, Walsh presented both aspects of the situation to Wilson. According to the reports of numerous newspapers, Walsh had exerted decisive influence on the president amidst the railroad crisis. The New York *Sun*, for example, announced the president's proposal in a large headline proclaiming "WILSON HEEDS WALSH'S PLAN." For his part, Walsh certainly grasped the significance of Wilson's intervention. He wrote at the time to a friend: "I am blazing with enthusiasm over the President's action in the railroad controversy. I consider it the most significant and far-reaching development in the industrial history of this nation. . . . It is a great world, and a glorious time to be in it."[34]

---

[33] Woodrow Wilson, "An Address to a Joint Session of Congress," August 29, 1916, in Arthur Link, *The Papers of Woodrow Wilson* (Princeton: Princeton University Press, 1966–); Wilson, "A Campaign Speech at Shadow Lawn," September 23, 1916, in Link, *The Papers of Woodrow Wilson*; Link, *Woodrow Wilson and the Progressive Era*, 235–9; Foner, *History of the Labor Movement*, 6:164–88; Lorwin, *American Federation of Labor*, 132–3.

[34] For newspapers reporting Walsh's role in passage of the Adamson Act, see the Boston *Journal*, August 24, 1916, and the New York *Sun*, August 22, 1916, Walsh Papers. For Walsh's appraisal, see his letter to Daniel Kiefer, August 30, 1916, Walsh Papers. On Walsh's view that workers' votes would be critical to the Democratic campaign, see his letter to Basil Manley, June 26, 1916, Walsh Papers.

The visible role played by Walsh presented a sharp contrast to the AFL leaders' awkward silence. The eight-hour day had been a chief objective of American workers since the mid-nineteenth century. One of the AFL's first major actions had been a widespread eight-hour campaign in 1886. As recently as 1906 the AFL had focused its resources on a fight by the International Typographers' Union for eight hours. Ironically, however, Gompers played little role in the passage of the Adamson Act. Organized labor's top legislative victory in the early twentieth century was won not by the AFL, but by the Railroad Brotherhoods – unions that had rarely participated in Gompers's political program during the previous decade.[35]

In fact, except in the case of government employees, the AFL formally opposed attempts to win shorter hours by legislative means. At the AFL's 1915 convention, the Executive Council opposed an effort to put the Federation on record as supporting the regulation of hours of work in private industry by law. As recently as March of 1916 Gompers had argued strenuously against legislating the hours of work because, as he described it, eight-hour legislation would only add

another obstacle to the achievement of a real, general eight-hour day. Instead of employees dealing directly with their employers, it would be necessary for the organizations to use their influence upon lawmakers to secure the enactment of an eight-hour law in all private industries and occupations.

As a major labor victory that the AFL had neither worked for nor supported, the Adamson Act indicated Gompers's failure to set the agenda for working-class politics. Luke Grant, a labor journalist who supported Hughes rather than Wilson in 1916, was one of many who noted Gompers's awkwardness on the issue of the Adamson Act. Because Gompers had fought so long and hard against legislation regarding the hours of work, Grant wrote to a friend, "it amuses me now to see him so ardently supporting Wilson who did . . . the very thing against which Sam has so often declaimed. Doesn't that bear out what I say, that we are all partisan in spite of ourselves?"[36]

Workers and the 1916 Presidential Campaign

The Adamson Act established the basis for a campaign in which the Democrats would present themselves as the party of labor, articulating a vision of the government's responsibilities that appealed deeply to many working people. By the

---

[35] On the history of the AFL's involvement with the eight-hour day, see Chapter Three, earlier; and David Roediger and Philip Foner, *Our Own Time: A History of American Labor and the Working Day* (New York: Verso Books, 1989). Roediger and Foner also provide a contrasting view of Woodrow Wilson and the Adamson Act (see pp. 194–9).

[36] Samuel Gompers, "Regulation by Law! Law!! Law!!!" *AF*, 23 (3), March 1916, 191–4; Luke Grant to John Walker, September 28, 1916, Walker Papers, University of Illinois. See also Samuel Gompers, "The Workers and the Eight-Hour Workday," *AF*, 22 (8), August 1915, 565–93.

standards of later decades or even by those of Woodrow Wilson's contemporary Theodore Roosevelt, who proposed a state tending toward command over society and the economy, this remained a limited view of the government's role. Wilson converted to it in the eleventh hour, eyeing his own reelection campaign and an impending strike that demanded urgent measures, and feeling pressure from Progressives and Socialists, and he most likely felt ambivalent about his own actions. His vision also remained limited to certain workers: Wilson would surely not, for example, use his governmental authority to protect the rights of African-American sharecroppers or domestic servants, or to assist the northwestern strike of Wobbly lumber workers. Yet despite its limitations, the view propounded by Wilson and the Democrats signaled a significant change in national-level politics. In the 1912 campaign, Wilson had stressed his opposition to government "paternalism" that would make workers unequal to other citizens. Such rhetoric disappeared entirely in 1916. Buttressed on the one hand by their recent legislative triumphs (the Adamson Act, the workmen's compensation act, and the child labor law), and on the other by Frank Walsh and his work with the Commission on Industrial Relations, the Democrats and Wilson could demonstrate their willingness, under certain circumstances, to employ the government on behalf of workers' struggles for social justice. This went well beyond the state Samuel Gompers envisioned: one capable only of interfering negatively with workers' rights, and hence one fundamentally distrusted by its citizens.

Thus, whereas the Democrats continued building on their efforts of previous years, and borrowed heavily from the prolabor sympathies William Jennings Bryan had placed at the party's heart, the substance and strategy of this campaign would differ profoundly from those of the past. The Democrats' new approach to the labor question made possible a very different coalition of supporters. While Samuel Gompers and the American Federation of Labor remained important allies, they now represented only one part of the Democrats' labor alliance. The Railroad Brotherhoods, Socialists, local trade unionists working for municipal reform, and the reformers clustered around Frank Walsh in the Committee on Industrial Relations emerged as central players in creating the Democrats' labor campaign.

The AFL leaders naturally sought to assist President Wilson's reelection effort in any way they could, but even so, their contribution remained limited compared to the mass mobilization efforts of 1906 and 1908. As in 1912, the AFL developed no extensive political program. Its leaders did not assess funds, assign organizers, or turn the AFL journal into a political instrument. They led instead a discreet campaign that formally followed the nonpartisan rituals begun in 1904, while in fact showing strong loyalty to Wilson and the Democrats. AFL leaders again visited each party's convention to ask that labor's demands be included in their platforms. They then used the Republican and Democratic responses as a basis for justifying their decision to support the Democrats. Having accepted the Clayton Act as a great victory, the AFL could argue that most of its demands since 1906 had been granted by the Democrats. In speeches and in political editorials, Gompers eloquently publicized the record of the Democratic Party on labor issues and praised Woodrow Wilson in particular. In a final editorial in the *American Federationist*, he wrote strongly in support of Wilson and concluded:

It lies with the working people – the masses – on Election Day to determine by their votes whether the policy of progress, justice, freedom and humanity shall prevail in the re-election of Mr. Wilson to the presidency of the U.S. or whether the pendulum shall swing backward and the policy of reaction shall be enthroned.

Gompers portrayed the 1916 campaign as a struggle between the "exploiters" and the "producers." Asking workers "On Which Side Are You?" Gompers stressed the President's support for the eight-hour day in suggesting that workers could vote only for him.[37]

Gompers's major contribution to the campaign consisted of a ten-day tour through the Midwest and Northeast in strong support of Wilson, accompanied by AFL organizer John Lewis. Midway through the journey Gompers wrote cheerfully to his secretary, "My meetings surpass expectation and from everywhere come the reports of bright outlook." The AFL also sent Grant Hamilton, who had headed the Democrats' labor campaign in 1908, to work with them again. However, once ensconced at Democratic headquarters, Hamilton had almost no contact with AFL leaders, making it difficult to confirm his precise role in the campaign.[38] The AFL's only other activities for the campaign consisted of distributing a pamphlet detailing the AFL's legislative achievements since 1906, a list that naturally benefitted the Democratic Party; sending a circular letter to all affiliated unions contrasting Wilson and Republican nominee Charles Hughes on issues of interest to labor; helping the Democrats write one pamphlet appealing to workers; and publishing a few pieces on politics in the *Federationist*. Political coverage in that AFL organ remained sparse, however: No more than half a dozen articles or editorials devoted to campaign politics appeared during the entire year, whereas in 1908, political questions dominated every issue from July onwards.[39]

---

[37] Gompers, "On Which Side Are You?" *AF*, 23 (11), November 1916, 1067–8.

[38] Memo for Frank Morrison, October 13, 1916, *AFL Records*, reel 81; Gompers to R. Lee Guard, October 27, 1916, *AFL Records*, reel 81; R. Lee Guard to Thomas Burke, November 6, 1916, *AFL Records*, reel 81; Florence Thorne to M. Grant Hamilton, October 17, 1916, Samuel Gompers Letterbooks, Library of Congress; R. Lee Guard to Hamilton, October 18, 1916, Gompers Letterbooks; Gompers to Hamilton, October 24, 1916, Gompers Letterbooks.

[39] Marc Karson, *American Labor Unions and Politics, 1900–1918* (Carbondale: Southern Illinois University Press, 1958), 83–8; for articles focusing on campaign politics in the 1916 *American Federationist*, see Samuel Gompers, "Promises and Performances," *AF*, 23 (7), July 1916, 537–42; "Men and Commodities," by the editor of *Metropolitan*, in *AF*, 23 (9), September 1916, 838–9; Samuel Gompers, "Lift the Burdens from Child Life," *AF*, 23 (9), 843–4; idem, "On Which Side Are You?" *AF*, 23 (11), November 1916, 1067–8. See also: "AF of L Building Dedicated," *AF*, 23 (7), July 1916, 658–64; and Samuel Gompers, "Economy of the Eight Hour Day," *AF*, 23 (10), October 1916, 959–60.

Across the country, observers saw trade unionists rallying behind President Wilson's reelection campaign. In Wilkes-Barre, Pennsylvania, a town considered strongly loyal to Theodore Roosevelt, workers turned the cold shoulder when the ex-president visited. Some five thousand gathered to march in protest against his attacks on President Wilson and the eight-hour day, but the mayor forbade their march. In Toledo, historically a safe town for the Republicans, party leaders feared mass defections to the Democrats. The Republicans sent scores of field workers out to proselytize among workingmen. Yet their attempt to organize a meeting among railroad workers, with the star speaker a Brotherhood of Locomotive Engineers member who denounced the Adamson Act, failed miserably. A crowd of Brotherhood men charged the stage, silenced the speaker, and then led all but a handful of the audience members out to another hall, where they passed resolutions praising the president and his eight-hour legislation. And, perhaps even more worrisome to Republican managers, unorganized workers likewise appeared supportive of the president. At the large factories, Democratic sentiment spread quickly. When Republican candidate Hughes visited a Toledo auto factory, the owner introduced him as "our candidate." The warm welcome did not prevent workers there from heckling Hughes "unmercifully."[40]

In industrial states like Indiana and Illinois, the votes of organized AFL workers had for years been drifting toward the Democratic Party, but the vote of railroad employees and of nonunion workers in mass production had remained predominantly Republican. Thus Republican campaign managers focused their efforts on preventing defections among these latter two groups of workers. They enjoyed little success, especially among railroad workers. Rank-and-file railroad workers hailed the president, as, for example, when some hundred of them surrounded his private car at Grand Central Station. The president came out to greet the men, listening to them call out: "Vote for Wilson, scratching Hughes; join the union, pay your dues!" Another yelled, "Three cheers for the man who's for the eight-hour day!" Railroad unions matched the energetic support provided President Wilson by rank-and-file workers, giving him unprecedented institutional support. The Order of Railroad Telegraphers assigned at least fourteen organizers to Wilson's campaign. Meanwhile, the Railroad Brotherhoods entered into campaign politics for the first time, sending out a strong appeal to members asking every man to support President Wilson. In the magazine of the Locomotive Firemen and Engineers, a leading editorial declared: "We have absolutely no doubt that Mr. Hughes owes his nomination to Wall Street, to the powers of wealth and special privilege, to the big employing interest – in short, to the master class – and that these interests are spending enormous sums of money in an effort to elect him President of the United States."[41]

[40] "Reports to Wilson Predict Landslide," *New York Times*, October 23, 1916, p. 3; "Toledo Labor Vote United For Wilson: Eight-Hour Law Turns the Scale to Democrats in Normally Republican County," *New York Times*, October 19, 1916, p. 5.

[41] "8-Hr Law Aids Wilson in Illinois," *New York Times*, October 25, 1916, p. 6; "Railroad Men Cheer Wilson," *New York Times*, October 19, 1916, pp. 1 and 3: H. B. Perham, president,

In states like Illinois where women could now vote, Republicans found it difficult to predict the outcome. Straw polls generated remarkably diverse results. A Republican analysis predicted 85 percent of the vote going to Hughes, whereas an independent poll estimated only 40 percent for the Republican candidate. All sides seemed to agree, however, that *working-class* women would vote overwhelmingly for President Wilson. In Chicago, the Women's Trade Union League was better organized than any other women's group, and its members favored Wilson by 85 percent. WTUL members like Agnes Nestor stood at the forefront of those Chicago activists who formed a Working Women's Independent Woodrow Wilson League in September. Thus, with female as well as male workers, the eight-hour issue seemed to be exerting an influence, though the peace issue clearly also helped Wilson win women's votes.[42]

As the Democrats developed their campaign strategy, they leaned heavily on all these groups – the AFL, the Brotherhoods, and the Women's Trade Union League. At the heart of the Democratic effort, though, stood Frank Walsh and his Committee on Industrial Relations. Over the years, and especially since his work with the Commission on Industrial Relations, Walsh had developed enviable ties to labor activists positioned across the political spectrum. Yet Walsh's politics contrasted sharply to that of conservatives like Gompers. He appreciated the advantages of state intervention on workers' behalf, and the final report issued by his CIR had proposed far-reaching solutions to the problem of industrial conflict, many of them unacceptable to pure and simple trade unionists. Though friendly with the conservative bloc that dominated the AFL as well as with the predominantly Republican leaders of the railroad Brotherhoods, Walsh's strongest alliances remained with activists in progressive unions like the United Mine Workers. And although Gompers had labored for years to define the "labor movement" in a way that excluded the Socialists, Walsh's vision embraced them and the IWW as well. Many Socialists rewarded Walsh's labors with unusual personal affection. The secretary of the Socialist Literary Society in Philadelphia asked Walsh in August 1916, for example, to visit her group: "You probably know that no group of people have followed your splendid, courageous work with greater eagerness and interest than the Socialists." Even Eugene Debs, campaigning for Congress in Indiana in 1916, asked Walsh to come and speak in his favor. As a local Socialist activist wrote on Debs's behalf, "We believe you can do more than anybody else to send Debs to Congress. . . . While you may not be a Socialist, yet, we know that you served this country perhaps as much or more than any other man. . . ." Walsh's correspondents over the years included

Order of Railroad Telegraphers, St. Louis, to Gompers, October 26, 1916, *AFL Records*, reel 81; "Railway Unions Ask Votes for Wilson," *New York Times*, October 27, 1916, p. 2; "Wants Hughes Defeated," *New York Times*, November 2, 1916, p. 6. Perham sent his organizers to work in Pennsylvania, Oklahoma, Maryland, New York, Indiana, Ohio, and Colorado.

[42] "Eight-Hour Law Aids Wilson in Illinois," *New York Times*, October 25, 1916, p. 6; and see the *Washington Trade Unionist*, September 22, 1916, p. 3.

such radical leaders as Emma Goldman, Joseph Ettor, Elizabeth Gurley Flynn, and Arthur LeSueur.[43]

Walsh also possessed strong ties to progressives allied with the Democratic Party such as George Creel, Frederick Howe, Rabbi Stephen Wise, Amos Pinchot, and Edward Costigan. In June, Walsh's associate Basil Manley proposed to Frederick Howe that they establish an organization of "radical Democrats," one separate from the Democratic National Committee so the radicals' agitation could not hurt its image, yet fully in support of President Wilson: "the radicals ought to concern themselves more with creating a democratic 'atmosphere' than with issues. What we ought to play for is reviving the same sort of atmosphere that carried Roosevelt in 1912." This should specifically include a labor group that would bring Democratic labor leaders together "with a few people like Walsh to give them punch and imagination."[44]

Manley's plan became a reality when a group of politically independent "Wilson Volunteers" formed to further the Democratic campaign. Besides Walsh, the group included Amos Pinchot, Rabbi Stephen Wise, Frederick Howe, Ray Stannard Baker, John Dewey, Walter Lippmann, Walter Weyl, George Creel, and Norman Hapgood. These volunteers worked for Wilson's reelection, but they focused on winning over specific social groups. Amos Pinchot described their target as the nation's workers, farmers, and small businessmen, and he declared in words that echoed the rhetoric of the AFL and the brotherhoods: "Wall St. was never so unanimous as it is today in its indorsement of Hughes."[45]

For his part, Walsh agreed to conduct an extensive speaking tour – nearly three weeks long – for the Democratic National Committee, but he insisted on carrying out his mission in an independent way. George West, his assistant on the CIR, traveled in advance of Walsh to arrange matters with local union activists. West remained independent of Democratic politicians and ensured, wherever he went, that Walsh would "speak alone and [be allowed] to handle subject in your own way. . . ." Behind the scenes, most of the work involved in planning Walsh's tour was carried out by Kacy Adams, the publicity director for the United Mine Workers, and by local union activists (especially those associated with the UMW) in towns across the country. When Walsh finally set off on his journey, William Harvey and two other men from the Democratic National Committee accompanied him to assist in all matters, but Walsh paid his own expenses.[46]

[43] Rosa Laddon Hanna to Walsh, August 15, 1916, Walsh Papers; Noble Wilson to Walsh, September 30, 1916, Walsh Papers. On Walsh's efforts in the 1916 campaign, see also Joseph McCartin, *Labor's Great War: The Struggle for Industrial Democracy and the Origins of Modern American Labor Relations, 1912–1921* (Chapel Hill: University of North Carolina Press, forthcoming).

[44] Basil Manley to Frederick Howe, June 22, 1916, Walsh Papers.

[45] "For a Drive on Privilege," *New York Times*, October 16, 1916, p. 3.

[46] "Wilson Will Greet Volunteers Today," *New York Times*, October 16, 1916, Personal Scrapbooks, Walsh Papers; George West to Walsh, October 2, 1916, Walsh Papers; Walsh to Dante Barton, October 3, 1916, Walsh Papers.

Walsh's tour began in New York State and stretched as far west as Kansas City, but he focused on mining districts in Ohio, Indiana, Michigan, and West Virginia. Sending the Democrats a list of local UMW leaders to contact in each location, Kacy Adams explained Walsh's appeal: The miners, he said, "are strong for Walsh; in fact he is their ideal in public life, and you will find that they will do everything possible to make his meetings a success." In addition to his popularity with labor crowds, Walsh could also, the Democrats believed, draw Socialists over to Wilson. Begging the Democratic National Committee (DNC) to send Walsh out to Kansas, a local politician wrote that the 15,000 miners in his region were mostly "red card" men, and "Frank P. Walsh is the only man in the world who can swing this Socialist vote to Wilson. . . ."[47]

Traveling across the country, through his speeches and writings, Walsh created a labor program that could attract larger numbers of American workers – especially trade unionists – to the Democratic Party. At its heart stood the issues raised by the Commission on Industrial Relations's final report. Walsh attributed the problems of working-class life to the unequal distribution of wealth and income in America; unemployment and the denial of workers' right to earn a living; the denial of justice to workers in the administration and adjudication of the law; and the denial of the right to form effective organizations for self-representation on the shop floor. According to the Commission's analysis, Walsh reminded audiences, the top 2 percent of America's population owned 60 percent of the wealth, whereas the "producers" who composed 65 percent of the population owned only 5 percent of the nation's wealth. Looking to the future, Walsh proclaimed that "In ten years it will be criminal that 10,000 persons shall live meagerly so that one person may live well."[48]

Having established these broad themes of social, economic, and legal justice for working-class Americans, Walsh turned to President Wilson's concrete achievements. He listed the many bills passed by the Democrats in workers' interests, for example, the Clayton and La Follette Seamen's acts, but he focused attention on the eight-hour day and Wilson's actions in the railroad crisis. The eight-hour day was not important simply for fighting fatigue and monotony on the job, but for giving workingpeople control over their lives. When the railroad workers began their struggle, "The eighteen railroad heads represented eighteen billions of capital – nine billions of it honest capital and nine billions of it unjust capital." The leaders of the railroad brotherhoods demanded "for themselves and their children opportunities in life second to those of no railroad President." When the railroads refused, the president of the United States "for the first time in all history" declared " 'I cast my vote for the eight hour day and say that society has reached the point where it does not want a man to work

[47] Walsh Itinerary, n.d., Walsh Papers; Kacy Adams to W. P. Harvey, October 6, 1916, Walsh Papers; no Signature to Democratic National Headquarters, October 17, 1916, Walsh Papers.
[48] See notes written on the back of William Harvey to Frank Walsh, October 12, 1916; Cleveland *Press*, October 21, 1916; and the Gloucester *Press*, November 2, 1916: all Walsh Papers, New York Public Library.

more than eight hours.' " In a ringing celebration of President Wilson that linked him to the heroes of working-class republicanism, Walsh proclaimed "His intelligence and bravery . . . has inspired a renaissance of Americanism as interpreted and lived by Washington. He has freed more slaves than Lincoln."[49] Wilson's reelection, in this context, would mark the end of an "industrial despotism" that allowed "a few men to exercise autocratic control over the lives . . . of millions of producers." When Theodore Roosevelt criticized the eight-hour bill, Walsh attacked him as "the political gunman of the exploiting interests" hired to "break the force of the nation's eight-hour movement."[50]

With Walsh as their star attraction, and assisted by the AFL, the railroad brotherhoods, the WTUL, and prominent labor representatives like John Lennon and William B. Wilson, the Democrats created a campaign in 1916 that appealed strongly to working-class voters. The president's action on the railroad crisis, especially when added to previous gains such as the child labor act, suggested to Democratic Party strategists that victory could come only by winning unprecedented support from workers. From all around the country came reports that businessmen felt enraged by Wilson's new politics. As a North Carolinian wrote to Josephus Daniels, "I am certainly receiving 'A Frost' from most of the bankers and cotton mill men. They are mad about the child labor law and the 8 hour law. Something ought to be done to straighten these matters out with these people." In the eyes of southern businessmen, Wilson "made an absolute surrender to organized labor." Consequently, the Democrats found it more difficult than usual to raise money for their campaign. Yet, for every alienated employer, dozens of workers appeared ready to support Wilson. These circumstances encouraged the Democrats to focus with greater intensity on the labor vote. William McAdoo, one of the president's leading advisors, worried aloud to his chief about the loss of business support and concluded, "we should pay especial attention to labor throughout the rest of the campaign . . . it is from that element that we can most certainly draw a large support." Party leaders thus devoted more money (approximately $35,000) to labor mobilization than to any other aspect of the campaign.[51]

How did the Democrats and their supporters define this elusive labor vote? Strategists did reach out to the working class somewhat more inclusively than in 1908, for example, and in this way, they pointed toward Democratic campaigns of future decades. They made an effort to attract the votes of unorganized

---

[49] Schenectady *Gazette*, October 17, 1916; Cleveland *Press*, September 9, 1916: both from Walsh Papers.

[50] Boston *Herald*, October 16, 1916; Los Angeles *Record*, September 9, 1916; Schenectady *Gazette*, October 17, 1916: all from Walsh Papers. See also "Walsh Likens T.R. to 'Gyp the Blood'," *New York Times*, October 17, 1916, p. 3.

[51] A. W. McLean to Josephus Daniels, September 13, 1916, Josephus Daniels Papers; McLean to Henry Morgenthau, September 25, 1916, Josephus Daniels Papers; Charles Adair to Democratic National Committee, Chicago, November 2, 1916, Thomas Walsh Papers; William Blackman to Thomas Walsh, August 24, 1916, T. Walsh Papers; Senator Thomas Gore to Henry Hollis, October 4, 1916, T. Walsh Papers; William McAdoo to President Wilson, September 24, 1916, William McAdoo Papers: all Library of Congress, Manuscripts Division.

male and female workers, unionized female workers, and tenant farmers, both in the substance and style of their campaign. Many of the themes propounded by Walsh and the Democrats could appeal to unorganized as well as organized workers, and as we saw earlier, the Democratic campaign repeatedly visited nonunion factories, and organizations such as the WTUL and often could reach groups like women workers more effectively than could the Democrats. The Democrats also made a determined effort to win the votes of Socialists and progressives who favored positive state action. This, too, suggested a significant transformation of Democratic strategy since the heyday of Samuel Gompers, who had carefully and deliberately portrayed Socialists as the pariahs of the labor movement. But despite these changes, Democratic Party strategy certainly did not speak to the entire working class. Still dominated by ideas of white supremacy, the Democratic Party was incapable of launching a campaign that would appeal to African-Americans or other nonwhite workers. Like Samuel Gompers had before them, the strategists clustered around the Democrats in 1916 centered their labor campaign around the union movement. Frank Walsh worked carefully with activists from the UMW and other unions wherever he toured, and he and the Democrats targetted unionized industries, regions, and factories when deciding where to focus their campaign. The party's effectiveness remained clearest among white and male trade unionists, and recruiting the "labor vote" meant, first and foremost, the vote of union workers. As Colonel Edward House described the campaign in his diary, "It is true we have organized wealth against us, and in such an aggregate as never before. On the other hand, we are pitting organized labor against it, and the fight is not an unfair one."[52]

Wilson's Republican opponent, Charles Evan Hughes, reinforced the Democrats' attractiveness to many workers. As associate justice of the U.S. Supreme Court in 1914, Hughes had voted to sustain that body's decision in the infamous Danbury Hatters' case, a decision that allowed the Hatters to be prosecuted for damages under the Sherman Anti-Trust Act on account of their boycott, which crossed state lines. We have seen how this Supreme Court decision fueled the AFL's political campaign after it was handed down in February 1908. Now in 1916, workers often heckled Hughes during his speaking engagements, taunting him for his vote on the Danbury Hatters' case, and local labor newspapers stressed that a vote for Wilson would bring justice to workers by helping to undo Hughes's Danbury vote.[53]

Hughes also hurt his hopes of winning unionists' votes by turning his fire onto the Adamson Act and the eight-hour day. Here was Wilson's chief vulnerability,

[52] See William Harvey to Walsh, October 11, 1916, Walsh Papers; Basil Manley to Fred Howe, June 22, 1916, Walsh Papers; for an example of Frank Walsh addressing the problems of agricultural workers, see *The Rebel*, July 1, 1916, Personal Scrapbooks, Walsh Papers; the House quote comes from Sarasohn, *The Party of Reform: Democrats in the Progressive Era* (Jackson: University Press of Mississippi, 1989), 217.

[53] S. D. Lovell, *The Presidential Election of 1916* (Carbondale: Southern Illinois University Press, 1980), 165; Washington *Trade Unionist*, November 3, 1916, p. 1.

Hughes believed, and he attacked the bill as dictatorial and as a ruse to fix wages. By late September, the Adamson Act had become a central part of Hughes's campaign repertoire, even in strong labor states. In Ohio Hughes campaigned tirelessly against eight-hour legislation, even in cities where the labor movement was strong and the eight-hour day was already entrenched. In Hughes's eyes the Adamson Act constituted a "surrender" to union blackmail. Yet when facing a working-class audience, he charged the bill was "gold-brick legislation" – rather than lessening workers' hours on the job, it would reduce their wages.[54]

While he denigrated the Adamson Act, Hughes's appeal to working-class voters remained weak and ineffective. Torn between the Republicanism of Theodore Roosevelt and that of William Howard Taft, Hughes never developed an effective campaign. For his themes, Hughes drew on previous Republican campaigns, yet by 1916, conditions had sufficiently changed to render them unpersuasive to many voters. He attempted to maintain his party's image as the standard-bearer of economic prosperity, an approach begun by William McKinley twenty years earlier. Because the country was enjoying significant economic growth under Democratic leadership, though, this approach would not suffice. Thus Hughes enlisted once again the old Republican emphasis on protectionism, claiming that without higher tariffs, the current prosperity would not outlast the war. He talked of American rights in world affairs and Americanism, and argued that although he wished not to take the United States into the war, he would also not subject her to international humiliation. Last of all, he replayed a theme used to great advantage by Republicans in 1908. As he declared in Terre Haute, "I understand that word has gone out through labor circles in official channels to vote against me, and I know perfectly well . . . that nobody can direct or control the labor vote of this country. That vote is going to be cast according to its sound judgment, according to what the men think is right and fair."[55]

The more that Hughes attacked Wilson for "surrendering" to labor unions, and the more that businessmen fled the Democratic Party, the more inclined Wilson became to center his campaign on a forthright appeal to working people. The president regularly spoke as an advocate for labor and a defender of the eight-hour day, noting in campaign literature, for example, that with the eight-hour day, a worker's "efficiency is increased, his spirit in his work is improved, and the whole moral and physical vigor of the man is added to." To critics who charged the unions had coerced him, Wilson defended himself by arguing that the eight-hour bill had been the right thing to do, and he had done it without asking either side what solution was preferred. The president also argued more

[54] Lovell, *Presidential Election of 1916*, 81–3 and 133–6; Sarasohn, *Party of Reform*, 204–5; "Hughes Turns East Predicting Victory," *New York Times*, November 2, 1916, pp. 2 and 8; and "Shall Force or Reason Rule?" speech by Hughes reprinted in *The Independent*, October 9, 1916.

[55] "Hughes Turns East Predicting Victory," *New York Times*, November 2, 1916, pp. 1 and 8; "Hughes Heckled on Eight-Hour Law," *New York Times*, October 17, 1916, pp. 1 and 3; "Hughes Asks Aid of Workingmen," *New York Times*, November 4, 1916, pp. 1 and 5.

broadly for his and his party's record on labor issues. In September, he accepted his party's nomination and declared he and the Democrats had given working people "a veritable emancipation," by recognizing their labor was not a commodity, exempting them from the Sherman Anti-Trust Act, freeing seamen from involuntary servitude, providing for employees' compensation, creating the machinery for mediation in industrial disputes, and making the Department of Labor's services available to workers searching for employment.[56]

If these issues were not enough to win workers' support, Wilson and the Democrats could add two additional and very powerful appeals: peace and prosperity. At the Democratic convention that summer, Wilson's campaign managers prepared to emphasize the theme of Americanism, but found that delegates preferred the peace issue. When speakers discussed Wilson's determination that the United States not enter the Great War, the crowds cheered and applauded wildly. "He Kept Us Out of War" became a prominent slogan of the campaign, and Wilson had the sense to embrace both the slogan and implicit leadership over the peace movement. The progressives and others fighting for social justice whom Wilson needed to win over, especially in the Middle and Far West, tended also to be pacifists. Certainly, the peace issue won for Wilson the support of many working people as well. Writing in pro-Democratic editorials, AFL organizer Grant Hamilton argued that workers' dislike of Hughes could be attributed to two key factors: their predisposition toward peace rather than war, and Hughes's record while in the Supreme Court on the Danbury Hatters' case.[57]

America's war-fueled prosperity also proved a bounty to Wilson's reelection campaign. Trade with European and Latin American countries soared as the Great War grew more intense. A recession that had stalled the U.S. economy from 1913 to the middle of 1915 let up as the Gross National Product and manufacturing output quickly grew. Total U.S. exports rose from $2.5 billion in 1913 to $5.5 billion in 1916. With the decline of immigration, also caused by the war, unemployment nearly disappeared and wages increased. The Democrats stressed their record in shaping a strong economy, and the general prosperity

---

[56] Woodrow Wilson, "A Campaign Speech at Shadow Lawn," to the Business Men's League, September 23, 1916, and "A Speech in Long Branch, New Jersey, Accepting the Presidential Nomination," September 2, 1916, in Link, *Papers of Woodrow Wilson*, 19:130–1 and 19:216; Lovell, *Presidential Election of 1916*, 83 and 201 n. 36; Sarasohn, *Party of Reform*, 204–7. The following leaflets produced by the Democrats suggest their approach to winning the workingman's vote: "President Wilson's Record for Labor," "The Whole Truth About the Eight-Hour Law," "Labor's Charter of Freedom," and "Record of Hughes as an Enemy of Labor."

[57] See Arthur Link, *Wilson: Campaigns for Progressivism and Peace, 1916–1917* (Princeton: Princeton University Press, 1965), 45–7 and 106–10; Grant Hamilton, "Labor Would Be Ignored," *Washington Trade Unionist*, November 3, 1916, p. 1; see also on labor and militarism, idem, "Issue Is Clearly Defined," *Washington Trade Unionist*, October 27, 1916, p. 1. Although the peace issue was undoubtedly important, my reading of the evidence concurs with scholars such as David Sarasohn, who see labor and social justice issues as more influential in the 1916 campaign. See Sarasohn, *Party of Reform*, chapter 7 and esp. p. 212.

clearly undercut Republican efforts to portray the Democrats as the party of depression.[58]

As the campaign wound down, most observers felt uncertain about which candidate would win. Eastern returns came in first, bringing apparent victory to Hughes. Only when western returns arrived, early the next morning, did it become clear that Wilson had won his reelection battle. Wilson won by 9,129,606 popular and 277 electoral votes to Hughes's 8,538,221 popular and 254 electoral votes. Hughes won the entire East and Middle West except for New Hampshire and Ohio. Wilson swept the South and West except for Minnesota, Iowa, South Dakota, Oregon, and West Virginia. Finally, Wilson achieved what Bryan and others had attempted since 1896: to unite the South and West. To many, this finally freed the party from bowing to eastern plutocrats. Others, like Frank Walsh's confidant Rabbi Stephen Wise, put a different and western spin on the victory: "To think that we can have a great forward-looking party and free that Party from the racial and social Toryism of the South and the industrial and economic reactionism of the East!"[59]

Yet this was also a triumph that transcended region. To win, Wilson had taken a step toward realizing the dream articulated by William Jennings Bryan: to unite farmers and workers together with those struggling toward social justice. The Democrats' campaign successfully polarized the electorate into left and right and brought more workers to their side. A Washington State trade unionist wrote to Gompers in exultation at Wilson's victory, saying: "We were never so united before." Throughout the campaign, polls predicted that workers would back Wilson. A poll of union officials by the *Literary Digest* in September found that of 457 who responded, 332 said their members supported Wilson. Forty-seven officials stated that their members would support the Socialist candidate Allan Benson, and a mere forty-three predicted support for Hughes.[60]

These predictions apparently were on the mark. In previous chapters, we have traced the voting returns in twenty-two counties across the United States where the AFL centered its political activism during the Progressive era. In 1916, these industrial counties developed a striking pattern of support for Woodrow Wilson: In every case, they gave Wilson a higher percentage of the vote than they had in 1912, and often by a very wide margin. Lucas County, Ohio, with Toledo as its major city, gave Wilson 24 percent more of its vote than in 1912; the vote for Wilson in Wayne County (Detroit), Michigan, rose by 19 percent; and in Los Angeles County, it rose by 10 percent. In addition, Wilson's campaign dramatically intensified a trend begun a decade earlier, whereby trade unionists

---

[58] Gilbert C. Fite and Jim E. Reese, *An Economic History of the United States*, 3rd ed. (Boston: Houghton Mifflin, 1973), 444–7.

[59] Arthur S. Link and William M. Leary, Jr., "Election of 1916" in Arthur M. Schlesinger, Jr., ed., *The Coming to Power: Critical Presidential Elections in American History* (New York: Chelsea House, 1971), 320–1; Stephen Wise to Frank Walsh, November 15, 1916, Walsh Papers.

[60] C. O. Young, Portland, OR, to Gompers, November 9, 1916, *AFL Records*, reel 81; Sarasohn, *Party of Reform*, 216; Lovell, *Presidential Election of 1916*, 165.

gradually shifted their loyalties to the Democratic Party. Eighteen out of these twenty-two counties gave Wilson more votes in 1916 than they had given any Democratic presidential candidate thus far during the twentieth century. Only in 1900 had the counties encompassing Chicago, New York, and Scranton and Williamsport, Pennsylvania, given the same or a larger percentage of their vote to the Democratic candidate.[61]

Especially in New Hampshire, Ohio, California, Washington, Idaho, and New Mexico, workers' votes seem to have gone largely to Wilson and contributed to his victory. The Ohio victory is particularly instructive for understanding trade unionists' reactions to the Wilson campaign. Frank Walsh and Woodrow Wilson as well as Charles Hughes campaigned energetically in this state. Historically voting Republican, Ohio gave Wilson a margin of some 90,000. Except for Cincinnati, with its large German-American population, every industrial city in the state went to Wilson.[62]

Socialists also supported Wilson in large numbers. Estimates of the numbers that defected from their party to vote Democratic range from 250,000 to 300,000. Particularly in the Rocky Mountain states, the Midwest, and New York State, Wilson made important gains among Socialists. In every one of the twenty-two industrial counties previously examined, the Socialist vote went down, often by a high percentage. For example, in 1912, Socialists won 12 percent of the vote in each of three counties: San Francisco, Mahoning County (Youngstown), Ohio, and in Cook County (Chicago). In 1916, the Socialist vote in each of these three counties dropped to 4 percent or lower. The president's support for labor and his administration's role in keeping the United States out of war persuaded many Socialists to support him.[63] Miners' leader John Walker of Illinois, for example,

---

[61] Voting data come from the Inter-University Consortium for Political and Social Research, Ann Arbor, Michigan, Data File 8611, principal investigators Jerome Clubb, William Flanigan, and Nancy Zingale. The counties examined were Los Angeles and San Francisco Counties; Pueblo County, Colorado; Fairfield and New Haven Counties, Connecticut; Cook County (dominated by Chicago) and Vermilion County (Danville), Illinois; Marion County (Indianapolis), Indiana; Knox County (Rockland), Maine; Essex County (Lawrence), Massachusetts; Wayne County (Detroit), Michigan; Jackson County (Kansas City), Missouri; Douglas County (Omaha), Nebraska; Atlantic County (Atlantic City), New Jersey; New York County and Kings County (Brooklyn), New York; Cuyahoga County (Cleveland), Lucas County (Toledo), and Mahoning County (Youngstown), Ohio; and Allegheny County (Pittsburgh), Lackawanna County (Scranton), and Lycoming County (Williamsport), Pennsylvania.

[62] See Link and Leary, "Election of 1916," 320; and Sarasohn, *Party of Reform*, 227. S. D. Lovell's findings reinforce my own. Examining the eight states and counties with the largest number of wage earners, all of them in the northeastern region, Lovell found that in every case, Wilson's vote increased in 1916 over the votes Democrats had received since 1904, and in most cases, the increase was quite dramatic. Lovell also demonstrated that in nearly every case, a Democratic vote this high would not be seen again until the 1928 or 1932 elections. Lovell, *Presidential Election of 1916*, 168–9 and 177.

[63] County-level voting statistics come from the ICPSR – see note 61. See also Sarasohn, *Party of Reform*, 220–1; Montgomery, *Fall of the House of Labor*, 365; "Through the Editor's Eyes," *Pearson's Magazine*, January 1917, Vol. 37, 92; Link, *Wilson: Campaigns for Progressivism and Peace*, 162.

joined better-known Socialists such as Mother Jones and Max Eastman in strongly supporting Wilson in the 1916 campaign. Ultimately, Walker's support for Wilson led to his expulsion from the Socialist Party. To Walker, Wilson deserved support both because of his commitment to peace and, more importantly, because of what he had done for labor. In particular, Walker cited the Adamson Act. He explained to a friend his position on eight-hours legislation: "I have always favored the getting of progress by whatever means it was easiest to get it, and . . . getting it by a legislative process was not only the easiest way, but was the most enlightened civilized way. . . ."[64]

A striking example of workers' support for Wilson was provided by the Bridge and Structural Ironworkers' Union. In the wake of the McNamaras' plea of guilty in the Los Angeles *Times* bombing case, a nationwide crackdown had resulted in the conviction and imprisonment of many members of the Bridge and Structural Ironworkers' Union. The union had hoped to win a pardon or commutation of their members' prison terms from Wilson, but he refused to consider it. Yet their president, J. J. McClary, wrote Gompers in October to say that 90 percent of the union members would support Wilson: "We are too broad minded and tolerant to let this disappointment overshadow what Wilson has done for organized and unorganized workers in this country." Indeed, McClary had just visited the seven union members still in prison at Leavenworth, and "They are not chagrined at Wilson's administration . . . they wished they could be out and have the privilege of voting for President Wilson. From this you can readily understand our sentiment and feeling on this all important subject. . . ."[65]

Rarely had workers and their interests been so central to a presidential campaign as they were in 1916. Arthur Link first pointed out the parallels between the 1916 presidential election and those of 1896 and 1936: In no other political battles during that forty-year period, he argued, did the United States see such a clear-cut political alignment. Wilson, allied with progressives in the labor movement and social justice camps, successfully polarized the electorate into right and left. This made the campaign, as Frank Walsh earlier envisioned to a friend, "a battle between big business and the people. . . ." Less visible were the costs this strategy entailed: By helping tie unionized workers to the Democratic Party, Walsh helped make both Socialist and labor party strategies less viable. Nonetheless, with the election won, Walsh happily proclaimed: "I am the happiest man in America over the Wilson victory."[66]

There were other happy men and women in America as the election results became clear, and Samuel Gompers was one of them. His political efforts since

---

[64] John Walker to Luke Grant, September 30, 1916, Walker Papers, University of Illinois; Walker to L. L. Jackson, November 6, 1916, Walker Papers; Walker to Adolph Germer, September 28, 1916, Walker Papers.

[65] J. J. McClary to Gompers, October 28, 1916, *AFL Records*, reel 81.

[66] Link, *Wilson: Campaigns for Progressivism and Peace*, 124; Frank Walsh to Basil Manley, June 26, 1916, Walsh Papers; Walsh to Dr. Wise, November 12, 1916, Walsh Papers.

the 1890s had helped make Wilson's triumph possible: He had successfully pushed a major party to take labor's demands seriously, and he raised the possibility that workers' votes could shape the outcome of a presidential campaign. The AFL's influence had been felt most dramatically during an earlier moment, however, and especially in the key years from 1906 through 1908.

While the AFL remained a central part of the Democratic coalition in 1916, and would continue in such a role during the war years to come, perhaps the most interesting aspects of the presidential campaign lay in the contributions made by people outside of labor's dominant institution. To observers with an eye for the future, these contributions might have suggested the future contours of American politics. Labor issues remained central to the campaign, but in a way that transcended the narrow outlook of Samuel Gompers and his pure and simple allies. The keys to Wilson's successful coalition had included a progressive program that spoke more broadly to the needs of working people, rather than focusing only on legalistic problems, and that accepted the need for state intervention; an inclusive strategy that reached out to Socialists as much as to moderate and conservative workers and that relied also on ties between labor activists and social justice progressives; and leadership offered by people, such as Frank Walsh, who stood outside of the AFL.

Only by taking action much broader than the AFL ever supported – using government intervention to achieve the eight-hour day for one group of workers – did Wilson and the Democratic Party succeed in uniting working people to such an unprecedented extent. His effort made the president a popular hero for American trade unionists in a way that superseded any presidential candidate up to that time, foreshadowing the impact Franklin Roosevelt would have on workers during the 1930s. This suggests an important contrast between the campaigns of 1916 and 1936. Although appeals to labor and workers' votes became central to each campaign, organized labor played a different role in each case. In 1936, workers and their unions exerted a dynamic political influence, and the Democratic Party reacted to their innovations. In 1916, on the other hand, Democratic Party leaders and activists like Frank Walsh emerged as the political innovators, dragging the AFL reluctantly behind them.

Conclusion

In the 1890s, Samuel Gompers and his allies first articulated their vision of pure and simple politics. It held that only trade union members and their leaders should shape and control American labor politics, and that they should follow a fiercely independent approach to politics, rejecting what unionists called "party slavery" as well as most forms of state intervention. By the beginning of the twentieth century, this vision dominated America's most influential labor organization and AFL unionists who embraced it worked energetically to achieve their modest and antistatist goals.

Over the next two decades, this political approach confronted a number of powerful challenges. Although initially AFL leaders pursued a modest lobbying strategy, changing relations between state and society made this strategy less tenable. In the first years of the new century, employers engaged in an open-shop drive, asserting their authority on shop floors across the country and, increasingly, in the political sphere. Allied with the Republican Party, open-shop employers skillfully worked through the courts and Congress to thwart organized labor's political ambitions. At the same time the federal government gradually expanded its powers. If at first this expansion could be seen most dramatically beyond the borders of the United States, in places like Cuba, the Philippines, and Panama, in more subtle ways the state began affecting workers' daily lives as well, through judicial actions, through limited regulatory legislation, and by employing rapidly growing numbers of working-class Americans. Together, the employers' anti-union movement and the expanding state led AFL leaders to reassess their emphasis on limited lobbying tactics.

Thus, in 1906 and again in 1908, AFL unionists embarked on an experiment in political mobilization. Trade unionists became more active politically and helped select, nominate, and work for candidates who supported labor's limited political goals – an eight-hour day for government employees and limits on the labor injunction. "Reward your friends and punish your enemies" became the slogan of AFL politics. The great experiment, meanwhile, taught some unexpected lessons. One was that rank-and-file workers envisioned the political sphere very differently than did their leaders. Whereas national leaders grew most active in attempts to defeat top congressional Republicans like Speaker of the House Joseph Cannon, local-level activists demonstrated greater interest in running positive campaigns for trade unionists or for strong allies of the labor movement. In addition, local activists proved indifferent to the narrow range of issues adopted by the AFL's national leadership. They tended instead to adopt more ambitious demands that spoke to the social needs of American working people.

The contested nature of AFL politics became particularly evident during 1908, as Federation leaders relinquished some of their vaunted independence to work closely with the Democratic Party. Determined to harness the political passions of AFL members behind the presidential bid of Democrat William Jennings Bryan, Gompers and his allies ran a highly disciplined single-issue campaign around the judiciary's antilabor hostility. Its intimate alliance with the Democrats, involving shared decision making and finances, enabled the AFL to centralize and discipline its operation – even to the extent of suppressing independent or socialist political initiatives. Although this strategy made labor a central issue in the year's campaign politics and encouraged a Democratic courtship of union workers, Republican strategists turned the AFL's maneuvers into a different sort of ammunition. Charging that AFL leaders sought to "deliver the labor vote" to Democrats, Republicans appealed to workers' pride and sense of independence by urging them not to follow the dictates of "foreigners" like Sam Gompers.

And, indeed, the AFL leaders found uniting American trade unionists behind the Democratic Party a more difficult task than they expected. AFL members divided sharply with their leaders over both the program and procedures for creating an American labor politics. Whereas many workers supported the alliance with the Democrats, many others refused to break from the Republican or Socialist parties. Regardless of their political leanings, workers united in criticizing the AFL leaders for the undemocratic way in which that strategy had been devised. Gompers clearly desired to limit popular political activity by rank-and-file workers. He feared he would lose control over labor's future if a robust political movement – whether labor party or socialist in its character – emerged. Rank-and-filers, however, saw things differently. After hearing for decades that labor must stay out of party politics, they watched their leaders shift gears and enter into a partisan alliance. No one asked for their participation in deciding labor's political strategy, or even for their opinions. In 1908, politics became yet another arena in which local and state workers experienced the undemocratic character of their labor movement. The result proved unfortunate for both the Democratic Party and the AFL leaders: Bryan lost the election by a wide margin. The available evidence suggests that trade unionists, especially in labor's stronghold in the Northeast, failed to support Bryan and the Democrats.

In the following years, AFL leaders rejected tactics based on grassroots mobilization but continued to nurture their alliance with the Democratic Party. After Democrat Woodrow Wilson won the presidency in 1912 with only weak support from trade unionists, he reached out to organized labor and quickly developed a close relationship with Samuel Gompers. This seemed to promise the AFL unprecedented influence in American politics, as Wilson sought its leaders' opinions on everything from antitrust legislation to nominations to the U.S. Supreme Court. Yet complex changes in American political culture after 1912 soon mounted the greatest challenges yet to pure and simple politics. The central question of the day became the state's role and its relationship to society; not *if*, but *how* the state should expand dominated political debate. In this context, and facing a tough reelection battle, independent reformers converted President Wilson to several measures that expanded the state's role in ensuring the well-being of working-class Americans. Significantly for the AFL, these reformers stood outside of, or at the margins of, America's trade union movement: Individuals like Frank Walsh and activists within the Women's Trade Union League were among the most important. Furthermore, they won the president's support for a key measure that AFL leaders adamantly opposed: a federal law mandating the eight-hour day for railroad workers. These changes signaled the failure and near collapse of pure and simple politics. Pushed from the center of American politics, Samuel Gompers watched as party politicians and independent reformers together crafted campaign slogans that would appeal to American trade unionists.

AFL politics, then, had evolved significantly since the 1890s. Although by 1917 Gompers's approach seemed defeated – or at least marginalized – by ascendant reformers such as Frank Walsh, it had exerted a significant influence on American labor politics. It may be useful to draw back from the details of our story and reflect on that larger political impact. Pure and simple politics shaped the Progressive era through its impact on relationships between the AFL and other groups, and within the Federation itself; and by helping make the "labor question" central to the political culture of the day.

At the heart of pure and simple politics stood the idea that trade unionists alone should determine the shape of American politics, yet this was never really feasible. From the AFL's founding onwards, political activity brought it into close contact with other organizations and with individuals outside of the labor movement, in ways that influenced organized labor, its friends, and its enemies. Determined to achieve political success, AFL leaders found that their aspirations inexorably pushed them into a broader political universe with a more diverse set of actors. By the first years of the twentieth century, the NAM, in alliance with Republicans, thwarted the AFL's drive for legislative reform and pushed it toward a strategy based on electoral mobilization. This decision in turn subjected the AFL to a host of influences, from Democratic and Republican Party politicians to Socialists, newspaper editors across the country, and even William Randolph Hearst and his supporters. Each of these happily passed judgment on AFL politics. As a result, Federation leaders and members felt buffetted by winds they could barely comprehend, much less control: Never during these years could the AFL leaders and members decide their political strategy without outside influences shaping the political universe in which they acted.

Yet, and sometimes even amidst political defeat, AFL activities influenced other groups such as the employers' associations and both mainstream and alternative political parties. The early efforts and successes of the AFL in large part prompted the NAM leaders to enter into a strenuous lobbying campaign during the first years of the twentieth century. Later, knowledge that AFL leaders would soon enter into electoral politics prodded the NAM to take the same step. The Republican party leadership also found its position on labor challenged by the AFL's new activism around political questions. Though most Republicans dug in their heels and placed their loyalty to open-shop employers above all else, they felt compelled to counter the AFL's accusations with a major attack on Gompers and his allies.

The AFL's pure and simple politics influenced the Democrats in a more complex way. Leaders like William Jennings Bryan first articulated the dream of uniting workers and farmers under the party's umbrella. Because this coincided with the AFL's growing commitment to political action, Democrats found it convenient to pursue an alliance with the Federation. This resulted in a far-reaching partnership between the two organizations in the 1908 presidential campaign, one in which the Democrats strongly supported labor goals such as injunction reform and the eight-hour day. By supporting the most progressive wing of the Democratic Party, the AFL helped Bryan win control over the Democracy's future. Moreover, support for labor's rights served to bring the conservative and reform wings of the party closer together; given the limited political demands of the AFL, even conservatives like Alton Parker could support them. This allowed the Democrats to embrace an image of reform without alienating more traditional members. In these ways, labor helped transform the Democrats from the party of "States' Rights" to the party of reform. In the following years the Democrats' support for organized labor's demands bolstered the party's image as the representative of progressive reform. Yet Democratic leaders also gleaned some important lessons from their alliance with the AFL. After Woodrow Wilson assumed control over the party in 1912, he and his allies increasingly realized that an alliance with AFL leaders did not hold the key to winning working-class votes more generally. Gradually, they established a political agenda that transcended Gompersism in order to speak to the needs of a more diverse, if still limited, group of workingmen.

How, then, did pure and simple politics change relations within the Federation? Its leaders hoped to politicize the outlook and behavior of AFL members by training them to take their class consciousness into the ballot box. Thus, AFL leaders warned trade unionists away from their affections for the Socialist or Republican parties, in favor of the Democrats. Although they failed to achieve their goals, this program had some clear consequences. Gompers and Morrison at first tolerated Socialist candidates and supported John Walker's bid for Congress in 1906, but soon they saw the need to run a disciplined campaign. In 1908, they led an aggressive battle against both socialism and independent politics. As Gompers's antisocialism grew more resolute, he increasingly defined loyal trade unionism to mean a clear rejection of socialism. He also began interpreting any independent actions by local workers, whether these involved a plea for more political discussion within the AFL or support for Republican candidates, as disloyalty. This tainted political viewpoints that ran counter to his views, thereby helping to make an alternative political movement vastly more difficult to achieve.

In these years, AFL politics became more than a battle to see which party or candidates trade unionists would support. Politics became as well an arena through which AFL members contested the meaning of their movement. As Gompers used the AFL political program to assert and consolidate his dominance over the movement in new and more rigorous ways, the dissent of rank-and-file members and their local-level leaders likewise carried a double meaning. Though AFL members were terribly fractious, many found a common unity in antipathy toward the undemocratic procedures that determined Federation political policy. When Republican leaders charged that Gompers behaved tyrannically and dictated to workers their political options, this resonated deeply among trade unionists who had already developed a similar critique on their own. As one Michigan worker complained to Gompers in 1908, "When you promised to hand me over to the Democratik Convention you sir counted without your slave."[1] Even with hundreds of paid and volunteer organizers, Gompers could not squash the growing criticisms of his political program voiced by local workers and state and national leaders. On the other hand, some workers simply felt indifferent toward the AFL program, and others refused to disavow their Republican or Socialist Party loyalties. Thus, AFL members denied Gompers his main goal: control over their political behavior. In the short run, this meant that Gompers and his allies would never again attempt a campaign strategy based on grass-roots mobilization. It also meant that although Gompers would remain president of the AFL until his death a decade later, his dominance, especially in the realm of politics, would never be complete. Instead, after 1908, rank-and-file members shifted their political gaze from Gompers and his allies. Increasingly, they looked directly for political guidance to party leaders in the Democratic, Republican, or Socialist parties, to independent reformers, or, after World War I, to unionists advocating more aggressive strategies such as a labor party.

One clear consequence of the AFL's political strategy during the early twentieth century lay in helping make the "labor question" central to political culture and in helping construct its character. Of course, by the first decade of the twentieth century, the tensions of industrialization helped put the problems of working-class Americans on the national agenda, with issues ranging from the cost of streetcars to conditions in tenements. And trade unionists were hardly the only Americans who sought redress of these problems. Many different sorts

---

[1] Thomas P. Maloney to Gompers, August 3, 1908; George H. Simmons, Auburn, Michigan, to Gompers, July 26, 1908: both *American Federation of Labor Records: The Samuel Gompers Era* (Microfilming Corporation of America, 1979) (hereafter cited as *AFL Records*), reel 66.

of people fought for reforms, whether members of women's clubs, activists in the Women's Trade Union League, lawyers linked to the American Association for Labor Legislation, or even machine politicians representing new immigrant constituencies. Nonetheless, the AFL could rightly claim that its political program moved the problems of "labor" to the center of *partisan* politics.

The political parties historically had represented the outlook of America's upper and middle classes. In their issues and platforms, the major parties only episodically reflected the needs and interests of working-class Americans. But from 1906 onwards, the relationship among candidates, parties, and the "labor question" became a central theme in party politics. On the one hand, this gave organized labor, and especially the AFL, a more visible role in American politics. Did a party or a candidate embrace the political demands of the AFL or did they reject AFL goals such as anti-injunction reform? This new prominence formed one part of a broader process in American politics whereby interest groups outside the party system exerted a greater influence. As we have seen, the AFL often failed to determine its own fate because powerful forces outside its parameters – such as the parties – regularly shaped its political fortunes. Yet during these years, the AFL became a visible force in national electoral politics, one that pushed candidates and party leaders to react to its demands. In this way, trade unionists proved central to Progressive era political discourse.

Yet the "labor question" involved far more than the AFL. If its campaign program helped make labor a central theme, trade unionists certainly failed to control the meanings of the theme itself. When Progressive era Americans spoke of "labor," they typically meant white male workers, and especially those engaged in industrial labor. If Samuel Gompers would place trade unionists at the center of "labor," others constructed the labor question around a different sort of worker. These diverse meanings became quite clear during the 1908 election, a high point in the AFL effort to make labor a central issue in campaign politics. While trade unionists strove to make their definition of the labor question dominant, with an emphasis upon injunction reform and the eight-hour day for government employees, Republicans skillfully developed a rival appeal for a different sort of worker. Reaching out to nonunion workers in large factories, Republican leaders stressed the importance of economic prosperity and the full dinner pail. Similarly, by 1916, even Democratic leaders had learned a lesson from the Republicans' broader construction of the labor question. Under Woodrow Wilson's leadership, they employed the powers of the state positively on behalf of railroad and other workers, demonstrating along the way that they had transcended the AFL's relatively narrow political intentions.

For every way that pure and simple politics contributed to shaping Progressive era America, then, there was another lesson of defeat and limitation to be learned. There exist many reasons for this. The AFL broke new ground in attempting to make itself into an influential political force, and it confronted a great many antilabor biases and prejudices along the way. Furthermore, the Federation represented only a segment of the working class and held many biases of its own when it came to the working men and women outside its institutional boundaries. Federation leaders could not conceive of building a "class vote," one that derived from different segments of the working class. Even a "trade-union vote," in the sense of a unified bloc, remained beyond their reach during these years. AFL members were too divided by craft, level of skill, region, partisan loyalties, ethnicity, gender, and race to rally around any political program in a uniform way.

Our story ends at a moment when the AFL leadership had become less influential in American labor politics. Keen allies of the Democratic Party, leaders like Gompers and Morrison had to watch as the federal government, pressed by reformers like Frank Walsh, took new steps to protect some workers' rights. By 1917, it appeared that circumstances offered AFL leaders a choice between two difficult options. They could watch as control and influence over American labor politics shifted toward groups and individuals outside of the AFL, such as Democratic Party politicians and independent reformers. Or they could reassess their relationship to the state. Led by Samuel Gompers, AFL leaders chose the second option, a decision that sheds light on organized labor's wartime partnership with the federal government. Though the course of American labor politics during and after World War I requires a study of its own, we might take a moment to place those events within the broader context of AFL politics in the era of Gompers.

After decades of antistatism, America's dominant trade union movement collaborated closely with government bureaucracies to support the nation's effort during the World War I. Although the men who dominated the AFL continued to hold only a limited view of state power, they proved quite willing in the military crisis to benefit from its protective mantle. In August 1916, Gompers received appointment to the new Council of National Defense, which held the responsibility to oversee American preparedness. When the United States entered the European war in April 1917, AFL officials enthusiastically supported the government and urged that labor leaders be placed on relevant boards and commissions to help build an efficient war effort. Many labor officials received appointments to government bodies during the war, most notably to the National War Labor Board, which included as its labor representatives Frank Hayes, William Hutchinson, and Victor Olander; and the president's Mediation Commission, whose members included Illinois UMW leader John Walker.[2]

The AFL's prowar activities also included establishing the American Alliance for Labor and Democracy to oppose pacifist and antiwar groups and individuals within the labor movement. With Gompers as chairman and Frank Walsh on its executive committee, the Alliance sought to combat the efforts of the People's Council, an antiwar organization that had been endorsed by several AFL unions, and to encourage support for the war among working men and

[2] Philip Taft, *The A.F. of L. in the Time of Gompers* (New York: Harper, 1957), 354 and 357; Joseph A. McCartin, *Labor's Great War: The Struggle for Industrial Democracy and the Origins of Modern American Labor Relations, 1912–1921* (forthcoming, University of North Carolina Press).

women. Toward this end, labor leaders revived tactics first used by the AFL in political work during 1906 and 1908, when it sought a broad mobilization of American workingmen. Alliance leaders created a weekly news service that churned out scores of leaflets and pamphlets on topics related to labor. Similarly as in 1908, when the Democratic Party funded the AFL's campaign work, now under a Democratic president the government assumed direct responsibility for financing the Alliance. George Creel of the Committee on Public Information (CPI), the government's main prowar propaganda agency, informed Gompers in July 1917 that the president had agreed to expand the Alliance into a national organization. All costs were thus ordered sent directly to CPI managers for payment. By November 1918, the Alliance had distributed approximately 1.5 million prowar pamphlets.[3]

In addition to running the labor arm of the government's propaganda campaign, the AFL collaborated with government agencies to suppress the Industrial Workers of the World in western industries like lumber and mining. In Montana, for example, the federal government relied on the military, the judiciary, and its own conciliation services to harass IWW members and convince them to join the AFL instead. As Melvyn Dubofsky found in his fine study of the IWW, giving up their Wobbly membership for an AFL card often brought workers few gains. In most cases when IWW agitation died down, neither the government nor employers had much interest in negotiating with the AFL. In some cases, such as Washington State's lumber industry, conservative trade unionists' enthusiasm for state intervention inflicted as much damage on the AFL as on the IWW. Gompers and Secretary of Labor Wilson gave their blessing to Lieutenant Colonel Brice Disque's plan to purge the spruce industry of Wobblies. Expecting Disque to organize workers out of the IWW and into the AFL, Gompers watched chagrined as the lieutenant colonel allied instead with industry employers. Disque won an eight-hour day for lumber workers, but at the cost of creating a company union with virtually compulsory membership and a required no-strike policy.[4]

Earlier in the twentieth century, the AFL had mobilized to further its own ends and build its influence over American labor politics, but now, during World War I, Federation leaders mobilized on behalf of the state and its military effort, even reinforcing the state's war at home against labor radicals. Yet if Gompers and his allies had confronted political circumstances beyond their control before, nothing quite matched the complex dynamics of the postwar period. Amidst tense confrontation between workers and employers and an atmosphere of anti-radical hysteria (which the AFL itself helped generate through its attacks on the IWW), the federal government with its bedridden chief executive failed to defend

[3] See Frank L. Grubbs, *The Struggle for Labor Loyalty: Gompers, the A.F. of L., and the Pacifists, 1917–1920* (Durham, NC: Duke University Press, 1968), 43–5; Philip Foner, *History of the Labor Movement in the United States*, vol. 7, *Labor and World War One, 1914–1918* (New York: International, 1987), 123–4.

[4] Melvyn Dubofsky, *We Shall Be All: A History of the Industrial Workers of the World* (New York: Quadrangle Books, 1969), chapter 16.

even the most modest conception of working-class rights. The government quickly dismantled its wartime bureaucracies and turned a deaf ear to labor's requests for assistance. Its most visible action in 1919 became the raids launched by presidential hopeful A. Mitchell Palmer. Meanwhile, employers mobilized to construct a new open-shop drive, known as the "American Plan," one more widespread and more devastating than that of nearly twenty years before. The government provided little protection, and the nation's courts grew more determined to buttress the employers' actions with antilabor decisions of their own. As a result, membership in AFL unions drastically declined, from a high of four million in 1920 to fewer than three million by 1924.[5]

Under these circumstances, the alliance between labor and the Democrats quickly came undone. By 1920, Frank Walsh, always a bellwether, coldly turned away from the Democratic Party and refused to support its candidate for the presidency. Angrily, Walsh declared in a widely reprinted article: "The next election will not be a political contest, it will be a coroner's jury on the corpse of the Democratic party."[6]

Although AFL leaders tried to sustain their alliance with the Democrats, their efforts grew feeble. Following the procedures they had relied on since 1908, members of the AFL Executive Council visited the major parties to request support for their demands. The *American Federationist* found the Democratic platform more congenial, though it noted that on many issues the Democrats were either silent or unyielding to labor's requests. For example, the AFL demanded that all restrictions on freedom of speech, press, and public assembly be removed as the United States completed its transition to peacetime. The Democratic platform, in response, noted simply, "We resent the unfounded reproaches directed against the Democratic administration for alleged interference with the freedom of the press and freedom of speech." Nonetheless, unlike Walsh, the AFL leaders continued urging support for the Democrats in the 1920 elections, and lamented the Republican victory that November. By 1924, even AFL leaders could no longer justify support for the Democratic Party. That year, the AFL officially endorsed independent presidential candidate Robert La Follette, breaking its tie to the Democrats for the first time in sixteen years. Knowing La Follette would lose, and divided amongst themselves over whom to support, AFL leaders did little beyond issuing their endorsement. They maintained an extremely low and awkward profile during the campaign.[7]

---

[5] Bernard Mandel, *Samuel Gompers: A Biography* (Yellow Springs, Ohio: Antioch Press, 1963), 505.

[6] Harold Charles Bradley, "Frank P. Walsh and Postwar America," Ph.D. diss., St. Louis University, 1966, 205–6.

[7] No author, "Read! Think! Choose! The Democratic and Republican Platforms," *American Federationist* (hereafter cited as *AF*), 27 (8), August 1920, 729–43; Samuel Gompers, "'Normalcy' vs. Progress," *AF*, 27 (10), October 1920, 913–18; idem, "Reaction in the Saddle," *AF*, 27 (12), December 1920, 1081–6; idem, "We Are in to Win," *AF*, 31 (9), September 1924, 741–3; idem, "Why Labor Should Support La Follette and Wheeler," *AF*, 31 (10), October 1924, 808–9; Mandel, *Samuel Gompers*, 517–23.

This awkwardness reflected two other key developments of the postwar period: Independent approaches to politics grew more popular among union activists, and the state, which had expanded during the war, would remain a permanent and important force in shaping industrial relations and, hence, working-class political consciousness. The Democrats grew less attractive to trade unionists during and after the war, alienating much of their 1916 constituency through their lackluster support for workers' rights, their antiradicalism, and their wartime support for Britain (which helped distance both Irish-American and German-American workers). Instead, independent labor politics underwent a revival. Predictably, it grew first at the local and state levels, in cities like Chicago and New York and in states like Indiana and North Dakota, as trade unionists, often allied with farmers, expressed preference for independent or labor party politics. By 1919, this movement had given rise to the founding convention of the American Labor Party, with twelve international unions and six state federations of labor represented. Among those initiating the movement stood AFL treasurer and Teamsters' leader Daniel Tobin of Indiana.[8]

A poor showing in the 1920 elections devastated the American Labor Party, but did not dampen enthusiasm for independent labor politics. Its next incarnation took shape in 1922, as members of the machinists, the railroad brotherhoods, and the stationary engineers issued a call for unionists to come together and discuss their political options. The resulting Conference for Progressive Political Action (CPPA) agreed to work for sympathetic congressional candidates. Socialists played a significant role on the national committee, which directed political policy for the CPPA. After some promising showings in the 1922 congressional elections, the CPPA reorganized in preparation for the next elections. Its delegates narrowly defeated a proposal to form themselves into a labor party, partly due to pressure from Gompers. Instead, the CPPA backed independent presidential candidate Robert La Follette in 1924, whose platform called for public ownership of the railroads and the nation's water power, protection of the right to organize, abolition of the injunction in labor disputes, denunciation of American imperialism, and independence for the Philippines. La Follette's poor showing in 1924 helped bring an end to the CPPA and, for the moment, to the chances for a powerful political movement centered around trade unionists' goals.[9]

Meanwhile, the federal government's prominent role now divided trade unionists in ways not seen before the Great War. At the heart of these independent

---

[8] A useful source on this movement is Philip Foner, *History of the Labor Movement in the United States*, Vol. 8, *Postwar Struggles, 1918–1920* (New York: International, 1988), 256–74; see also Taft, *The A.F. of L. in the Time of Gompers*, 476–88, esp. 478.

[9] Mandel, *Samuel Gompers*, 517–21; David L. Waterhouse, *The Progressive Movement of 1924 and the Development of Interest Group Liberalism* (New York: Garland, 1991); David Montgomery, *The Fall of the House of Labor: The Workplace, the State, and American Labor Activism* (New York: Cambridge University Press, 1987); James Weinstein, *The Decline of Socialism in America, 1912–1925* (New York: Monthly Review Press, 1967), 272–323.

political movements lay a more positive view of the state than Gompersite approaches would ever countenance. The initiative taken by railroad unions during these years provides an instructive example. Just as they had pioneered in the weeks before the 1916 election, pushing President Wilson to employ state power on their behalf, the railroad brotherhoods took a firm stand in favor of government ownership after the war. Their Plumb Plan dominated working-class politics in these years, and helped inspire foundation of the CPPA in 1922. Nor was the issue of the government and the railroads fought out only among the brotherhoods. When AFL delegates debated the issue of government ownership of the railroads at their convention in 1919, longtime AFL Secretary Frank Morrison stood prominently among those who spoke in favor of the measure, which passed overwhelmingly by a vote of 29,159 to 8,349.[10]

Amidst this changing political environment, some AFL officials continued to oppose positive state action as vehemently as they derided independent labor politics. Gompers and others energetically denounced not only the labor party movement but any independent effort as divisive and wasteful.[11] Fewer unionists were listening now. A decade earlier, Gompers controlled the higher echelons of AFL leadership, enabling him significant influence over the character of political discourse within the Federation. Now his trusted secretary was publicly advocating government ownership of the railroads, and his treasurer was off agitating for a nationwide labor party. These changes suggested the fading of pure and simple politics and a larger transition as well, as the era of Gompersism gradually waned and came to an end. The labor chief's failing health emblematized these changes. Since 1919, Gompers had suffered from deteriorating eyesight that left him virtually blind during the last years of his life. Although he insisted on continuing in his duties until the very end, by 1923 he was enfeebled. While in Mexico City to attend the Congress of the Pan-American Federation of Labor, Gompers grew very ill. Rushed by train back to the United States, he died in a San Antonio hotel during the early morning of December 13, 1924.[12]

With the death of Samuel Gompers, the pure and simple approach to politics that he promoted would seem to have ended as well. Gompersite antistatism never again ruled the labor movement as it once had, and instead the state by the 1930s would become a major influence in the relationships between workers and employers, particularly in manufacturing. Yet a distinct suspicion of the state has appeared in various incarnations throughout American labor history. More generally, the legacy of pure and simple politics has reached across the

[10] Taft, *The A.F. of L. in the Time of Gompers*, 470.

[11] See, for example, the AFL National Non-Partisan Political Campaign Committee, "A Bugle Call to Duty," *AF*, 29 (11), November 1922, 809; J. W. Sullivan, "Other Movements – Transitory; Fruitless; Disruptive," *AF*, 29 (11), November 1922, 813–15.

[12] Mandel, *Samuel Gompers*, 529; no author, "The End of a Gallant Struggle," *AF*, 32 (1), January 1925, 17–23; no author, "Six Years in the Shadow," *AF*, 32 (1), January 1925, 39–41; Frank Duffy, "The Old – The New," *AF*, 32 (3), March 1925, 165–7.

decades of the twentieth century and down to our own times in the 1990s. Most compelling and constant has been the nonpartisan orientation Gompers founded.

The labor movement from the 1930s onward would be different from its predecessor in crucial ways. The labor vote, in the sense of a united bloc of workers, would become a force in American politics in ways Gompers could hardly have imagined. With the rise of the Congress of Industrial Organizations and the shaping influence of the Communist Party, the labor movement at last reached beyond the native-born white workers who dominated the skilled crafts. By the end of World War II, trade unionism included a larger and more diverse proportion of American workers than ever before. And many of these gains were made possible by an aggressive political strategy in which organized labor pressured the Democratic Party and the state for reforms.

Yet for all these differences, organized labor has adhered to key tactics pioneered during the Progressive era. The pure and simple strategy – nonpartisan principles combined with a careful courting of the Democratic Party – has dominated twentieth-century American labor history, bringing with it distinct costs and benefits. When the Democratic Party needs allies, when its leaders feel vulnerable, when its candidates seek reelection, or when the labor movement enjoys a period of particular power, this strategy can produce significant and sometimes dramatic gains. One need only look back to the political reforms that preceded the elections of 1916 and 1936, each of them pathbreaking for their time, to see the advantages that could accrue from labor's friendship with the Democratic Party. Yet that friendship could easily turn cold, and repeatedly during the twentieth century, it has done so. After both world wars, for example, the Democratic Party found its partnership with labor to be an awkward encumbrance, with consequences that greatly damaged labor's struggle for equal rights in the workplace. The weakness of labor's nonpartisan strategy remains the same today as in the time of Gompers and Morrison: With no independent base of political power, labor becomes vulnerable to the whims of a powerful party over which it possesses, ultimately, no control.

Ironically, the leaders of today's organized labor movement fear losing control over the course of labor politics, just as Gompers did before them. Somehow they have learned to fear the loss of control an independent political movement of American workers seems to promise more than the loss of control their alliance with the Democratic Party actually delivers. In the last two decades, the Democratic Party has turned its back on American workers, apparently rejecting its old friendship with labor more completely than ever before. During the same period, labor has faced the most powerful anti-union movement among employers of the century, resulting in a precipitous fall in union membership.

In the autumn of 1994, tensions generated by all these pressures began to come to a head within the AFL-CIO. As the Executive Council of the AFL-CIO met to decide on a response, its conservative leadership confronted new demands from affiliated unions like the Oil, Chemical and Atomic Workers and the Teamsters for new strategies and new approaches. Finally, Ronald Carey, president of the Teamsters' Union and a member of the Executive Council, pro-posed that they form a labor party. AFL-CIO President Lane Kirkland responded: "We don't need a labor party, we already have one – it's called the AFL-CIO Committee on Political Education."[13] In Kirkland's reaction, one could sense Samuel Gompers's long reach stretching down across the century.

Even as he spoke, Kirkland's tenure as president of the AFL-CIO drew slowly to an end. Facing overwhelming pressures from below, Kirkland stepped down from the presidency later that year. In the election that followed, Service Employees' International Union chief John Sweeney defeated Kirkland protégé Thomas Donahue to become the new president of America's union federation. Although Sweeney's new leadership brought promising hope of innovation and change in the labor movement, troubling old questions about politics remained. President Sweeney put approximately $35 million into rewarding friends in the Democratic Party and defeating Republican enemies during the 1996 campaigns. By most accounts, these expenditures resulted in only disappointing gains, because the Republicans retained control over both houses of Congress. Mean-while across the country another political movement could be heard rumbling, as 1,500 union activists met in Cleveland to found a new Labor Party in June 1996.[14] Whichever way labor steps in the future, it seems, the movement will grapple with the vision made dominant by Samuel Gompers and his friends at the century's dawn.

---

[13] News of this exchange at the AFL-CIO's Executive Council meeting comes to me indi-rectly from a conversation with Judy Ancel of the Institute for Labor Education, Kansas City, Missouri. My thanks to her for this information.

[14] Glenn Burkins, "Labor Faces Harsh Payback," *Wall Street Journal*, November 7, 1996, p. A15; Steven Greenhouse, "Despite Setbacks, Labor Chief is Upbeat over Election Role," *New York Times*, November 15, 1996, p. A20; Philip Dine, "Surge of Interest Puts New Labor Party on the Political Map," *St. Louis Post-Dispatch*, June 14, 1996, p. C11.

Index

Adamson Act, 242, 257–9, 267, 272, 276

African-American workers, 5, 10, 23–4; and Commission on Industrial Relations, 252; exclusion from AFL, 39; and Knights of Labor, 32; and the vote, 49–50

American Alliance for Labor and Democracy, 280–1

American Anti-Boycott Association, 90, 154–5

American Federation of Labor: attacks on socialism, 65, 76–8, 87, 135–6, 169, 189–90, 277–8; the Bill of Grievances, 108–9; 1904 campaign strategy, 97–8; 1906 campaign strategy, 99–104, 108–18, 121–5, 131–41; 1908 campaign strategy, 158–70, 175–9, 197–204, 211–14; 1910 campaign strategy, 226–9; 1912 campaign strategy, 231–40; 1916 campaign strategy, 260–2, 272–3; campaign finances, 112–13, 161, 165–6, 226–7; centralization in, 138, 168–70, 179, 192, 193–5, 213–14, 275; Congressional races, 116–17, 120–4, 127–30, 133–4, 183–4, 197–202, 227–8; demographic character of, 11; eight-hour politics, 94–5, 97, 110, 257–9; ethnicity of members, 20, 22; Executive Council and politics, 114–16, 186–8; founding of, 19, 35;

growing exclusivism, 38–41; impact of 1890s depression, 37–8; Industrial Workers of the World, 99, 281; injunction politics (before 1905), 84, 93–4, 96; injunction politics (1906–1908), 110, 159, 163, 177–9, 189, 198, 212–13; injunction politics (1909–1914), 85, 225, 226, 246–8; internal dissent within, 134–6, 168–70, 213–14, 275, 278; Labor Representation Committee, 107, 112, 161–2, 200; lobbying activities (1895–1904), 65, 81, 84–5, 86–7, 93, 97; lobbying activities (1906–1916), 110, 157, 225, 246–8, 274; Morgan program, 61–4; Panama Canal, politics of, 100–2, 133–4; and party politics, 137–8, 178, 280; during postwar period, 282; power structure of, 42–4; relations with international affiliates, 11, 42n59, 44, 165; relations with Knights of Labor, 35, 37; salaried organizers in, 43–4, 113, 162–4, 167, 228, 260; volunteer organizers in, 43, 113; workers' criticisms of AFL politics, 133–6, 185, 187, 188–93, 194–6; workers' support for AFL politics, 118–19, 182–3; during World War One, 280–2; *See also* Samuel Gompers; Democratic party; and local labor activism

AFL-CIO, in 1990s, 285

287